Teaching and Learning
in the Arab World

Teaching and Learning in the Arab World

Christina Gitsaki (ed.)

PETER LANG

Bern·Berlin · Bruxelles · Frankfurt am Main·New York · Oxford·Wien

Bibliographic information published by Die Deutsche Nationalbibliothek
Die Deutsche Nationalbibliothek lists this publication in the Deutsche
Nationalbibliografie; detailed bibliographic data is available on the Internet
at ‹http://dnb.d-nb.de›.

British Library and Library of Congress Cataloguing-in-Publication Data:
A catalogue record for this book is available from *The British Library*,
Great Britain.

Library of Congress Cataloging-in-Publication Data

Teaching and learning in the Arab world / Christina Gitsaki (ed.).
p. cm.
Includes index.
ISBN 978-3-0343-0408-5
1. Education–Arab countries. 2. Educational change–Arab countries. I. Gitsaki, Christina.
LA1491.T43 2011
370.917′4927–dc22
2011002069

ISBN 978-3-0343-0408-5

© Peter Lang AG, International Academic Publishers, Bern 2011
Hochfeldstrasse 32, CH-3012 Bern, Switzerland
info@peterlang.com, www.peterlang.com, www.peterlang.net

Printed in Switzerland

Table of Contents

This book is dedicated to His Highness Sheikh Dr. Sultan bin Muhammad Al Qassimi, Ruler of Sharjah and Member of the Supreme Council of the United Arab Emirates, for his financial support of the UNESCO Chair Program at the Sharjah Higher Colleges of Technology, and for his unwavering commitment to the development of education in the Arab world.

Preface

Education is undergoing significant change globally and locally. In the Arab States, globalization and economic development have had a significant effect on education. The *Arab Knowledge Report* (2009) by the United Nations Development Program (UNDP) expressed serious concerns over the state of education in the Arab world which has resulted in the lack of a critical mass of highly skilled professionals capable of responding to the needs of the 21st century marketplace. Even in the oil-rich Gulf States, with over 200 higher education institutions, education is problematic with a notable lack of emphasis on specialized science and innovative learning. The Gulf States are in a race to become 'knowledge economies' and as a result they are promoting educational reforms such as the application of bilingual education models and education curricula adopted from the west. However, 'the lack of extensive public debate in Arab countries, together and individually, on the nature, goal and challenges of education reform, and the dearth of published studies, research, and documents on these issues have caused reform efforts to turn in on themselves, exposing them to the dangers of oversimplification' (MBRF & UNDP/RBAS, 2009:129). This book is an attempt to fill this gap by providing a collection of studies on the state of education in Arab countries with a special focus on the Arabian Gulf where currently there is increased activity and investment in education.

There are three major sections in the book. The first section is a collection of nine papers on current practices and challenges in education in the Arab world. In the first chapter Abbad Alabbad with Christina Gitsaki provide an in-depth investigation of Arab students' attitudes towards learning English and the negative effects of the traditional English teaching practices used across most of the government schools in Saudi Arabia and other Arab countries. In chapter two, Michael Fields, prompted by the poor language learning outcomes of Arab students, describes his study of learner motivation and language learning strategy use by Arab university students. Chapter three deals with the problem of school drop out rates especially among Arab male students. Georgia Daleure delves into the factors that contribute to male persistence with post-secondary education in the United Arab Emirates. In chapter four, Rana Raddawi addresses the issue of critical thinking skills among Arab university students and foregrounds cultural and pedagogical factors that may impede the teaching of such skills to Arab students. Chapter five documents how an undergraduate research project headed by Lauren Stephenson and Barbara Harold led to the development of leadership skills among Emirati university students. In chapter 6, Khawlah Ahmed raises the issue of the Arabic culture being marginalised in the English curriculum in the United Arab Emirates and poses important questions pertaining to the English language domination in Arab countries. The wide-spread use of English in the Arabian Gulf is also the topic of chapter seven, where Keith Kennetz, Melanie van den Hoven, and Scott Parkman describe their study of Arab students' attitudes towards different varieties of English and the effects of these attitudes on students' education. The last two chapters in the first section of the book address educational issues from the teachers' perspective. In chapter eight Ahmad Al-Issa with Aida Abou Eissa provide an investigation of teachers' attitudes and their current practices towards providing feedback to Arab students' writing, while in chapter nine Jonathan Aubrey and Christine Coombe discuss the issue of occupational stressors among EFL teachers in the United Arab Emirates and their repertoire of coping strategies.

The second major section in the book is devoted to the educational reforms that are being implemented in the Arabian Gulf. Chapter ten provides an overview of the Madares Al Ghad model applied to schools in the United Arab Emirates and Robin Dada discusses the challenges and issues faced in the first three years of the model. In chapter eleven Nettie Boivin provides a critical perspective of the educational reforms in Qatar and other Gulf states, while in chapter twelve Stephanie Knight and her colleagues provide a description of the educational reforms implemented in Qatari elementary schools and a thorough investigation of the outcomes of those reforms. In chapter thirteen, Iqtidar Ali Shah and Neeta Baporikar question the suitability of the imported education curricula used widely in Omani tertiary institutions. The last two chapters in the second section of the book provide examples of teacher education programs adopted in Bahrain and Palestine in an effort to facilitate attempts for educational reform in these countries. In chapter fourteen Mary Ellis, Anitha Devi Pillai and Ali Al Raba'i describe the development and implementation of the new bilingual teacher education program adopted at the Bahrain Teachers' College, while in chapter fifteen, Hala Al-Yamani discusses the use of drama-based techniques in teacher training in Palestine in an effort to help teachers develop constructivist approaches to classroom teaching.

The third and final section of this book is a collection of papers describing new approaches to teaching and learning in the Arab world. In chapter sixteen Rida Blaik Hourani, Ibrahima Diallo and Aleya Said provide a convincing argument for the deconstruction of the current educational model in Arab countries that emphasizes rote learning and passive transmission of knowledge. They then propose a constructivist model for education using the study of subjects in the field of humanities as an example. In chapter seventeen, Mick King discusses the outcomes of the implementation of problem-based learning with university students in Qatar, while, in chapter eighteen, Sabina Ostrowska investigates the effects of the introduction of local materials on student motivation in the Emirates. In chapter nineteen Melanie Gobert documents a teaching approach designed to increase Arab EFL students' phonological and orthographic awareness and in chapter twenty Katherine Hall provides best practice examples for teaching composition and rhetoric to Arab learners. Finally, in the last chapter Josephine O'Brien provides a series of arguments for the development of a pedagogical grammar for Arab learners of English.

While the collection of papers in this book is not an exhaustive account of the whole spectrum of educational issues in the Arab world, it does provide an overview of the kinds of issues and challenges that need to be addressed in any public discussion of educational reforms in the Arab states. Given the breadth and scope of the research studies included in this book, it is my intention that these papers make a significant contribution to the field as it continues to grow and evolve.

Christina Gitsaki, Ph.D.
UNESCO Chair in Applied Research in Education
Sharjah Higher Colleges of Technology, UAE

References

MBRF & UNDP/RBAS. (2009). *The Arab Knowledge Report.* Dubai: Al Ghurair Printing and Publishing House.

Part I: Current Practices and Challenges in Teaching and Learning in the Arab World

ABBAD ALABBAD & CHRISTINA GITSAKI

Chapter 1
Attitudes toward Learning English: A Case Study of University Students in Saudi Arabia

Abstract

This chapter discusses Saudi students' attitudes toward learning English as a foreign language (EFL) and their satisfaction with the current teaching methods used by teachers of English. Data were collected from 215 university students using an attitudinal questionnaire. Seventeen students from the subjects who completed the questionnaire participated in semi-structured interviews to discuss in detail their concerns and suggestions about the current EFL teaching method in Saudi Arabia. The findings revealed the students' negative attitudes toward learning English largely due to the didactic, teacher-centred approach and the limited use of teaching aids in the classroom. Student suggestions and recommendations confirmed that it is necessary to take practical steps to move from passive learning approaches towards a more learner-centred approach incorporating modern digital technologies.

Introduction

Teachers and researchers in countries where traditional English as a foreign language (EFL) teaching methods are practised have been calling for a change in classroom teaching practices. For example, in China (Jin, 2007; Ling, 2008), in Iran (Hayati, 2008), and in Japan (Cooker & Torpey, 2004; Tanaka & Stapleton, 2007), investigations are being directed towards replacing the traditional, didactic, teacher-centred approaches with practices that accommodate learners' communicative objectives in language learning. In learning environments that still adhere to the traditional teaching methods, such as the grammar-translation method and the audio-lingual approach, students are seen merely as recipients of the information taught to them, and one of their highest motivations to learn is to pass examinations (Chang, 2002). Since the emphasis in such traditional teaching methods is primarily on the forms of the language rather than their functions in real life communication (Cooker & Torpey, 2004), the students end up with poor speaking (Lu, 2005) and listening abilities (Ling, 2008), which are important skills needed for effective communication in the target language.

One country which has experienced similar drawbacks in EFL outcomes is Saudi Arabia. There is a common perception among educators that teaching English in Saudi Arabia is a fairly unsatisfactory process (Al-Ahaydib, 1986; Al-Hajailan, 2003; Alhamdan, 2008), while students in Saudi Arabia consider learning English as one of the most difficult subjects to study in school.

This chapter discusses the extent of the inadequacy of the current instructional language teaching approaches in Saudi Arabia, and explores the impact of traditional teaching approaches to student attitudes towards learning English.

Background

The English language has a significant status in Saudi Arabia as it is the medium of instruction in many academic programs (Abalhassan, 2002). There is also a growing emphasis on English proficiency as a requirement for employment by most of the major companies in Saudi Arabia. EFL in Saudi Arabia has, therefore, received significant attention from the Ministry of Education (MoE) as an essential subject in schools. In 1930, the MoE initiated the teaching of EFL in elementary schools. This was revised in 1942 to start EFL teaching in the newly created intermediate and secondary school programs (Alfallaj, 1995). From 1942 until 2006, EFL continued to be an essential part of the education system from Grade 7 until Grade 12. In 2006, the MoE decided to start EFL earlier, in the 5th Grade. During intermediate and secondary education, students receive four 45-minute sessions of EFL each week. By the time they enter university, students have completed between six to eight years of studying EFL.

At the tertiary level, all students must complete one compulsory EFL course during their four years of Bachelor's degree study. This compulsory EFL course is completed in one semester, with students attending a 50-minute lecture three times a week over 15-17 weeks. The course is purely instructional and focuses on grammar skills and short reading passages followed by comprehension questions. The common teaching method in this course, as in all the other EFL courses in the Saudi government education system, is either the grammar-translation or the audio-lingual method.

While students' unsatisfactory achievements in EFL education in Saudi Arabia are well documented in the literature (Al-Hajailan, 2003; Alhamdan, 2008) and the Saudi media (Aldakheel, 2009; Alisa, 2004), studies that have explored the problems of EFL teaching in Saudi Arabia are limited to secondary education and not directed toward finding a remedy. There is still uncertainty as to what causes the unsatisfactory EFL achievement of Saudi students, with studies pointing to factors such as teachers' skills inadequacy and the students' late start in EFL learning (Alshaer, 2007). For decades, researchers in Saudi Arabia have highlighted the serious shortfall in EFL teaching and learning in Saudi Arabia. A quarter of a century ago, for example, Al-Shammary (1984) pointed out that after six years of EFL study in public secondary schools, the Saudi students

were still unable to express themselves in correct English. Still, after
many years, things have not changed as Saudi researchers continue to
investigate the shortcomings of the current EFL teaching practices,
and indicate that despite the time and effort dedicated to EFL
teaching and learning in Saudi Arabia, students' achievements are
still not satisfactory (Al-Hajailan, 2003; Alhamdan, 2008). It was not
only the Saudi researchers who were worried about the inadequate
EFL achievement by Saudi students; parents and members of the
public were also concerned about this, with this concern being
repeatedly raised in the Saudi media. Seventeen years ago *Okaz*
newspaper pointed out:

> After thirty years of introducing the teaching of English in the country, the
> Ministry of Education in the studies that it conducts, discovers the weakness of
> the achievement of students. [Even]…after six years spent in learning English,
> students may not be able to write their names in English. (*Okaz*, 1991, p. 16)

A decade and a half later, the media still complain about the
unsatisfactory situation of EFL teaching in Saudi Arabia (Aldakheel,
2009; Alisa, 2004; Asiri, 2009). One of the Saudi journalists, in
Alriyadh newspaper, remarks:

> […] most of the students graduate from the secondary schools with almost no
> results in English proficiency although they have been studying English for six
> years. This fact is known by everybody who had access to the acceptance
> results in the higher education institutes. (Alisa, 2004, p. 23)

In some of the early studies in Saudi Arabia, the students'
unsatisfactory performance in their EFL studies were related to their
low motivation and their negative attitudes toward learning EFL (Al-
Ahaydib, 1986; Zaid, 1993). Al-Bassam (1987) and Alfallaj (1995)
found a relationship between the students' EFL achievement and
their instrumental motivation scores, but they did not directly
investigate the factors influencing such attitudes. Surur (1981) also
found that Saudi students were critical of the teachers' quality, the
teaching methodology, and the content of the EFL program. In a

study that investigated the textbook used in secondary schools (AlShumaimeri, 1999), it was found that the most important reason for studying English was for passing the final exam and the most significant skills needed to accomplish this objective were grammar and writing.

What these early studies of EFL in Saudi Arabia have shown is that, for the past three decades, Saudi secondary students have had negative attitudes and low motivation towards learning EFL mainly due to poor teaching methodology. These results are not surprising given that the dominant language teaching approaches in Saudi Arabia have been the audio-lingual and the grammar-translation methods (Al-Kamookh, 1983; Al-Mazroou, 1988; Rabab'ah, 2005; Zaid, 1993). How can a teaching method that focuses mainly on grammar or on drill and practice exercises, and which neglects other language skills and authentic communication, produce learners who are effective communicators in the target language? Alawad (2000) related students' low achievement in EFL learning to the lack of computer-based resources and the explicit focus on passing EFL examinations. As a result of the intensive focus on form and grammar instruction, students in the Saudi context and in other Arab countries score well in grammar tests, but they have serious communication problems in the target language (Al-Hazmi & Scholfield, 2007; Rabab'ah, 2005). This small number of research studies on the effectiveness of English language teaching in Saudi Arabia were conducted mostly in the secondary education context. It would be useful to investigate the current teaching methods in a tertiary EFL context, exploring students' attitudes toward EFL and the contributing factors toward such attitudes. The results of such a study could then be used to help improve EFL teaching in Saudi Arabia and in similar contexts.

The Study

The main research question underpinning this study was:

- How does the current teaching methodology in Saudi Arabian universities affect students' attitudes toward learning EFL?

This study utilized a quantitative research methodology that was supported by qualitative measures. Quantitative data were collected through an attitudinal questionnaire. Qualitative data were collected through semi-structured interviews. Both instruments were administered in Arabic.

The study was conducted at a major university in Riyadh, in Saudi Arabia, which was established approximately 50 years ago, and is one of the largest universities in the country, with 75,000 students enrolled across 33 different departments (Almarshad, 2008). Like most universities in Saudi Arabia, it is a government-funded body, and as such it is representative of the government education system in Saudi Arabia.

The sample was obtained through the School of Languages and Translation, which is the school responsible for teaching the compulsory English course, i.e. Eng 101, to all the undergraduate students in the university. All subjects were male, similar in age (18-20 years old), and were fairly similar in their English proficiency level. They had all studied English during their secondary (Grades 7-9) and high school (Grades 10-12) education. The attitudinal questionnaire was distributed to 250 students and 215 of them responded. Among the 215 respondents, 17 subjects volunteered to participate in the semi-structured interviews.

Attitudinal Questionnaire

The attitudinal questionnaire contained three parts.

- Part 1 comprised twenty-two statements and students were asked to evaluate them using a 5-point Likert-scale ranging from 1 (*strongly disagree*) to 5 (*strongly agree*).
- Part 2 included fifteen multiple choice items. Each item provided three statements from which the subjects chose one as their response. Responses were coded from 1-3 according to how positive (Code 3) or negative (Code 1) they were.
- Part 3 contained four open-ended questions.

Interviews

Among the 215 subjects who responded to the questionnaire, 17 respondents volunteered to be interviewed about their attitudes towards learning English at university. The purpose of the interviews was to explore how students evaluated the pedagogy used in teaching EFL and their suggestions to remedy the situation. The individual interviews were semi-structured, with eight starting questions, which highlighted three main categories: a) attitudes towards learning English; b) factors affecting students' EFL performance; and c) their view towards a better EFL teaching methodology. The length of each interview was between 10 and 20 minutes.

Results

Together, the two instruments (the Attitudinal Questionnaire and the Interviews) used for the data collection yielded important findings.

They helped to provide an in-depth explanation for the students' attitudes toward the current teaching methodology. The results of the students' responses to the Attitudinal Questionnaire are given below. Table 1 provides the means and standard deviations to the Likert-scale questionnaire items, while Table 2 provides the results to the multiple choice items.

Table 1. Attitudinal Questionnaire – Likert scale items - Means and standard deviations *(n=215)*

Questionnaire Items (Likert Scale)

	Students' attitudes toward learning EFL	Mean	Std Deviation
1	English is an important part of the school program.	3.93	1.45
2	I feel happy when I come to the English class.	2.70	1.34
3	I plan to continue studying English further after this course whether inside or outside the university.	3.64	1.43
4	Learning English is difficult for me.	3.06	1.27
5	I would rather spend my time on subjects other than English.	3.43	1.21
6	I think learning English is boring.	2.81	1.46
7	I think we should not dedicate much time and effort for learning English because it is not worth it.	1.76	1.16
8	When I finish studying the compulsory English courses, I have no intention to take more English courses.	2.39	1.35
	Students' attitudes toward the course	Mean	Std Deviation
9	I feel that the current design of the content of the course Eng 101 makes learning English effective.	2.60	1.29
10	During this course I achieved the language-learning goals that I hoped to achieve.	2.16	1.17
11	I think that the contents of the course do not reflect the real use of the foreign language.	4.15	1.12
12	If I had the opportunity to choose a different method of learning English (e.g. computer based or multimedia based),	4.19	1.21

		Mean	Std Deviation
	I would choose a method that is different from the current one.		
13	I didn't get much benefit from the course.	3.54	1.36
14	I feel that the materials used in the course are not interesting.	4.20	1.05
15	I feel that the contents of the course's textbook are not related to each other (coherent) in a way that helps me remember them.	3.29	1.16
16	I am happy with the teaching method of the course.	2.31	1.20
17	I think that the number of contact hours is enough for the course.	3.49	1.25

Students' attitudes toward Assessment	Mean	Std Deviation
18 Even if I work hard in the English course, I will still be scared of failing or getting low grades.	3.39	1.51
19 I prefer that there were better assessment methods (e.g. assignments, collaborative projects, self-learning tasks, etc.) other than the current traditional paper-based tests.	4.00	1.26
20 I think I can pass the course by simply focusing on the sample questions of the previous final exams.	3.39	1.22

Students' attitudes toward Task-based learning	Mean	Std Deviation
21 I wish that there were an opportunity for task-based learning activities in this course.	4.12	1.04
22 I wish we had a chance to work in groups in this course.	3.46	1.21

Scale: 1= strongly disagree, 2= disagree, 3= not sure, 4= agree, 5= strongly agree

Table 2. Attitudinal Questionnaire – Multiple Choice Items – Means and standard deviations *(n=215)*

Multiple Choice Items

Students' motivational intensity	Mean	Std Deviation
If English were not taught in school, I would:		
23 1) not bother learning English at all	2.22	.68
2) try to obtain lessons in English somewhere else		

	3) try to practise speaking English whenever possible (i.e. read English printed materials, speak it in hospitals, on the Internet, in the airport and wherever I can)		
24	**When it comes to English homework, I:** 1) just skim over it 2) put some effort into it, but not as much as I could 3) work very carefully, making sure I understand everything	1.77	.77
25	**Considering how I study English, I can honestly say that I** 1) will pass on the basis of sheer luck or intelligence because I do very little work 2) do just enough work to pass the course 3) really try to learn English regardless of the exam	1.86	.60
26	**My aim in the English course is to** 1) pass the final exam 2) get a good academic score to help raise my GPA 3) benefit as much as I can from this opportunity to learn English	1.94	.72
27	**If my teacher wanted someone to do an extra English assignment (which is not graded), I would:** 1) definitely not volunteer 2) only do it if the teacher asked me directly 3) definitely volunteer	1.34	.69
28	**When I am in the English class, I** 1) never say anything 2) answer only the easier questions 3) volunteer answers as much as possible	1.90	.83
	Students' desire to learn English	**Mean**	**Std Deviation**
29	**During English classes, I would like:** 1) to have more Arabic spoken than English	2.23	.75

2) to have a combination of speaking in English and Arabic

3) to have as much English spoken as possible

Compared to my other compulsory courses (e.g. Arabic, Islamic studies) I like English:

30 1) least of all   1.88   .79

2) not different from the other subjects

3) the most

Compared to my major's courses (e.g. statistics, math, administration, law) I like English:

31 1) least of all   1.93   .80

2) as much as the other subjects

3) the most

If there were an English club in my school, I would:

1) definitely not join

32   1.79   .72

2) attend meetings once in a while

3) be most interested in joining

If it was up to me whether or not to select studying English, I:

33 1) would definitely not select it   2.11   .78

2) do not know whether I would select it or not

3) would definitely select it

If the opportunity arose and I knew enough English, I would watch English TV programs:

34 1) never   2.58   .67

2) sometimes

3) as often as possible

If I had the opportunity, I would read English magazines and newspapers:

35 1) never   2.23   .70

2) not very often

3) as often as I could

	Students' orientation	Mean	Std Deviation
36	**If English was not important in getting a good job:** 1) I would never be keen on learning it 2) I would learn it only if I had extra time and money 3) I would learn English even if it was not important in getting a job	2.14	.78
37	**The current methodology in teaching English has made me:** 1) hate learning English, and therefore, it has negatively affected my performance 2) teaching methodology has had no impact on my attitude toward English or on my performance 3) love learning English and am keen on acquiring it	1.70	.67

Scale: 1= Negative,   2= Neutral,   3= Positive

The open-ended questions and the interview data were coded and analysed thematically. The issues that emerged from the data analysis are discussed in the following section.

Discussion

The aim of the present study was to investigate Saudi university students' attitudes toward the current English language teaching methodology and elicit their suggestions on how to improve it. The most significant issues that emerged from the study were the inadequacy of the current teaching method, teacher competency, and the lack of resources and teaching materials. Each of these issues is addressed in the following sections. The final section discusses the students' suggestions and recommendations.

Students' Concerns about the Current Teaching Methodology

The majority of the students in the present study complained that the current method of teaching English was inadequate for supporting them in the achievement of their language learning goals. The current language teaching method that is used widely in Saudi Arabia corresponds to a large extent to the grammar-translation method. This is a textbook-centered method of working out the grammatical system of the language with little or no emphasis on the speaking of the target language or on listening to authentic speech. The learner is expected to study, memorize, and master rules and examples of grammar structure. All interviewed subjects commented on their total dissatisfaction with the current teaching method. One of the students reported:

> In fact, the teaching of English has never been satisfactory during all my English studies starting from secondary school until university level. Believe me, if the native speakers of English knew that we studied English like this they would be disappointed. (Student 5, Interview, Lines: 10-13)

The current English teaching method also failed to motivate the students to learn the target language, with over a third of the subjects (36.2%) reporting that English is boring. As one of the students put it:

> I like English as a language and I like learning English in general, but the thing that my classmates and I do not like is how the language is being taught to us. It is boring and not beneficial. (Student 6, Interview, Lines: 12-14)

More than half of the subjects criticized the traditional teaching method as mainly focusing on grammar and giving only minor attention to the other language skills. Students were frustrated that the current teaching method gave little attention to oral communication skills, as one of the subjects pointed out:

> One of the main factors that has caused the current teaching method to be unsatisfactory is its over-focus on grammar and its neglect of the other

language skills, like conversations. The student studies the Present-simple Tense and the Past Tense along with the other grammatical rules but he does not know how to read properly. Giving the students chances for conversations and discussion is more important in learning than injecting the grammatical rules. (Student 2, Interview, Lines: 12-17)

The other major concern about the current teaching method was that it did not reflect the real use of the target language. This was apparent from the students' answers in the questionnaire (Table 1, Items 11, 13, 14) and from the interviews. Students commented that despite the years they had spent learning English they still could not express themselves in the target language. They knew how to answer the examination questions about grammar and other drill and practice activities, but they were unable to participate in conversations using English. They even felt that watching movies in the target language outside the classroom was more helpful for learning real-life English than attending English classes. This excerpt from a student interview reflects these views:

Our problem is not with studying the foreign language itself, however, our real problem is with the content we study in the English courses. We merely study the language rules which are irrelevant to the real goal of language learning. Our way of learning is similar to bringing an English speaker who wants to learn Arabic and you give him the grammar of Arabic. How would this learner use the language for communication without knowing any language skills beyond the grammar rules? The results we get from watching English-speaking TV channels and English movies are more beneficial than the English courses at the university. (Student 12, Interview, Lines: 8-16)

The learners' passive role was repeatedly mentioned by the students as a major drawback of the current teaching method. The lack of learner engagement and the teacher-centred classroom are among the features of the grammar-translation method (Jin, Singh, & Li, 2005; Li & Li, 2004). In a didactic classroom the students are passive listeners to the teacher's instruction and have limited interaction opportunities. This is exactly what the study found the traditional classroom in the Saudi university to be. The majority of the subjects

(76%) complained about being passive in the classroom. The learners in the English classroom would take notes and often photocopy other students' notebooks that summarized the lesson's grammar rules in a way that they could be easily memorized and regurgitated in the final examination. One of the students reported that:

> The problem with the teaching method that we have been using is that it is just injecting the information into our heads and this has created negative results, and made the students hate the course. (Student 6, Interview, Lines: 17-20)

However, the present study also found that the students wanted to be able to use not only grammar but also to put into practice the other language skills as much as possible. They mentioned 42 times in the open-ended questions that they wanted to have conversations in the classroom since they thought that would be the best way to practise their speaking and listening skills in authentic contexts. In fact, effective language learning cannot be accomplished unless students have an active role in learning, where they effectively participate in the learning process and negotiate meanings to complete classroom activities (Littlewood, 2007). EFL learners need sufficient opportunities to achieve their communicative objectives in the classroom.

From the discussion above it is clear that the grammar-translation teaching method that Saudi students encounter in their language learning has failed to motivate them and enhance their communication skills in the target language. An over-reliance on grammar teaching, a didactic teaching style, and passive learning in the classroom are the key factors that led to the students' dissatisfaction with the traditional teaching method in Saudi Arabia. The main cause of the problem with current teaching was the saturation of the students with language forms without providing corresponding practical situations on how to use those forms in daily life. As previous research found, studying the structure of the language for more than six years does not help the students much in gaining the skills needed for effective communication in the target language.

Teachers' Competency

An issue that emerged from the data was the students' concern about
the competency of their English teachers. 54 subjects indicated that
their English teachers were incompetent: '...The quality of the
teachers is poor' reported one of the subjects (Student 24, Attitudinal
Questionnaire, Open-Ended Questions). As the data were collected
from different groups who were taught by different teachers, this
indicates that the perceived teacher incompetence was a common
problem across different classes. It is true that there could be
instances where teachers were incompetent in language teaching.
However, the generalization that the teachers' incompetence was the
cause for the shortfall of the current teaching method may not be
completely accurate.

Most of the English teachers at the School of Languages and
Translation at the university have a MA degree in Teaching English
to Speakers of Other Languages (TESOL) or in Linguistics, and there
are also others who have a doctorate in TESOL. The subjects'
assumption that the teachers were not adequately qualified, however,
can be explained in several ways. First, the English curriculum is not
flexible in terms of content and teaching methodology. At the
institutional level all teachers must follow the predetermined course
objectives and help their students pass the final examination, which is
designed and administered centrally by the University Examination
Committee. Most of the teachers will not, therefore, risk skipping or
not covering all the units in the textbook from which the questions of
the final examination are drawn. This policy gives teachers little
room to provide learning opportunities beyond the textbook or to
focus on other language skills such as oral conversation. The lack of
course flexibility coupled with the limited teaching resources at the
teachers' disposal may be legitimate explanations as to how the
students developed the idea that their teachers were incompetent.
This, however, does not exclude the possibility that some teachers
may indeed be incompetent or poorly trained in language teaching.

Teaching Resources

About one third of the students reported that the traditional teaching method used limited teaching aids, such as computer programs and multimedia. The teaching resources in the traditional classroom are the textbook, the blackboard, and the chalk. Some of the teachers would write the new vocabulary and the irregular verbs on sheets of paper and distribute these as handouts to their students. The students, on the other hand, reported seeing the rapid development of new technologies and their use in their daily lives without seeing any application of such technologies in their classrooms. From the 215 subjects, 165 (77%) mentioned in the Attitudinal Questionnaire (Table 1, Item 12) that they would like a different teaching methodology where more teaching aids and resources are used. As one student commented:

> There has been a great development in modern learning aids beyond the traditional textbook and the blackboard. There are modern teaching aids that can help better in teaching such as projector presentations, and real conversation in simulation using computer programs. (Student 7, Interview, Lines: 27-30)

Not only did the lack of resources affect their language proficiency development, but it also affected their attitudes and motivation to learn the language. As one of the subjects pointed out:

> I personally like to learn English, but there are no motivational tools for learning and there are no modern aids for learning beyond the traditional chalk and board. (Student 48, Attitudinal Questionnaire, Open-Ended Questions)

Students were confident that introducing more teaching aids and new technologies into the English classroom would enhance their learning experience and would increase their motivation to learn the target language.

An interesting question may be raised at this point as to why the teachers did not use more resources and teaching aids, such as computers and the Internet, in language teaching in the context of the study. One of the reasons could be the lack of computer literacy or sufficient training to allow the teachers to implement technology into their classrooms. The lack of computer skills or inappropriate training styles can result in low levels of technology use by the teachers (Becta, 2004; Preston, Cox, & Cox, 2000). However, even when the teachers have sufficient knowledge of the computer applications, there are still other possible factors that may negatively affect the proper implementation of these technologies in the classroom. Dawes and Selwyn (1999), for instance, found that a major barrier to the use of computers by teachers was the teachers' anxiety and fear that their students may possess more knowledge of computers than they do, or the suspicion that they could be replaced by computers in the future (Darus & Luin, 2008). Resistance to change could also be a deterrent to the integration of technology in language teaching by the teachers and the institutions alike. The teachers may be unwilling to change their teaching practice, while the institutions may also find that the new technologies are difficult to implement in terms of infrastructure and organization which could be beyond their ability (Cuban, Kirkpatrick, & Peck, 2001).

There are also possible social factors that could have affected the use of technology by teachers in the study context. Being a Muslim country with strong religious norms, Saudi Arabia is culturally and religiously different from the English-speaking countries in the world. The content and the materials presented to the students are carefully selected so that they do not violate cultural and religious restrictions, such as exposing the female body. These restrictions, which are well-known to be delicate in the Saudi context, may have also hindered the teachers in Saudi Arabia from using the materials available on the Internet or in computer programs for teaching English.

Students' Suggestions and Expectations

During the interviews, students were asked to provide suggestions and solutions to improve their attitudes toward learning English. Many of the students saw the use of multimedia, computers and other audiovisual aids as key elements to improving students' attitudes. More than one third of the interviewees suggested changing the whole curriculum and the teaching methodology and trying different teaching methods as a solution. One of the students commented:

> I wish that the decision makers would respond to our requests and change the curriculum and the teaching method in high schools and universities as well, so that we could achieve our language learning goals. The current teaching method, however, is merely a waste of money and effort and the outcome is not satisfactory. (Student 17, Interview, Lines: 20-24)

In the discussion about the possibility of having collaboration and group-work integrated into the EFL course, the overwhelming majority of the subjects (82%) supported the idea and they reported that they would be excited to have such activities as part of the course (see also Table 1, Items 21 & 22). One of the major advantages of group-work that students mentioned was that they would be able to exchange information and learn from each other. More than one third of the students expected that they would feel more comfortable to ask each other questions about what they do not know than to ask the teacher directly. An additional advantage of group work mentioned by the students was the possibility for peer-editing where students would correct each others' mistakes. Some of the respondents thought working in groups was easier than working individually. Other students mentioned advantages not directly related to learning, such as increasing their feeling of responsibility and enhancing the relationship among the group members. Overall, the students expected that group-work would add excitement and be more enjoyable than the traditional way of learning. Other subjects stated that it would not only add joy to learning, but it would also allow them to have a better chance to practise speaking the target language. The participants also expected the student's role to be more active using this mode of learning. One of the participants illustrated:

> There are many benefits in group-work. The student will have the chance to take an active role in the class, which we do not get in the traditional classroom. They will also be more excited to practise using the target language than in the passive learning mode. (Student 7, Interview, Lines: 39-42)

The interview also sought to explore the students' views regarding substituting the traditional test-based evaluation with a task-based assessment. The majority of the subjects (82%) favoured task-based assessment over traditional tests (see Table 1, Item 19). About one third of the students thought that the new assessment method would keep students in a continuous learning process, in contrast to the test-based evaluation method where students do not study seriously until just before the examinations. The subjects also suggested that this mode of assessment would allow for longer retention of what had been learnt in class. A further advantage mentioned by the students was that the new assessment method would make the students use the target language more frequently.

The last issue addressed during the interviews was related to the students' perspectives towards the use of technology for learning English. Subjects expressed a positive attitude towards the introduction of computers and the Internet in the EFL classroom and reported the advantages that they expected from the integration of such technologies and resources in their lessons. Students suggested that they would be excited to use chat programs to enhance their learning. About one quarter of the interviewees thought that searching the web in the target language would be a great way to learn English. A similar number of subjects suggested exchanging emails in English for learning the target language. Participating in games in the target language was also seen as helpful.

With regard to how the use of technology would improve their language skills, the subjects reported the following ideas. More than one third stated that they would improve their reading skills by browsing websites in the target language. One quarter of the subjects thought that using word processing programs would enhance their writing. A subject suggested that word processing programs might improve their spelling as well. Browsing English websites could also increase the students' vocabulary acquisition according to some participants. Students also reported that not only would the use of technology have practical effects on the acquisition of different language skills but it would also make learning more enjoyable compared to the traditional teaching method. Another feature that computers and the Internet were expected to offer was that learning could take place beyond the time and space of the regular classroom, allowing students to learn anywhere and at any time. One student also expected technology to provide better opportunities for authentic use of the target language. An important point raised by another student was the ability to learn beyond the curriculum and to open new learning opportunities for the students through the use of technology:

> I think that the biggest advantage of this new technology is that it would be real practice of what we learn. Also we would be able to get more learning opportunities outside the book, and get to know new things beyond the curriculum. (Student 11, Interview, Lines: 38-41)

Conclusion

The aim of the present study was to investigate the effects of the current teaching method used in traditional EFL classrooms in Saudi Arabia on the students' attitudes towards language learning. Upon analysing the students' responses on the Attitudinal Questionnaire and the interviews, it became apparent that university students in Saudi Arabia overwhelmingly held negative attitudes toward the current EFL teaching method. They attributed the causes of this negative attitude to several factors, such as the lack of resources and teaching aids, the didactic teaching method, the focus on grammar and the complete disregard for oral communication skills. Major concerns of the students regarding the current teaching method were the passive learner role and the reliance mainly on the instructor to teach the language. Students felt that their English class was boring and lacked enjoyment, which had negative effects on their motivation to learn English.

The students' suggestions were to change the current grammar-translation approach to another teaching method that would allow students to become active in the classroom and to practise a range of language skills. They also needed to move from learning the abstract grammar rules of the language to the practical application of these rules in authentic language learning situations. They thought that collaboration and group-work would improve language learning. Finally, the adoption of new technological learning aids, such as computers and the Internet was another important suggestion that the students discussed. They thought that computers and the Internet with their infinite capabilities would provide the language learner with a wide range of learning opportunities that are beyond the time and space of the traditional classroom.

Even though the study was conducted at one particular university in Saudi Arabia, the findings reflect the current status of EFL teaching in the government education system. Saudi Arabian schools and universities still use the didactic teacher-centred approach, which advocates a passive learner role in the learning process and focuses mainly on grammar and how to prepare students for exams, rather than on teaching communication skills that the students really need in order to communicate effectively in the target language. The findings of the study provided further evidence to why Saudi students cannot express themselves in the target language after years of EFL education at school and at university.

The unsatisfactory results in EFL by Arab students (Aldakheel, 2009; Alisa, 2004) are an indication that there is no point in persisting with the instructional grammar-based teaching approach any longer. Even though the current teaching methodology has been used in Saudi Arabia for a long time, this does not justify preserving such teaching practices, particularly after it has become apparent that their effectiveness does not go beyond training the students to pass their examination, and does little to enable them to express themselves or communicate properly in the target language. There is a need for a thorough evaluation and revision of current EFL teaching methods in terms of the objectives they intend to achieve and the needs of the students. On a larger scale, the findings of the study provide insights and implications for other Arab contexts where EFL classroom teaching follows similar didactic approaches.

Acknowledgement

This project received assistance from King Saud University, Riyadh, Saudi Arabia.

References

Abalhassan, K.M.I. (2002). *English as a foreign language instruction with CALL multimedia in Saudi Arabian private schools: A multi-case and multi-site study of CALL instruction.* Unpublished Ph.D., Indiana University of Pennsylvania.

Al-Ahaydib, M.E.A. (1986). *Teaching English as a foreign language in the intermediate and secondary schools of Saudi Arabia: A diagnostic study.* Unpublished Ph.D., University of Kansas.

Alawad, K.A.M. (2000). *The concerns of teaching EFL in intermediate schools from the teachers' perspective.* Unpublished M.A. thesis, Riyadh.

Al-Bassam, M.M. (1987). *The relationship of attitudinal and motivational factors to achievement in learning English as a second language by Saudi female students.* Unpublished Ph.D., University of Florida.

Aldakheel, T. (2009, February 11). English for Arabs. *Alwatan.*

Alfallaj, F.S. (1995). *The effect of students' attitudes on performance in English language course at the College of Technology, Buraydah, Saudi Arabia.* Unpublished Ph.D., University of Toledo.

Al-Hajailan, T. (2003). *Teaching English in Saudi Arabia.* Riyadh, Saudi Arabia: Aldar Alsawlatia.

Alhamdan, B. (2008). *Survey of students', teachers', and supervisors' attitudes toward EFL learning, CALL, and the design and the use of Bedouin society-based software in EFL classes in secondary schools in nomadic areas in Saudi Arabia.* Unpublished M.A. thesis, The University of Queensland.

Al-Hazmi, S.H., & Scholfield, P. (2007). Enforced revision with checklist and peer feedback in EFL writing: The example of Saudi university students. *Scientific Journal of King Faisal University, 8*(2), 237-267.

Alisa, A. (2004, April 28). About English teaching: The ministry is right. *Alriyadh.*

Al-Kamookh, A. (1983). *A survey of the English language teachers' perceptions of the English language teaching methods in the intermediate and secondary schools of the eastern province in Saudi Arabia.* Unpublished Ph.D., University of Kansas.

Almarshad, A. (2008, March 3). 75,000 is the number of students enrolled in King Saud University and 50 contracts with international research centres. *Alriyadh.*

Al-Mazroou, R.A.Y. (1988). *An evaluative study of teaching English as a foreign language in secondary schools in Saudi Arabia as perceived by Saudi EFL teachers.* Unpublished M.A. thesis, Southern Illinois University, Carbondale.

Alshaer, M. (2007). *Our students and their EFL problems.* Retrieved February 5, 2009, from http://pulpit.alwatanvoice.com/content-91546.html

Al-Shammary, E.A.S. (1984). *A study of motivation in the learning of English as a foreign language in intermediate and secondary schools in Saudi Arabia.* Unpublished Ph.D., Indiana University.

AlShumaimeri, Y.A.N. (1999). *Saudi students' perceptions of their textbook: English for Saudi Arabia, (EFSA), secondary year one.* Unpublished M.A., University of Leeds.

Asiri, H. (2009, February 22). The worst 10 problems. *Alwatan.*

Becta. (2004). *A review of the research literature on barriers to the uptake of ICT by teachers.* Retrieved August 28, 2008, from http://partners.becta.org.uk/index.php?section=rh&rid=13642

Chang, M.M. (2002). Learning foreign language through an interactive multimedia program: An experimental study on the effects of the relevance component of the ARCS model. *CALICO Journal, 20*(1), 81-98.

Cooker, L., & Torpey, M. (2004). From the classroom to the self-access centre: A chronicle of learner-centred curriculum development. *The Language Teacher, 28*(6), 11-16.

Cuban, L., Kirkpatrick, H., & Peck, C. (2001). High access and low use of technologies in high school classrooms: Explaining an apparent paradox. *American Educational Research Journal, 38*(4), 813-834.

Darus, S., & Luin, H. W. (2008). Electronic feedback: Is it beneficial for second language writers? *Teaching English with Technology: A Journal for Teachers of English, 8*(3), 1-9.

Dawes, L., & Selwyn, N. (1999). Teaching with the dream machines: The representation of teachers and computers in information technology advertising. *Journal of Information Technology for Teacher Education, 8*(3), 289-304.

Hayati, A.M. (2008). Teaching English for special purposes in Iran: Problems and suggestions. *Arts and Humanities in Higher Education, 7*(2), 149-167.

Jin, L., Singh, M., & Li, L. (2005). *Communicative language teaching in China: Misconceptions, applications and perceptions.* Paper presented at the AARE 2005 Education

Research 'Creative Dissent: Constructive Solutions', the Australian Association for Research in Education.

Jin, Y. (2007). Adapting communicative language teaching approach to China's context. *Sino-US English Teaching, 4*(10), 29-33.

Li, X., & Li, H. (2004). On developing oral communicative competence in TEFL. *Sino-US English Teaching, 1*(4), 13-18.

Ling, C. (2008). Study on affective factors on listening performance of English majors in Xinjiang Agricultural University. *US-China Foreign Language, 6*(3), 32-38.

Littlewood, W. (2007). Communicative and task-based language teaching in East Asian classrooms. *Language Teaching, 40*(3), 243-249.

Lu, J. (2005). On improving students' spoken English in classes. *Sino-US English Teaching, 2*(11), 70-74.

Okaz, N. (1991, May 27). The English language in school curriculum. *Okaz Daily Newspaper,* 16-17.

Preston, C., Cox, M. J., & Cox, K. M. J. (2000). *Teachers as innovators: An evaluation of the motivation of teachers to use information and communications technology.* MirandaNet.

Rabab'ah, G. (2005). Communication problems facing Arab learners of English. *Journal of Language and Learning, 3*(1), 180-197.

Surur, R. S. (1981). *Survey of students', teachers', and administrators' attitudes toward English as a foreign language in the Saudi Arabian public schools.* Unpublished Ph.D., University of Kansas.

Tanaka, H., & Stapleton, P. (2007). Increasing reading input in Japanese high school EFL classrooms: An empirical study exploring the efficacy of extensive reading. *The Reading Matrix, 7*(1), 115-131.

Zaid, M.A. (1993). *Comprehensive analysis of the current system of teaching English as a foreign language in the Saudi Arabian intermediate schools.* Unpublished Ph.D., University of Colorado at Boulder, Boulder.

Michael Fields

Chapter 2
Learner Motivation and Strategy Use among University Students in the United Arab Emirates

Abstract

Students in the United Arab Emirates (UAE), before commencing their undergraduate degree, are required to demonstrate adequate English proficiency by obtaining a score of Band 5-6 on the International English Language Testing System (IELTS) exam. Many students fail to achieve the required score, and are often criticised for lacking motivation and appropriate study skills. This is a serious issue not only in the UAE but also other countries in the Gulf region where students are taught in Arabic at school and then have to attend university through the medium of English. The study described in this chapter used semi-structured interviews with five Emirati students who scored 6 on the IELTS exam to explore the issue of learner motivation and strategy use among Arab university students. Results showed that participants were mainly instrumentally motivated, seeing English as a tool that is necessary for study and work in the UAE. In terms of learner strategies, participants showed developed social/affective strategies, learning through using language in authentic situations, and by speaking with teachers and colleagues. Cognitive strategies appeared to be limited to language practice in authentic situations, such as reading the English press and watching films. Metacognitive strategies were largely absent. Students put little effort into formal study, and there was little evidence of the use of strategies for learning grammar or developing reading and writing skills.

Introduction

Motivation and learner strategies are generally considered to be the most important individual differences that influence success in language learning. They are far more important than age, aptitude, past success, and the effects of the teacher, the physical environment or study materials (Naiman, Frohlich, Stern, & Todesco, 1996). Most universities in the UAE and the rest of the Gulf States are English medium. In order to begin a university course, students must qualify by attaining a Band of 6 on IELTS. While some students achieve this, many do not. Average band scores in 2008 for the IELTS academic module were 5.0 for the UAE, 5.26 in Saudi Arabia, 5.33 in Kuwait, and 4.81 in Qatar (*IELTS Test-taker Performance, 2008*). Teachers often complain that students are unmotivated and have no study skills, though little research has been done to determine the type of motivation and the strategies used by students who do succeed in passing their IELTS test. To address this gap, this research study used semi-structured interviews with five Emirati university students who achieved Band 6 on IELTS, in order to examine their motivation and employment of learner strategies.

Background

Motivation

Motivation has been defined as 'effort expended to achieve the goal, desire to achieve the goal, and attitudes toward the activities involved in achieving the goal' (Gardner, 1985, p. 51). The classic motivational model in second language learning was proposed by Gardner and Lambert (1972) and Gardner (1985). This model holds that motivation has two orientations: integrative and instrumental. Integrative orientation is the desire by learners to identify with the target language community, develop an interest in the people and the culture, and take on their speech habits. This is seen as a stronger motivation than instrumental orientation, which originates in the desire to attain good marks or to benefit professionally by using the language (Gardner & Lambert, 1972).

There has recently been much criticism of Gardner's model. Most of the research was done in Canada, using English speakers learning French. The need to learn a foreign language in a bilingual society is a special case which cannot be generalised to most other language-learning situations (Mitchell & Myles, 2004). Dornyei (1990), Oxford and Shearin (1994), and Warden and Lin (2000) have suggested that integrative motivation is less important than instrumental motivation in contexts where English is taught as a foreign language (EFL). A more general criticism is that motivational research is 'largely dominated by a Euro-Anglo English as a Second Language perspective', while other contexts, especially EFL contexts in Asia, have not been adequately researched (Gan, Humphries, & Hamp-Lyons, 2004, p. 231).

Ushioda (1996) distinguished *intrinsic* motivation from Gardner's integrative and instrumental orientations. Intrinsic motivation is the desire to learn created by the enjoyment of the learning process itself. While both of Gardner's orientations relate to the ultimate use of language, Ushioda posited that most learners in classroom situations have no motivation whatsoever, other than what can be created by the teacher. Intrinsic motivation can increase interest in tasks, so that students will become good language learners. Integrative or instrumental motivation may occur later, when language proficiency is well enough developed that there is potential for real-life use.

Furthermore, the concept of integrative motivation has been reappraised in the era of globalisation. Lamb (2004) argued that a young generation is emerging around the world which is bicultural: both rooted in the local culture and having a global identity, which includes speaking English to communicate with other global citizens. Motivation to learn English is integrative, but not toward any particular Anglophone society. Rather, learners wish to integrate with both English-speaking global citizens in their local culture (most likely in the urban middle class), and English-speaking members of the global culture around the world. Dornyei (2005) has added that the lines between types of motivation may be blurred by today's globalised generation. He defined Intrinsic-Instrumental-Integrative Motivation as a general international orientation. Today many people learn English because it is enjoyable to communicate with others all over the world and use the internet (intrinsic). They also have opportunities to work or study abroad (instrumental) and wish to develop a cosmopolitan, globalised world-citizen identity (inte-grative). Yashima, Zenuk-Nishide, and Shimizu (2004), in a study on young Japanese learners of English, stated that 'Those who are conscious of how they relate themselves to the world tend to be more motivated to study English as they probably visualize "English-using selves" clearly' (p. 119).

Since 2001, a new paradigm has been developed, mainly through the work of Dornyei and Ushioda. Dornyei (2001) argued that motivation is dynamic over time, not static as Gardner's theory implied. The teacher's behaviour is the single most important factor in influencing motivation. Ushioda (2001) developed a model of *the Ideal L2 Self*, the person the learner would like to become who speaks a foreign language (L2). Ushioda (2001) and Dornyei (2005) have both stated that learners who are intrinsically motivated are much more likely to succeed than those who are motivated by marks or monetary gain.

Gan et al. (2004), in a large scale study of successful and unsuccessful English learners at university level in China, found that successful learners had positive language experiences before university, and they had high levels of intrinsic motivation, due partly to teacher praise, encouragement and enthusiasm. Instrumental motivation also played a part, as successful learners were planning to go on for international examinations such as IELTS and possibly study in the US or UK, while unsuccessful learners found exams a source of anxiety and panic.

Learner strategies

Learner strategies are defined as 'specific actions, behaviours, steps, or techniques...used by students to enhance their own learning' (Oxford, 2003, p. 2). While several taxonomies of learner strategies have been suggested (Wenden & Rubin, 1987; Oxford & Nyikos, 1989; Naiman, Frohlich, Stern, & Todesco, 1996) it is O'Malley and Chamot's (1990) taxonomy that is the most widely accepted today. They proposed a division of learner strategies into *metacognitive*, *cognitive*, and *social/affective* strategies. Metacognitive strategies are those which allow for the planning, monitoring and evaluation of a learning activity. Cognitive strategies are those which operate directly on the information, such as repetition, grouping, note-taking, elaboration, summarizing, inferencing and deduction. Social/affective strategies are those which involve either interaction with another person (for example, questioning for clarification or cooperation with other group members) or control over affect (for example, maintaining a positive attitude or dealing constructively with negative feelings). Cognitive strategies are the most commonly used by all learners, while social/affective strategies are used the least.

Wenden (1987) carried out semi-structured interviews with language students on their use of strategies. He was able to group learners according to distinct ideas about learning strategies. The most commonly reported set of beliefs was simply to *use the language*, for example living and studying where the language is spoken, practising as much as possible, concentrating on meaning without concern for grammar, and not worrying about mistakes. Another set of learners reported that their strategy was based on *learning about the language*, studying grammar and vocabulary, keeping a vocabulary log, using dictionaries and grammar books, taking a formal course, and paying primary attention to formal aspects of language. Finally a third, smaller group had very *emotional connections* with the language, relying on feelings of personal aptitude, being motivated by positive reactions of those with whom they used the language, and being aware of self-concept when using the language and having vivid memories of feelings while in learning situations.

There is a general consensus in the literature (O'Malley & Chamot, 1990; Oxford, 2003; Gan et al., 2004) that good language learners use strategies more often and more effectively than poor language learners. Good learners constantly use strategies, though the particular strategy will depend on the task, the learner and his ability to use it effectively.

In a wide-ranging study of Chinese university level students of English (Gan et al., 2004), it was found that the difference between successful and unsuccessful learners (defined by external exam scores), in terms of learning strategies, was often their use of metacognitive strategies. For example, while both successful and unsuccessful learners made lists and memorized vocabulary items, successful ones reported checking themselves, trying to use the words in daily life, and revising the lists, while unsuccessful learners often forgot them. Similarly, successful learners used at least four metacognitive strategies to prepare for upcoming lessons, while unsuccessful learners did nothing. Finally, successful learners set short and long term goals for themselves, while unsuccessful learners did not.

With regards to student motivation and strategy use in the context of the study, low motivation and lack of appropriate study skills have been noticed at every level of society in the UAE. Local education authorities have run workshops on motivation and study skills (Zeitoon, 2001), and human resource officers have also remarked on the need for Emiratis to improve motivation and develop skills in order to succeed in the workplace (Hoath, 2001). Of all Emirati students entering universities, 94% must take remedial English language courses in foundation programmes before beginning their university coursework (Lewis & Bardsley, 2010). For those who enter university, some take as long as eight years to complete their undergraduate work, due to poor performance, and this is to a large degree blamed on low motivation (Thomas, 2010). This study set out to identify both the motivational types and learner strategies employed by Arab students who achieved a Band 6 on IELTS. A better understanding of their motivation and learning strategies may inform both teaching methods and curriculum planning.

The Study

Semi-structured interviews were conducted to research motivation and learner strategies among successful EFL learners in the UAE. Participants were five male Emirati students who had scored Band 6 or more on IELTS and were enrolled in an undergraduate course in a public university in the UAE. They were between 20 and 24 years old and used Arabic as their native language. None of them had lived or studied outside the UAE. All participants were unknown to the researcher.

Participants signed informed consent forms and understood that their participation was voluntary. Each participant was interviewed for an hour. The interviews were modeled on questions from two similar interview-based studies (Wenden, 1987; Naiman et al., 1996). The research questions were divided into two parts: motivation and learner strategies. Motivation was broken down into the following categories: integrative, instrumental (Gardner, 1985); integrative in the globalised era (Lamb, 2004); intrinsic (Ushioda, 1996); and the Ideal L2 Self (Ushioda, 2001). Two models of learner strategies were used for the interviews. First was the standard division into metacognitive, cognitive and social/affective strategies (O'Malley & Chamot, 1990). Second was the division of using language, studying about language, and emotional connection to language (Wenden, 1987). Questions were constructed to discriminate which learner strategies were used most effectively by the participants. The interviews were recorded and transcribed.

Results

Motivation

The analysis of the interview transcripts showed that motivation for all participants tended to be mainly instrumental. English was seen as a tool for study in English-medium universities. As one student stated, 'All our courses are in English, so I had to learn English' (Student 1, Line 60). English was also seen as necessary to communicate with the foreign staff in their future jobs as another student makes clear '...when I am working in the lab, there are staff from the Philippines and India, I am dealing with them in English' (Student 2, Lines 49-51). In reaction to the interview statement *Learning English is hard work, but it will pay off* (meant to test the students' instrumental motivation), all participants agreed that

English would pay off, though all modified the statement to reflect the idea that learning English is not difficult.

There was also evidence of integrative motivation in a globalised world. In answer to the first question in the interview, *What are your reasons for learning English?* most responses included the idea that English is today the international language. Another question examining integrative motivation in a globalised world was *Do you feel part of the globalised world? How does English help you be a part of it?* For these participants, globalisation meant not only extending themselves into the world outside the UAE, but also interacting with what they perceive as their own globalised country. The following interview excerpts illustrate this point:

> I am using all the time the internet, and seeing what is going on all over the world. ... the world is becoming like one country, one culture. ...We communicate with others in English. (Student 2, Lines 92-7)

> Student 3: [In] Dubai, we have all people from different countries, it's become like a global village.
> Interviewer: And do you feel a part of this?
> Student 3: Yes, of course.
> Interviewer: When do you interact with people from outside your country?
> Student 3: Like, in work, in study, in malls, anywhere.
> Interviewer: Do you ever use websites in English?
> Student 3: Yes, for news, CNN.
> (Student 3, Lines 72-76)

> Yes, I use the internet. I travel. I do many things. English is very useful, for example when you travel and meet some people from other countries and they speak about their countries, you know about it. And also when you get in the internet, and read about something, the information is not in Arabic, so English is very useful for me. (Student 4, Lines 84-87)

There was evidence of intrinsic motivation for most of the participants, who reported enjoying studying English. All students reported that teachers made classes more interesting, and that they enjoyed working with their classmates.

[Teachers] are using many things to make it interesting. For example, now they are using some websites, and there are some exams or challenging tests, and we must solve it in groups. (Student 2, Lines 124-6)

Learning new languages is an enjoyable thing. … Every teacher has his own skills and his way to teach you. I had a teacher called Mary, she is very good in English. I learned a lot about English. (Student 3, Lines 106-12)

… they tried to bring new stuff to us, like reading stories and novels, watching movie scenes…(Student 5, Lines 122-3)

There was no evidence of traditional integrative motivation, the idea that students learn a language to assimilate the culture of the target language group. No participant responded positively to the idea of going abroad to live for work or study, and the anecdotes that they told about their travels abroad generally tended to be negative.

I'm not interested in traveling at all. … I prefer to stay here. (Student 1, Line 5)

Interviewer: Have you ever visited or would you like to visit the UK, America, or another English-speaking country?
Student 2: Yes, the UK for six weeks. It was very difficult. … as a foreigner, I felt homesick, I wanted to come back to my country. I can't stay there … for me, living in my country is better. Studying here is better.
(Student 2, Lines 71-8)

I'd prefer to work here. I'd be close to family and friends. It's very difficult to live outside your country, experience new things there. You have to start your whole life again there. (Student 3, Lines 65-7)

Interviewer: Do you think you would enjoy living with the people in England or America?
Student 4: No, because our culture is different.
(Student 4, Lines 74-5)

To test the concept of the Ideal L2-Self, participants were asked to comment on the following statement: *The person I want to be can speak Arabic and English, and can work and travel easily in the UAE and outside the UAE.* All participants strongly agreed with this statement.

Intrinsic-Instrumental-Integrative motivation which creates a general international orientation (Dornyei, 2005) may not fit the profile of these participants, who use English more out of necessity to study, work, and communicate with foreigners in their own country. No response indicated that the participants wanted to develop a cosmopolitan, world-citizen identity. The following interview excerpt illustrated this point:

> ...it's not matter if I learn about other cultures, that's okay with me, but my culture is the most important thing. I want to keep it. English is a tool, but nowadays, everyone must learn it. But if I learn it, it will not affect my culture. (Student 4, Lines 131-4)

Learner strategies

Participants preferred language practice to formal study, focusing on meaning with little regard to form. All reported using English in authentic situations as their most meaningful learning experiences. Exposure to English was through reading authentic materials and watching films. However, the activity most mentioned was group discussion in class.

> Student 2: I just want to practise speaking English every day.... I am listening to music, reading news, these kinds of things. Before I couldn't talk English, but now I can.
> Interviewer: So it was mainly by using it.
> Student 2: Yeah, by using it and practising, this is the best way to learn.
> (Student 2, Lines 56-61)

> If you try to speak in class and participate, it will be helpful for you to learn more. (Student 3, Line 217)

> Interviewer: What do you think is the most important factor in your learning?
> Student 4: Talking to people.
> (Student 4, Lines 159-60)

In terms of study, all participants had taken formal courses. However, formal study of grammar, reading and writing is not the preferred learning strategy for these participants.

> I don't study at all. I just stay in class. For like progress test and like this, I don't study. I only attend the classes. (Student 1, Lines 158-9)

> Interviewer: Do you like analysing grammar?
> Student 2: No. It's difficult. I don't like it at all.
> (Student 2, Lines 192-4)

> Student 5: I don't really study it. I practise it. See, studying for me is a boring thing, but I don't take English as a boring thing. I take it as something that I really enjoy.
> (Student 5, Lines 246-8)

> Interviewer: So when I said grammar, you immediately thought of how to speak correctly. You didn't think of sitting down and trying to learn the rules?
> Student 5: No, it's really boring.
> (Student 5, Lines 179-81)

Cognitive strategies were in almost all cases related to learning vocabulary in context while reading, often by using a bilingual dictionary and writing translations directly in the books. Most students reported reading in English outside of university assignments, as one student remarked: 'I read Harry Potter. I read The National newspaper' (Student 2, Line 221). While this is a cognitive strategy, the context is again authentic language practice.

> Student 2: When I see a new word, I open the dictionary. ...And if I have a book, and I see a word I don't know, I open the dictionary, then I take a pencil and write it down in English in the book.
> Interviewer: Did you turn these into lists later? Did you keep a book?
> Student 2: Actually no need. Because I tried to repeat it five or ten times and then it was stuck in my mind.
> (Student 2, Lines 167-75)

> When I hear a new word, I write them down, and when I go home I try to translate them into Arabic. (Student 3, Lines 159-60)

Independent study outside the context of language practice in authentic situations was also largely absent, as Student 1 reported that he only 'followed the assignments that the teacher gave me.' None suggested any conscious reading or writing strategies.

> Interviewer: You don't have any special techniques for writing.
> Student 4: We took that you must write introduction, body and conclusion. That's it. No special technique. What is in your mind you can write it.
> (Student 4, Lines 198-200)

> Writing, no special strategy. I just write. And after I finish, I take another look, to find out if there is something wrong. That's it.
> (Student 5, Lines 189-90)

Metacognitive strategies were almost entirely absent. When asked to describe how they organised their study of English, participants made comments such as the following:

> Interviewer: How do you plan and organise your study time?
> Student 4: Not too much.
> Interviewer: Do you set short term goals and long terms goals for your English study?
> Student 4: No. No goals. No planning. We study only before the exam. Two days before the exam or three days before the exam, that's all.
> (Student 4, Lines 202-11)

Social strategies were the most developed among the participants, who reported many strategies for practising speaking.

> Student 2: Yeah, with my friends. Sometimes, for example, when we are sitting in the coffee shop, I will say to the guys, 'We will talk in English now.' And we talk in English.
> Interviewer: They don't mind?
> Student 2: No, it's okay with them. Actually they are better than me in English. So I talk with them in English. I want to get the language from them. Two of them got 7, and one of them, 7.5 [on IELTS].
> Interviewer: Do you ever find it artificial, to speak English with your friends who know Arabic?

Student 2: Not strange. Before it was strange. I sitting with my friends, and two Emiratis sitting there also, they are speaking English, and we are laughing at them. 'Why they are speaking English, they are Emiratis?' We don't know what the purpose. But now I understood why. They wanted to get the language. They wanted to practise it.
(Student 2, Lines 252-60)

I have to speak. Lucky for me, I have my classmates. Whenever I say something wrong, he embarrass me, in front of everybody. He say 'No, you have to say this.' I learn from him. ... When I go to a restaurant, and I order something, and I spend maybe five or ten minutes talking to the guy, just telling him anything.
(Student 5, Lines 177-80)

In terms of affective strategies, four participants reported experiencing negative emotions such as confusion, frustration, and impatience while studying, though these tended to be at moderate levels. Three reported constructive affective strategies for dealing with these emotions. Two dealt with these emotions by themselves.

Saying to myself, 'Calm down, you can do it, you can understand this word, so just look in the dictionary,' so then when I know the word's meaning, I feel better. I feel relaxed. (Student 2, Lines 265-7)

While Student 3 had another approach:

Going and asking the teachers, tell them about your feeling, so they can give you some good examples and try to encourage you in your learning.
(Student 3, Lines 234-6)

Discussion

The present research has shown that Emirati students are mainly instrumentally motivated. Their own local culture creates a deep sense of comfort and identity. They do not want to give this up to be global citizens and have no desire to work or study abroad. While integrative motivation in a globalised world and the Ideal L2 Self come into play, these are ultimately functions of the practical necessity of using English in their local context and should be seen as sub-factors of a dominant instrumental motivation.

Most Emirati students do show some level of intrinsic motivation. Teachers could be a primary source of increasing intrinsic motivation through their planning of classroom activities. Data showed that teachers should attempt to make classes as fun, interesting, relevant and appealing as possible to students. Use of film, reading local English newspapers, and promoting practice through conversation, pair and group work are all ways to increase intrinsic motivation. Foreign textbooks could be supplemented with local sources on parallel topics (Dornyei, 2001).

Based on the participants' responses, there is obviously a mismatch between learner expectations and teachers' expectations for language study in a formal environment. As in Wenden's (1987) study at Columbia University, Arab students prefer to acquire language by using it, instead of through formal study. Participants seemed to concentrate on using language in authentic situations, especially conversation, reading, and watching films, and had few resources available to manage a formal learning environment. Teachers need to recognise the learning strategies of the Emirati student population. Students, for their part, need also to conform to teacher expectations for formal study in a university setting.

Although teachers commonly complain of students' lack of study skills, the present study showed that students do in fact use learning strategies. They do not, however, use optimal learning strategies (and most likely not ones which teachers expect them to use). The students in this study used relatively developed social/affective strategies. While cognitive strategies are what learners throughout the world rely on the most (Oxford, 2003), the students in this study were much weaker in using them. The only cognitive strategy for formal study mentioned by the students in the present study was in vocabulary development. Entire aspects of foreign language learning, notably grammar, reading and writing, seem outside their ability to approach effectively in terms of formal study. Participants in this study used almost no metacognitive strategies, while research shows that successful learners constantly use them, and it is often the ability to employ metacognitive strategies which can make the difference between successful and unsuccessful learners (Oxford 2003; Gan et al., 2004).

Conclusion

Increasing learners' motivational levels and increasing their use of learning strategies could improve learning outcomes in two ways. First, higher levels of performance could be achieved by those who are already enrolled in university courses. Second, if the motivation levels and learner strategies have somehow led the students in the study sample to achieve Band 6 on IELTS and enrollment at university, then lower-scoring test-takers may be even less motivated and have fewer strategies at their disposal. Increasing motivation and improving learning strategies could increase the rate of success in the total student population.

The connections between motivation and strategy use create a virtuous circle. Not only do more motivated learners employ more strategies, but the use of strategies leads to greater proficiency, which in turn increases motivation (Oxford & Nyikos, 1989). Students will be more effective learners if they can study independently. Though not dealt with in this study, learner autonomy is the third piece of the puzzle that is linked to motivation and learner strategies. Both motivation (Ushioda, 1996) and effective use of learner strategies (Oxford, 2003) enable learners to become more independent, self-directed and autonomous learners.

In addition to learner autonomy, the present research study suggests several areas for further investigation. First and foremost, cognitive and metacognitive strategies are usually regarded as the keys to successful language learning, while the results of the present study indicate that among Emirati learners cognitive and metacognitive strategies are underdeveloped. Research with a more narrow focus should be undertaken, specifically on Arab university students' employment of cognitive and metacognitive strategies. Research on motivation and learning strategies with learners who failed to achieve Band 6 on IELTS could also be undertaken, and especially important would be a comparison of learners who achieved Band 6 with those who failed to do so.

Low rates of success in attaining a Band 6 on IELTS among Emirati students can, in many ways, be seen as a result of low levels of motivation, and perhaps the wrong kinds of motivation on the part of Emirati and other Arab students. As Gan et al. (2004) pointed out, motivation at the university level may be influenced more by learners' secondary school experience than by anything they experience while at university. Motivation and strategy use are not issues that can be addressed quickly and corrected at the point of entering university. Neither will a semester-long study skills course be sufficient to develop the kinds of learner strategies that Arab students need to be successful in their studies. These issues must be addressed throughout the students' primary and secondary education in order to increase the rates of success among university students in the Gulf.

References

Chamot, A. (1987). The learning strategies of ESL students. In A. Wenden & J. Rubin (Eds.), *Learner Strategies in Language Learning* (pp. 71-83). Englewood Cliffs, NJ: Prentice Hall International.

Dornyei, Z. (1990). Conceptualizing motivation in foreign language learning. *Language Learning 40*, 45-78.

Dornyei, Z. (2001). *Motivational strategies in the language classroom.* Cambridge: Cambridge University Press.

Dornyei, Z. (2005). *The psychology of the language learner: Individual differences in second language acquisition.* Mahwah, NJ: Laurence Earlbaum Associates.

Dornyei, Z. (2009). *The psychology of second language acquisition.* Oxford: Oxford University Press.

Dornyei, Z., & Schmidt, R. (2001). *Motivation and second language acquisition.* Honolulu, HI: University of Hawaii Press.

Dornyei, Z., & Ushioda, E. (2009). *Motivation, language identity and the L2 self.* Bristol: Multilingual Matters.

Ellis, R. (2008). *The study of second language acquisition.* Oxford: Oxford University Press.

Gan, Z., Humphries, G., & Hamp-Lyons, L. (2004). Understanding successful and unsuccessful EFL students in Chinese universities. *The Modern Language Journal, 88*(2), 229-244.

Gardner, R. (1985). *Social psychology and second language learning: The role of attitudes and motivation.* London: Edward Arnold.

Gardner, R., & Lambert, W. (1972). *Attitudes and motivation in second-language learning.* Rowley, MA: Newbury House.

Hoath, N. (2001, December 8). Motivation, skill improvement key to success. *Gulf News.* Retrieved September 22, 2010 from http://gulfnews.com/news/gulf/uae/general/motivation-skill-improvement-key-to-success-hr-expert-1.431960

IELTS Test-taker performance 2008 (n.d.). Retrieved September 22, 2010, from: http://www.ielts.org/researchers/analysis_of_test_data/test_taker_performance_2008.aspx

Lamb, M. (2004). Integrative motivation in a globalizing world. *System, 32,* 3-19.

Lewis, K., & Bardsley, D. (2010, February 23). University remedial English to end. *The National.* Retrieved September 22, 2010 from

http://www.thenational.ae/apps/pbcs.dll/article?AID=/20100223/
NATIONAL/702229804&SearchID=73393762668150

Mitchell, R., & Myles, F. (2004). *Second language learning theories.* London: Hodder Arnold.

Naiman, N., Frohlich, M., Stern, H.H., & Todesco, A. (1996). *The good language learner.* Toronto, ON: Multilingual Matters Ltd.

O'Malley, M., & Chamot, A. (1990). *Learner strategies in second language acquisition.* Cambridge: Cambridge University Press.

Oxford, R. (1996). *Language learning strategies around the world: Cross-cultural perspectives.* Honolulu, HI: Second Language Teaching & Curriculum Center.

Oxford, R. (2003). *Language learning styles and strategies: An overview.* Retrieved September 22, 2010 from http://web.ntpu.edu.tw/~language/workshop/read2.pdf.

Oxford, R., & Nyikos M. (1989). Variables affecting choice of language strategies by university students. *The Modern Language Journal, 73*(3), 291-300.

Oxford, R., & Shearin, J. (1994). Language learning motivation: Expanding the theoretical framework. *Modern Language Journal, 78*(1), 12-28.

Rubin, J. (1987). Learner strategies: theoretical assumptions, research history and typology. In A. Wenden & J. Rubin (Eds.), *Learner strategies in language learning* (pp. 18-30). Englewood Cliffs, NJ: Prentice Hall International.

Thomas, J. (2010, April 11). F is for fail, and financial disincentive in federal schools. *The National.* Retrieved September 22, 2010 from http//www.thenational.ae/apps/pbcs.dll/article?AID=/20100412/OPINION/704119946

Warden, C.A., & Lin, H. J. (2000). Existence of integrative motivation in an Asian EFL setting. *Foreign Language Annals, 33,* 535-547.

Wenden, A. (1987). How to be a successful language learner: Insights and prescriptions from L2 learners. In A. Wenden & J.

Rubin (Eds.), *Learner strategies in language learning* (pp. 103-118). Englewood Cliffs, NJ: Prentice Hall International.

Wenden, A., & Rubin, J. (1987). *Learner strategies in language learning.* Englewood Cliffs, NJ: Prentice Hall International.

Ushioda, E. (1996). *Learner autonomy: The role of motivation.* Dublin: Authentik Language Learning Resources Ltd.

Ushioda, E. (2001). Language learning at university: Exploring the role of motivational thinking. In Z. Dornyei & R. Schmidt (Eds.), *Motivation and second language acquisition* (pp. 91-124). Honolulu, HI: University of Hawaii Press.

Yashima, T., Zenuk-Nishide, L., & Shimizu, K. (2004). The influence of attitudes and affect on willingness to communicate and second language communication. *Language Learning, 54*(1), 119-152.

Zeitoon, D. (2001, September 17). Workshops try to rescue under-performing students. *Gulf News.* Retrieved September 22, 2010 from http://gulfnews.com/news/gulf/uae/general/motivation-skill-improvement-key-to-success-hr-expert-1.431960.

GEORGIA DALEURE

Chapter 3
Factors Affecting Persistence in Post-Secondary Education: A Case Study of Emirati Males

Abstract

In the United Arab Emirates (UAE), Emirati males drop out of secondary and post-secondary education in significantly higher numbers than Emirati females, a phenomenon which can lead to severe economic and social consequences. This chapter approaches the issue from the perspective of Emirati males who persisted into post-secondary education. A study was conducted with 294 Emirati male students attending a College of Higher Education in the UAE to gain insight into their attitudes, beliefs and important factors contributing to their persistence in post-secondary education. Persistence factors found included the perceived support from parents and siblings, students' own dream of continuing education, and the existence of high quality public post-secondary education institutions. Emirati males showed awareness of the importance of education for career development. The chapter concludes with a set of recommendations such as increasing career development support in the secondary schools, redeveloping educational policies to better prepare Emirati males for the realities of the workplace, and admitting continuing students to public post-secondary institutions so that experienced Emirati males who left the educational system before completing a full Bachelors degree can return to upgrade their qualifications. Further studies are urged to add to the limited body of literature on this topic.

Introduction

Much of the literature on educational persistence addresses the needs of females with the assumption that boys will automatically benefit (Ridge, 2009a; Daleure, 2005). Examples include the *Arab Human Development Report* (AHDR), (United Nations Development Program [UNDP], 2006), *Gender and Development in the Middle East and North Africa* (World Bank, 2004), *Global Education Digest* (United Nations Educational, Scientific and Cultural Organization [UNESCO], 2004), *Education For All (EFA)Global Monitoring Report* (UNESCO, 2008), *Girls Continue to Face Sharp Discrimination in Access to School* (UNESCO, 2003), and *The EFA 2000 Assessment: Country Reports United Arab Emirates* (UNESCO, 2001). The reports describe the difficulties faced by females in the Middle East and emphasize the social and economic benefits of females obtaining as much education as possible. Difficulties faced by males in obtaining education, factors which may promote early male withdrawal from the educational system, or the economic and social issues that can surface when males are undereducated and/or underemployed were absent in these reports (Ridge, 2009a; Daleure, 2005). Even more strikingly, when specific data were presented showing considerable imbalances in the educational persistence of males and females, no discussion was undertaken to examine the causes, consequences, or potential remedies as was done when females were underrepresented in education. For example, the EFA *Global Monitoring Report* (UNESCO, 2008) and the *Middle East North Africa (MENA) Development Report: The Road Not Travelled* (World Bank, 2008), reported the following figures:

Table 1: Gender Parity Index for Gross Enrollment in UAE for year 2005

Education Level	Male % (out of total males in age group)	Female % (out of total females in age group)	Gender Parity Index
Primary	85	82	.97
Secondary	62	66	1.05
Tertiary	12	39	3.24

Source: *EFA Global Monitoring Report* (UNESCO, 2008)

There is a clear imbalance shown in Table 1 through the gender parity index value of 3.24 in favor of females. Rather than leading to a discussion of the factors disadvantaging boys at the tertiary level, this information was reported as a success in the battle to increase the number of females in the educational system with the rationale being that increasing the number of educated females in developing countries has a positive effect on the economy and society (UNESCO, 2008; World Bank, 2008). Not addressed were the consequences of males not achieving similar increased education levels as the females.

The early withdrawal from education of Emiratis of either gender raises concerns about the stability of the UAE economy and society in the future (Al-Qassimi, 2010). In 2005, UAE nationals comprised about 20 percent of the total population and about 10 percent of the eligible workforce. Nearly half the UAE nationals were under age 20 and slightly more than half were male (Ministry of Economy, 2006; MIC, 2008). Despite the low number of UAE nationals in the general population, unemployment figures remained as high as 13 percent overall (Glass & Bowman, 2009) with youth unemployment as high as 60 percent in unofficial figures (Ridge, 2009a, p. 183). In the past, Emirati males could enter the military, police, or other public sector area relatively easily with a secondary school diploma or less (Ridge, 2009a; Labi, 2008; Wagie & Fox, 2008). However, in recent years, the public sector 'has reached saturation point and is, therefore, incapable of absorbing the thousands (15,000 to 20,000) of nationals entering the job market each year' (MIC, 2008, p. 217). Future employment opportunities lie in the private sector representing about 52 percent of the jobs in UAE. Emiratis hold only about 2 percent of the private sector jobs (Wagie & Fox, 2008). In *Plan Abu Dhabi 2030* published by the Abu Dhabi Urban Planning Council (ADUPC, 2007) and *Highlights: Dubai Strategic Plan: 2015* (Government of Dubai, 2010) emphasis is placed on developing and expanding participation of UAE nationals in the private sector. However, less than 5 percent (Ministry of Education, quoted in Wagie & Fox, 2008) of the Emirati secondary school graduates are prepared to enter college or university without completing an English and math foundations program, and more than two thirds of the students do not choose the technical majors needed to fill the private sector jobs (Wagie & Fox, 2008).

Emiratization policies or 'governmental intervention in the form of employment quotas for nationals in certain sectors' (Ministry of Information and Culture [MIC], 2008, p. 218), have been put into place to assist Emiratis in securing jobs. However, Emiratization policies did not show the intended results in any sector except the banking sector where UAE national employment increased over 300 percent from years 2000 to 2005 (Moussly, 2009; Glass & Bowman, 2008; MIC, 2008; Shaiba, 2008). The banking sector has had more success than other sectors because Emiratis have been hired in positions requiring minimal education such as tellers, clerks, and customer service officers with little chance of advancement. According to the MENA Report (World Bank, 2008), over the next 25 years, more highly educated adults will enter the workforce displacing those who have less education. Employees who have gained skills and experience on the job but do not possess desired academic qualifications could be bypassed for advancements and promotions or be terminated in favor of fresh college graduates (Assaad, 2008; Chaaban, 2008; Issa, 2008; World Bank, 2008). Emiratis wishing to continue their education are excluded from public post-secondary institutions because priority is given to fresh high school graduates (Wagie & Fox, 2008).

Highlights: Dubai Strategic Plan: 2015 (Government of Dubai, 2010) and *Plan Abu Dhabi 2030* (2007), emphasized the need to develop a 'workforce for the high-value, knowledge-driven economy,' requiring highly skilled, qualified, and motivated Emirati employees (Government of Dubai, 2010, p. 22). As a result, the number of public post-secondary institutions has been increased and scholarships to study abroad were given to 410 students in 2010 (National Admissions and Placement Office [NAPO], 2010). Few countries encourage and subsidize post-secondary education to the extent that the UAE does (Wagie & Fox, 2006). Even so, Emirati males lag behind in taking advantage of the abundant opportunities to continue their education.

This chapter approaches the issue of educational persistence from the viewpoint of the Emirati males who have persisted to the post-secondary level. The literature review sets the groundwork to understand issues affecting the gender imbalance in post-secondary education along with potential economic and social consequences. A survey was formulated incorporating information from the literature and a series of focus group interviews designed to gain insight into factors and attitudes leading Emirati males to persist into post-secondary education. The findings of this study and others can be used to develop strategies to retain Emirati males in the educational system longer.

Background

The Public Education System in the UAE

The Kuwaiti Mission opened the first school in the UAE in 1953. Other schools opened soon after with support and personnel from a variety of other counties. After gaining independence from Britain in 1971, the government of the UAE began setting up a standard public education system from scratch (Farah & Ridge, 2009) and prioritizing educational attainment for all. By 1985, only 14 years after independence from Britain, the Ministry of Education managed to bring the newly established standard National Curriculum Project into full use across the UAE (Farah & Ridge, 2009).

In 2001, UAE Ministry of Education submitted a comprehensive study analyzing the public education system in the UAE to the *International Conference on Education* in Geneva. The *National Report on the Development of Education in the United Arab Emirates During the period 1990/91 to 1999/2000* (*National Report*) (Ministry of Education, 2001) pointed out deficiencies in the public education system and gave recommendations for correcting the deficiencies. Problems reported included assessment and evaluation practices in all levels, exams focusing on memorization and lacking critical thinking, written exams derived exclusively from textbook material, and pass/fail comprehensive final exams (Ministry of Education, 2001). English language teaching in public secondary schools was particularly problematic with students being taught English by poorly trained non-native English speakers who often conducted the classes in Arabic and gave students little or no opportunities to practise (Mustafa, 2002; Ridge, 2010).

The *National Report* (Ministry of Education, 2001) recommended the development and implementation of major educational reforms to remedy the problems. The main challenges facing national education reform included funding and facilities restructure, the effects of globalization on culture and society, and a generational gap in educational attainment. According to Al-Taneiji (2001) due to the lack of educational experience, many parents did not perceive the importance of their children maintaining regular attendance at school, completing homework assignments on time, and working independently. However, Al-Taneiji noted that low parental involvement occurred in both distinguished schools (with high performance levels) and non-distinguished schools (with satisfactory performance levels) leading the researcher to conclude that parental involvement or lack thereof was not a contributing factor in the academic performance of their children.

In a more recent report, *Key Findings From School Inspections 2009-2010* (Knowledge and Human Development Authority [KHDA], 2010), it was found that overall the quality for both public and private schools had improved. The number of Emirati males that dropped out of school in Grade 12 decreased from 10 percent in 2008 to 7 percent in 2009 while the number of Emirati females dropouts in Grade 12 increased slightly from 2 percent in 2008 to 3 percent in 2009 (McArthur, 2010). Most students dropped out in the first non-compulsory year of schooling.

Despite the deficiencies in the primary and secondary education in public and private institutions in the UAE, both males and females progress to post-secondary education with the number of females more than double the males. The next section explores reasons for differences in male and female educational persistence in the UAE.

Factors Leading to Differences in Male and Female Educational Persistence

Ridge (2009a) conducted a study of the public schools in the Emirate of Ras Al Khaimah. Findings concluded that although the funding and facilities were the same among boys' and girls' schools, there were important differences disadvantaging the male students such as the learning environment, family expectations, and perceived returns to investment in education. Teachers in boys' schools were non-Emirati males who were earning a relatively low salary, gave their minimum during the school day, and then supplemented their income delivering private lessons in the evenings. The schooling facilities were bare with graffiti on the walls (Ridge, 2010, p. 25). In the girls' schools teachers stayed longer during the school day, and the facilities reflected a more student-friendly learning environment with decorations and student work displayed on the walls. There were no major issues with classroom management in the girls' schools and more was expected of the students in terms of participation and assignment completion (Ridge, 2010; 2009a; 2009b).

Family expectations differed between males and females in the study (Ridge, 2009a). At home, boys reported that they were not encouraged to do their homework and were free to spend time outside the home. In contrast, 'girls were expected to stay home and do their homework' (Ridge, 2009a, p. 185). Ridge reported that males from less affluent families, or families with widowed or divorced mothers, or families with fathers who had taken another wife often quit school to work. Girls faced pressure to 'complete school to improve future prospects of work or marriage' (2009b, p. 3). Perceived returns on education for males were lower than for females as many students and teachers 'felt that it was immaterial whether the boys received a high-quality education, as they were all guaranteed jobs, housing, health care, and other social benefits by virtue of being Emirati' (2009a, p. 182). Zuraik (2005) conducted a study of public schools in the emirate of Sharjah with findings similar to Ridge's study except that secondary educational experience was similarly poor in both the boys' and girls' public schools in terms of quality of teaching, facilities, low expectations of students, and negligible parental involvement.

Daleure (2005) conducted a study exploring the perceived motivations, supports, rewards, and challenges for Emirati women enrolled in post-secondary education in Sharjah and Dubai. Women reported the encouragement from family and friends, the desire to do something other than sit at home, and the desire to give back to society and country as their major motivations to continue their education. The reported supports included a society and government promoting women's education, separate high quality single-sex women's institutions (also mentioned in Perry, 2000), access to transport, and no expectation to quit studying to work. Women perceived the following as the rewards for continuing their education: a sense achievement, future employment, and a bit of independence. The major reported challenges faced by Emirati women included the preference for males in the workplace and, for those who were single, the possibility that their future husband might not support their decision to work.

Social and Economic Consequences of Undereducated Emirati Males

Studies conducted since the late 1990s (Al-Oraimi, 2004; O'Hara, 2003; Bahgat, 1999) describe societal changes from the perspective of the Emirati females. Women believed that the responsibility of the development of Emirati society had fallen to them. As women assumed the additional roles of responsibility, pressure was lifted from the men. Emirati men began opting for less education and settled for occupations such as the military or the police carrying lower salaries. At the same time, the costs associated with marrying UAE national females such as elaborate weddings, honeymoon holidays, bridal gifts of gold and expensive clothing and so on increased dramatically causing many young men to borrow beyond their means to satisfy future inlaws' requests. To avoid postponing marriage or going into debt, some Emirati males opted for marriage with non-Emirati females. In the UAE, nationality and national benefits are passed along to children only through Emirati males, effectively prohibiting Emirati women from marrying non-Emirati men. Consequently, a growing number of Emirati women remain unmarried through their twenties and thirties or do not marry at all (Al Qassimi, 2010; Daleure, 2005; Khatib, 1994).

The educated Emirati women who do marry increasingly continue to work. Family sizes have been decreasing over the last 50 years with couples married in the 1960s and 1970s having an average of six to seven children. Couples married from the 1990s to present began limiting family size to an average three or four children. In a country where nationals constitute only around 20 percent of the population, Al Qassimi (2010) recommends that the society and government must make the necessary policy changes to support rather than penalize Emirati women for developing themselves to their full potential. In another study, Chaaban (2008) discussed the economic costs of 'youth exclusion,' a term referring to 'youth unemployment, youth joblessness, school dropouts, adolescent pregnancy, and youth migration' (p. 6) in several countries in the Middle East. The most significant outcome applying to the UAE is the overall loss of economic power resulting from youth exclusion mostly due to high dropout rates from primary, secondary, and tertiary education. Consequences include increased unemployment, low skilled youth competing for the existing low skilled jobs, and inability of young people to secure jobs requiring higher skill sets. All factors lead to lower personal income yield and lower quality of life. According to Chaaban (2008) 'the real costs extend beyond the economic costs to include psychological and mental costs that are difficult to measure' (p. 22) (see also Al Qassimi 2010; Daleure, 2005; Khatib, 1994).

Given the profound economic, social and psychological effects that male early withdrawal from education has, it is important to tease out the factors that motivate Emirati males to continue their post-secondary education. The following section describes one such study undertaken at one of the major federal institutions in the UAE.

The Study

The Participants

The participants of the study were 294 male UAE nationals attending a men's college at one of the campuses of the Higher Colleges of Technology (HCT), the largest federal tertiary institution in the UAE. They were between 18 to 27 years old and they were studying courses in business, information technology and engineering. Table 2 shows the number of participants in each program of study.

Table 2: Respondents by Program and Level *(n=294)*

	Diploma	%	Higher Diploma/ Bachelors	%
Business	134	46%	47	16%
IT	32	11%	9	3%
Engineering	43	15%	29	10%
Total	209	71%	85	29%

Most participants came from Sharjah, Ajman, and Umm Al Quwain (UAQ) with 7 percent or 22 students coming from the outlaying areas as shown in Table 3. The majority of the students, 77.9 percent had attended a public secondary school.

Table 3: Respondents by Location *(n=294)*

Location	Respondents	%
Sharjah	179	61%
Ajman	50	17%
UAQ	31	11%
Dubai	6	2%
Khorfakhan	5	2%
RAK	4	1%
Dibba	4	1%
Dhaid	2	1%
Kalba	1	0%
N/A	12	4%

Nearly one third (31%) of the respondents indicated that they were working but only 22 percent attended evening classes. Therefore, about 10 percent of the respondents attended day classes while working evenings, weekends, or rotating shifts.

Data Collection

The data were collected in two stages. First, four focus group interviews were conducted with 4 to 6 students each from a mix of levels and programs. Students were asked open-ended questions with probing follow up prompts to gain rich information and insight needed to develop the questions for the survey. The students' responses were arranged in themes. Two distinct areas of interest emerged: factors for persistence, and attitudes and beliefs about education and the workplace.

In the second stage of the data collection, students were asked to complete a survey. In the first part of the survey, participants had to rate the importance of the different factors in their decision to continue into post-secondary education using a Likert scale (3-extremely important, 2-very important, 1-a little important, 0-not important, NA- not applicable). The second part of the survey explored students' attitudes and beliefs about education in general and perceived return on education using a 5-point Likert scale (from 1-strongly disagree to 5-strongly agree). Each section of the survey contained a space for students to add an open-ended explanation to any response.

To ensure that students answered the questions thoughtfully, each question was asked in at least two ways with opposite orientations. The survey instrument was written in simple English to avoid language difficulties and administered by either the researcher or one of three native Arab speaking research assistants, all of whom administered the surveys using a preapproved interactive presentation lasting about 10 minutes taking the students through the survey question by question giving explanations and clarifications to minimize the chances of incomplete or careless answers.

Results and Discussion

The survey data were analyzed using the Statistical Package for Social Sciences (SPSS) software. The mean, variance, and standard deviation were calculated for each item in part 1 and part 2 of the survey. Then the means were calculated for each of the selected demographic attributes including program, credential, school type, location, and employment. *Chi*-tests and *t*-tests were used to detect differences among the different groups, but there were no statistically significant variances among the different demographic subsamples.

The survey showed that the most important factors for attending university were the students' parents, their own dream, their siblings, the HCT reputation, and the program choices offered at the college (see Table 4 below).

Table 4: Significant Factors for Persistence *(n=294)*

Factors	Mean*	Standard Deviation
Parents	2.51	0.80
Dream	2.35	0.88
Siblings	2.17	0.98
College Reputation	2.16	0.89
Program Choices	2.05	0.97

*Scale: 3-extremely important, 2-very important, 1-a little important, 0-not important, NA- not applicable

Although the previous literature (Ridge, 2010, 2009a; Al-Taneji, 2001) suggested that parents have little to do with the educational experience of their children, the findings of the present study suggest that parents somehow exert a positive influence in the home. It would seem that the parents are at least supportive and perhaps even encouraging their sons to attend university/college. The second important factor, the students' own dream, suggests that students who persist with their education have an internal desire to achieve an education despite the perceived barriers. The third important factor, the students' siblings, indicates that students took the opinion or advice from their older brothers or sisters and received some sort of familial support in addition to the support provided by their parents. The last two factors, college reputation and program choices, indicate that students were generally familiar with their options in the public post-secondary education. Other factors which were non-existent or of little importance were recruitment visits from colleges to their high schools, visits they made to colleges, and input from high school staff. 50 percent of the students responded 'N/A – not applicable' to each of these factors indicating more should be done at the secondary school level to raise the students' awareness of the abundant post-secondary education options and post-secondary education institutions should involve students and parents in recruitment events both on college campuses and in the community.

The second part of the survey looked at students' attitudes and beliefs about education in general. The results are shown below in Table 5.

Table 5: Students' attitudes and beliefs about education in general and perceived return on education *(n=294)*

Themes	Mean*	StD
Importance of Education		
Everyone should study after high school.	3.99	1.10
Only smart people should study after high school.	2.43	1.40
Return on Education		
UAE nationals get better jobs if they have better qualifications such as Diploma, Higher Diploma, Bachelor's Degree.	4.26	.97
Salaries and promotions are easy for UAE nationals to get without degrees after high school.	3.07	1.25
UAE nationals get better salaries and promotions if they have completed a degree after high school.	4.12	1.00
The salaries that UAE nationals get with a high school diploma are high enough to live comfortably in the UAE.	3.07	1.34
UAE nationals can get good jobs with only high school certificates, no need to continue studying after high school.	2.63	1.29
Connections are more Important than Qualifications		
UAE nationals can get good jobs with connections so they don't need to study after high school.	3.09	1.43
Even with connections, UAE nationals need to have a qualification such as Diploma, Higher Diploma, or Bachelors Degree to get good jobs and promotions.	3.71	1.29
Awareness of Increasing Cost of Living		
Life is getting more expensive.	4.41	.86

UAE nationals will need to get higher paying jobs.	4.26	.93
Awareness of Emiratization		
UAE nationals can get good jobs with a high school certificate because of emiratization.	3.19	1.20
Emiratization can only work if UAE nationals get higher qualifications such as Diploma, Higher Diploma, or Bachelors Degree.	3.41	1.22
Encouragement to Females		
UAE national females should study after high school.	3.56	1.08
UAE national females should not study after high school.	2.58	1.37
UAE national females should study after high school even if they are not going to work.	3.83	1.17
UAE national females should have the option to work if they want.	3.84	1.08

*Scale: 1-strongly disagree, 2-disagree, 3-no opinion, 4-agree, 5-strongly agree

Participants generally agreed on the importance of education for all (Mean:3.99). This supports the assertion in the literature that the UAE is a society that supports education for all and confirms the results of the first part of the survey showing students' own dream to be an important factor for persistence in education. Participants generally agreed that better qualifications lead to better jobs (Mean:4.26), better salaries and promotions (Mean: 4.12), however, they were not sure that a degree is a necessary prerequisite. This aligns with the results of previous studies (Ridge, 2010, 2009a, 2009b; Chaaban, 2009; Zuraik, 2005) that UAE nationals perceive that good jobs can be had with only a high school diploma or less, especially with access to connections. Despite this widely-held perception, the participants in this study chose to enroll in post-secondary education.

The survey also found that participants are aware of the increasing cost of living (Mean:4.41) and the need to earn more money in the future (Mean:4.26). This raised level of awareness may be due to the trend described in the literature in which fresh graduates enter the workplace and compete with workers already in the workplace (see Chaaban, 2009) or may be simply reflecting an awareness of increasing cost of living associated with a more mature lifestyle, i.e. marriage, raising children, supporting a family, supporting parents in old age, and so on.

Results also showed that participants did not have strong opinions about emiratization (Mean:3.19), not surprisingly since emiratization has not been particularly effective (Glass & Bowman, 2009; Issa, 2008; Shaiba, 2008). Finally, participants in the study showed moderate support for female participation in education (Mean:3.56) whether the females choose to work or not (Mean:3.83). That is, the males who have themselves persisted into post-secondary education are supportive of female participation in post-secondary education. These results are in line with previous studies showing females being encouraged to continue through post-secondary education (Al Qassimi, 2010, Ridge, 2009a, 2009b; Daleure, 2005; Khatib, 1999).

Recommendations and Conclusion

This chapter has dealt with the subject of male educational persistence in the Middle East, and specifically in the UAE. It was shown that this issue must be further explored in order to effect positive change in society whereby both males and females develop themselves to their full potential. The literature review described aspects of the educational system and society that have disadvantaged males, and the severe consequences to the economy and society as a whole if the situation is not examined and rectified. In this study, the subject of Emirati male persistence was approached from the perspective of males who have persisted with post-secondary education in order to shed light on the most important factors promoting persistence such as the positive influence of parents, siblings, the students' own dreams, the college reputation, and the program choices on offer. Young Emirati males appeared to be aware of the importance of education for economic benefits, and the inadequacy of connections for career advancement. Male Emiratis were less aware of the benefits of Emiritisation policies, and provided moderate support for the participation of females in education and the workplace.

The UAE is a young country in the growth stage of development (Government of Dubai, 2010) which has invested heavily in its citizens. Females have benefitted from this investment more than males. The literature review and the findings of this study indicate that UAE national males are concerned with providing for their families for which they have sole responsibility. Females, on the other hand, are motivated by family and society to continue their education, to pursue self-fulfillment and to give back to their countries (Al Qassimi, 2010; Ridge, 2009a, 2009b; Daleure, 2005; Khatib, 1999; Al-Abed & Vine, 1998).

More should be done at the secondary level in both public and private schools to raise the awareness of the abundant post-secondary educational opportunities available to young Emiratis. Specifically, abundant jobs available in the private sector in which Emiratis are solely under-represented (Government of Dubai, 2010) must be highlighted to students in time to make important decisions in study options. Parents must to be involved in the awareness process so that they will come to understand the future benefit of their young men remaining longer in the educational system rather than opting for the short-term gains.

Policies must be developed and implemented to support Emirati men in their overall career management including educational experience. Emirati males must obtain more education to compete in the job market and must adjust their attitudes and perspectives in order to gain employment in the private sector. As more highly skilled and educated Emiratis enter the workforce, competition for jobs and promotions will necessitate the re-entry of working Emiratis back into the education system to 'catch up' educationally with the younger more highly educated but less experienced workers. The public post-secondary institutions should examine their policy of giving priority and funding only to fresh high school graduates and reserve spaces for Emiratis returning to education to enhance their qualifications or credentials and offer more part-time evening undergraduate and post-graduate programs. This is in line with what is happening in the western world where professionals build experience and gain qualifications throughout their careers not just at the beginning. Finally, more studies need to be conducted on the subject of Emirati male educational persistence in order to gain more information about the educational experiences of Emirati males and the kind of support they need, similar to the studies which have been examining the experiences of Emirati females for the last 20 years.

References

ADUPC. (2007). *Plan Abu Dhabi 2030: Urban structure framework plan*. Abu Dhabi Urban Planning Council.

Al-Qassimi, S.S. (2010, May). *Expectations haven't advanced with UAE Women*. Dubai School of Government. Retrieved August 19, 2010, from:
http://ww.dsg.ae/NEWSANDEVENTS/DSGNews.aspx?udt_755_param_detail=2212.

Al-Shaiba, A. (2008, November 4). Long term strategy to tackle unemployment. *Gulf News*. Retrieved November 14, 2009, from:
http://archive.gulfnews.com/aricles/08/11/04/10259367.http.

Al-Taneiji, S.O. (2001). The relationship between parental involvement and school success in the United Arab Emirates. Doctoral dissertation, University of Colorado. Dissertation Abstracts International, 62/2: 2291A. (UMI No. AAT 3021496). Retrieved 22 July, 2004, from: UMI ProQuest Digital Dissertations database.

Assad, C. (2008). *Gender equality in the United Arab Emirates: A driver for increased competitiveness?* Policy Brief No. 5. Dubai School of Government.

Canadian Career Foundation. (2007). Persistence in post-secondary education. Retrieved March 3, 2009, from: www.millenniumscholarships.ca/images.publications/PokVol4_Ch3_backgrounder.pdf

Daleure, G.M. (2005). *Reflections of post-secondary educational experience of selected women of the United Arab Emirates (UAE): A qualitative analysis investigating the motivations, supports, rewards, and challenges encountered by seven Emirati women in the year 2004.* Doctoral Dissertation, Ball State University. Retrieved November 2, 2009, from: http://liblink.bsu.edu/uhtbin/catkey/1317929

Farah, S., & Ridge, N. (2009, December). Challenges to curriculum development in the UAE. Policy Brief no. 16. Dubai School of Government.

Glass, A., & Bowman, D. (2009, May 7) Less than 4% of workforce Emirati by 2020. *Arabian Business.* Retrieved on May 10, 2010, from: www.arabianbusiness.com/515875-less-than-4-of-workforce-emirati-by-2020

Government of Dubai, UAE. (2010). *Highlights: Dubai Strategic Plan (2015).* Government of Dubai.

Issa, W. (2008, April 5). UAE national workforce could double to 500,000 by 2020. *Gulf News.* Retrieved May 17, 2009, from: http://archive.gulfnews.com/articles/08/11/17/10260228.

KHDA. (2010). *Key findings from school inspections 2009-2010.* Government of Dubai.

Khatib, M. K. (1995). *Beyond the mysterious and exotic: Women of the Emirates (and I) assess their lives and society.* Doctoral dissertation, Brown University. Dissertation Abstracts International, 55/7: 2025A. (UMI No. AAT 9433384). Retrieved July 22, 2004, from UMI ProQuest Digital Dissertations database.

Labi, A. (2008, February). World Bank urges sweeping changes in higher education across the Arab world. *The Chronicle of Higher*

Education, *54*(23), A30. Retrieved April 28, 2008, from: www.proquest .umi.com

Lohfink, M.M., & Paulsen, M.B. (2005). Comparing the determinants of persistence for first-generation and continuing-generation students. *Journal of College Student Development*, *46*(4), 409-428.

McArthur, R. (2010, 8 June). More Emirati girls drop out. *ZAWYA*. Retrieved June 10, 2010, from: http://www.zawya.com/Story.cfm/sidZAWYA20100620044403/More%20Emirati%20girls%20drop%20out%3A%20report/

Ministry of Economy, UAE. (2006). *Preliminary results of population, housing, and establishments census 2005, United Arab Emirates*. Unpublished statistics.

Ministry of Education, UAE. (2001, September). *National report on the development of education in the United Arab Emirates during the period 1990/91 to 1999/20* [Electronic version]. Geneva: International Conference on Education.

Ministry of Information and Culture, UAE. (2008). *United Arab Emirates Yearbook: 2008*. London: Trident Press.

Moussly, R. (2009, 3 April). Target: Emiratization. *Gulf News*. Received May 17, 2009, from: http://archive.gulfnews.com/articles/09/04/03/10300632.

Mustafa, G.S. (2002). *English language teaching and learning at government schools in the United Arab Emirates*. Unpublished doctoral dissertation, University of Exeter, U.K.

Perry, P. (2000, April 9). Culture at the crossroads: The education of women. Is there a future for women's colleges in the new millennium? Retrieved November 12, 2004, from ERIC database (ED447279): http://eric.ed.gov

Ridge, N. (2009a). *Privileged and penalized: The education of boys in the United Arab Emirates*. Doctoral Dissertation: Teachers College, Columbia University, 2008.

Ridge, N. (2009b, August). The hidden gender gap in education in the UAE. Policy Brief no. 12. The Dubai School of Government.

Ridge, N. (2010, May). Teacher quality, gender and nationality in the United Arab Emirates: A crisis for boys. Working Paper No. 10-06. Dubai School of Government.

Sharjah Higher Colleges of Technology. (2009). Annual Foundations Survey. Unpublished statistics.

Suliman, O.M. (2001). *A descriptive study of the educational system in the United Arab Emirates.* Doctoral dissertation, University of Southern California. Dissertation Abstracts International, 62/6: 2055A. (UMI No. AAT 3018132) Retrieved August 30, 2004, from: UMI ProQuest Digital Dissertations database.

UNDP. (2006). *Human development report: Economic growth and human development.* Oxford, UK: Oxford University Press.

UNESCO. (2001). *The EFA 2000 assessment: Country reports United Arab Emirates.* Retrieved August 19, 2010, from: www.unesco.org/education/wef/countryreports/united_arab_emi rates/contents.html

UNESCO. (2003). *Girls continue to face sharp discrimination in access to school.* Paris, France: United Nations Educational, Scientific and Cultural Organization. Retrieved May 16, 2004, from: http://www.unesco.org

UNESCO. (2004). *Global Education Digest 2004: Comparing education statistics across the world* [Electronic version]. Montreal, Canada: UNESCO Institute for Statistics.

UNESCO. (2008). *Gender and equality for all: The leap to equality. Global Monitoring Report.* (Report No. 2003/4) [Electronic version]. Paris, France: United Nations Educational, Scientific and Cultural Organization.

UNESCO Institute for Education. (1996). *Women's educational and empowerment.* In Report of the international seminar (Hamburg, Germany, January 27 - February 2, 1993). Hamburg, Germany: United Nations Educational, Scientific, and Cultural Organization. Retrieved November 10, 2004, from: www.unesco.org.

Georgia Daleure

U.S. Department of Education, National Center for Education Statistics. (2008). *The condition of education 2008* (NCES 2008-031), Indicator 24. Retrieved from: nces.ed.gov/programs/digest/d07/tables/dt07_191.asp.

Wagie, D., & Fox, W. (2006). Transforming higher education in the United Arab Emirates (UAE). *International Journal of Learning, 12*(7), 277-289.

World Bank. (2008). *MENA development report: The road not travelled, Education reform in the Middle East and North Africa.* Washington, DC: MENA.

World Bank. (2003). *Middle East and North Africa face unprecedented employment challenge. Washington.* Retrieved September 6, 2004, from: http://web.worldbank.org/WBSITE/EXTERNAL/NEWS/content MDK:20129457

Zuraik, E. (2005). *A study of success and failure patterns in the public high schools of the Emirate of Sharjah in the United Arab Emirates.* UNESCO Chair Program, Center of Applied Studies in Education (CASE), Sharjah Higher Colleges of Technology.

Rana Raddawi

Chapter 4
Teaching Critical Thinking Skills to Arab University Students

Education is more than filling a child with facts.
It starts with posing questions.
(D.T. Max, *The New York Times*)

Abstract

This chapter aims to highlight cultural and pedagogical issues that arise within, and at times impede, the teaching of critical thinking skills to Arab students in a university setting in the United Arab Emirates (UAE). A quantitative study that extended over a period of two years was conducted with 200 student participants, amongst whom 180 were Arabs. Students at a private university in the UAE were enrolled in the Advanced Academic Writing course, which aims to develop students' critical thinking along with academic writing competencies and enable them to produce a research paper using their newly acquired analytical and critical skills. The study addressed some of the principal cultural differences that the students were exposed to while researching and writing their papers, such as their social background, education, religious beliefs, ethnicity, instructor and peers' views, and the university mission statement. The study found that these elements can hinder free critical thinking in students, thus undermining the main objective of the academic writing skills course and impeding the teaching of such indispensable skills for the youth to challenge the competitive job market. The chapter concludes with recommendations based on experiential learning theories, interactive instruction strategies, and critical thinking approaches that would serve to enhance the effectiveness of teaching critical thinking and analytical skills in English academic writing classes to Arab students in the Gulf region.

Introduction

Barnt and Bedau (2005) define the term 'critical' as 'searching for hidden assumptions' which can be seen as 'noticing various facts and evaluating what is most significant' (p. 3). The etymological meaning of the word 'critical' comes from the Greek word 'krinein' which means to 'separate,' 'to choose' (p. 3). According to Booth, Colomb and Williams (2008), critical thinking is 'trying to support our position and also trying to see the other side' (p. 3). Furthermore, Barnt and Bedau (2005) share the same definition of critical thinking stating that 'the heart of critical thinking is a willingness to face objections to one's own beliefs' (p. 45). This implies that whether a student who is carrying out a research project shares or not the same beliefs and values of his/her peers, he/she should be ready to take the challenge to the next level and to confront the peers with newly perceived arguments. Chafee (2009) explains critical thinking as thinking 'independently' and 'actively'. It is 'viewing situations from different perspectives' (p. 123) but in an organized way, i.e., through presentation of reasons followed by evidence and arguments.

Historically, the teaching of critical thinking can be traced to Dewey's philosophy of thinking, developed during the early part of the twentieth century (Dewey 1916, 1933, 1938). However, according to Beyer (1985), it was not until the 1950s that educators began to teach critical thinking skills in the classroom as an integral component of the curriculum. Marwan Muasher, a senior World Bank official (as cited in Gavlak, 2008), stated in a report that:

> The time has come for countries to focus their energies on the quality of education and making sure that students are equipped with what they need for the labor market needs now-the ability to solve problems, critical thinking, innovation, and teacher retraining. (p. 28)

Muasher's report pointed out that unemployment in the Arab world reached 14% in 2008, which is higher than in other areas in the world except in Sub-Saharan Africa and Palestine. Muasher also pointed out in the report that '100m new jobs will need to be created over the next 10 to 15 years in the Arab world,' and he ended his statement by affirming that 'if we are to create such jobs, then we have to start with education' (p. 2).

Speaking about Arab education mainly in the Middle East and North Africa, Rugh (2002) stated that:

> ...education will need to impart skills enabling workers to be flexible, to analyze problems, and to synthesize information gained in different contexts.... By all indications, education systems in MENA (the Middle East and North Africa) do not reward these skills. (p. 3)

Moghraby (1999) also advocated 'reform in the educational system' (p. 303) in order to promote rational and critical methods of thinking and to enhance creativity and innovation.

Critical thinking skills in education is what is urgently needed in the GCC (Gulf Cooperation Council) countries in particular and the Arab world in general in order to keep up with the demands of the labor market (Moghraby, 1999; Al-Suwaidi, 1999; Abi-Mershed, 2009) if the Gulf region and the Middle East wish to keep up with global growth and development and build 'an Arab knowledge society' (UNESCO, 2005).

Background

Calls to 'build a knowledge society' and the importance of critical skills have become a key feature of present day discourses in the Middle East (Mazawi, 2010, p. 201). In the Arab world, few studies were conducted to research and investigate critical thinking in education (Rugh, 2002; Coleman, 2006; Amir, 2008; Roth, 2008; Gavlak, 2008; Selim, 2008; Bataineh & Alazzi, 2009). For example, Bataineh and Alazzi's study (2009) on the teaching of critical thinking in Jordanian secondary schools revealed that most teachers are not aware of the definition and teaching strategies of critical thinking. In brief, all of the referenced studies confirmed the lack of emphasis on critical pedagogy in educational institutions in the Middle East and the Gulf region. Hence, there is an urgent need for awareness and attention to the teaching of critical thinking which are indispensable skills in the competitive global world today.

This chapter explores the teaching of critical thinking skills at a mid-size university in the United Arab Emirates (UAE). The university hosts more than 80 different nationalities. According to the university's recent statistics, 73% of the students are Arabs and 93% are Muslims. All students, regardless of their major, are required to take General Education courses such as Advanced Academic Writing. The main objective of this course is to develop critical thinking and analytical skills in students. Thus, the students learn basic skills such as how to summarize, paraphrase, and quote effectively and apply those techniques to critique non-literary texts. Furthermore, one of the main course assessments is the writing of a research paper (term paper), which is usually allotted 40% of the total grade of the course. Students are required to submit an eight- to ten-page-long research essay on a topic of their choice − preferably argumentative and raising controversy. Whilst choosing their topics, the students are confronted with several obstacles stemming from many factors, which are scrutinized in this chapter. These mainly cultural hindrances not only affect the freedom of choice for the students' discussion topics and restrict the key freedom of opinion and speech necessary to build a knowledge society (Mazawi, 2010; UNESCO, 2005), but also undermine the main objective of the course – to instill critical thinking skills in students. This contradicts the mission statement of the university which calls upon the quest for in-depth knowledge and social responsibility to relate to the outside community. The following section reports the details of the case study.

The Study

This research is based on a mixed-method approach of investigation. Data were collected using surveys, interviews, classroom observation, students' research papers, syllabi and course handouts. A list of 690 students' research topics was compiled. These topics were categorized as follows:

- Topics related to the Arab world vs. topics not related to the Arab world;
- Topics related to Islam vs. topics not related to Islam;
- Culturally challenging topics vs. non-culturally-challenging topics.

Ten individual student interviews were also conducted. The interviewees were selected from the list of participants in the study based on the type of their research topics. The interviewees' topics tackled culturally challenging topics or what Bataineh and Al-Azzi labeled as 'untouchable issues' (2009, p. 8). The students were asked only one open-ended question: why they considered their topics 'culturally challenging' and how they would handle such subjects. Participants were given the choice either to be recorded during the interview or to just allow note-taking. Both methods were used.

Some selected students' papers and presentations were also used to confirm some theoretical statements used to explain the concept of critical thinking. Finally a survey was also conducted with 180 Arab students (male and female) who had taken the Advanced Academic Writing. They were chosen out of 200 students from nine sections of the course offered over four consecutive semesters. Informed consent was sought from all participants. The survey comprised three multiple-choice questions, aimed to determine the factors that affect the participants' choice of research topic and subsequent procedural behavior/action. The survey also allowed the researcher to specify the cultural hindrances that students are confronted with whilst choosing their research topic and available alternatives. The results from the analysis of each set of data are presented and discussed in the following section.

Results and Discussion

Research Topics

The distribution of the research topic selection among the 690 topics compiled over several semesters, showed that 73% of the chosen topics were not related to the Arab world (501 topics), while only 27% dealt with issues related to the Arab world (189 topics). Only 8% of the 690 topics were related to Islamic issues (52 topics). Similarly, topics on culturally challenging issues comprised 8% (58 topics) of the total sample of topics.

Surveys

The survey aimed to explore the factors that affected students' choice of topic, the factors that limited their choice of topic and the students' reaction to cultural hindrances. The results are shown below in Figures 1-3.

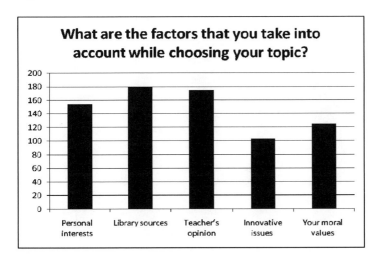

Figure 1. Factors that affect students' choice of topic.

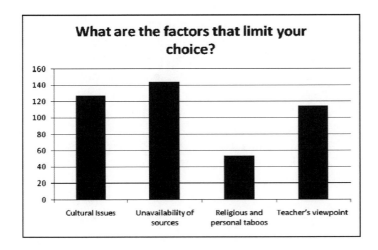

Figure 2. Factors that limit students' choice of topic.

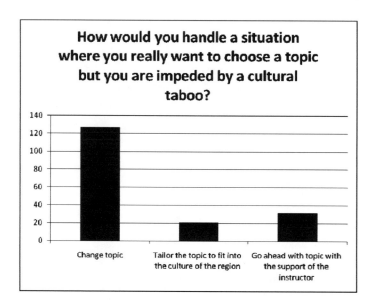

Figure 3. Students' reaction to cultural hindrances.

As shown in Figure 1, in choosing their topic, 86% of students considered their personal interests and 69% considered their moral values. This indicates the role that the students' cultural background plays in the research process. The fact that 97% were influenced by their teacher's opinion illustrates the crucial position of the teacher in the elaboration of the students' research topic. All surveyed students took into account the availability of library resources whilst choosing their topic, revealing their awareness of the importance of resources in conducting a research paper.

With regards to the other two questions, of the 180 surveyed students, 71% considered the weight of culture in their research, whilst 80% saw the lack of reference sources as a hindrance to the choice of their topic. 29% of the participants viewed religious and personal taboos as limiting factors in their research, which was also mentioned in the interviews. The students' answers revealed that their religious background and perception of their surroundings played a significant role in their choice of research topic.

Furthermore, 63% regarded the teacher's viewpoint as a hindrance. Only 18% of the students would choose a culturally challenging topic if they had their instructor's support, and this explains why 70% of students would change their topic when there is discrepancy between the teacher and their own opinion. Finally, 12% of students reported they would try to fit the topic into the cultural context of the region.

To better understand why the cultural background of the students plays such an important role in choosing their topics (71% look at their culture while selecting the topic), it is essential to examine the concept of culture as defined by scholars in the field of intercultural communication studies. Today, culture is referred to as a self-sustaining community with a large population that shares beliefs, values, experiences about life that guide their behavior (Thill & Bovee, 2007). Griggs and Louw (1995) describe culture as 'every individual difference that affects a task or relationship' (p. 55). According to Bennett and Bennett (2001) culture can be defined in two ways: 'Objective' culture and 'Subjective' culture. These terms created initially by Berger and Luckmann (1967) explain the significance of culture as referred to in modern times. Objective culture or 'Culture with a big C' as described by Bennett and Benenett (2001) refers to 'the institutional aspects of culture such as political and economic systems and to its products such as art, music, cuisine, etc.', while subjective culture or 'culture with small c' refers to the experience of the social reality formed by a society's institution, in other words the worldview of a society's people (p. 27).

Based on these definitions of culture, one can infer that culture is a set of values, behaviors and learned experiences shared by groups of interacting people defined by the political, economic and social systems in addition to personal characteristics such as verbal and non-verbal communication and individual social behavior. When Hofstede (2001) studied the cultural dimensions of a society, he classified cultures into individualist and collectivist. Collectivism here has no political meaning but refers to one's belonging and loyalty to the group. In collectivist societies, people from birth onwards are integrated into strong, cohesive in-groups and are concerned about the harmony and the heritage of their society. Whereas in individualist societies the person is in general self-centered and cares about his/her well-being in the first place and is somehow detached from the family and community's interests. Usually Arabs are described as collectivist societies (Hofstede, 2001; Jandt, 2007; Samovar, Portier, & McDaniel, 2009). This could explain why Arab students give so much value to their moral principles and their cultural roots in the selection of their research topic. They possess a spirit of belonging to their group cultural origins.

Fortunately, culture is not viewed as static but rather 'dynamic' (Samovar, et al., 2009, p. 12). If culture is defined by shared experiences (Jandt, 2007), it is implied that the more we share the more our cultural luggage increases. The fact that culture is a constantly changing phenomenon opens up a wide horizon for the students to conduct inquiry and seek innovation. This is the reason why teachers at all levels of education devote their lives to research and governments spend billions on it. It is 'the world's biggest industry' (Booth et al., 2008, p. 9). According to Booth et al. (2008), those who cannot participate in innovation, or support others in their pursuit of innovative thinking, will find themselves 'sidelined' in a world based on sound inquiry supported with evidence and clear and accurate arguments. The student participants of this study are no exception. If 127 (70%) out of 180 students change their research topic because of its culturally challenging aspects, then they will find themselves confined to the task of paraphrasing what the others have said and maintaining the status of an 'outside observer.'

Interviews

The researcher interviewed 10 out of the surveyed 180 students to shed light on the type of topics that the students consider 'culturally challenging' and the way they handle them. The following interview question was used: *Was there a time you wanted to discuss a culturally challenging topic but you were impeded by any external factor?*

The following quotes taken from the interview dataset summarize the participants' responses:

> Yes, I wanted to talk about the double facades of Dubai, but I could not because I am Emirati and my mother is an expatriate, so I feared discrimination and blame. This subject could be a social and political taboo, so I decided to discuss another challenging issue but more personal, which is the discrimination that mixed-blood Emirati girls endure by pure blood Emirati females. (Participant 1)

> Yes I wanted to tackle prostitution in Dubai, but the instructor opposed and asked me to change the topic. (Participant 2)

> I wanted to discuss youth and atheism: Why Pakistani youth is sweeping away from Islam. But then I changed my mind because I did not want to get in trouble with my peers, so I shifted to how Islam can answer youth questions. (Participant 3)

> I wanted to convince my teacher and my classmates that Hijab (the veil) in Islam is a must. I had to struggle hard to make a point because the instructor had the opposite viewpoint. He came from a different cultural and ethnic background. I had to recur to other religions and establish analogy in my arguments. I mentioned Christianity and used the example of the Virgin Mary who is always portrayed veiled and the nuns. It was not easy to persuade my instructor but I made it! (Participant 4)

> I wanted to talk about Islam and whether it is a religion of backwardness but had a hard time locating sources with the two sides of the argument to better support my view, so I changed the topic to genetically modified food. (Participant 5)

> I wanted to discuss suicide bombing and defend it but was not allowed by the instructor. (Participant 6)

I wanted to discuss transsexuals in the Arab world but had some reservations about how my instructor and my peers would perceive me. Yet, I went ahead with the topic thanks to the support of the instructor. (Participant 7)

I wanted to focus my research on the Armenian genocide in Turkey, but the instructor advised not to do it as it may create a sort of tension with some of my multicultural peers in class, in addition to the possibility of the subject not being very attractive to all my 22 classmates! (Participant 8)

I initially wanted to discuss the factors that lead many Khaleeji males and females to behave outside their morals and traditions when they are outside the Gulf Region and especially in western countries. I was very interested in the topic, but prior to submitting my proposal, I tried to search for sources to support the topic, and I couldn't find a reasonable number of references so I changed the topic. (Participant 9)

I was keen to talk about sex education in the Arab world but feared the reaction of my peers as some of them were very religious and conservative, then went to the professor's office to have her opinion. She welcomed the idea and told me that as long as I had convincing reasons, sufficient evidence, and strong arguments, I could go ahead with the topic. In fact I did, and my paper was a success! (Participant 10)

From the participants' responses, we can infer that 'culturally challenging' topics tend to be those which may contradict the 'common sense' of the local society – including authorities, peers, and even teachers. The topics students found challenging were mostly culturally sensitive, and some were taboos – such as Dubai's double façades, prostitution, atheism, suicide bombing, sex education, homosexuality, and transsexuality. The unavailability of library sources was also sometimes a hindrance to students. The apparent lack of resources for certain topics reflects the avoidance of culturally sensitive issues in the region in general as well as the lack of encouragement and support for research and critical thinking. In the Arab world 'inadequate resources for higher education and scientific research' (Moghraby, 1999, p. 299) are some of the setbacks of the educational system.

If students are to develop critical thinking skills, they should be encouraged to voice their ideas and assumptions regardless of their initial acceptance by the audience. Students need to learn how to further organize and present their ideas supported by evidence, and subsequently crowned by their own arguments. At this level, the students should be motivated and encouraged to challenge not only their peers, but also the opinions of the broader research community. This presupposes taking critical thinking skills to the next level of creative thinking, that is presenting one's arguments in a unique fashion. This implies that the researcher advances arguments that can be not only useful, but also valuable for further research. Chaffee (2009) calls these progressive steps in research the 'stages of knowledge'. The first stage is the 'Garden of Eden,' where knowledge is clear and certain and is provided by authorities (Chaffee, 2009, p. 170). The role of the audience, including the student who is conducting the research, is to 'learn and accept information from authorities without question' and 'anyone who disagrees with the authorities is wrong' (p. 171). It is akin to following the crowd and holding the same evidence and arguments. The second stage is 'Anything Goes,' when even authorities disagree with each other and no one knows where the truth lies (p. 171). In this case, all arguments are of equal value. The third stage is the 'Thinking Critically' stage, whereby some ideas are better than others not because the authorities said so, but because there are valid reasons to support these viewpoints (p. 171). In this case, student researchers analyze these arguments, evaluate them, and take the responsibility of presenting them to their peers with a new insight.

To better illustrate these steps of knowledge advanced by Chafee, a research paper about polygamy presented by a student in one of the Advanced Academic Writing courses will serve as an example. In the research proposal, the student explained the rationale of the topic and defended polygamy, by stating the reasons why men would subscribe to it as follows: firstly, when a woman cannot have a child; secondly, when she has a chronic disease; and thirdly, to solve a problem of spinsterhood – a global problem in the Islamic world.

The student based his beliefs on what authorities say through the media and partially through education, without questioning the accuracy of the information. The instructor asked him to verify the evidence in support of these reasons – typically done through religious resources such as the holy book, the Prophet statements, or by consulting different religious authorities. In the first draft of the research, the student was able to consult with various religious scholars, yet came away with the same arguments. The instructor intervened again and asked the student to refer this time to religious texts and present new arguments in the final draft. The student did the task successfully and found out that there is no evidence in the Quran (the first reference for Muslims as to the reasons for polygamy) to support his original statements. There was no single verse that gives men the right to seek another wife in case the first woman is infertile or ill or even if there are many spinsters. At this stage, the student achieved the stage of 'thinking critically,' or the third stage of knowledge – as stated by Chaffee.

If the student's critical thinking skills were to be pushed further, a thorough revision of the concept of religion – which is meant to put humans on the path of justice, mercy, and love – could have been expected. How would this concept match the perception of polygamy discussed in the paper? How would religion as a means of seeking justice for humans be a way of oppression and suppression at the same time? Reasoning is essential to all research studies. Chaffee (2009, p. 305) advises to consider the 'ethic of justice and care' in our critical thinking skills. This echoes the results of the survey where 124 (69%) students said their moral values were an important factor in their choice of topic. They chose to be moral individuals. Yet, these moral values are not always universal. They are usually aspects of someone's life experiences, and this is why they may be challenging, especially in a multilingual and multicultural class environment. However, does this mean that the student should give up on his or her values or stop presenting them through research? An example would be Participant 4 who was trying to defend the wearing of Hijab, or veil in English. However, the teacher, who came from a different cultural and ethnic background, argued that Hijab was not ordered in the Quran. The student used analogy in her arguments to convey her viewpoint and better illustrate the dilemmas arising when social and moral values are challenged.

Making one's culture explicit requires a critical attitude and helps the students understand their own culture compared with others. Thinking, as a mental activity, is not sufficient to make a strong argument; there must be a sound decision to be made and a wise multidimensional critical thinking that voices the researcher's point of view. According to Strenberg (as cited in Lang & Evans, 2006), a 'wise' researcher seeks three kinds of interests that should be informed by values: 'intrapersonal' as one's own, 'interpersonal' (other people's), and 'extra personal' or 'institutional' (p. 447). A good researcher is the one who can satisfy all three requirements. Yet, this process does not relate only to the student or the critical thinker alone but also to all stakeholders of the research and mainly the instructor. The first level of interests refers to critical and creative thinking that serves the ego of the researcher. The second interest, or 'interpersonal' interest, serves three parties: the student (researcher) and the others (peers and instructor) and can be called 'alterism' or 'otherness' from the intercultural perspective. Finally, the third interest, or 'extra personal' level of thinking, serves the institution – which, in the case of this study, is the academic setting to which the student belongs. This interest is reflected by the university mission statement which calls upon the quest for in-depth knowledge and social responsibility to relate to the outside community. There is also an invitation to faculty and students for research and scholarship to improve teaching and learning and to contribute to the growth of the nation. Yet, at the academic institution were this study took place, although Arabs comprise 73% of the total student population and the number of Muslim students is high (93%), only a few students (27% and 8% respectively, according to the survey analysis) were attracted to topics that relate to their own culture and religion. This implies that the first level of interest, or intrapersonal, is not satisfied. It is rather the second, or the 'interpersonal,' that most of students seek.

This also partially explains why only 8% of the students (58 out of 690) selected 'culturally challenging' research topics.

The role of the teacher has changed tremendously in the past few decades. No more just an instruction provider, a teacher has also become a mentor, collaborator, and good advisor. There is no doubt that a good teacher is the one who can find a balance between the direct instruction and the experiential or constructivist method of teaching. In the first approach, the teacher has the role of an 'initiator,' providing basic information for the student to begin with; in the second role, the teacher is a guide, facilitator, and resource person. The student in the latter approach is an active learner engaged in activities, motivated and involved in focused imaging and experiments. The student plays the role of an investigator through the constructivist approach; 'students construct knowledge linking new information to pervious knowledge' (Lang & Evans, 2006, p. 341). Through constructivism, students raise questions and build understanding to the extent of shifting roles with the instructor. When students are conducting a research project, they should have the courage to take the responsibility of being a teacher who presents facts, reasons, evidence, and arguments in an organized and intelligent way. In addition, if they can come up with unique ideas that would change the audience's perspectives about a certain issue, they would be shifting to the next level – that of the creative thinker. With the many existing theories and programs in education, in addition to advances in technology and ease of communication, the teacher's role of a 'colonizer' (Severino, Guerra, & Butler, 2008, p. 105) in the classroom should change. As the survey results show, around 97% of students take the teacher's viewpoint into account whilst choosing their topic. This reflects a certain level of excessive authority from the instructor's side. The number of students who change the topic because of their teacher's viewpoint is also not to be neglected. Therefore, there must be a shift in roles, whereby the student becomes an instructor and the teacher a learner.

Implications

To form a distinguished generation of young people who are ready to compete in the outside world, leading academic institutions such as the one under scrutiny in this chapter must seek to foster the teaching and learning of critical and creative thinking. This entails giving a leeway to the learner in terms of thinking, raising questions, and discussing issues that relate to their own culture. One's culture is the product of a series of shared experiences in all areas of life. Students should be given the chance to fully voice their opinions and either support them with existing reasons and arguments or come up with new viewpoints. Bakhtin (as cited in Severino et al., 1997) calls it a 'double-voiced discourse,' where half of the argument is attributed to what others have said on the subject and the other half is the student's own voice.

Sometimes students are torn between their cultural background, the way they were raised and taught things, and their inner powerful voices that want to be heard. They wish to stay loyal to these values instilled in them since childhood, but, at the same time, they want to set themselves free of these restrictions. They want to let their creative voice go out to the world and express their feelings through their research paper. Students should be given permission to challenge religious misconceptions related to issues such as polygamy, adoption, education, segregation, racism, and fanaticism – which are mostly misconceived by a small number of uneducated or insufficiently informed individuals. Students should be encouraged to foster their identity without giving up the essence of academic writing, the rules for critical thinking and ethics, and the consideration of others' feelings. The solution probably lies in instilling critical thinking skills in students. As a mental process, critical thinking requires intelligence and practice in order to become a norm. Many great thinkers such as Albert Einstein, Carlos Castaneda, and Bill Gates were not good students at school or in college, but their proficiency at applying their knowledge to problems they faced set them apart as the great minds in modern history. According to McCarthy (2006), one does not have to be book-smart to be a critical thinker; instead, all they need is a clear mind and the passion to find out new things and the way those things work.

Universities in the Gulf region should continue their systematic support for students' research with comprehensive state-of-the-art printed and electronic resources. Yet, often the lack of library resources can be traced to the absence of critical thinking required to provide a multiplicity of resources. The teacher's role should be defined with a modern and professional perspective, i.e., that of a facilitator and motivator, rather than a lecturer. The students' role is to be enhanced by encouraging leadership and decision-making skills. This can be developed through critical and creative thinking skills – i.e., intentionally separating and choosing arguments. This would keep the student abreast with the latest breakthroughs and take learners and their academic institution to the next level at the forefront of educational settings in the world.

Conclusion

The present study aimed to shed light on a crucial component of modern teaching: critical thinking. Qualitative and quantitative research was carried out to analyze and evaluate the factors that hinder the development of critical thinking skills in Arab students of a chosen university. Results showed that there is a need to continue fostering the teaching of critical thinking skills. Not only the case study institution but all academic institutions and decision makers in the Gulf should develop their education systems and set them free of biases and misconceptions to encourage critical and creative thinking and critical analysis skills that would prepare Arab students to face the challenges of today's globalized world. A new generation of critical thinkers, knowledgeable and smart, with free mindsets is needed to face the challenges of a highly competitive world. Education is accessible to almost everyone today, but it is the way one acquires and uses the information that makes the difference. We do not need to teach our students how to think, nor what to think. We just need to provide the necessary tools, such as language skills, research opportunities and freedom of choice, and let them think for themselves.

References

Abi-Mershed, O. (2009) .*Trajectories of education in the Arab World: Legacies and challenges.* London: Routledge.

Al-Suawidi, J. (1999). Education and human resources development in the Gulf: Challenges of the twenty-first century. In ECSSR (Ed.), *Education and the Arab World: Challenges of the Next Millennium* (pp.331-333). Abu Dhabi: The Emirates Center for Strategic Studies and Research.

Amir, K.A. (2008). Arab unemployment likely to rise 14%. *Gulf News.* Retrieved June 6, 2010 from http://gulfnews.com/business

Barnt, S., & Bedau, H. (2005). *Critical thinking, reading and writing: A brief guide to argument* (5th Ed.). Boston: Bedford/St.Martin's.

Bataineh, O., & Alazzi, K. (2009). Perceptions of Jordanian secondary schools teachers towards critical thinking. *International Education, 38*(2), 56-72.

Bayat, A. (2005). Transforming the Arab world: The ADHR and the politics of change. *Development and Change, 36*(6), 1225-37.

Bennett, M., & Bennett, J. (2001). Developing intercultural sensitivity: An integrative approach to global and domestic diversity. Proceedings from *The Diversity Symposium*, Bentley College, Waltham, MA.

Bennett, M. (2003). *Lecture at The Intercultural Communication Institute.* Portland, Oregon.

Berger, P., & Luckman, T. (1967). *The Social construction of reality.* Garden City, NY: Doubleday.

Beyer, B.K. (1985). Critical thinking: What is it? *Social Education, 42,* 270-276.

Booth, W., Colomb, G., & William, J. (2008). *The Craft of Research.* Chicago & London: The University of Chicago Press.

Chafee, J. (2009). *Thinking critically.* Boston: Heinle Cengage Learning.

Coleman, I. (2006). The Arab World is experiencing the first tremors of a youthquake. Retrieved June 7, 2010, from: http://www.cfr.org/ubicayions

Dewey, J. (1916). *Democracy and eduaction.* New York: Macmillan.

Dewey, J. (1933). *How we think.* Chicago: Henry Regnery.

Dewey, J. (1938). *Experience and education.* New York: Collier Books.

Gavlak, D. (2008). Arab education 'falling behind'. *BBC News.* Retrieved June 13, 2010 from: http://news.bbc.co.uk.

Griggs, L.B., & Louw, L. (1995). *Valuing diversity: New tools for a new reality.* New York, NY: McGraw-Hill.

Hofstede, G. (2001). *Culture's consequences, comparing values, behaviors, institutions, and organizations across nations.* Thousand Oaks CA: Sage Publications.

Jandt, F.E. (2007). *An introduction to intercultural communication.* London: SAGE Publications.

Lang, H., & Evans, D. (2006). *Models, strategies, and methods for effective teaching.* Boston: Pearson Education, Inc.

McCarthy, C. (2006). *What is critical thinking?* Retrieved May 4, 2010 from: http://www.scottsdalecc.edu/ricker/critical_thinking.

Mazawi, A. (2010). Naming the imaginary. In O. Abi-Mershed (Ed.), *Trajectories of education in the Arab World.* London and New York: Routledge.

Moghraby, A. (1999). Human development in the United Arab Emirates: Indicators and challenges. In ECSSR (Ed.), *Education and the Arab World: Challenges of the next millennium* (pp.279-307). Abu Dhabi: The Emirates Center for Strategic Studies and Research.

Roth, J.H. (2008). Beyond literacy in the Arab World. Retrieved June 9, 2010 from: http://www.commongroundnews.org.

Rugh, A. (2002). Arab education: Tradition growth and reform. *Middle East Journal, 56*(3), 396-414.

Samovar, L., Porter, R., & McDaniel, E. (2009). *Intercultural communication.* Boston, MA: Wadsworth Cengage Learning.

Selim, H. (2008). Unemployment in the Arab World. Retrieved June 8, 2010 from: http://www.asharq-e.com/news

Severino, C., Guerra, J., & Butler, J. (1997). *Writing in multicultural settings.* NY: The Modern Language Association of America.

Thill, J., & Bovee, C. (2009). *Excellence in business communication.* NY: Pearson.

UNESCO. (2005). *Literacy and adult education in the Arab World.* Hamburg: UNESCO Institute for Education (UIE).

Wellington, J. (2007). *Educational research. London:* Continuum.

LAUREN STEPHENSON & BARBARA HAROLD

Chapter 5
Emergent Leadership Development through Undergraduate Research in UAE Classrooms

Abstract

This chapter provides an account of the serendipitous elements of tacit leadership development in a pre-service teacher education college in the United Arab Emirates (UAE). Drawing on socio-cultural theories of learning and using case-study techniques, data were drawn from student reflections on the collaborative research project process, the authors' own reflections about their role as research supervisors, supervision notes and course syllabi. The data were analysed using an inductive process of identifying themes. Some of the findings reflected the themes in the wider literature on communities of practice and the value and benefits of collaborative undergraduate research. These related to the nature of learning and emergent leadership development from the self through to the collective. This chapter is concerned with these key leadership learning findings and the following themes are discussed for their relevance to the Arab region: developmental growth in confidence and skills; improved knowledge of self; communication and negotiation; collaborative processes and teamwork; and improved research and leadership practices. The chapter contributes to the knowledge base on leadership education by identifying opportunities for leadership and research capacity building within undergraduate research programs in the UAE and the Gulf region.

Introduction

UAE leaders have called for a greater focus on improving professional practice in the schools, and the need for beginning Emirati teachers to develop the skills for classroom inquiry, to improve their critical analysis of educational literature, to develop a better understanding of practical issues in their curriculum specialty and to take on the role of 'change agents' in local schools (see Al Qassemi, 2010; Constantine, 2010). To this end a college of pre-service teacher education at one of the federal tertiary institutions in the UAE has increased its emphasis on practitioner research and inquiry. Much of the emphasis elsewhere has been on the in-service level and less attention has been paid to the pre-service context and how undergraduate students are introduced to classroom research. While it is normal for student teachers to read and analyze educational research done by others, the use of a systematic collaborative approach to becoming researchers in a community of practice is far less common in pre-service programs in the UAE. This chapter draws on female Emirati student experiences in such a program in research practice undertaken in their final year of their Bachelor of Science in Education. A review of the first five years of the capstone seminar program was conducted to investigate its development, successes, challenges and lessons learned to meet teaching and learning needs in the UAE context. One unexpected success was the development of communities of practice and the significant leadership development that occurred as a result of students undertaking collaborative research projects and this is the focus of this chapter. The review of the undergraduate research program provided an unexpected opportunity to make explicit previously implicit leadership learning.

Background

The UAE is a collective society where the importance of tribe, family and social networks is significant and, as such, suggests that collective approaches to learning may resonate with Emirati students' learning styles and preferences. The UAE government has recently promulgated its broad educational objectives in a document entitled *Vision 2021* (which includes goals such as 'Confident, socially responsible Emiratis', 'Cohesive and prosperous families', 'Strong, active communities', 'Sustainable and diversified economy', 'Knowledge-based and highly productive economy', and a 'First rate education system' (*Vision 2021*, website).

The current project (a review of five years of the undergraduate capstone project) was initiated in part by the authors' ongoing interest in the changes that were occurring in student learning over time and in part by unexpected, unplanned outcomes relating to student leadership practices. The overview of the literature has thus drawn on the four perspectives of learning, communities of practice, undergraduate research processes and leadership to reflect how all of these were inextricably intertwined in the capstone seminar and informed the analysis of the data.

Learning

From a socio-cultural perspective, learning may be viewed as a dynamic social activity that is situated in context and distributed across people and activities. Leadership learning may therefore also be considered in this way. Research (see Garrick, 1998; Gherardi, Nicolini, & Odella, 1998; Rogoff, 2003) suggests that throughout the learning process informal learning opportunities occur through social interactions and they are usually tacitly transmitted. A distinction between tacit and explicit knowledge is necessary to understand individual learning in context. Tacit knowledge is concerned with personal insights, intuitions and abilities. In contrast, explicit knowledge is knowledge which can be shared and communicated (DiBella, Nevis, & Gould, 1998).

According to Spender (1995), tacit knowledge can be defined as that which has not yet been distracted from practice. Tacit knowledge, acquired by individuals through personal experience, can range from new insights to a more wholistic understanding of a situation. Some researchers (e.g. Davenport & Prusak, 2000; Easterby-Smith, 1997), suggest that tacit knowledge cannot be codified or verbalised and can only be communicated informally or through example. Similarly, they also believe that certain knowledge is something implicit that can only be acquired, utilised, shared and transferred through long term observation of people who have such knowledge.

Reber (1993) distinguishes between informal learning and formal or deliberative learning. Informal learning is implicit, unintentional learning that leads to knowledge acquisition 'independently of conscious attempts to learn and in the absence of explicit knowledge about what was learned' (Reber, 1993, p. 55). Neither learning intention nor any awareness of learning at the time it happens is apparent. Such learning leads to both tacit and explicit knowledge. Eraut (2000) introduces an additional category of learning which he terms reactive learning. Reactive learning is spontaneous and unplanned. The major distinction for each learning type is the level of intention to learn. Implicit learning is at one end of the continuum and deliberative learning is at the other. Reactive learning occurs between implicit and deliberative learning and describes situations where the learning is explicit but takes place almost spontaneously in response to a current situation. This is often referred to as 'just in time' learning.

For Nonaka (1994) learning is the result of continuous dialogue between explicit and tacit knowledge. Nonaka's spiral of knowledge creation is about tacit knowledge being converted into explicit knowledge by individuals, then groups and finally organisations.

The theory of situated learning, a result of the influence of social learning and socialisation theories, also views learning as typically unintentional rather than deliberate. According to Clancey (1995),

> Situated learning is the study of how human knowledge develops in the course of activity, and especially how people create and interpret descriptions (representations) of what they are doing' (p. 49).

It is concerned with how learning occurs every day and explores the situated character of human understanding and communication (Clancey, 1995; Lave & Wenger, 1991). Social interaction is a critical component of situated learning theory. Because situated learning focuses on the relationship between learning and the social situations in which it occurs, learning is therefore situated in a particular context which includes a location, a set of activities to which knowledge either contributes or is embedded, and specific social relations which give rise to these activities. It views action as situated in individual's roles as members of communities:

> Understanding how learning is a process of conceiving an activity, and activities are inherently social, puts emphasis on improving learning addressing issues of membership, participation in a community, and identity. (Clancey, 1995, p.50)

The basic premise has been that knowledge, skills and capabilities are embedded in collective work processes. Learning ceases to be an attribute of an individual and instead manifests itself through changes in knowledge and/or performance in the interaction of individuals grounded in the context of its use (Brown & Duguid, 1991; Rogoff & Lave, 1984).

This raises the question about the extent to which a given piece of knowledge is individually or socially constructed within that context. According to Clancey (1995, p. 54), cognitive anthropologists such as Lave (1988), Lave and Wenger (1991), and Suchman (1987) have overemphasised social perspectives encouraging the idea that social views and group activity are more fundamental than cognitive individual views. In response, Clancey (1995, p. 55) advocates a situated cognition theory of learning which views learning as the integration of individual identity and social participation (see Brown, Collins, & Duguid, 1989). It constitutes evolving membership, varied forms of social participation and results in the creation and development of communities of practice.

The above views of learning reflect the ways in which the students in the capstone program drew on their individual tacit knowledge and developed new perspectives through the collective group processes with which they were involved. In this way they formed a 'community of practice' at the specific group level and also at a wider level when they met as a full class group to discuss the research process.

Communities of Practice

A community of practice is referred to in the literature on situated learning and cognition as a group of individuals with different roles and experience engaged in common practice (Brown & Duguid, 2000; Clancey, 1995). Individuals become involved in communities of practice, which embody certain beliefs and behaviours to be acquired (Lave & Wenger, 1991). Learning, from this point of view, requires developing the disposition, demeanour and outlook of the practitioners, rather than merely acquiring information (Brown & Duguid, 2000, p. 26). According to Brown et al. (1989), as newcomers move from the periphery of a community of practice to its centre, they become enculturated. That is, the more active and engaged they are with the culture, the more they can assume the role of 'expert' (Bransford, Brown, & Cocking, 1999; Lave & Wenger, 1991). Lave and Wenger (1991) call this process 'legitimate peripheral participation'. Clancey (1995) summarises the community of practice analytic framework as:

Knowledge is the ability to participate in a community of practice. Learning is becoming a member of a community of practice and tools [for carrying out socially organised activity] facilitate interaction in a community of practice. (p. 55)

Clancey (1995), Lemke (1997), Wenger (1998), and Wenger, McDermott, and Snyder (2002) believe situated cognition and social practice are the fundamental processes by which we learn and so become who we are. Wenger (1998) views learning as an act of membership in a 'community of practice.' He argues that:

learning changes who we are by changing our ability to participate, to belong, to negotiate meaning [and] this ability is configured socially with respect to practices, communities, and economies of meaning where it shapes our identities. (p. 226)

Similarly to Clancey (1995), Brown and Duguid (2000) and Wenger et al. (2002) believe knowledge resides in the skills and understanding of individuals in relationships that allow them to learn together. They argue that informal communities of practice, formed by people as they pursue shared enterprises over time, are the primary unit for analysing the learning process.

The communities of practice concept assumes that learning is fundamentally a social phenomenon; knowledge is inseparable from practice and is integrated in the life of communities that share values, beliefs, languages, and ways of doing things. According to Wenger et al. (2002), circumstances in which individuals engage in real action that have consequences for themselves and their communities of practice create powerful learning environments. Similarly, Dixon (1994) states that information that is generated through direct experience of members is shared, interpreted collectively, and leads to a learning cycle in which organisational members take responsible action. Dixon's (1994) view supports the theory that learning occurs through participation in a changing world (Geertz, 1995). It also draws on the work of Revans (1970), action learning, which focuses on the need to integrate cognition, action, theory and behaviour. The practical application of this view of organisational learning occurs when colleagues work together to solve problems and challenges in the work context. Dixon (1994), Nevis, DiBella, and Gould (1995), and Wenger's (1998) models complement each other by focusing on social, cyclical and action oriented aspects of learning where learning and unlearning are constants in an ever changing world.

Similarly, for Wenger et al. (2002), sharing tacit cultural and procedural knowledge requires interaction and informal learning processes such as conversation, telling stories and informal mentoring of the kind that communities of practice provide. Through communication and networking individuals develop relationships and individuals and groups collaborate to achieve together (Garrick, 1998). Through involvement with others, decisions are made, work is done and people learn collectively (Garrick, 1998; Wenger, 1998). Learning is spread through social encounters with friends, colleagues, role models and mentors. Such social interaction allows for continued dialogue, negotiation of meaning and creation of new meanings.

The context for the socially constructed learning of the undergraduate students was the implementation of a research project and we now turn to an account of the value and benefits of undergraduate research for student leadership learning.

Undergraduate Research Processes

The Council for Undergraduate Research (n.d.) in the USA defines undergraduate research as 'an inquiry or investigation conducted by an undergraduate student that makes an original intellectual or creative contribution to the discipline'. Undergraduate research is an emerging practice in UAE higher education although it has been commonplace in higher education internationally for some time, and thus the authors draw on literature from the latter field.

There is general agreement on the value of undergraduate research. For example Moore and Avant (2008, pp. 231-235) highlight a range of benefits to students that helps them to:

- Think critically and solve problems
- Value subjects and outcomes that affect them
- Read their discipline's literature more critically
- Develop communication skills and effective teamwork skills
- Learn to work independently
- Develop mentoring relationships with faculty

Lopatto (2006) also comments on the value of undergraduate research because it may afford what he terms empowered learning (communication, problem solving and teamwork), informed learning (study of the natural and cultural world), and student engagement (active collaborative learning, intense student-faculty interaction). With colleagues, he undertook qualitative and quantitative studies at four liberal arts colleges in the US (Lopatto, 2006; Seymour, Hunter, Laursen, & Deantoni, 2004). They found that students reported growth in specific skills (e.g. design and hypothesis formation, data collection and interpretation, and information literacy). In addition the studies found accompanying gains in professional advancement and professional development. A significant finding was what Lopatto termed 'seen out of the corner of the eye' (Lopatto, 2006, p. 23) – growth that was not specifically planned for but that included positive gains in self confidence, interest in the discipline and a sense of accomplishment and pride in one's new knowledge.

Waite and Davis (2006) report on an action research investigation into the student experience at undergraduate level in a UK university. Students worked in groups through a collaborative learning process. The researchers found four features of the collaborative tutorials that were stimulating for students:

- Peer comments and ideas introduce elements of surprise that pique students' curiosity and encourage further exploration.
- Peers provide models of expertise that others can emulate.
- Peers provide benchmarks for monitoring one's own level of accomplishment, which may in turn increase the belief in self efficacy.

- Persistence is enhanced when working with others because there is an obligation to the group and a collaborative goal. (Waite & Davis, 2006, p. 410).

Moore and Avant (2008) discuss another kind of collaboration – that between faculty and undergraduate students - which helps students develop their professional and disciplinary interests and discover new areas of research opportunity. It also improves their self esteem and confidence.

Leadership

The preceding sections have identified some key benefits of undergraduate research that are discussed in the literature, including its value as a basis for leadership learning. In this respect it is helpful to briefly comment about the literature on leadership education. Along with Ashforth (2001) the authors believe that a person has multiple identities that vary in relation to their 'readiness to act out an identity' (p. 26). Communities of practice (Brown & Duguid, 1991; Wenger, 1998) highlight the connections between identity and learning and the role practice has in constructing and maintaining individual and collective identities. Typically leadership identities are developed as learners move through stages focusing initially on the self and gradually moving toward a collective leadership focus (see Komives, Owen, Longerbeam, Mainella, & Osteen, 2005). What is common is the shift from theory to practice, from arts to systems, from states and roles to processes, from knowledge to learning, from individual action to collective action and from detached analysis to reflexive understanding (Taylor, de Guerre, Gavin, & Kass, 2002). According to Allio (2005) effective leadership development should be learner focussed and link contemporary theories to actual experiences. Komives, Lucas, and McMahon (1998) define leadership development as developing a personal approach to leadership, most often through opportunities and experiences extending to co-curricular activities, in-class assignments, internships and scaffolded experiences (Sagaria, 1988).

The overview of the literature indicates clearly how new learning and practice can develop from the interrelationship between tacit and explicit knowledge and this occurs as learners form and engage in communities of practice. It also highlights that undergraduate research programs can offer rich insights into student learning, including leadership practices. These ideas thus underpinned our program review and allowed us to analyze the capstone seminar process from a multi-faceted stance.

The Study

As part of their final year, UAE students at a College of Education participate in a course (known as the capstone seminar) where they complete collaborative research projects that provide a summative response to the broad goals and objectives of their teacher education program. At this time they also do an intensive internship in UAE schools and their projects are based on authentic curricular and instructional issues occurring across the Emirates. This paper reports on a study done by the authors that reviewed five years of the capstone seminar program. During this period more than one hundred senior female university students completed research projects. This final semester is also when they do their intensive internship in local schools and during the last five years the rationale for this process has been to introduce student teachers to the development of basic research skills through classroom inquiry, to assist them to improve their critical analysis of educational literature and to help them develop a better understanding of practical issues in their internship and curriculum specialty and some methods to investigate these. Before going on internship the students attend a series of workshops run by the course teachers to provide guided support for the initial research processes. They work collaboratively to prepare an introduction and rationale for their topic, conduct a literature review, develop their methodology and prepare research instruments. In addition they prepare an introductory letter of information and consent forms for their participants. During this stage they are provided with resources and support from their teachers. As their projects are implemented they attend further workshops to develop techniques of data analysis and reporting.

Using case study techniques, data were drawn from student written reflections on the research process, the authors' own reflections about their role as research supervisors, supervision notes and course syllabi. The data were analysed retrospectively using an inductive process. Miles and Huberman (1994, p. 9) identify a set of 'analytic moves' which we used in this study. We began with some general themes derived from the literature and subsequently added more themes and sub themes. Gradually, after reading and rereading the data, some indicative themes and significant events emerged. This process occurred before, during and after data collection (Ryan & Bernard, 2000). As such, analysis of the data was interpretive and interaction occurred reflexively between the researcher, the research questions, data collection and interpretation. This yielded rich, descriptive data about our undergraduate research seminar and the leadership learning that occurred over the five year period. These data are discussed in the following section. Psuedonyms are used to protect the identity of the participants.

Results

As previously discussed, this paper focuses solely on the area of leadership learning, specifically the improved student leadership practices as experienced through the development of communities of practice as students engaged in the collaborative undergraduate research process. The following key leadership themes emerged:

- Developmental growth in confidence and skills
- Improved knowledge of self
- Communication and negotiation
- Collaborative processes/teamwork
- Improved leadership practices
- Improved research practices

Development of Confidence and Skills

At the beginning of the capstone seminar it was common for students to feel some trepidation about what might be involved, but this feeling gradually dissipated and students grew in confidence as they worked with their team. Shaima's comment was typical of this perspective:

> *Before writing our capstone I was very nervous and I thought it was a very difficult task to do. I thought that working in a big group would reduce the value of the project; however this idea quickly vanished. Working with this team gave me the energy to do my tasks on time.* (Shaima)

In addition to feelings of anxiety, students were often unsure about the kinds of skills required for their project but with perseverance their confidence improved:

It was a little difficult to collate and collect the data all together but by working hard and dedicating our time to the project our mission became somehow easier. (Maitha)

In the beginning I didn't believe I could write that much with such proficiency. Now I can confidently ask anyone who needs help to come and ask me for any help especially in terms of writing. (Sara)

For some, the project increased their confidence to a level where they wanted to do more research:

I feel now I am willing to take my Master's degree next year because of the good job we have done as a team as well as the amount of information and skills we learned from the project. (Najla)

I learned how to write an academic research paper. I think this experience will help me when I will do my Master's degree. (Leyla)

Improved Knowledge of Self

Alongside development in confidence, the collaborative research process allowed students to see themselves in a different light. Amal, for example understood more about how her emotions affected her work:

During working on the research paper I gained much positive experience which has affected my life. This research gave me the chance to develop my skills and become patient while seeking information because sometimes you lose your patience when you do not find a certain thing. (Amal)

Alia benefited from having to contact participants and conduct interviews with them:

I learned that I can do better things by overcoming some of my personal problems such as getting rid of shyness and stress. (Alia)

Communication and Negotiation Skills

A key part of working as a team was learning to negotiate with each other and to communicate tasks and content effectively. Sohaila's and Boshra's comments typify the elements of this process:

> *As a group we cooperated through meeting each other, collecting and gathering information together, discussing ideas, sharing opinions, solving problems related to our project and also expressing our experiences and feelings which contributed a lot in improving and strengthening our project.* (Sohaila)

> *Working as part of a team was one of the challenging tasks for me during this project, because I had to deal with people who had different personalities, different abilities and different ways in working.* (Boshra)

Collaborative Processes/Teamwork

Working collaboratively with a team of peers to carry out a research project in some depth was a new experience for most of the students. As they reflected on the experience, the value of collaboration became clear as noted, for example, by Alanood and Nahla:

> *The project was very beneficial for me. It helped me to realize how much work could be done if only we co-operated. Working in groups and sub-groups increased the quality and the quantity of the research content. I never realized how group work is effective until we have done this project.* (Alanood)

> *I have come to recognize the importance of collaborative group work. I learned not to be discouraged by working in a big group. Even though our group consisted of fourteen participants...by thoroughly working on this research study I have obtained the knowledge to professionally construct a research study.* (Nahla)

The students were also aware of the challenges inherent in working as a group, as Alia notes:

> *The challenges I faced are teamwork, self-learning, responding to difficulties and delays, and finding new methods in terms of using technology, knowledge gathering, and goal setting. I learned how to convince my team, advise them, take advice from them, manage the time and collect data from the group as well as giving data to the group.* (Alia)

Alanood benefited from the team experience and highlighted the need for management skills as well as leadership:

> *Being part of a big group handling such complicated research [led] me to have different experiences such as developing my management skills as well as leadership skills. Also, it is great to have such team who help in being cooperative by sharing ideas, thoughts and experiences.* (Alanood)

Abla and Faiza commented on how the collaborative processes involved in teamwork developed specific leadership skills and resulted in a better quality product as a result:

> *Working in a group enabled me to develop my academic and social skills such as decision making, problem solving, critical thinking and taking responsibility for one's own actions. Moreover, I learned that working as group is one of the best ways to increase the quality and quantity of the research.* (Abla)

> *Working on this project as a group allows me to be more cooperative with my group members in order to accomplish this huge research. The team work also enables me to gain important ideas and skills that benefit both me and my partners on our topic. In fact, as this project is huge, I feel more comfortable to work and share what I have with the group.* (Faiza)

Improved Leadership Practices

The faculty supervisors encouraged student teams to think about the logistics of their research task and about group leadership. Their reflective comments revealed some interesting insights about how they perceived and enacted the leadership role. Asra's comments, for example indicated that she was approaching the task from a distributed leadership perspective:

> *My group members chose me to become the leader of the group. I tried hard to manage everything. I encouraged my group members to work hard and write the best they could. I was flexible with my members because I wanted them to not feel that they were under pressure... We benefited from each others' ideas, suggestions, skills, experiences and much more...Working with my friends helped me to understand their personalities and appreciate them more.* (Asra)

Maryam's experience of team leadership had significantly changed her perspective from individual to collective practice:

> *Working as a team was the most challenging part because I am a ... person who prefers to work individually. I decided to accept the challenge to be the capstone coordinator for my team. Being the coordinator taught me to respond to each team member differently, to react to problems differently, to accept the criticism differently. I have to say that the capstone experience helped me to develop my team work skills and now I am an excellent team player and individual leader.* (Maryam)

She was successful in her role and gained a deeper meaning of leadership practice:

> *Being a leader is more than giving orders, making decisions and dividing tasks. It is about empowering and motivating team members, sharing ideas and thoughts, working together for the benefit of all.* (Maryam)

Fatma too, had developed her leadership practice and others now saw her in a different light:

> *The most practical skill that I gained through this journey is leadership. I have succeeded in managing time, tasks, relations, and coordination and communication skills. I gained my friends' and my supervisor's trust in accomplishing this project.* (Fatma)

Improved Research Practices

Almost all the student reflections commented on growth in understanding and skill in research practice. Some commented on this development in broad terms:

> *Working on this study gave me a great opportunity to enhance and develop my research and analytical skills. It gave me the chance to develop a proper research paper that I am so proud of ...I feel that this research helped me by developing my social, communication, interpersonal, teamwork and leadership skills.* (Maryam)

Others identified where they had developed specific skills:

> *I had learnt how to use journals and databases as a way to get the required information for the project. Also it was a way to know how to use different methods in order to collect the data and how to analyze them. I have learnt how to organize the findings taking into consideration the percentages and the statistics used in it.* (Aisha)

> *I also learned some of the professional methods to analyze data, discuss it and link it to the literature review provided at the beginning of the project. The literature review itself was a challenge because we had to look for various resources, evaluate them in order to choose the most credible ones, and read between the lines to find the information we need.* (Mona)

Athaba's experience in data collection had improved other more generic skills:

> *Furthermore, the interviews and surveys helped me to improve my communication skills. I used to speak in front of many people and interviewed them in many public schools.* (Athaba)

Discussion

The data clearly indicate that the development of communities of practice through collaborative research created an environment conducive to learning that many Emirati students found comfortable. As student groups worked collaboratively through the research process their learning trajectory showed a distinct pattern. At the very beginning most reacted initially from an individual perspective, showing anxiety and uncertainty about what was required. As they moved into a group context and were provided with specific information and resources to scaffold their learning these feelings began to change (see also Brown et al., 1989; Clancey, 1995; Lave & Wenger, 1991). The collaborative processes of teamwork began to emerge and negotiation occurred within the teams about leadership, task responsibilities and deadlines. These various forms of social participation resulted in the creation and development of communities of practice where membership and the learning process were inseparable and the ability to contribute to the community of practice created the potential for learning (Wenger, 1998).

There was a spiral of knowledge creation (Nonaka, 1994) where increased knowledge of self enabled the students to better integrate their own identity with that of the collective and therefore contribute more effectively. This is an example of Lave and Wenger's (1991) legitimate peripheral participation process and Nonaka's (1994) continuous dialogue between explicit and tacit knowledge. The very fact of engaging in collaborative research placed the individuals in real action with shared goals, values, beliefs and ways of doing things, resulting in consequences for themselves and their communities of practice. These consequences provided powerful learning environments as found by Wenger et al. (2002). The very nature of the capstone seminar program thus acknowledges that knowledge is inseparable from practice and is integrated in the life of communities. The program recognises that an understanding of the self and how personality, experience and social participation integrate into leadership practice is also an important aspect of leadership development.

The process of reflection on action enabled the students to surface and negotiate tacit knowledge creating an explicit collective knowledge (Spender, 1995). We found, similarly to Easterby-Smith (1997) that tacit knowledge was best communicated informally or through example. Supporting Davenport and Prusak's (2000) view it was long term interaction, negotiation with, and observation of people within the community of practice that generated collective learning opportunities. By the very nature of the research process which was complex, messy, fluid and organic there were many opportunities for Eraut's (2000) reactive learning. This 'just in time' learning occurred as students took on team coordination roles, for example, or dealt with contextual constraints or unexpected challenges and issues in the research process.

The way the capstone seminar was set up enabled us to utilise Reber's (1993) distinctive types of learning. This included the formal deliberative learning arising from course notes, lectures and support materials (Sagaria, 1988). It also unexpectedly enabled students to develop a personal approach to leadership (Komives, et al., 1998) through formal and informal learning opportunities. The informal unintentional learning, i.e. 'the acquisition of knowledge independently of conscious attempts to learn' (Reber, 1993, p. 55), resulted in both tacit and explicit knowledge of self, research and leadership.

The key leadership skills emerging from this study such as thinking critically, problem solving, effective teamwork, increased confidence and relationship building were also identified as key benefits in the literature on undergraduate research (Moore & Avant, 2008; Lopatto, 2006; Seymour et al., 2004).

Conclusion

Since leadership exists in communities, across fields, in team collaboration, collaborative undergraduate research therefore provides the perfect learning context for leadership practice and reflection on that practice. Such a context acknowledges that leadership is located in collective as much as in individual action, it is premised on interdependence and networking as well as hierarchical influence, and it should be concerned with common goals rather than the interests of a few.

The undergraduate research program that was developed through the capstone seminar has resulted in some important opportunities for Emirati female students to develop deeper understanding of self, research and leadership. They are now better able to critically reflect on practice, continue to develop their own research skills in a systematic and scaffolded way and develop teacher leadership potential. As a result we have a richer process and product in undergraduate research. The capstone process has enhanced Emirati pre-service teacher individual and collective learning about classroom inquiry and developed knowledge and skills that will continue to be of value as they enter the profession. Like Simmons (2006), we believe that the pursuit of undergraduate research is not only worthwhile but is essential if the broader socioeconomic objectives of the UAE are to be achieved and if the full potential of emerging Emirati leadership is to be realized:

> *Making a commitment to develop an undergraduate research program is an extensive one and should not be taken lightly. The institution and the related faculty are embarking on a journey that will require sacrifice in time and resources. It is my firm belief that at the end of that journey is a brighter future for the fortunate young people who are the direct beneficiaries of that effort* (Simmons, 2006, final para.).

There is little literature on the value of undergraduate research in the Gulf region and the value of collaborative research in developing leadership knowledge, skills and attitudes in Arab students. Further research is needed in the area of learning styles and preferences, Emirati experiences in leadership development, and gender and leadership development.

References

Allio, R.J. (2005). Leadership development: Teaching versus learning. *Management Decision,43*, 1071–1077.
Al Qassemi, S. (2010, 6 June). An education vision with an eye on all Emiratis. *The National.* Retrieved on June 6, 2010, from http://www.thenational.ae/apps/pbcs.dll/article?AID=/20100606/OPINION/706059946/1080/yourview?template=opinion
Ashforth, B. (2001). *Role transitions in organizational life: An identity-based perspective.* Mahwah, NJ: Lawrence Erlbaum Associates.
Bransford, J.D., Brown, A.L., & Cocking, R.R. (1999). *How People Learn.* National Research Council.
Brown, J.S., Collins, A., & Duguid, S. (1989). Situated cognition and the culture of learning. *Educational Researcher, 18*(1), 32-42.
Brown, J.S., & Duguid, P. (1991). Organizational learning and communities of practice: Toward a unified view of working, learning and innovation. *Organization Science, 2*, 40-57.
Brown, J.S., & Duguid, P. (2000). *The social life of information.* Boston: Harvard School Press.
Clancey, W.J. (1995). *A tutorial on situated learning.* In J. Self (Ed.), *Proceedings of the international conference on computers and education* (pp. 49-70). Charlottesville, VA: AACE.
Constantine, Z. (2010, 15 September). New start for schools as teachers learn a better model. *The National.* Retrieved on September 15, 2010, from

http://www.thenational.ae/apps/pbcs.dll/article?AID=/20100915/
NATIONAL/709149810&SearchID=73403446955368
Council for Undergraduate Research (n.d.). Retrieved on June 10,
2010 from http://www.cur.org/about.html

Davenport, T.H. & Prusak, L. (2000). *Working knowledge: How
organizations manage what they know.* New York. McGraw-
Hill.

DiBella, A.J., Nevis, E.C., & Gould, A. (1998). *How organizations
learn.* San Francisco: Jossey- Bass.

Dixon, N.M. (1994). *The organizational learning cycle. How we can
learn collectively.* London: McGraw-Hill.

Easterby-Smith, M. (1997). Disciplines of organizational learning:
Contributions and critiques [electronic version]. *Human
Relations, 50,* 1085-1113.

Eraut, M. (2000). Non-formal learning and tacit knowledge in
professional work. *The British Journal of Educational
Psychology, 70*(1), 11-133.

Garrick, J. (1998). *Informal learning in the workplace.* London:
Routledge.

Geertz, C. (1995). *After the fact: Two countries, four decades, one
anthropologist.* Cambridge, Mass: Harvard University Press.

Gherardi, S., Nicolini, D., & Odella, F. (1998). Toward a social
understanding of how people learn in organizations [electronic
version]. *Management Learning, 29*(3), 273-297.

Komives, S.R., Lucas, N., McMahon, T.R. (1998). *Exploring
leadership: For college students who want to make a difference.*
San Francisco: Jossey-Bass.

Komives, S.R., Owen, J.E., Longerbeam, S., Mainella, F.C., &
Osteen, L. (2005). Developing a leadership identity: A grounded
theory. *Journal of College Student Development, 46,* 593–611.

Lave, J. (1988). *Cognition in practice: Mind, mathematics, and
culture in everyday life.* Cambridge, UK: Cambridge University
Press.

Lave. J., & Wenger. E. (1991). *Situated learning: Legitimate peripheral participation.* Cambridge: Cambridge University Press.

Lemke, J. (1997). Cognition, context, and learning: A social semiotic perspective. In D. Kirshner, & J. A. Whiston (Eds.), *Situated cognition: Social, semiotic, and psychological perspectives.* Mahwah, NJ: Lawrence Erlbaum Associates.

Lopatto, D. (2006, Winter). Undergraduate research as a catalyst for academic learning. AAC and CU, *Peer Review, 8*(1), 22-25.

Miles, M.B., & Huberman, A.M. (1994). *Qualitative data analysis: An expanded sourcebook.* London: Thousand Oaks, Sage.

Moore, L.S., & Avant, F. (2008). Strengthening undergraduate social work research: Models and strategies. *Social Work Research, 32*(4), 223-235.

Nevis, E.C., DiBella, A.J., & Gould, J.M. (1995). Understanding organizations as learning systems [electronic version]. *Sloan Management Review, 36*(2), 73 – 85.

Nonaka, I. (1994). A dynamic theory of organizational knowledge creation [electronic version]. *Organization Science Linthicum, 5*(1), 14 – 38.

Reber, A.S. (1993). *Implicit learning and tacit knowledge: An essay on the cognitive unconscious.* Oxford: Oxford University Press.

Revans, R.W. (1970). The managerial alphabet. In G. Heald (Ed.), *Approaches to the study of organizational behavior* (pp. 141-161). London: Tavistock.

Rogoff, B. (2003). *The cultural nature of human development.* Oxford, England: Oxford University Press.

Rogoff. B., & Lave. J. (1984). *Everyday cognition: Its development in social context.* Cambridge: Harvard University Press.

Ryan, G.W., & Bernard, H.R. (2000). Data management and analysis methods. In N.K. Denzin, & Y.S. Lincoln (Eds.), *Handbook of Qualitative Research.* Thousand Oaks: Sage.

Sagaria, M.A.D. (1988). *Empowering women: Leadership development strategies on campus.* San Francisco: Jossey-Bass.

Seymour, E.A., Hunter, B., Laursen, S.L., & Deantoni, T. (2004).

Establishing the benefits of research experience for undergraduates in the sciences: First findings from a three-year study. *Science Education, 88*(4), 493-534.

Simmons, K.M. (2006). *Developing an undergraduate research program in economics.* Retrieved on June 15, 2010 from http://www.abe.sju.edu/proc2006/simmons.pdf

Spender, J.C. (1995). Organizational renewal: Top management's role in a loosely coupled system. *Human Relations, 48*(8), 909-927.

Suchman, L.A. (1987). *Plans and situated actions: The problem of human-machine communication.* Cambridge: CUP.

Taylor, M., de Guerre, D., Gavin, J., & Kass, R. (2002). Graduate leadership education for dynamic human systems. *Management Learning, 33*(3), 349–369.

UAE Vision 2021. UAE Government. Retrieved on July 10, 2010, from http://www.vision2021.ae/

Waite, S., & Davis, B. (2006), Developing undergraduate research skills in a faculty of education: Motivation through collaboration. *Higher Education Research and Development, 24*(4), 403-419.

Wenger, E. (1998). *Communities of practice, learning meaning and identity.* Cambridge: CUP.

Wenger, E., McDermott, R., & Snyder, W. (2002). *Cultivating communities of practice: A guide to managing knowledge.* Cambridge: Harvard Business School Press.

KHAWLAH AHMED

Chapter 6
Casting Arabic Culture as the 'Other': Cultural Issues in the English Curriculum

Abstract

Education is said to be the key venue that supports globalization and its ideologies where certain values and information are prioritized and others are disregarded. The emphasis on English in many curricula around the world is beginning to dominate and erase weak languages and cultures or blur and overshadow stronger ones. Some curricula in the Arab world are using English as the medium of instruction in schools and universities. This emphasis is expected to increase due to the growing global demands, especially in countries like those in the Arab Gulf which are becoming major players in a competitive global market and where western academic institutions and curricula are being imported. Many are skeptical about this education and concerns are now beginning to be voiced about the Arabic language being sidelined and relegated as 'non-useful' and the Arabic culture being cast aside. This chapter presents these concerns and examines samples of the English as a Foreign Language (EFL) textbooks being taught in the public schools in one of these Arab countries to see if the Arabic culture is incorporated in these curricula and if there is any basis for such concerns. Results suggest that the Arab culture is minimally represented in the English curriculum, and usually only superficially, validating the concerns that it is marginalized.

Introduction

Terms like 'language,' 'culture' and 'identity,' have recently resurfaced in discussions, debates and controversies relating to education in light of globalization in many parts of the world, the Middle East included (Kreiger, 2008a; Hellyer; 2008; Mill, 2008). Globalization, a highly controversial phenomenon sometimes viewed from a narrow perspective, has brought with it changes in all aspects of life. In education, those changes are reflected in curriculum development and language policies, with computer education and English language teaching being two of the most important new initiatives introduced into the curricula. It appears that globalization has initiated a great deal of concern in regards to the increasing use of English and its role in 'perpetuating global inequalities... [and] homogenizing local cultures and traditions' (Rizvi, Engel, Rutkowski, & Sparks, 2007, p. 13). Globalization is seemingly producing, using Kramsch's (as cited in Hinkel, 1995) terms, 'surface cultures' portrayed merely by 'foods, fairs, folklore, and statistical facts' (p.5). Today's globalized system of education may be aiding in either erasing weak cultures or blurring and overshadowing stronger ones. The Middle Eastern culture, with its relatively strong background, is not an exception. In many parts of the Arab World region, the imported education and rampant spread of and emphasis on English, accompanied by a relatively American pop culture, is beginning to sideline Arabic resulting in the linguistic and cultural loss of those who identity with it. Of course there are many factors that this may be a result of, but the most prominent is the impact of globalization on education and the manifestation of ideologies through the use of language. Many are now voicing concerns that Arabic is being relegated as 'non-useful' and the Arabic culture is being cast as the 'other' (Findlow, 2006).

Background

To many, globalization is seen as a new form of western cultural colonialism. In the past, as Rasool (2007) explains, colonialism shaped the linguistic habitus of societies, cultures and individuals and the ways in which language-in-education policy interacted with history, politics, culture and economics ultimately impacted societal development possibilities. A great deal of the analysis of the relationship between education and development in developing countries was provided by people from the 'outside' and only economic goals were incorporated into educational policy, planning, and practice with little or no attention given to issues such as culture and empowerment (Leech & Little, 1999). With globalization and 'the shift in composition of the control of many domestic economies, away from national and towards global and regional,' questions are being raised about 'whose economic and cultural goals and interests are being served by education' (Leech & Little, 1999, p. 4)

According to Stromquist (2002), education and the knowledge it brings may have 'intended and unintended consequences.' She sees that education has become the key venue to support globalization and is the primary site for the creation and transmission of ideologies which are now seen in

> (1) the adoption of economistic values and the naturalization of new objectives and comitant practices in schools and universities, (2) the priority assigned to certain subject matters and fields of study over others, and (3) the disregard, and sometimes plain erasure, of certain knowledge, particularly that which might contest points 1 and 2. (p. xiv)

It also appears that higher education is being reshaped according to a 'standardized Anglo-American model' that is molded into 'neoliberal economic reforms and managerial styles' (Stomquist & Monkman, 2000).

The Arab World: Current Situation and Concerns

Today's globalized education in many Arab world countries has led to incorporating institutional policies that require courses to be taught in English to the exclusion of Arabic. English, described as the language of colonialism and the 'Neoliberal Empire' (Phillipson, 1992; 2008), is believed to be redefining national and individual identities (Graddol, 2006, p. 12). This is predicted to have far-reaching social and cultural effects on these societies (Karami, 2005). Globalization appears to be challenging the social, political and economic structures, especially of countries like those in the Arab World that do not have the prerequisites to resist it (Shorish, 1999). In many cases, this is rapidly changing the goals, policies, curricula, contents and methods of education, which according to Arani (2004), is causing education researchers, policy-makers, and practitioners to differentiate and re-think education and learning, both within and outside the school system.

Many of the Arab countries are, to some extent, still considered part of the 'third', 'non-developed', or 'emerging' world. The Arab region has been identified by a 2005 UNESCO report, as the least research-and development-intensive area in the world, while Arab educational institutions have been described by The World Bank report, released in 2008, as not yet fully equipped to produce graduates with the skills and expertise necessary to compete in a world where knowledge is essential to making progress (Krieger, 2008b). In a globalized world system with a highly competitive market Arab countries need to develop their populations' skills and technical knowledge, or human capital, in order to compete in the 21st century global economy (Gonzalez, Karoly, Constant, Salem, Goldman, 2008). To do so, as Kireger (2008a) states, countries such as those in the Arab Gulf, have redirected massive amounts of money and effort to education. They have also, as Mills (2008) explains, recruited universities from around the world to set up outposts in these countries and are tapping Western academics to run their education system. However, this expansion of education in the area has brought about an imported education that comes with its own ideals and values, which many see as exclusively Anglo-American. It is also given precedence and priority in many school curricula with English becoming the medium of instruction in the social sciences and humanities in many elementary and primary schools and the language of instruction in the majority of tertiary level institutions. This comes at the expense of the Arabic language and culture that are, to some extent, being curtailed in the new curricula.

The current situation raises language as well as cultural concerns. Any assessment of conflict involving ethnic identity requires delicate treatment of language (Chroist, 2003). A cultural system, which is the outcome of the political and economic system, is most obviously, and importantly, represented by language (King, 1997). Language is the main ingredient in any discussion on culture and cultural identity (Maalouf, 2000; Kramsch, 2005). Words in a language are 'microcosms of human consciousness' (Vygotsky, 1962), and as Bakhtin (1981) says, language is not a neutral medium but it is overpopulated with the intentions of others. Phillipson (1999 as cited in Chroist 2003) argues that language policy becomes a central concern to sociology and political science since language issues have been important in many of the major ethnic upheavals of recent decades. Linguistic identity is not only a 'powerful means of exercising social control' (Thornborrow, 2004, p. 158), where language policies are employed as mechanisms of political and social control (Tellefson, 2002), but serves as a powerful symbol of the social solidarity of those who speak it (Sapir, as cited in Kramsch, 2005). Culture, which goes hand in hand with language, is believed to be the ideological battleground of the modern world system (United Nations Development Program, 1999).

Language and cultural issues are now being addressed on the academic as well as the political level in the Arab world, especially in the Arab Gulf (see Helleyer, 2007; Al Baik, 2008; Shaheen, 2009). Officials are voicing their opinions about the need to maintain Arabic as the language of the land and the society (Al Baik, 2008), and trying to take steps towards a unified educational policy that stresses the national religious and cultural values that will help develop a generation that is proud of its national identity (Shaheen, 2009). Some see that teaching courses in English is technically a violation of the general education law (that applies to all the Arab world) which mandates that the language of instruction in schools is Arabic (Shaheen, 2009). Al Kitbi (2006) sums up many of the sentiments about the decision to change the language of instruction to English in many school curricula in the social sciences and humanities in the primary and secondary levels of education. She explains that this decision has profound implications for education:

> The increasing reliance on English is an example of the sort of proposed changes in educational systems that serve foreign interests more than they serve the societies of the Gulf. The insistence of foreign powers on a change in the educational philosophy in the Arab Gulf region comes within the context of the control and suppression...of youth so that their world view in the future will be compatible with and serve the interests of those powers. (para. 3)

Of course, not everyone is adverse to the current situation. Some view the current development and modernization in these parts of the Arab World as direct results of this imported knowledge, but others are beginning to be skeptical about issues that range from curriculum content to the open society being created. Mills (2008) says that in many institutions Arabic has been all but eliminated as the language of instruction in favor of the more universal English and entire university systems, from classroom instruction to institutional accreditation, are being overhauled to conform to American standards. At the law school, for example, Mills says that the study of Shariah Islamic law and jurisprudence, which once played a significant role in the curriculum, has now been significantly curtailed.

The imported education, with 'marquee American universities,' may improve these countries' 'international cachet,' as Kreiger (2008a) explains, but questions if it is the best way for these countries to improve their education systems. They may, as he says, be getting more than they bargained for. He quotes specialists like

Haykel, Ezzine, and Tetreault that support this view. Suffice it here to mention Tetreault, a professor of international affairs and a gulf specialist at Trinity University in Texas, who states that one problem these countries will be faced with is having a huge generation of people coming out of these institutions that will not be connected in any kind of organic way to society as a whole, a generation of people who cannot even speak to their parents. This, Tetreault believes, is going to have massive social repercussions that may not just be positive, but negative as well.

English may have become one of the few enduring facts of global modern life, but Arabic, unlike many other languages, is not just a language of communication, it is the basis of the religion which is pivotal to the whole way of life, the culture and cultural identities of its members. This culture is now seen as being threatened from internal as well as external forces. Samuel Huntington's (1993) prediction of the 'Clash of Civilizations' has had its impact on Arabic because of it carrying linguistic as well as religious implications. It has created a scenario in which the Arabic language is now connotated with terrorism, leading to a repression of not only the language, but also those who identify with it.

Rising Sentiments: Feelings of being 'lost'

Many feel that marginalization and cultural loss is inevitable in such circumstance. Those who are affiliated with the Arabic language and culture feel they are being erased. Mills (2008, para. 48) quotes one professor as saying 'it is not just knowledge' that is being passed over to these societies 'It is deeper than that' because 'We knew our culture and our values…Now we don't even know our neighbors.' To Mills, this is a crucial point, especially in countries which he describes as appearing to be in the throes of national identity crisis. In some contexts in the world, plurality is accepted and fostered, but when factors such as 'unity, and coherence of identities' are perceived to be under threat, as Tsui and Tollefson (2007, p. vii) explain, efforts are made to preserve them. The latter is true in many Arab Gulf countries whose demographic makeup is overwhelmingly made up of non-Arabic speakers with expatriate communities accounting for 90 percent of the country's population (Krieger, 2008a). Though the natives of these countries tend to be, according to Krieger, relatively conservative, the governments have been happy to afford great social liberties to foreigners. As Maalouf (2000) says, if these governments relaxed their vigilance and just let market forces and the power of numbers have it all their own way, the national language would soon be used for domestic purposes only and would end up as a mere local dialect. This current situation has therefore caused questions to be posed. Findlow (2006) asks:

> How far should the requirement for native Arabic speakers to pursue their...studies in the language be seen as an inevitable response to market needs, and how far a symptom of neo-colonist power politics in which Arabic is relegated as non-useful, and Arab culture is cast as 'other'? (p.21).

Questions such as those posed by Green (1997) become relevant to the Arab World context. He asks: 'How far can states promote 'national culture' through education and what forms should these take in pluralistic societies?' (p.2). This brings us to the topic of the curriculum and the role that the curriculum plays in promoting and preserving cultures or marginalizing and casting them aside.

Culture in the Curriculum

The term 'culture' was described as one of the 'most contentious concepts in academia' in the second half of the 20th century and remains 'very much a burning issue at the beginning of the 21st century' (Atkinson, 2004, p. 279). Culture, defined from an anthropological perspective, is 'the ever-changing values, traditions, social and political relationships, and world view created and shared by a group of people bound together by a combination of factors that can include a common history, geographic location, language, social class, and or religion' (Nieto, 1996, p.138). Cultural identity, therefore, is an image of the behaviors, beliefs and norms (i.e. culture) that each person maintains and which is deemed appropriate to members of the ethnic group (Ferdman, 1990).

Inclusion and representation of cultures in the curriculum have been shown by empirical research and theoretical formulations to have important consequences for students, both on the social and academic level. Students may feel that whatever is not valued by school is not worth learning (Banks, 1995; Diamond & Moore, 1995). Seeing oneself portrayed and recognized, gives the student a sense of belonging and pride, which in turn can motivate students to learn and become or feel successful (Au, 1993; Nieto, 1996). Problems can arise if students with strong cultural backgrounds do not see their culture in the curriculum (Takaki, 1993). Identity and pride in one's self and cultural heritage can have psychological effects on individuals. From a social psychological perspective, it gives people a sense of belonging to a group (Ferdman, 1990), answers the question 'Who am I?' (Gordon & Browne, 1996), and legitimizes one's existence in the eyes of others.

Literacy, school achievement and the culture that the students identify with (in the home or at school) are closely related (Ferdman, 1990). Schools are viewed as the institutions most responsible for literacy education and socialization in a society (Apple, 1996). According to Ferdman, 'When a child perceives a writing task, or text, and its symbolic contents as belonging to and reaffirming his or her cultural identity, it is more likely that he or she will become engaged [in the task] and individual meaning will be transmitted or derived' and the opposite is also true (p. 195). Therefore including students' culture in the curriculum is seen as an essential factor for not only fostering a sense of identity and self-worth in students, but also as important for academic success. Not including students' cultures in the curriculum, can be a matter of concern. As far as the English language curriculum is concerned, it is not neutral, neither on the political, social, economic, or cultural level (see Phillipson, 1992,

2008). It too, plays a powerful role in the construction of roles, relations and identities (Pennycook, 1994; Duff & Uchida, 1997).

The Study

The study described in this chapter is based on a research project conducted by Lie (2002) on the Indonesian English as a Foreign Language (EFL) curriculum to determine, as Lie explains, whether the textbooks used in the EFL classrooms incorporate multicultural aspects of student life and their cultural environment. The current study examined the EFL school textbooks in Grades 6, 9, and 11 used in the United Arab Emirates (UAE), one of the Arab Gulf countries, to see if the native Arabic culture is incorporated in these curricula. These textbooks were published by Longman (EIPL in Egypt), Garnet (in the UK), and McGraw Hill (in the UK). The dates of publication range from 2006 to 2008. The study focuses on textbooks because in Arab countries they tend to be the dominant instructional media in the classroom (Patrick, 1988; Lockheed & Verspoor, 1990) and they are also good indicators of the learning and teaching process, as Lie (2002) explains. The study examined the written curriculum (Glatthorn, 1987) in the EFL textbooks in terms of text content. Texts here refer to reading passages which include passages, conversations, dialogues, stories, etc. (which may or may not be supported with pictures and/or illustrations). The texts considered were those that dealt with or contained terms and terminology that denote the Arabic culture from names, beliefs, values, ideals, etc. The text-supporting pictures considered were those that represented anything 'Arabic' from traditional dress to geography and landmarks. The term 'Arabic' is used very loosely here as there are many varying cultures within it. The texts and the text-supporting pictures are used as data in examining the frequency of cultural representations. To sharpen the focus of the study, only two sets of categories were constructed in collecting the data (in-text supporting pictures and in-text supporting terms), those that reflected Arab culture and those that did not.

Results and Discussion

The findings of the cultural representations of in-text supporting pictures, show that out of a total of 80 pictures in the Grade 6 textbook, only 6 were representative of the native culture; out of 143 pictures in textbook 9, 63 pictures reflected Arabic culture (mostly pictures of native Arab students in or outside their classrooms, i.e. in the school context, as well as landmarks and maps); and out of 119 pictures in the Grade 11 textbook, 10 reflected the Arabic culture (see Table 1).

Table 1. Arab Culture Representation- in-text Supporting Pictures

Book Grade	Arab	Non-Arab	Total # of pictures	Arab Culture Representation
Grade 6	6	74	80	7.5%
Grade 9	63	80	143	44%
Grade 11	10	109	119	8.4%

The frequency results in terms of the overall cultural representation from in-text supporting pictures show that the Arabic culture was represented in 7.5 % of the pictures in the Grade 6 textbook; in 44% of the pictures in the Grade 9 textbook; and in 8.4% of the pictures in the Grade 11 textbook.

The study also looked at the representation of the Arab culture in regards to the Arabic terms used. Results showed that in the Grade 6 textbook, out of the 53 text passages only 6 referred to Arabic terms; out of the 36 passages in the Grade 9 textbook, 23 referred to Arabic terms (mainly names of individuals or countries); and out of the 63 passages in the Grade 11 textbook, 21 referred to Arabic terms (see Table 2).

Table 2: Arab Culture Representation-In-text Supporting Terms

Book Grade	Arab	Non-Arab	Total # of Texts	Arab Culture Representation
Grade 6	6	47	53	11.32%
Grade 9	23	13	36	63.88%
Grade 11	21	42	63	33.33%

With regards to the in-text terms that are representative of the Arabic culture, frequency results show that the Arabic culture was represented 11.32% in the Grade 6 textbook; 63.88% in the Grade 9 textbook; and 33.33% in the Grade 11 textbook.

The findings of the study call for some reflection on the material presented in the textbooks. The textbook that contained the greatest number of cultural representations in terms of pictures and terms was the textbook for Grade 9. However, in reviewing the information included in the data in terms of the pictures, one notices that the pictures were predominantly pictures of native Arab students in their school uniforms in the classroom environment. These pictures were being repeatedly shown throughout the book. The majority of the rest of the pictures with an Arabic reference, in all the textbooks, were maps that contained either Arab countries or landmarks in these countries.

The reading passages with Arabic references in the textbooks discussed diverse topics, and were included in the data only because they contained Arabic names or names of Arab countries. Generally speaking, there were no references to Arabic traditions, values, or beliefs except for the Grade 11 textbook which had sections in one of its units that mentioned the holy month of Ramadan in terms of activities and food items. The unit contained a poem that spoke about Ramadan mentioning *praying, fasting* and paying *zakah* and had one picture of a group of boys praying. In summary, a closer look at the data showed that what was presented in terms of Arabic culture in these textbooks reflected what Kramsch described as 'surface culture.'

According to the literature reviewed in this chapter, cultures are maintained by curricula and the learner's experiences and backgrounds are important considerations in the curriculum content. The students' cultural backgrounds, histories, and values are socially as well as academically important. What is included, excluded, or even neutrally represented in curricula, is equally important, carries consequences and may have major effects on students.

The findings of the present study show that the inclusion of the Arabic culture in these EFL textbooks leaves room for improvement. There are inequalities in the curriculum in terms of including the Arabic culture and the learning materials reflect that. There may be state policies that call for 'a unified educational policy that stresses the national religious and cultural values...to develop a young generation that is proud of its national identity' (Shaheen, 2009), but as can be seen from the results of the present study, these policies have yet to be implemented. Based on the rhetoric and the concerns being voiced one would assume that the curriculum will include material that reflects more of the native Arabic culture. In societies where there are concerns about casting the native culture as the 'other' and being engulfed by other more dominant cultures, where the make-up of the native population is sometimes less than 10% of the overall population, the curricula need to include and present as much information about the native culture as possible. However, the EFL curriculum in the UAE seems to mirror the larger society. The textbooks portray the more dominant cultures present in society. Representation or inclusion of the native culture in the EFL curriculum may not make a significant difference in the large scheme of things, but when all that is around one is seemingly foreign, as is increasingly the case in the UAE and many of the Gulf countries, any mention of one's culture, no matter how simple, may help maintain it. Issues such as student vulnerability, personal worth, and alienation need to be examined. Policy makers, curriculum developers and materials writers need to be aware of the consequences of their decisions and the long term repercussions these decisions will have on the society. The material chosen from cultural artifacts to cultural values infiltrated in the curriculum has major effects on the students. In cases where there is a shortage of specialized individuals from the native culture, where local educators and scholars may not be ready to develop their own materials, curriculum developers and textbook writers coming from outside cultures should involve their local counterparts as partners and empower them as local resources who can later develop their own curricula.

What gets included in the curriculum has political (Tollefson, 2002) and socio-cultural implications and implicitly determines which cultural values are important and which are given secondary status (Troudi, 2007). According to Pennycook and Karmani (2005), changing the curricula in the Muslim countries to reflect life in the West may be based on a desire to eliminate anti-western ideas, however to advocate 'a more secular curriculum', in this case with the emphasis on English and western culture, 'is to advocate a set of changes that may have profound religious affiliations, social movements....' (Pennycook & Karmani, 2005, p. 158). The stakeholders who have implemented such policies in their education systems without reflecting on their long term effects (Findlow, 2006) may need to revisit these policies in light of the growing concerns in the area.

Conclusion

It seems that 'globalization has brought with it unease and mistrust of the new global culture in its present form' (Maalouf, 2000, pp. 92-93). Rather than leading to a 'great enrichment' and 'diversification of opinion', as Maalouf explains, globalized education seems to be resulting in 'impoverishment' and producing 'simplistic conformism...an intellectual lowest common denominator' (pp. 92-93). Globalization has been considered by many people in developing countries as a threat to culture and identity because globalization demands some degree of structural change in the various dimensions of a society which, according to Shorish (1999), are expected to affect the normative and value systems of developing countries in a most dramatic way. One of these changes that may affect the Arab culture is seemingly coming in the form of education and curriculum policies. The long term socio-cultural effects of the rampant spread of English in the Arab Gulf region, the presence of more dominant cultures outside and inside the classrooms and curriculum, and the evident sidling of the Arabic language and culture are concerns worthy of consideration and further research.

References

Al Baik, D. (2008). It is not acceptable to drop Arabic language from our lives. *The Nation*. Retrieved December 5, 2008, from: http://archive.gulfnews.com/articles.html

Al Kitbi, E. (2006, May 29). Gulf States: Education reform's real goals: Arab Reform Bulletin. *The Emirates Economist*.

Apple, M.W. (1996). *Cultural politics and education*. New York: Teachers College Press.

Arani, M.R.S. (2004). Policy of education for the 21st century in developed and developing countries: Focus on Japan and Persian Gulf region. *Journal of International Cooperation Studies*, *11*(3), 101-130.

Atkinson, D. (2004). Contrasting rhetorics/contrasting cultures: Why contrastive rhetoric needs a better conceptualization of culture. *Journal of English for Academic Purposes, 3*, 277-289.

134   *Khawlah Ahmed*

Au, K.H. (1993). *Literacy instruction in multicultural settings.* United States: Bolt, Rinehart & Winston.

Bakhtin, M. (1981). *The dialogic of imagination.* Austin: University of Texas Press.

Banks, J. A. (1995). Multicultural education: Characteristics and goals. In J.A. Banks, & C. Banks (Eds.), *Multicultural education: Issues and perspectives* (pp. 3-28). Needham Heights, Massachusetts: Allyn & Bacon.

Chriost, D.M.G. (2003). *Language, identity and conflict: A comparative study of language in ethnic conflict in Europe and Eurasia.* London: Routledge.

Diamond, B., & Moore, M. (1995). *Multicultural literacy: Mirroring the reality of the classroom.* New York: Longman Publishers.

Duff, P., & Ushida, Y. (1997). The negotiation of teachers' sociocultural identities and practices in postsecondary classrooms. *TESOL Quarterly, 31*(3), 451-486.

Ferdman, B. (1990). Literacy and cultural identity. *Harvard Educational Review, 60*(2), 181-204.

Findlow, S. (2006). Higher education and linguistic dualism in the Arab Gulf. *British Journal of Sociology of Education, 27*(1), 19-36.

Glatthorn, A. (1987). *Curriculum leadership.* Glenview, Illinois: Scott, Foresman & Co.

Gonzalez, G., Karoly, L.A., Constant, L., Salem, H., & Goldman, C.A. (2008). *Facing human capital challenges of the 21ˢᵗ century: Education and labor market initiatives in Lebanon, Oman, Qatar, and the United Arab Emirates.* RAND Corporation (ED503118).

Gordon, A., & Browne, K. (1996). *Guiding young children in a diverse society.* Needham Heights, Massachusetts: Allyn & Bacon.

Graddol, D. (2006). *English Nest: Why global English may mean the end of 'English as a foreign language'.* United Kingdom: British Council.

Green, A. (1997). *Education, globalization and the Nation State.* United Kingdom: Macmillan Press Ltd.

Hellyer, P. (2008, November 11). *The National,* 22.

Hinkel, E. (1999). *Cultures in second language teaching and learning.* Cambridge: Cambridge University Press.

Karmani, S. (2005). Petrolinguistics: The emerging nexus between oil, English, and Islam. *Journal of Language, Identity & Education, 4*(2), 87-102.

King, A.D. (1997). *Culture, globalization and the world-system: Contemporary conditions for the representation of identity.* Minnesota: University of Minnesota Press.

Kramsch, C. (2005). Language, thought, and culture. In A. Davies, & C. Elder (Eds.), *The Handbook of Applied Linguistics (pp. 235-261).* United States: John Wiley & Sons.

Krieger, Z. (2008a, March 28). An academic building bloom transforms the Persian Gulf. *Chronicle of Higher Education, 54*(29).

Krieger, Z. (2008b, August 26). Desert Bloom. *Chronicle of Higher Education, 54*(29).

Leach, F.E., & Little, A.W. (1999). *Education, cultures, and economics: Dilemmas for development.* New York: Falmer Press.

Lie, A. (2002). *Multicultural issues in the 1994 English curriculum in Indonesian senior high schools.* Singapore: SEAMEO Regional Language Center.

Lockheed, M., & Verspoor, A. (1990). *Improving primary education in developing countries: A review of policy options.* Washington, D.C.: World Bank.

Maalouf, A. (2000). *On Identity.* London: The Harvel Press.

Mills, A. (2008, September). Emirates look to the West for prestige. *Chronicle of Higher Education, 55*(5).

Nieto, S. (1996). *Affirming diversity: The sociopolitical context of multicultural education.* New York: Longman Publishers.

Patrick, J. (1988). High school government textbooks. *ERIC Digest,* ED301532.

Pennycook, A. (1994). *The cultural politics of English as an international language*. New York: Longman.

Pennycook, A., & Karmani, S. (2005). Islam, English, and 9/11. *Journal of Language, Identity and Education, 4*(2), 157-172

Phillipson, R. (1992). *Linguistic imperialism*. Oxford: Oxford University Press.

Phillipson, R. (2008). The linguistic imperialism of neoliberal empire. *Critical inquiry in language studies, 5*(1), 1-43.

Rassool, N. (2007). *Global issues in language, education and development: Perspectives from postcolonial countries*. United Kingdom: Multilingual Matters Ltd.

Rivzi, F., Engel, L., Rutkowski, D., & Sparks, J. (2007). Equality and the politics of globalization in education. In, G.K.Verma, C.R. Bagley, & M.M. Jha (Eds.), *International perspectives on educational diversity and inclusion* (pp. 3-20). London: Routledge.

Shaheen, K. (2009). FNC: Use of Arabic in federal universities. *The National*. Retrieved on November 11, 2009, from: http://www.thenational.ae

Shorish, M.M. (1999). Globalization and culture. *Journal of International Cooperation in Education, 2*(2), 15-24.

Stromquist, N.P. (2002). *Education in a globalized world*. United States: Rowman & Littlefield Publishers.

Stromquist, N.P., & Monkman, K. (2000). *Globalization and education: Integration and contestation across cultures*. Lanham, Maryland: Rowan & Littlefield Publishing.

Thornborrow, J. (2004). Language and identity. In L. Thomas, S. Wareing, I. Singh, J.Peccei, J. Thornborrow, & J. Jones (Eds.), *Language, society and power* (pp. 157-172). New York: Routledge.

Tollefson, J.W. (2002). *Language policies in education: Critical issues*. Mahwah, New Jersey: Lawrence Erlbaum.

Takaki, R. (1993). *A different mirror: A history of multicultural America*. Canada: Little, Brown and Company Ltd.

Troudi, S. (2007). The effects of English as a medium of instruction. In A. Jendli, S. Troudi, & C. Coombe (Eds.), *The power of language: Perspectives from Arabia* (pp. 3-19). Dubai: TESOL Arabia Publications.

Tsui, A.B.M., & Tollefson, J.W. (2007). *Language policy, culture and identity in Asian contexts*. New Jersey: Lawrence Erlbaum Associates, Publishers.

United Nations Development Program. (1999). *Human Development Report 1999*. New York: United Nations Development Program.

Vygotsky, L. (1962). *Thought and language*. Cambridge: MIT Press.

KEITH KENNETZ, MELANIE VAN DEN HOVEN, & SCOTT PARKMAN

Chapter 7
Arab Student Attitudes towards Varieties of English

Abstract

Over the past two decades, there has been theoretical support for
viewing English as an international language, which, in turn, has
generated practical suggestions for the teaching of English as a
Foreign Language (EFL). The perceptions of learners who encounter
English in all of its many varieties, however, has been underexplored
in general, and, notably, in the Arab world where English is
increasingly used as the language of instruction at schools and
universities. This study aims to better understand Emirati students'
attitudes toward international varieties of spoken English by using
perceptual methods taken from Preston (1989, 1999) and theoretical
constructs used in the discourses of World Englishes (McKay, 2001;
Jenkins 2000, 2006). The study used two surveys that asked seventy-
four respondents in their first year of college to rate six varieties of
English prevalent in the Arabian Gulf. The first survey featured a
questionnaire that asked respondents to rate the varieties for
pleasantness, correctness and understandability. The second survey, a
modified matched-guise experiment was employed to elicit
participants' perceptions of the six varieties after listening to short
speech samples. Respondents were asked to identify the nationality
of the speaker and rate the speech sample using the same variables of
pleasantness, correctness and understandability. The study suggests
that while students demonstrate clear preferences towards different

varieties of English, they are not accurate at identifying these varieties when tested. This study also supports the development of EFL teaching materials which promote phonological awareness of different varieties of English spoken in the Gulf and the mediation of negative associations of certain varieties.

Introduction

Over the past twenty years, the recognition that the English language is used in many diverse contexts all over the world and its role in intercultural communication has had increasing prominence in TESOL and Applied Linguistics discourses (Jenkins, 2006). Interest in teaching English with a view of its emerging global role in media, business and trade (Crystal, 1997) has led to a number of suggestions for both EFL teachers and curriculum developers. One widely supported suggestion is to promote an awareness of the many different varieties of spoken English (Ur, 1999; McKay, 2000, 2003; Berns, 2008). While identifying the plural nature of English usage is admirable and deemed especially relevant for 'East Asia, Europe, and to a lesser extent, Latin America' (Jenkins 2006, p. 162), research providing empirical evidence of learners' experiences of English varieties both inside and outside these regions is warranted (Jenkins, 2006) especially in terms of intelligibility and linguistic tolerance (Berns, 2008, p. 332). In addition, the use of English in diverse Middle Eastern contexts has been under-theorized. Given the recent impact of socio-cultural factors (such as educational reforms, the increased use of English alongside Arabic in public settings and a globalized workforce), it becomes apparent that more research is needed into the use of English in the Arab world (Dahan, 2007).

In the Arabian Gulf, in such countries as Kuwait, Saudi Arabia and the United Arab Emirates, for instance, the importance of English as a subject of academic study in high school and increasingly as a medium of instruction in higher education has prompted research into learners' perceptions of English (Alam, Hussain, & Khan, 1988; Al-Haq & Smadi, 1996; Malallah, 2000; Mustafa, 2003; Findlow, 2006; Dahan, 2007; Qashoe cited in Randall & Samimi, 2010). The results indicate that students learning English in higher education view the language positively and see the perceived benefits of studying it. However, the English language has been consistently presented in these studies as a singular, monolithic language reflecting Western cultural norms and so questions as to the students' specific perceptions towards diverse varieties of English arise. For example, a recent study by Randall and Samimi (2010) surveyed members of the Dubai police force in order to explicitly measure attitudes towards English given its status as a lingua franca used by many of the city's multicultural residents. However individual varieties of English were not investigated in this study.

The perceptions and reactions to international varieties of spoken Englishes as used in local contexts, while recommended in the literature for World Englishes (Jenkins, 2006), have not, as of yet, been a strong focus for researchers. More research which generates data on learners' perceptions of the different varieties of English is critical for a better understanding of how the sounds of international varieties of spoken English may be a source of challenge to learners of English, particularly those outside of native-English speaking contexts, such as British, Australian and North American (BANA) contexts. This is especially relevant for tertiary-level students in multicultural contexts such as the Arabian Gulf, where English is often used as a lingua franca alongside Arabic (Syed, 2003; Randall & Samimi, 2010).

As a result of the increasing internationalization of English, many English textbook series commonly used in the region have Middle East editions (e.g. *Tapestry and Interactions*) and incorporate multiple varieties of English (Hartmann & Gill, 2005; Tanka & Baker, 2007). For students not familiar with these varieties, this can be a considerable source of stress and confusion, especially since their understanding of such varieties can affect their performance on proficiency tests. As evidenced in a college in the United Arab Emirates (UAE), the use of unfamiliar accents on a listening exam generated student complaints of unfair assessment practices. Further anecdotal evidence, such as the following statements made by UAE students, typify a range of prevalent attitudes students have to the varieties of English encountered in educational settings: 'We usually use only US and British not another like New Zealand' and '...one kind [of English] it make me feel boring [sic]'. Both statements illustrate student awareness of English varieties and concern for appropriate forms of English for language learning.

In general, because of the multicultural identities of teachers in the UAE, the recognition that English serves as an international language is well accepted (Dahan, 2007). For instance, in the UAE, the rapid growth of education has resulted in a massive influx of expatriate teachers, including expatriate English teachers (Clarke, 2006). In this sense, the theoretical arguments supporting the incorporation of World Englishes into the English language curriculum are not inherently problematic as they reflect the real-world contexts of teaching and learning in schools. However, questions remain for many teachers about implementation (ibid). Although teachers may recognize that students in the Arabian Gulf will need to communicate with speakers of many varieties of English several issues immediately arise. How will students respond to diverse accents and lexis when presented in the classroom? Which varieties are most suitable for classroom instruction? How can lessons on variation within the English language be best incorporated into the school curriculum? However difficult these questions might be, if biases toward and against prevalent varieties of English are influencing students' interaction with the language and its myriad of interlocutors, then those biases need to be uncovered and, perhaps, mediated.

Background

An investigation of Emirati student perceptions of international varieties of spoken English can be informed by three lines of discourse: 1) World Englishes, namely the recognition of English as an International Language in English language teaching contexts; 2) English and Higher Education within the context of the UAE; and 3) perceptions of language in general, and, in particular English. In this section, these lines of discourse are discussed.

World Englishes and Teaching English as an International Language

The English language has been steadily expanding its role in an increasingly globalized world and this rapid expansion of use, beyond the traditional areas where English has historically functioned as a first language (L1), has led to situations where the language is being transformed in a variety of significant ways by second language (L2) users in their own areas to meet their own particular sociolinguistic needs (Brutt-Griffler, 2003). These changes can be semantic, lexical and grammatical but are specific to the local area where the language is being used. As these changes are solidified and regularized across the local community, we can say that new varieties of English have emerged and the reference of its plurality is seen in the coinage of the term World Englishes (Jenkins, 2006). Although Asian countries like Singapore and India are often cited as having distinct varieties of English (Strevens, 1992; Kirkpatrick, 2002) its relevance extends to many countries in the Middle East.

There is much interest in the teaching and learning of international varieties of English. However, what is meant by variety, and how the different varieties can be categorized and distinguished from one another warrant clarification. To this end, there are two main frameworks which are useful in the consideration of international varieties of English. An influential early framework, proposed by Kachru (1985), argues that there are three main groups into which varieties of English can be organized. Kachru theorizes these three groups as different circles of English. The first circle, called the inner circle, is where English is the historical L1, such as in the United Kingdom and the United States. The second circle, the outer circle, consists of places where English is not the historical L1, but has risen to a high level of prestige and intra-national use, as in India and Singapore, but also includes many African countries where English enjoys a legal status. In the final circle, the expanding circle, are the countries where English is in very limited use, used primarily to support international communication. Korea, China and Brazil are some examples of countries in this category.

While Kachru highlights the role of English in various countries, Holliday (1994) proposes a different model to characterize the professional identities of English-speaking teachers. According to Holliday (2002), there are two broad positions of English speakers traditionally known as native-speaker and non-native speaker. In order to account for the different ways English is taught internationally, he introduces a BANA-TESEP model which characterizes the two positions of language educators in terms of power and privilege (ibid). The first group consists of those who have learned English in predominantly English speaking countries, which he names BANA, an acronym for Britain, Australia and North America. The second category, TESEP, includes those who teach English in the so-called Periphery, which includes any area where English is not the dominant L1. In other words, TESEP refers to TEachers who work in SEcondary and Primary schools whose culture of teaching English is influenced by mainstream educational policies.

Missing in the literature are overt references to the classification of the status of English in the Middle East, including its status in the Arabian Gulf peninsula. The usage of English in the United Arab Emirates is a good example of how intra-national use and the prestige of English is influenced by educational policy (Anon, 2006). In the UAE English has been mandated as the language of instruction at the tertiary level. In addition, it is a key subject taught in secondary schools to enhance admittance into higher education. In this regard, the use of English parallels usage in many outer circle countries. At the same time, English has been taught as a foreign language with an exam-focused methodology similar to those used in many countries in the expanding circle. The BANA-TESEP model is thus useful in explaining how the identity of teachers in some ways could be related to socially constructed notions of linguistic prestige and student perceptions of different varieties of English.

English and Higher Education in the UAE

Due to its international profile, English has spread as a medium of instruction in higher education to much of the Arab world, and quite notably in the UAE. Although religious and cultural subjects are taught in Arabic, most other subjects, especially science and technical subjects are taught in English. Students who pursue a college degree face the two-fold challenge of having to achieve academically while at the same time mastering a second language. Despite this, in a study looking at the different domains of English within the UAE, Findlow (2006) reported that college students have an overall positive view towards English, seeing it as a medium of openness, modernity and progressiveness. It was suggested that both English and Arabic are seen as equally important for young people in the UAE and, for the time being, Emirati students do not perceive English as an oppressive post-colonial language: 'English is the language of the world, Arabic the language of my country' (Findlow, 2006, p. 21). However, this study and other studies conducted in the wider Arabian peninsula (Alam et al. 1988, Al Haq & Smadi 1996; Malallah 2000) do not explore the perceptions students hold towards the varieties of spoken English found in the region.

Perceptions of Language

Unlike most students in outer circle countries who learn English mostly from non-native speakers of their own language group, Emirati students learn English in a multi-cultural schooling environment with their teachers coming from a variety of BANA and Peripheral countries (Shaw, Badri, & Hukul, 1995) and, thus, are exposed to a wide range of World Englishes. Understanding just how they view different varieties of English, and the people who speak these varieties, is therefore of critical importance to the teaching and learning of English in this region.

The concept of varieties of English, as used in this chapter, refers to much more than just accent. The concept of accent is based on the observation that some people and groups speak differently from others (Lippi-Green, 1997). Despite the simplicity of this notion, the term accent is a loaded construct; it connects linguistic patterns with social and economic divisions between both individuals and groups. Cavanaugh (2005, p. 29) argues that accents must be treated as 'acoustical things in the world, indexing both speakers (subjects), as well as qualities detachable from these speakers, and at times even places themselves (objects).' This characterization does not only apply to accents but can also be suitable for linguistic features that have achieved stereotype status (Labov, 1966). Language differences do not exist in a neutral socio-political context, and patterns of cultural subjugation typically lead to linguistic subordination (Lippi-Green, 1997). Therefore, some varieties are deemed 'better' than others for socio-economic reasons.

Researchers conducting experiments in the field of language attitude and perception studies have found evaluative categories useful in researching perceptions of language. Ryan, Giles, and Sebastian's (1982) categories of social status and group solidarity have been further refined by Preston (1989, 1999) who pioneered the use of the descriptors 'pleasantness' and 'correctness' to study perceptions of dialects of a single language. Understandability, or intelligibility, is also a common descriptor featured not only in sociolinguistic work but in TESOL research as well (McKay, 2002). Each of these descriptors is explained below.

Correctness

The general public in societies across the world usually has very strong opinions about what qualifies as 'good' language and what qualifies as 'bad' language, although they may not agree on exactly what that is, even within the same speech communities (Niedzielski & Preston, 2000). In this sense, correctness is designed to measure individual attitudes held about perceived standard and non-standard varieties of a certain language. Such evaluations might be confined to certain grammatical or phonological features of a dialect or may encompass beliefs about different languages.

Pleasantness

Leaving issues of correctness aside, pleasantness is another variable which captures associations of a particular language variety. Even though a language variety may be deemed not correct, often times it can be considered pleasant, friendly and casual by members of a speech community. In other words, a particular language variety may be considered incorrect but valued as a symbol of group solidarity by the speakers of such a variety (Preston, 1999; Niedzielski & Preston, 2000).

Understandability/Intelligibility

From the perspective of English teaching professionals, it is important to investigate which varieties students perceive to understand the best. Understandability is also a common variable in perceptual sociolinguistic work, and has been used to study how far certain varieties are perceived to be from the standard (Preston, 1996). Intelligibility is a similar variable, more commonly used in second language acquisition and World Englishes research to capture the degree to which the utterance is deemed understandable and meaningful to diverse speakers of English in international contexts (Berns, 2008; Nelson, 2008).

In the study described in this chapter, the three variables of pleasantness, correctness and understandability are operationalized to measure Emirati students' perceptions of several varieties of English.

The Study

This research focuses on three basic questions:

1. What are Emirati college students' attitudes towards different varieties of English?
2. How well can they distinguish between the various accents that they hear?
3. Do their ratings of varieties of English match their ratings of actual speech samples of English-speaking academic professionals?

The study was conducted at a teachers' college in the United Arab Emirates. The mission of the college is to train Emirati pre-service teachers for the nations' primary schools who can teach English, Maths and Science to Arabic speaking students with English as the medium of instruction. The faculty members at the college are international and English speaking with instructors coming from over twenty different countries.

For this study, surveys were distributed and collected from seventy-four (74) first-year students in an academic bridging program. All of the students were Emirati females between the ages of 18 and 21. The students had high school diplomas and an English proficiency level between IELTS 4.5 and 5.

This study employed two bilingual attitudinal surveys administered in the same session. The first survey was designed to capture general attitudes held towards six common varieties of English commonly heard in the UAE: three from the BANA nations (North American; British; Australasian); and three from TESEP nations (Gulf-Arabic; non-Gulf Arabic and South Asian). These varieties were selected due to their prevalence in the region and their alignment with the theoretical frameworks of Holliday (1994) and Kachru (1990) as discussed in the previous sections. Students were asked to rate each of these varieties of English based on their correctness, pleasantness and understandability using a 5-point Likert scale. This survey was delivered with no linguistic input, so students were expected to draw upon their own experience of these varieties.

The second survey was a modified form of the Matched Guise Technique (MGT). MGT is designed to capture student perceptions of spoken English and is an approach which elicits listener responses to sets of linguistic performances that differ in specific qualities. Much of this work contrasts different languages (Lambert, 1967) or language varieties (Giles & Billings, 1990) although other aspects have been investigated, including speech rate (Ray & Zahn, 1990) and powerful versus powerless language strategies (Ruva & Bryant, 1998). Although traditional MGT studies use the same speaker to create different speech samples in order to ensure that differences in reactions can be attributed to the selected variables under investigation, this was not viable for the current study due to the large number of accents under investigation. Therefore, different speakers were used to capture the authenticity of the accents under investigation but all were controlled for content and lexis. The speech sample selections featured the same six varieties as in the first survey. The speakers were educated teaching professionals living and working in the UAE. They each read an identical, pre-written script and this was done to ensure that, to some extent, the register remained consistent. This also ensured that students were evaluating each speech sample based on its phonological features (rather than its content), but it also meant that much of the natural variety (lexical choices, word ordering, etc.) was eliminated from the samples. The script used for the samples was delivered as a segment from a lecture and featured a neutral explanation of the differences between facts and opinions. The samples selected for the survey were taken from a pool of samples and were pilot-tested by independent judges for authenticity and representativeness.

After completing the first survey, students were asked to listen to a randomized recording of the six speech samples and judge them on perceived pleasantness, correctness, and understandability on a 5-point Likert scale. In addition, they were asked to identify where they thought each speaker was from.

Results and Discussion

The results of the two-part survey shed light on Emirati college students' attitudes towards different varieties of English. For the first survey (i.e. without linguistic input) a 5-point Likert scale was employed to capture student preferences. In response to prompts the informants could chose from 'strongly agree', 'agree', 'not sure', 'disagree', or 'strongly disagree' then numerical values '2', '1', '0','-1',and '-2' were assigned to these descriptors respectively. These values were added up for all respondents and mean scores calculated for each English variety and perceptual category (see Table 1).

Table 1. Survey 1: Student Perceptions of Varieties of English – Without Speech Samples *(n=74)*

Variety of English	Correctness	Pleasantness	Understandability	Composite Score	Overall Rank
Gulf Arabic	1.07	0.99	1.30	1.12	1
North American	1.12	0.99	0.91	1.00	2

Variety of English	Correctness	Pleasantness	Understandability	Composite Score	Overall Rank
United Kingdom	1.08	0.88	0.92	0.96	3
Non Gulf Arabic	0.64	0.38	0.92	0.64	4
Oceanic	0.59	0.43	0.46	0.50	5
South Asian	-0.30	-0.24	-0.41	-0.32	6

Scale: Strongly Agree: 2, Agree: 1, Not Sure: 0, Disagree: -1, Strongly Disagree: -2

Looking at Table 1, it is clear that students had strong preferences concerning the English varieties tested. In particular there were high ratings for North American and UK Englishes in all three criteria. This is not surprising given the high status often afforded to native-speaking English teachers. However, while North American English was ranked the most correct and the most pleasant of the six varieties tested, it was Gulf-Arabic English which received the highest ratings for understandability. It was, in fact, the extremely high rating of Gulf-Arabic English for understandability which was responsible for this variety achieving the top position in the overall rankings. Similarly, non-Gulf Arab speakers of English also rated highly for understandability but it was the weak rating of pleasantness which lowered its overall composite score. The results of the first survey also show a clear bias against the South Asian and Australasian varieties, with the former being the only variety to receive an overall negative rating in all three categories.

The results of the second survey showed clear differences between the attitude of students towards the tested varieties of English with and without speech samples (see Table 2). Again mean scores were calculated for each variety of English and perceptual category.

Table 2. Survey 2: Student Perceptions of Varieties of English – With Speech
       Samples *(n=74)*

Variety of English	Correctness	Pleasantness	Understandability	Composite Score	Overall Rank
North American	1.38	1.14	1.33	1.28	1
South Asian	1.37	0.78	1.10	1.08	2
Non Gulf Arabic	0.81	0.62	1.03	0.82	3
Oceanic	1.23	0.37	0.62	0.74	4
Gulf Arabic	0.92	0.19	0.9	0.67	5
United Kingdom	0.78	0.19	0.52	0.50	6

Scale: Strongly Agree: 2, Agree: 1, Not Sure: 0, Disagree: -1, Strongly Disagree: -2

While the Gulf-Arabic variety was rated very highly in all three criteria in the first survey, it received some of the lowest scores when rated in the second survey and received an overall rank of 5. Interestingly, the students' perceptions of the Australasian and South Asian varieties were much more positive in the second survey, with the South Asian variety receiving an overall rank of 2. In addition, the UK variety, which initially received high scores, received the lowest scores in the second survey and was ranked 6th.

Students were also asked to identify the varieties of English they heard in the second survey. The results are given in Table 3.

Table 3. Accuracy in Identifying Varieties *(n=74)*

Speech Samples	% of Correct Identification	% of Correct Pan Arabic
Gulf Arabic	49.30	76.06
Non Gulf Arabic	27.78	70.83
North American	25.35	
United Kingdom	10.29	
Oceanic	7.35	
South Asian	2.99	

Perhaps considering our informants' level of English, it was not surprising that they demonstrated a low level of accuracy when asked to identify the varieties of English they heard from the speech samples. While respondents were quite good at identifying samples of pan-Arabic origin (i.e. respondents judged the speech sample to be from an Arabic speaker origin but could not discriminate whether the speaker was a Gulf or non-Gulf Arabic speaker) with scores of 76% and 71%, only 25% could accurately identify the North American sample and only 10% or less could identify the UK and Australasian speech samples.

In sum, the results of this study indicate that although the students surveyed indicated that they have strong preferences for certain varieties of English such as North American, British and Gulf Arabic, when listening to authentic input of the six varieties their preferences for certain varieties (such as South Asian) was quite different. Students were also found to be weak in their ability to identify correctly the different English varieties. These findings suggest that knowledge of the diverse speech patterns found among different users of English is quite weak among Emirati students.

There are a number of pedagogical issues raised by the results of these surveys, which warrant further investigation. One of the most interesting findings was the clear preference that the students have for their own variety of English. The Gulf-Arabic variety of English was rated highly in all three criteria, being seen as nearly as correct as the North American and UK Englishes, slightly more pleasant than UK English, and significantly more understandable than any other variety. This is an interesting point considering how much emphasis is being placed on native-English speaker models when teaching English in the country's classrooms.

According to Phillipson (1992) in many countries with colonial pasts, the language of the colonizer is often resisted. In contrast to this view, the results of this study support a previous study conducted in Saudi Arabia, which concluded little perceived resentment and resistance to learning English (Al-Haq & Smadi, 1996). The high ratings of Gulf-Arabic English in this study are also indicative of a desire to assert the respondents' own national solidarity. Further qualitative research is needed to better interpret how Emirati students perceive and evaluate English spoken by Arab Gulf nationals.

Another important consideration raised by this study is the students' lack of awareness of different varieties of English. For example, students demonstrated very little awareness of what Australasian English is or how it sounds. Most likely, our respondents, while being aware that English is a language spoken around the world, do not have the linguistic resources to categorize different varieties accurately. Providing students with linguistic resources for international varieties of academic English is the responsibility of English teachers, native and non-native (Smith cited in Berns, 2008). A lack of resources led to unexpected implications for our respondents. For example, in the first survey South Asian English was ranked 6th overall with negative ratings in each of the three categories. However, in the second survey (using a speech sample as a prompt), South Asian English was ranked second scoring higher in all three categories than the UK English. This means that students who are taught by teachers from a South Asian background may have a negative perception of their teachers' English variety and evaluate the teacher as difficult to understand or speaking incorrect English. Correlations between student evaluations of teacher performance and positive or negative associations attributed to specific varieties of English warrant further investigation. In addition, the results of the present study suggest that a follow-up investigation into the interpretations students bring to the variable 'correctness' is needed. Given that all speech samples used in the study contained grammatically correct English and identical lexis, why did students perceive some varieties to be more correct than others? How did students interpret correctness? Are pragmatic functions influencing student conceptions of correctness?

The results taken in sum imply that the development of teaching materials for the EFL classroom in the Gulf Arabian context should be considered carefully. In terms of listening materials, it is advisable to feature varied input in order to help students become aware of the basic phonological variations between different varieties of English which are prevalent in the region. There is also a need for teaching materials to mediate students' attitudes and negative associations towards different varieties of English that are less popular, such as the South Asian and Australasian Englishes.

There are several limitations to this study which should be taken into consideration when interpreting the results. Firstly, the informants surveyed were from a homogeneous group of female students in a B.Ed. program from one college in the U.A.E.; therefore, the results cannot be seen as representative of a larger, more diverse sample pool. Further research into male perceptions and mixed gender studies would add to the discussion. Reactivity is another drawback of this study. During the implementation of the survey students were given instructions by a faculty member at the college, who, undoubtedly, spoke one of the featured varieties of English. It is impossible to gauge the effect that this may or may not have had on the students' perceptions of the varieties that they were surveyed about. Lastly, this study used self-reported data. While it is hoped that respondents are aware of their own beliefs and honest in their reporting, the accuracy of self-reported data introduces some bias into the study's results.

Conclusion

The results show that Emirati students in our study have strong preferences regarding the different varieties of English that they encounter in their daily lives. Students had clear beliefs about the correctness, pleasantness and understandability of the different varieties of English. However, they were not accurate at identifying spoken varieties of English. This finding reveals a strong disconnect between respondent beliefs and their linguistic resources (i.e. their ability to accurately identify varieties of English when provided with authentic linguistic input) and highlights the influence cultural stereotypes play in the development of attitudes and beliefs towards different varieties of the English language. The study also showed a clear preference for local varieties of English (i.e. Gulf English) mainly due to perceived understandability. Future follow-up studies need to expand on these findings and hopefully shed further light on the status of World Englishes in the Gulf region. Given the important role of English as a language which is taught and learnt with increasing fervor in this region, it is hoped that further empirical studies will contribute to a deeper understanding of perceptions towards the varieties of English prevalent in the wider Arab world.

References

Alam, M.A., Hussain, S.M., & Khan, B.A. (1988). *A study of the attitudes of students, teachers, and parents towards English as a foreign language in Saudi Arabian public schools.* Ministry of Education, Educational Development, The General Directorate of Research and Evaluation, Saudi Arabia.

Al-Haq, F., & Smadi, O. (1996). Spread of English and westernization in Saudi Arabia. *World Englishes 15*(3), 307-317.

Anon (2006). *The UAE class of 2020: Critical choices for educating the next generation of Emiratis.* Ministry of Higher Education and Scientific Research, Abu Dhabi: Office of Higher Education Policy and Planning.

Berns, M. (2008). World Englishes, English as a lingua franca, and intelligibility. *World Englishes, 27*(34), 327-324.

Brutt-Griffler, J. (2002). *World English: A study of its development.* Clevedon, UK: Multilingual Matters.

Cavanaugh, J. (2005). Accent matters: Material consequences of sounding local in northern Italy. *Language and Communication, 25*(2), 127-148.

Cambridge ESOL (2009). *Academic and general English.* Retrieved May 28, 2009, from: http://www.cambridgeesol.org/exams/academic-english/ielts.html

Clarke, M. (2006). Beyond antagonism? The discursive construction of 'new' teachers in the United Arab Emirates. *Teaching Education, 17*(3), 225-237.

Crystal, D. (1997). *English as a global language.* Cambridge: Cambridge University Press.

Dahan, L. (2007). English as an international language in the Arabian Gulf: Student and teacher views of the role of culture. In S. Midrij, A. Jendli, & A. Selammi (Eds.), *Research in ELT Contexts.* Dubai: TESOL Arabia.

Giles, H., & Billings, A. (1990). Assessing language attitudes: Speaker evaluation. In Davies, A., & Elder, C. (Eds.), *The handbook of applied linguistics* (pp. 187-209). Blackwell: Oxford.

Hartmann, P., & Gill, M. (2005). *Tapestry – listening and speaking 2 – Middle East edition.* London: Heinle.

Holliday, A. (1994). *Appropriate methodology and social context.* Cambridge: Cambridge University Press.

Holliday, A. (2002). The struggle against 'us'–'them' conceptualizations in TESOL as the ownership of English changes. In Z. Syed, C. Coombe, & S. Troudi (Eds.), *Critical reflection and practice – Selected Papers from the 2002 International Conference.* Abu Dhabi: TESOL Arabia.

Holliday, A. (2009). *The struggle to teach English as an International language.* Oxford: Oxford University Press.

Findlow, S. (2006). Higher education and linguistic dualism in the Arab Gulf. *British Journal of Sociology of Education, 27*(1), 19-36.

Jenkins, J. (2006). Curent perspectives on teaching World Englishes and English as a lingua franca. *TESOL Quarterly, 40*(1), 157-181.

Jenkins, J. (2000). *The phonology of English as an international language.* Oxford: Oxford University Press.

Kachru, B.B. (1985). Standards, codification and sociolinguistic realism: The English language in the outer circle. In R. Quirk, & H.G. Widdowson (Eds.), *English in the world: Teaching and learning the language and literatures* (pp. 11-30). Cambridge: Cambridge University Press.

Kachru, B.B. (1992). *The other tongue: English across cultures.* Chicago: University of Illinois Press.

Kirkpatrick, A. (2002). *Englishes in Asia: Communication, identity, power and education.* Melbourne: Language Australia.

Labov, W. (1966). *The social stratification of English in New York city.* Washington: Center for Applied Linguistics.

Lambert, W. (1967). A social psychology of bilingualism. *Journal of Social Issues, 23,* 91-109.

Lippi-Green, R. (1997). *English with an accent.* New York: Routledge.

Malallah, F. (2000) English in an Arabic environment: Current attitudes to English among Kuwait nuiversity students. *International Journal of Bilingual Education and Bilingualism, 3*(1), 19-43.

McKay, S.L. (2000). Teaching English as an international language: Implications for cultural materials in the classroom. *TESOL Journal, 9*(4), 7-11.

McKay, S.L. (2003). Towards an appropriate EIL pedagogy: Re-examining common ELT assumptions. *International Journal of Applied Linguistics, 13,* 1-22.

Nelson, C. (2008). Intelligibility since 1969. *World Englishes, 27*(34), 297-308.

Niedzielski, N., & Preston, D. (2000). *Folk linguistics.* New York: Mouton de Gruyter.

Phillipson, R. (1992). *Linguistic imperialism.* Oxford: Oxford University Press.

Preston, D. (1989). *Perceptual dialectology: Nonlinguists' views of areal linguistics.* Providence, RI: Foris Publications.

Preston, D.R. (1996). Where the worst English is spoken. In E.W. Schneider (Ed.), *Focus on the USA* (pp. 297-360). Amsterdam.

Preston, D. (1999). *The handbook of perceptual dialectology* (Vol.1). Philadelphia: John Benjamin Publishing Company.

Randall, M., & Samimi, M. (2010). The status of English in Dubai. *English Today, 26*(1), 43-50.

Ray, G.B., & Zahn, C.J. (1990). Regional speech rates in the United States: A preliminary analysis. *Communication Research Reports, 7*, 34-37.

Ruva, C., & Bryant, J. (1998).The impact of age, speech style, and question form on perceptions of witness credibility and trial outcome. Paper Presented at the American Psychology–Law Society Biennial Conference.

Ryan, E., Giles, H., & Sebastian, R. (1982). An integrative perspective for the study of attitudes toward language variation. In E. Ryan, & H. Giles (Eds.), *Attitudes toward language variation* (pp. 1-19). London: Edward Arnold.

Shaw, K.E., Badri, A.A.M.A., & Hukul, A. (1995). Management Concerns in the United Arab Emirates State Schools. *International Journal of Educational Management, 9*(4), 8-13.

Strevens, P. (1992). English as an international language. In B.B. Kachru (Ed.), *The other tongue: English across cultures* (pp. 27-47). University of Illinois Press: Chicago.

Syed, Z. (2003). TESOL in the Gulf. *TESOL Quarterly, 37*(2), 337-41.

Tanka, J., & Baker, L. (2007) *Interactions 2 – listening and speaking – Middle East edition.*Berkshire: McGraw-Hill Education.

Ur, P. (1999). *Teaching listening comprehension.* Cambridge: Cambridge University Press.

AHMAD AL-ISSA & AIDA ABOU EISSA

Chapter 8
Teachers' Attitudes and Practices toward Providing Feedback on Arab EFL Students' Writing

Abstract

Teacher feedback serves many purposes and it is an important part of being a teacher. Pedagogically, while teacher feedback is important, it is not an easy task, partly because of the teachers' attitudes toward providing feedback. Providing second language (L2) students with written feedback on their writing assignments is a challenge for many teachers in the Arab world. This study investigated L2 teachers' attitudes towards and practices on writing assessment and feedback. The study sample comprised 51 secondary teachers of English in the United Arab Emirates (UAE). Data were collected using a questionnaire and semi-structured interviews. The results revealed that L2 teachers in the UAE, in general, hold negative attitudes towards providing written feedback on their students' writing. The results also presented examples of these teachers' assessment practices and showed that L2 teachers in the UAE need training on assessing their students' writing tasks.

Ahmad Al-Issa & Aida Abou Eissa

Introduction

Research on language teaching has emphasized the significance of teachers' feedback on L2 writing as an integral part of second language learning (Brown, 2004; Ferris, 2002, 2003, 2007; Hyland, 2003; Hyland & Hyland, 2006a, 2006b; Sugita, 2006; Weigle, 2002, 2007; White, 1995). Since writing has always had, and will continue to have, a fundamental role in the assessment of students' general academic achievement and development, assessing writing has long been considered a challenge for teachers and educators (Weigle, 2002). However, despite the numerous studies that have been conducted on the significance of teachers' feedback in L2 writing classrooms and its impact on students' writing abilities (for a comprehensive review, see Lee, 2003, 2004, 2007, 2008a, 2008b; Montgomery & Baker, 2005), little has been done on the issue of L2 teachers' attitudes towards writing assessment/feedback in the Arab world in general, and in the United Arab Emirates (UAE) L2 context specifically.

Our extensive experience as English teachers and teacher educators in the UAE has led us to observe that many L2 teachers encounter challenges when responding to students' writing. Most L2 teachers in UAE government schools still depend on impressionistic criteria when assessing students' writing and many of them appear to have negative attitudes towards writing assessment as they believe that it is tiresome and time consuming. Many of the teachers we encountered felt that they are unsure about how to respond to student writing because they have not received training in this field. Although there have been no empirical studies done on this specific subject in the UAE or other Arab countries, our personal observations echo those of other scholars who also work in the Arab educational context (see Coombe, Jendli, & Davidson, 2008; Shine, 2007). The current empirical study aims to fill this gap in the literature. Unless teachers are aware of their own attitudes and practices there will be fewer opportunities for improvement in any facets of teaching, including responding to or assessing student writing. Therefore, this study is an attempt to explore L2 teachers' attitudes toward responding to students' writing in UAE government secondary schools and to investigate teachers' actual practices when responding to their students' writing.

Background

There are studies about students' attitudes towards their writing and the comments they receive, but little has been written about what the teachers think about this very important part of their teaching practice. This issue is important to study mainly in terms of teacher training and how knowledge of their own attitudes towards feedback will assist them in their teaching and in understanding how best to motivate their students through their comments (see Fathman & Whalley, 1990; Ferris & Roberts, 2001; Hedgecock & Lefkowitz, 1996; Leki, 1990, 2003).

Feedback is viewed as 'the biggest and most significant part' (Ferris, 2007, p. 179) of a teacher's job. Despite the challenges inherent in assessing L2 writing, research has shown the importance of teachers' feedback on developing students' writing abilities and skills (Ferris, 2007; White, 1995) through teaching or reinforcing a particular aspect of disciplinary content, teaching specific academic writing conventions, indicating strengths and weaknesses of a piece of writing, explaining or justifying a grade, and suggesting how a student may improve their next piece of writing (Coffin, Curry, Goodman, Hewings, Lillis, & Swann, 2003). According to Hyland (2003), feedback can provide students with 'a sense of audience and sensitize them to the needs of readers [and] offers an additional layer of scaffolding to extend writing skills, promote accuracy and clear ideas, and develop an understanding of written genres' (p. 207). Commenting on the quality of teachers' feedback, Hyland further argues that the written feedback that teachers provide on their students' writing should be 'more than marks on a page' and that teachers should take into consideration all aspects in student writing such as the structure, organization, style, content, and presentation (p. 208). Furthermore, L2 students, who are developing writers acquiring the L2 lexicon, morphological and syntactic systems, need 'distinct and additional intervention from their writing teachers to make up these deficits and to develop strategies for finding, correcting, and avoiding errors' (Ferris, 2002, p. 4).

While feedback is important, it is not an easy task. One of the questions that needs to be examined is how L2 teachers view and respond to L2 students' written work. Many teachers look at it as an unpleasant task instead of being a 'central aspect of teaching that has the potential to be beneficial to both teacher and students' (Weigle, 2007, p. 194). Part of the problem is that most writing teachers believe it is their responsibility to correct most of the errors, especially since their students expect it (Lee, 2003). Bitchener (2008) examined the effectiveness of written corrective feedback on three pieces of descriptive writing in the pre-test, immediate post-test, and delayed post-test of 75 low-intermediate international L2 students in New Zealand. His findings showed that students who received written corrective feedback in the immediate post-test achieved higher levels of accuracy than those in the control group who did not receive any corrective feedback. However, marking all student errors can be a fatiguing process for teachers and a sometimes irritating experience for students themselves (Lee, 2003). In a study conducted by Lee (2004) in order to examine existing error correction practices in secondary writing classrooms in Hong Kong from both the teachers' and students' perceptions, results indicated that teachers had a tendency to mark students' writing errors comprehensively rather than marking them selectively. However, according to Ferris (2002) error correction can be most effective 'when it focuses on patterns of error' as this would allow both the teachers and students to focus on just two or three major kinds of mistakes instead of trying to view and correct 'dozens of disparate errors' (p. 50). Teachers need to become more aware of the variety of assessment tools that are available and understand 'what the essential qualities of a good assessment instrument are and how to develop assessments that maximize these essential qualities within the constraints of time and resources that teachers face' (Weigle, 2007, p. 195).

To conclude, in L2 writing, teachers' feedback is considered a helpful pedagogical instrument which is implemented to improve not only the teaching but also the learning of writing. Teachers require certain abilities and skills, as well as awareness of the issues and difficulties that they might encounter when giving feedback. They also need to be cognizant of their own attitudes and concerns. As the UAE is currently moving towards the use of English as the medium of instruction in all higher education institutions (see Guefrachi & Troudi, 2000; Troudi 2007) having L2 teachers at the secondary level aware of the importance of their own attitudes as they teach writing will have long term benefits for teachers, students, and university instructors.

The Study

Although the medium of instruction in UAE government schools is Arabic, there is a strong emphasis on teaching English at all levels, particularly at the secondary level. At that level, writing is an obligatory element in both monthly tests and final English exams throughout each semester. Each writing test is composed of two parts: the first section has students write simple and compound sentences, and the second section requires they write a well-structured piece of writing. For instance, Grade 10 students are asked to write a one-paragraph composition of 100-150 words. Grade 11 students have to write a multi-paragraph composition of 150-200 words; and senior students write an essay of 200-250 words. The topics that students are required to write are theme-based and related to the content of their textbooks (for more information, see the UAE Ministry of Education website www.moe.gov.ae).

A total of 51 teachers (24 males and 27 females) participated in this study (see Table 1). All of them were experienced secondary level teachers who taught English to Grades 10, 11, and 12 in eight different government secondary schools (four boys' and four girls' schools) in the Sharjah Educational Zone, in the UAE. All teachers were non-native speakers of English from different Arab countries (Egypt, Jordan, Palestine, Syria, Tunisia, and the UAE), with teaching experience ranging from five to thirty years.

Table 1: Teacher Demographics *(n=51)*

	% of teachers (number of teachers)
Nationality	
Emirati	6 (3)
Jordanian	35 (18)
Tunisian	4 (2)
Palestinian	14 (7)
Syrian	18 (9)
Egyptian	24 (12)
Teaching experience	
5–10 years	18 (9)
10–20 years	24 (12)
Over 20 years	59 (30)
Classes teachers taught	
Grade 10	33 (17)
Grade 11	22 (11)
Grade 12	33 (17)
Grades 11+12	12 (6)
Average class size teachers taught	
15 – 20 students	2 (1)
20 – 30 students	94 (48)
Over 30 students	4 (2)

In order to discover what types of attitudes teachers share, as well as their practices concerning providing feedback on students' written assignments in L2 classrooms, the teachers first completed a questionnaire. The questionnaire was divided into two parts and aimed at eliciting information about teachers' attitudes and practices. For the first 15 statements, teachers were asked to indicate the extent to which they agreed with each statement using a 5-point Likert-type scale (from strongly agree to strongly disagree). For the last 14 statements, participants were asked to choose from four options (always, usually, sometimes, and never) that described their usual practices in responding to student writing.

In addition to the questionnaire, semi-structured interviews were utilized to collect data for this study and obtain more in-depth information about teachers' perspectives and practices on the subject of providing feedback. Interviews were conducted with eight teachers (four males and four females). These eight were selected based on their response to the final question on the instrument requesting volunteers. The interviews concentrated on various domains such as the teachers' main focus when responding to student writing, their views about effective methods when responding to writing, and their responsibility when providing feedback.

The data collected from the questionnaires were analyzed descriptively. Data from the open-ended questions and interviews were analyzed qualitatively to gain more insights into teachers' responses to the questionnaire, by using deductive and inductive logic (Best & Kahn, 1998). For the purpose of this chapter, only those statements that are directly related to the topic under discussion are reported here. The presentation of the findings is divided into two sections: English teachers' attitudes about providing feedback on students' written assignments in the L2 classroom, and teachers' practices when responding to their students' writing in UAE government secondary schools.

Results and Discussion

Teachers' Attitudes about Providing Feedback

Confirming our observations as teachers and teacher educators, findings of this study showed that the majority of the participating teachers expressed a negative attitude towards assessing writing. More than half of the teachers (57%) strongly agreed/agreed that responding to student writing is boring, 73% of them thought it is stressful and tiresome, and almost half of them strongly agreed/agreed that it is time-consuming (see Table 2).

Table 2: Teachers' General Attitude *(n=51)*

Statements	Strongly Agree & Agree	Undecided	Strongly Disagree & Disagree
Responding to students' writing is boring.	29 (57%)	5 (10%)	17 (33%)
Responding to students' writing is stressful and tiresome.	37 (73%)	5 (10%)	9 (17%)
Responding to students' writing is time consuming.	25 (49%)	7 (14%)	19 (37%)

These findings are consistent with others in the field who indicate that assessing writing can be difficult, time-consuming, and tiring, all of which pose a challenge to L2 teachers (Brown, 2004; Ferris, 2007). UAE teachers' negative attitudes towards writing assessment is not surprising, since as the interviews showed L2 teachers in the UAE government schools are under-paid, have heavy teaching loads, do not have the proper training in assessing writing, and work under a lot of pressure to meet the deadlines of covering their mandated curricula. These challenges for teachers in the UAE are well-documented in newspaper articles and the literature (see Bardsley,

February 11 & 20, 2010; Coughlin, Mayers, & Wooldridge, 2009; Lewis, 2010).

Several statements on the survey were meant to examine teachers' attitudes regarding their actual practices when commenting on students' writing. Interestingly, 63% (32 out 51 teachers) strongly disagreed/disagreed that it is the teacher's responsibility to underline and correct all errors in written assignments (see Table 3).

Table 3: Teachers' Attitudes About the Use of Responding Methods to Students' Writing *(n=51)*

Statements	Strongly Agree & Agree	Undecided	Strongly Disagree & Disagree
It is the teachers' responsibility to underline and correct all the errors in written assignments.	13 (25%)	6 (12%)	32 (63%)
Teachers should not only correct errors but also write comments when responding to students' writing.	35 (69%)	3 (6%)	13 (25%)
It is acceptable to refer to errors only, without providing feedback on students' writing.	14 (27%)	7 (14%)	30 (59%)

Furthermore, 59% of the participants in this study strongly disagreed/disagreed that teachers should point out errors without providing corrective feedback. For them, as elucidated from the interviews, teachers should identify student errors and correct them at the same time. Reviewing these findings reveals the wide ranging differences of opinions among teachers concerning how to deal with student errors. It is important to remember, that all participating teachers in this study worked in the same educational zone and they all taught similar grades; therefore, the disparity in their responses is quite revealing. Although teachers were not expected to have the exact same attitudes towards any topic, the differences of opinion in this case point to a lack of training with regards to assessment and a lack of knowledge about their options. Despite the many years of teaching experience found in this group of teachers, there appear to be some major gaps in their knowledge of writing assessment. For example, in one of the statements, seven teachers were undecided on what to do: refer to the errors only or refer to the errors *and* provide corrective feedback/comments. This is a problem that needs to be addressed through training sessions, reflections, or other types of professional development activities.

The study also revealed that the majority of respondents (74%) strongly agreed/agreed that it is essential that teachers receive training on how to assess and respond to student writing (see Figure 1).

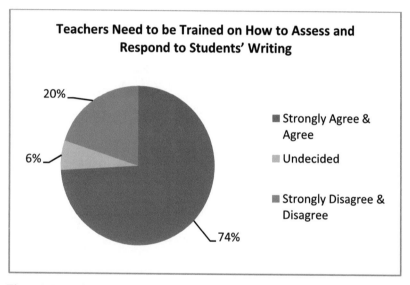

Figure 1: Need for Training

Although 86% of the teachers confirmed that they had received some formal training on writing assessment, most of them referred to the CEPA (Common Educational Proficiency Assessment) training sessions that were arranged by the UAE Ministry of Education. Others mentioned training sessions that focused on process writing, teaching writing in general, and raising teachers' performance in assessing the four language skills. However, the current study showed that teachers' attitudes varied in regards to the usefulness of these training sessions. While some considered them useful, the majority of them viewed them as unhelpful.

English Teachers' Practices when Responding to their Students' Writing

Findings of this study provide insights on which aspects of students' writing receive the most attention from teachers when providing feedback. Findings further provide information on the type of teachers' feedback – direct vs. indirect, as shown in Table 4.

Table 4: Teachers' Practices When Responding to Students' Writing *(n=51)*

Statements	Always	Usually	Sometimes	Never
I respond to students' writing by underlining all their writing errors.	18 (35%)	20 (39%)	10 (20%)	3 (6%)
I underline and correct all grammatical errors.	10 (20%)	17 (33%)	19 (37%)	5 (10%)
I underline and correct all lexical errors.	5 (10%)	19 (37%)	19 (37%)	8 (16%)
I refer to the writing errors without correcting them (indirect feedback).	5 (10%)	12 (24%)	21 (41%)	13 (25%)
I meet with students individually to discuss their errors.	3 (6%)	11 (21%)	35 (69%)	2 (4%)

The majority of respondents (74%) always and/or usually point out (e.g., underline) all student mistakes in writing. More than half of the teachers (53%) focus on grammatical errors in student writing, 47% tend to focus more on lexical errors, and the majority of the teachers (66%) favor providing students with direct feedback. Underlining or pointing out all errors/mistakes to students is something that is expected in UAE schools. The English exam focuses on accuracy of grammar and vocabulary. Due to these factors, students themselves want their grammar to be perfect and want their teachers to pay attention to their grammatical errors in writing. From the interviews we conducted it was quite apparent that the nature of the exams, in addition to the students' expectations, is the rationale for what teachers direct their efforts to when grading writing. Furthermore, discussions with the teachers showed that most of them learned English by focusing on grammar. This is an important factor as it indicates that most of the teachers teach the way they were taught. Although some of them realize they need to look at other factors when assessing writing, they still find themselves directing their efforts towards grammatical accuracy.

The results also indicated that most of the teachers preferred providing students with comprehensive direct error correction feedback. According to Ferris (2002) direct feedback is suitable for beginner students with untreatable errors such as grammatical and lexical ones, and when teachers want to illustrate error patterns which require students' self correction. However, Lee (2003), on the other hand, warns against providing direct feedback as she believes that teachers may change the gist of what their students have written by misinterpreting their meaning. Furthermore, over-marking student errors can be a tiring process for teachers (Lee, 2003).

Finally, it was important to address the various factors that affect teachers' current practices when responding to student writing. Participants were given a list of factors to choose from and also to add their own, if any (see Figure 2). The major factor for choosing how to assess a piece of writing was based on the students' grade level (82%). This meant that the teachers were not allowing for any differences in proficiency level within the group. Teachers essentially assessed all Grade 10 students in the same manner, and assumed that at that level certain factors needed to be assessed, mostly grammar. However, this virtually eliminates any hope for higher achievers to be noticed. Students with good grammar skills should be assessed in terms of the content of their papers or at least with a more holistic vision (see Cooper, 1977; Fathman & Whalley, 1990; Ferris & Roberts; 2001; Perkins, 1983; Shine, 2007; Truscott, 1996). However, as these teachers only viewed students as a homogenous group, there was little hope for any good writers to be recognized.

This can be discouraging for both the students and the teachers. Recognizing a 'good' paper in the midst of many with grammatical errors can often make the whole job of teaching writing a more positive and enriching experience.

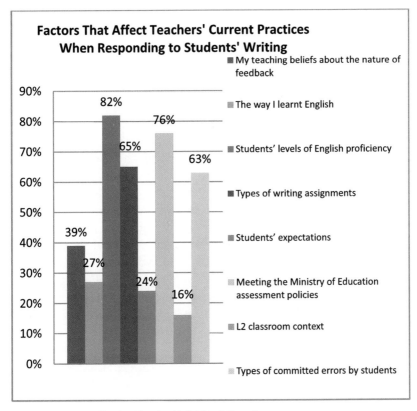

Figure 2: Factors affecting Teachers' feedback Practices

The second most predominant factor that affected teaching practices was related to meeting the assessment policies of the UAE Ministry of Education. 76% of the teachers indicated that these policies affect their practices as they are required to follow them. The role of the Ministry is ever-present in everything teachers do and are able to do in the UAE. The rules and regulations of the Ministry influence how teachers carry out their duties including how they evaluate their students' performance. Therefore it is not surprising that so many of those who participated in the study indicated that their teaching practices were related to the processes prescribed by the Ministry.

Data obtained from the interviews revealed that a great many Ministry edicts were burdensome to teachers and a cause of consternation. For example, an English teacher in a UAE government secondary school teaches three classes with an average number of 20 to 30 students in each class and a total of eighteen contact hours per week. The teaching loads imposed upon teachers are heavy and for those attempting to teach and mark large numbers of writing tasks the process becomes even more tiresome. Furthermore, the Ministry-set curriculum is quite extensive and getting through it each year is often stressful for teachers (see Lewis, 2010; Thomas, 2010). Additionally, teachers have no input or say in the materials that are used in each course, and therefore must utilize and deal with those assigned to them as best they can. Finally, from the interviews it was apparent that in many ways the teachers were quite overwhelmed by the amount of work they were required to do and the lack of input they had in these matters. Therefore, when it comes down to their ability or perhaps even desire to give extensive feedback, they tend to look at surface types of corrections due to their heavy workload, lack of time, and lack of training.

Conclusion

The main objective of this study was to examine L2 teachers' attitudes about providing feedback on student writing. Findings showed that teachers in this study had more negative than positive attitudes toward responding to student writing. They viewed it as a demanding and time-consuming practice. The data also revealed that teachers need to be trained on how to assess and respond to students' writing. While these teachers received training from the UAE Ministry of Education, the majority of them viewed these training sessions as unhelpful. Furthermore, teachers who participated in this study admitted that they not only paid equal attention to all writing errors, but they also underlined and corrected all of them, in particular the grammatical and lexical errors. Finally, the study also showed that students' grade level, the Ministry of Education's assessment policies, the types of writing assignments, and the types of students' errors were among the most predominantly reported factors that affected these English teachers' practices when responding to their students' writing.

The results of this study highlight the need for further teacher training with regard to assessing writing. Since responding to students' writing is thought of as an essential part of learning how to write successfully in L2 contexts, it is important for English teachers in the UAE secondary schools to become conscious of the significance of feedback and its impact on student writing. This can be achieved when English teachers have opportunities to explore different means of offering feedback. For example, teachers can provide direct feedback to less proficient students as well as for errors that students cannot deal with on their own. Moreover, they should encourage self and peer editing practices and giving oral feedback through conferencing with students on an individual or group basis in order to support their written feedback. When appropriately applied, peer feedback can produce a rich intercultural interaction, and grant students a sense of group solidarity. When used effectively peer reviews go beyond being a step in the writing process and become an important stage in helping L2 writers develop (Liu & Hansen, 2005). The importance and usefulness of peer review cannot be overlooked; from a socio-cognitive perspective it can be seen as a 'formative developmental process that gives writers opportunities to discuss their texts and discover others' interpretations of them' (Hyland & Hyland, 2006a, p. 6).

In addition, the UAE Ministry of Education needs to provide teachers with opportunities for professional development and training programs in order to raise teachers' awareness about various techniques and error correction strategies in L2 classrooms. These sessions must be tailored to fit teachers' needs, both novice and experienced teachers. The Ministry will have to evaluate the effectiveness of these training sessions and ensure their appropriateness.

Finally, it is apparent from the current study, that much time and effort is being aimed at correcting mechanical errors. However, at some point, it would be beneficial to both teachers and students to look holistically at their writing, to view the content and build upon that as opposed to consistently seeking out errors. L2 students in the UAE are bilingual writers, which makes them special. They are the 'global souls' who are raised in a multicultural environment, the UAE, and feel comfortable crossing linguistic and geographic borders (Li, 2007, p. 260). What they write encompasses a richness often not found among native speakers, and it is this uniqueness that needs to be looked at by their teachers. If teachers help students celebrate their writing, perhaps in finding their voices therein they may begin to enjoy peer-review interactions, they may self-correct more readily, and find ways to ensure that what they have to say is written with fewer errors.

References

Bardsley, D. (2010, February 20). Teaching candidates ready – and waiting. *The National, 2*(310), 4.

Bardsley, D. (2010, February 11). Initiatives fail to silence criticism: Education standards have not kept pace with growth. *The National, 2*(301), 4.

Best, J.W., & Kahn, J.V. (1998). *Research in education* (8th edition). Boston, MA: Allyn and Bacon.

Bitchener, J. (2008). Evidence in support of written corrective feedback. *Journal of Second Language Writing, 17*(2), 102–118.

Brown, H.D. (2004). *Language assessment: Principles and classroom practices.* NY: Pearson Education, Inc.

Coffin, C., Curry, M.J., Goodman, S., Hewings, A., Lillis, T.M., & Swann, J. (2003). *Teaching academic writing: A toolkit for higher education.* NY: Routledge.

Coombe, C., Jendli, A., & Davidson, P. (2008). *Teaching writing skills in English: Theory, research and pedagogy.* Dubai: TESOL Arabia Publications.

Cooper, C.R. (1977). Holistic evaluation of writing. In C.R. Cooper & L. Odell (Eds.), *Evaluating writing: Describing, measuring, judging* (pp. 3-31). Urbana, Illinois: National Council of Teachers of English.

Coughlin, C., Mayers, G., & Wooldridge, D.G. (2009). History of public kindergarten in the United Arab Emirates: Past, present, future. *Delta Kappa Gamma Bulletin, 76*(1), 14-19.

Fathman, A.K., & Whalley, E. (1990). Teacher response to student writing: Focus on form versus content. In B. Kroll (Ed.), *Second language writing: Research insights for the classroom* (pp. 178-189). Cambridge: Cambridge University Press.

Ferris, D. (2007). Preparing teachers to respond to students' writing. *Journal of Second Language Writing, 16*(3), 165-193.

Ferris, D. (2003). Responding to writing. In B. Kroll (Ed.), *Exploring the dynamics of second language writing* (pp. 119-140). Cambridge: Cambridge University Press.

Ferris, D. (2002). *Treatment of error in second language student writing.* Ann Arbor: The University of Michigan Press.

Ferris, D.R., & Roberts, B. (2001). Error feedback in L2 writing classes: How explicit does it have to be? *Journal of Second Language Writing, 10,* 161-184.

Guefrachi, H., & Troudi, S. (2000). Enhancing English language teaching in the United Arab Emirates. In K. Johnson (Ed.),

Teacher education: Case studies in TESOL practice series (pp. 189-204). Alexandria, VA: TESOL Inc.

Hedgcock, J., & Lefkowitz, N. (1996). Some input on input: Two analyses of student response to expert feedback in L2 writing. *The Modern Language Journal, 80*(3), 287-308.

Hyland, K. (2003). *Second language writing*. Cambridge: Cambridge University Press.

Hyland, K., & Hyland, F. (2006a). *Feedback in second language writing: Contexts and issues*. Cambridge: Cambridge University Press.

Hyland, K., & Hyland, F. (2006b). Feedback on second language students' writing. *Language Teaching, 39*, 83–101.

Lee, I. (2008a). Student reactions to teacher feedback in two Hong Kong secondary classrooms. *Journal of Second Language Writing, 17*(3), 144-164.

Lee, I. (2008b). Understanding teachers' written feedback practices in Hong Kong secondary classrooms. *Journal of Second Language Writing, 17*(2), 69–85.

Lee, I. (2007). Feedback in Hong Kong secondary writing classrooms: Assessment for learning or assessment of learning? *Assessing Writing, 12*(3), 180-198.

Lee, I. (2004). Error correction in L2 secondary writing classrooms: The case of Hong Kong. *Journal of Second Language Writing, 13*(4), 69–85.

Lee, I. (2003). L2 writing teachers' perspectives, practices and problems regarding error feedback. *Assessing Writing, 8*(3), 216-237.

Leki, I. (2003). A challenge to second language writing professionals: Is writing overrated? In B. Kroll (Ed.), *Exploring the dynamics of second language writing*. Cambridge: Cambridge University Press.

Leki, I. (1990). Coaching from the margins: Issues in written responses. In B. Kroll (Ed.), *Second language writing: Research insights for the classroom*. Cambridge: Cambridge University Press.

Lewis, K. (2010, February 24). Give schools money to improve facilities. *The National, 2*(314), 4.

Lewis, K. (2010, February 11). Public school curriculum needs reform, advisers say. *The National, 2*(301), 1 & 4.

Li, X. (2007). Souls in exile: Identities of bilingual writers. *Journal of Language, Identity, and Education, 6,* 259-275.

Liu, J., & Hansen, J.G. (2005). Guiding principles for effective peer response. *ELT Journal, 59*(1), 31-38.

Montgomery, J.L., & Baker, W. (2007). Teacher-written feedback: Student perceptions, teacher self-assessment, and actual teacher performance. *Journal of Second Language Writing, 16*(2), 82-99.

Perkins, K. (1983). On the use of composition scoring techniques, objective measures, and objective tests to evaluate ESL writing ability. *TESOL Quarterly, 17,* 651-671.

Shine, A. (2007). More writing, less grading. In A. Jendli, S. Troudi, & C. Coombe (Eds.), *The power of language: Perspectives from Arabia* (pp. 164-174). Dubai: TESOL Arabia.

Sugita, Y. (2006). The impact of teachers' comment types on students' revision. *ELT Journal, 60*(1), 34-42.

Thomas, J.Y. (2010). Internationalization and education reform in the UAE. *Paper presented at The Gulf Comparative Education Society Symposium, Hilton Hotel, Ras Al Khaimah, UAE.* Retrieved July 10, 2010, from: http:// gces2010.webs.com/ presentations.htm

Troudi, S. (2007). The effects of English as a medium of instruction. In A. Jendli, S. Troudi, & C. Coombe (Eds.), *The power of language: Perspectives from Arabia* (pp. 3-19). Dubai: TESOL Arabia.

Truscott, J. (1996). The case against grammar correction in L2 writing. *Language Learning, 46*(2), 327-369.

Weigle, S.C. (2007). Teaching writing teachers about assessment. *Journal of Second Language Writing, 16*(3), 194–20.

Weigle, S.C. (2002). *Assessing writing.* Cambridge: Cambridge University Press.

White, R.V. (1995). *New ways in teaching writing.* Bloomington, IL: Paragraph Printing.

JONATHAN AUBREY & CHRISTINE COOMBE

Chapter 9
An Investigation of Occupational Stressors and Coping Strategies Among EFL Teachers in the United Arab Emirates

Abstract

Research has shown that professionals who do 'people work' or care giving are prime candidates for occupational stress. Teachers, especially those working in foreign contexts, are particularly susceptible to stress in the workplace. This mixed method study investigates the types of stressors that tertiary-level ELT educators encounter in their day-to-day working environment and deals with how these educators cope with stressors. The quantitative findings from 75 ELT professionals working at tertiary-level institutions in the United Arab Emirates (UAE) reveal that there are generally two categories of stressors in the workplace, namely stressors dealing with the institutional context and those dealing with how teachers are evaluated. Qualitative findings from 10 participants show that five themes of coping strategies were exhibited in those educators who reported low stress levels. These themes ranged from establishing a support system to the ways in which one should volunteer for additional responsibilities.

Introduction

The topic of stress in the workplace has attracted considerable attention in recent decades as evidenced by more than 100,000 books, journals and articles on the subject (Gmelch, 1988). Adding to the voluminous literature, has been a wealth of research related to stress in educational contexts, much of which has pointed to teaching as being one of the most stressful professions (Kyriacou & Sutcliffe, 1987a, 1987b; McShane & Von Glinow, 2005). A prominent concern expressed within the literature on teacher stress, is the mounting evidence that prolonged exposure to it can lead to ill-health and, in return, impact the overall quality of classroom instruction. Although teacher stress research has been ongoing for quite some time, few studies have investigated the occupational stress experience of university-level teachers of English as a foreign language (EFL) overseas. Fewer still, are teacher stress studies conducted in Arab countries, where a considerable number of expatriate teachers live and work.

Background

Although the phenomenon of teacher stress has been under consideration over the past 35 years or so, its prevalence is on the rise and expanding world-wide (Forlin, 2001; Gmelch, 1993). Kyriacou (2001) (cited in Wragg, 2004) aptly points out that:

> there are differences in the main sources of teacher stress between countries based on precise characteristics of national educational systems, the precise circumstances of teachers and schools in those countries and the prevailing attitudes and values regarding teachers and schools held in society as a whole. (p. 266)

This explains, in part, the reason why teacher stress has received considerable attention in the international literature. There have been numerous studies conducted in several countries, including Australia (Pithers & Fogarty, 1995; Tuettemann & Punch, 1990), the United Kingdom (Brimblecombe, 1995; Chaplain, 1995; Troman, 2000; Wilson & Hall, 2002), the United States (Millicent & Sewell, 1999; Schonfeld, 1990), New Zealand (Manthei & Soloman, 1988), Hong Kong (Hui & Chan, 1996), Canada (Bryne, 1996; Dussalt, Deaudelin, Royer, & Loiselle 1999), Greece (Okebukola, 1992), Egypt (Mohammed, 2000), Turkey (Sari, 2004) and Qatar (Al-Mohanndi & Capel, 2007). Kyriacou (2000) has pointed out that the general level of stress reported by teachers appears to be quite similar, and studies suggest that approximately 25 to 30 percent of teachers view their profession as very to extremely stressful (Chaplain, 1995; Manthei, Gilmore, Tuck, & Adair, 1996).

It should be noted that most previously reviewed studies date back to the 80s and 90s with very few studies conducted in the last decade. These studies do not take into consideration some of the important stressors that are now in existence in the Gulf educational context. In the past five years alone, tertiary level educators have had to cope with increased class size (from 15-18 students in 1999 to 40 in 2008), increased work load (i.e. from 15 contact hours in 1999 to 20 in the present day), cuts in vacation time and the pressures resulting from increased accountability for intuitional accreditation purposes. Most recently, despite the fact that most tertiary level teachers have received salary increases, these increases have not kept pace with rapidly rising prices and inflation (L. Barlow, personal communication, March 10, 2009).

In the literature, the overwhelming majority of teacher stress studies have been concerned with primary and secondary schools and the paucity of research involving EFL Teachers is alarming; to the best of our knowledge, there have not been any teacher stress studies conducted in the United Arab Emirates. Thus, the aim of this study was to investigate teacher stress among university-level EFL teachers in the UAE. The researchers sought to explore the general level of teacher stress, the specific sources of teacher stress and coping strategies used by teachers. The study focuses on the following main research questions:

1. What sources of stress do university-level EFL teachers have in the workplace?
2. How do university-level EFL teachers in the UAE rate various occupational stressors?
3. What coping strategies do teachers who exhibit low levels of stress use?

Higher Education in the UAE

The history of higher education in the UAE is a relatively short one as far as histories of education are concerned. The country was established in 1971 and six years later UAE University opened its doors in Al Ain as the nation's first institution of higher education. In the decades that followed, the government established a series of colleges throughout the country that cater exclusively to students of local origin and also augmented its university system with the creation of Zayed University, adding university campuses in Dubai and Abu Dhabi. More recently, private foreign-affiliated universities have entered the educational arena and their rapid expansion into the market has been ongoing from the late 1990s to present day. The American University of Sharjah, the American University of Dubai, the British University in Dubai, the Canadian University of Dubai, and the University of Wollongong all serve as examples that can attest to the dynamic and ongoing state of educational expansion in the region (see Barlow, 2009; Osmond, 2008).

This study was conducted within an academic bridge program at a large university in the UAE. As is customary in the Middle East, the university had separate campuses for male and female students and the program's goal was to help freshman become proficient in mathematics, English and computer skills prior to delving into their major areas of study at the university, many of which use English as the medium of instruction. The program consisted of four proficiency levels: low false beginner, false beginner, low intermediate and intermediate.

The Study

The present study used a mixed methodology approach. An online survey was used to explore the general level and sources of teacher stress. The survey comprised a bio-data section, and occupational stressor sections that pertained to student issues, teacher assessment and classroom teaching, and was designed in accordance with the procedures suggested by Brown (2001) and Dornyei (2003). Participants were asked to rate the survey items using a six-point Likert scale.

A follow-up interview schedule consisted of seven open-ended and semi-structured questions; it aimed to gather qualitative data related to stress coping strategies and to provide further insights of participants' personal experiences with teacher stress. A total of 110 full-time expatriate teachers on two campuses were invited to participate in the study (see Table 1 for detailed demographic information). The participants were initially contacted via email and sent a letter that explained the purpose of the study, along with a detailed set of instructions for completion and a confidentiality agreement. The invitation letter also contained a link to the online survey, which was made available for a period of ten days. The surveys were completed anonymously and were subsequently checked by the researcher for complete responses. Of the 110 surveys that were made available, 75 were completed in full, giving a response rate of 68.1%. Ten teachers were contacted for follow-up interviews and two declined, stating busy schedules as their main reasons. The eventual sample consisted of eight teachers; five women and three men. The participants for the interviews were selected based upon their online survey responses which indicated that only 20% or less of stress in their lives came from work; they were identified by completing an optional contact information section on the online survey. The teachers were interviewed in person by the researchers. Each interview lasted 30-45 minutes in length.

The quantative data collected in this study were made available in real-time by the online software used to create the survey. Upon completion, the data were analyzed using the Statistical Package for the Social Sciences software (SPSS).

The individual interviews were directed by the researchers and digitally recorded. The responses were then transcribed verbatim and read many times as a way of entering into the teachers' perceptions of stress. Elbow (1986) refers to this as a process of self-insertion and asserts that it is a useful way of coming to know the participants' experiences. Over time, a sense of themes emerged from the data and these were then used to label and categorize the data. The final step was to compare these themes across all eight participants, noting the similarities and differences as to how the various aspects of teacher stress were perceived.

Results

Demographic Information

A total of 75 online surveys were completed in full. 56% of the respondents were males and 44% were females. All respondents were over the age of 25. 21.3% were between the ages of 26-35; 20% were between 36-40; 50.7% were between 41-55; and 8%: were over the age of 55. A breakdown of the sample can be found in Table 1.

Table 1: Online survey participants *(n=75)*

Variable	Demographic Categories	N	%
Religion	Non-Muslim	66	88
	Muslim	9	12
Mother	English	68	90.7
Tongue	Arabic	3	4
	Berber	2	2.7
	Hindi	1	1.3
	Other	1	1.3
Nationality	American	38	50.7
	British	13	17.3
	Canadian	11	14.7
	Australian	6	8
	Algerian	2	2.7
	Other	3	4
	Egyptian	1	1.3
	New Zealander	1	1.3
Qualifications	Masters degree	72	96
(completed or	RSA/Trinity Diploma	16	21.3
currently	USA state teacher	12	16
studying)	certification	9	12
	Doctorate	6	8
Teaching	10-14 years	25	33.3
Experience	15-20	19	25.3
	Over 20	17	22.7
	5-9	13	17.3
	0-4	1	1.3

Sources of Stress

Analysis identified eight important sources of stress that received an average score of 3 and above on the 6-point Likert scale (1=no stress, 2=slight stress, 3=slight to moderate stress, 4=moderate stress, 5=moderate to excessive stress, 6=excessive stress).

Jonathan Aubrey & Christine Coombe

Table 2: The most important sources of stress *(n=75)*

Rank	Sources of Stress	1*	2*	3*	4*	5*	6*	N/A	Mean
1	Poorly maintained teaching equipment	4% (3)	12% (9)	17% (3)	20% (15)	19% (14)	**27%** **(20)**	1% (1)	**4.19**
2	Teaching disinterested students	4% (3)	13% (10)	13% (10)	**29%** **(22)**	**29%** **(22)**	11% (8)	0% (0)	**3.99**
3	Lack of transparency of teacher evaluation criteria	12% (9)	15% (11)	8% (6)	17% (3)	11% (8)	**27%** **(20)**	11% (8)	**3.96**
4	Increased workload	3% (2)	15% (11)	19% (14)	**24%** **(18)**	23% (17)	15% (11)	3% (2)	**3.92**
5	Being observed	4% (3)	20% (15)	12% (9)	20% (15)	**24%** **(18)**	16% (12)	4% (3)	**3.90**
6	Going through a contract renewal	8% (6)	16% (12)	9% (7)	**24%** **(18)**	16% (12)	15% (11)	12% (9)	**3.77**
7	Too many course objectives	11% (8)	17% (3)	17% (3)	**21%** **(16)**	11% (8)	20% (15)	3% (2)	**3.66**
8	Teaching repeaters	15% (11)	19% (14)	**20%** **(15)**	**20%** **(15)**	8% (6)	9% (7)	9% (7)	**3.18**

*Scale: 1=no stress, 2=slight stress, 3=slight to moderate stress, 4=moderate stress, 5=moderate to excessive stress, 6=excessive stress

From the table, one can see that two stressors were found to cause the highest level of stress with participants: poorly maintained teaching equipment and lack of transparency of teacher evaluation criteria. From the data above, one can interpret that the major stressors fall within two major categories. The first major category of stressor relates to factors within the intuitional context. The number one stressor, poorly maintained teaching equipment, falls into this category. The students themselves are represented in two areas. Faculty reported teaching disinterested students to be the number two stressor in the study and teaching multiple repeating students ranked as number eight amongst participants. Another stressor falling into this category is the feeling of overload, both in terms of curricular objectives and work overload in general. The second category of stressors relates to the way teachers are evaluated at their respective institutions. Particularly worrisome for participants was a perceived lack of transparency with evaluation criteria. Being observed and going through the contract renewal process were also reported as being important stressors amongst study participants.

Interview Data

Equipment and Environment

In the follow-up survey interviews, participants equated 'poorly maintained' teaching equipment with an overall loss of control and a downgrading of classroom teaching practices. Six out of eight teachers felt that quality of equipment and their surroundings influenced their ability to have control over their teaching environment. Although half of the teachers noted that this issue did not cause a great deal of stress to them personally, most participants were quick to tell of their various classroom mishaps and frustrations. One teacher recalled a time when the video equipment failed:

> I decided to use video, but the plug didn't work.... I was just wringing with sweat, running all over the place and I ended up dismissing the class early....So that is when I get stressed...when something doesn't work and I'm depending on it... They just don't seem to care ... (Teacher 3, Lines 151-156)

In another example, a different teacher explained his difficulties with writing classes:

> It's so frustrating when I can't teach the way I want to. How can I teach writing when I don't even have a proper OHP? In the end I have to make copies of everything for every student and pray that the copy person can get it all done. The writing classes are the most stressful of all... (Teacher 7, Lines 130-132)

The general undertone amongst the teachers was that poorly maintained equipment not only caused them stress, but it also lead to a feeling of disrespect, believing that a lack of repair or working equipment meant that they were not cared about as employees. Some teachers seemed more cynical than others and some attributed the equipment issue to the overall low status often placed upon English teachers in comparison to academic staff in other departments.

Furthermore, the majority of the teachers reported that the students were the ones who ultimately suffered from the poorly maintained classroom equipment. One teacher explained her opinion this way:

> I think it's just basically a mistake when a teaching institution doesn't see the importance of having equipment working ... it really slows you down, it makes you less efficient and it impacts on classroom choices. (Teacher 1, Lines 101-104)

Another teacher expressed similar feelings:

> I've gone back to chalk and talk methods here because things are consistently *not* reliable...how can we do listening in the labs if they don't even have working headsets? That's one reason why I don't get stressed, I've taken the attitude that if they don't care about equipment then I don't care... I just throw it all out the window and forget about it, which isn't good teaching practice because I'm getting 'de-skilled'... (Teacher 4, Lines 181-188)

Here the participants expressed the view that the lack of working equipment made available to them had a direct impact on the methods that they used in the classroom, which resulted in limiting the types of practice for their students. Overall, the teachers stated that having to compensate for the lack of working equipment decreased their productivity in the classroom as well as the way they taught the class. This translated into valuable classroom time being wasted and a feeling of not being able to keep up-to-date with their profession.

Coping Strategies for Dealing with Stress

Teachers were asked to share the various techniques and coping strategies that they used to reduce the amount of stress they have in the workplace. They responded with a variety of strategies that were psychological, physical and proactive. All of the teachers provided specific examples of the strategies that they used intentionally, but many admitted, too, that much of what they do has become so second nature to them that there were probably other strategies that they were unaware of. The responses that they shared were categorized into common themes.

Seek Support from Friends and Family

One strategy used by all of the participants to cope with work stress was the seeking of support from others. One teacher explained it this way:

> One way that I deal with stress is to focus on my leave when I will be home with family. This is one area where those with families have it better than singles. Their families are with them and help them deal with problems. (Teacher 2, Lines 122-124)

Another teacher expressed similar sentiments:

> I think one of the things that I'm lucky... like I'm a couple. And I think sometimes couples fair better than singles because they've got somebody, 'cause if they work with the same person, in the same place or in the same profession, they've got somebody who understands, often you're under the same pressure at the same time so we actively go for a swim or go to the movies, we go to Dubai and do some retail therapy or you deal with it in other ways. (Teacher 6, Lines 209-217)

Overall, teachers who exhibited low levels of stress felt that empathizing with other teachers was an important factor in reducing their stress levels. Many pointed out that it was important for the 'listener' to have first-hand knowledge of the actual situation that was being discussed, and for this reason they preferred talking things over with other teachers. Single teachers tended to seek support from other friends, and married couples from their spouse. Interestingly, half of the teachers interviewed were also married to teachers who worked at the same university.

Vent Quickly and Let it Go

This theme is related to the previous one and the remark of 'just let it go' or 'don't dwell on it' was a suggestion made by all of the participants. One teacher noted:

> I'm one of these people who gets stressed very quickly and it's quite intense and then five minutes later it's all gone. I have my freaky moment ...and then afterwards move on....I don't hold on to stuff. If I'm stressed on Monday, I don't go on Tuesday morning still boiling over what happened before – it's forgotten. Invariably, Tuesday will bring something new, you know. But that's quite as far as I deal with it. (Teacher 1, Lines 375-382)

Another teacher mentioned that letting go is not always as easy as it sounds, and sometimes it leads to the avoidance of others:

> It is really kind of an avoidance strategy. I try to keep myself out of the... the 'bitch club' [laugh], not to, you know, and ah... I think that really helps me a lot. I really remove myself from the minutiae of people's problems and, you know, I can be a sympathetic listener, but once it turns into a 'bitch session', I just sort of leave. (Teacher 8, Lines 94-99)

A third teacher explained how not dwelling on the past was consciously part of his philosophy:

> I read a book a number of years ago by the Dalai Lama, who is really spot on. He said that if you have a problem that has a solution, you don't need to spend time worrying about it, you just act to solve it. And if you have a problem that has no solution, then equally there is no point spending time worrying about it as there is nothing than can be done about it. (Teacher 3, Lines 304-307)

When teachers sought the support of others, they thought that venting their frustrations was important, but that it should be done quickly and it was equally important to move on to a different point of focus. In general, teachers stated that they were conscious of this strategy being employed and tended to shift their concerns to family matters outside of the workplace.

Stay Organized

A third strategy used by teachers who exhibited low levels of stress was staying organized. One teacher stated that 'Over the years I've learned how to organize myself and multitask. Because I have many systems in place for various types of work duties, I save time and this reduces the stress I feel.' (Teacher 1, Lines 317-319). To quote another teacher:

> I'm a hoarder so, that's one of the ways in which I cope. I file and re-use. And ah, I also use the FTP and other online resources and I save them and keep them.... I think that makes life a lot easier. Just put in the legwork and produce something. Then you can put it on your portable drive or whatever and access it the next semester without having to start from scratch again. (Teacher 2, Lines 282-286)

Two teachers also mentioned that staying well organized was a particularly helpful strategy for dealing with students who they felt lacked motivation. One of them recalled how they prepared for teaching their IELTS classes:

> I know that students on Sundays are pretty tired ...So every Sunday I coped by offering them a timed test activity that we would do and then correct together... so what I'm saying is that a lot of the Sunday lessons were well pre-prepared and it was just a case of administering them and dealing with them. The more interactive eliciting type lessons came Mondays, Tuesdays, Wednesdays. Thursdays were usually games and a whatever day...That was a coping thing for me on a Sunday. No matter what sort of weekend I had it was certainly a way to cope with students who probably didn't want to be there. (Teacher 5, Lines 363-370)

Teachers who employed this strategy felt that staying organized was an important way of coping with their duties and they emphasized the recycling of previously prepared materials. Having these prepared in advance provided the educators with a more relaxed timeframe which they could devote to other aspects of their teaching; several teachers considered creating a bank of lessons and sharing materials with others to be essential.

Choose What you Want, Be Careful about Volunteering

Choosing what teachers wanted or didn't want to do also played a role in how they coped with stress. As one teacher put it, 'I choose carefully which classes I'm going to ask for and know what I'm getting into before it happens...' and another added 'the university is really great with scheduling... that is one area where they do actually seem to help' (Teacher 4, Lines 350-352). Other teachers explained that they were careful about volunteering for any additional work-related duties and did so only because it involved an area of high personal interest:

> Rather than volunteer for extra stuff at work, I focus my attention on TESOL Arabia, the local English language teaching affiliate. With TESOL Arabia I can work on what I'm interested in and with people I like. In fact, my work with TA means I work more, but because it is so rewarding, it's a stress reliever, believe it or not. (Teacher 1, Lines 200-203)

Another teacher shunned volunteering altogether, especially for administrative tasks, as he feared that it would open the door for further targeting at a later point in time:

> Volunteer? Oh yeah, I never do that! [laughing]... I have in the past only because it suited me and I had oodles of time and realized that what I was volunteering for would take me ten minutes... but generally, yeah, I don't volunteer for anything and I try to avoid it. (Teacher 7, Lines 338-342)

Overall, six teachers stated that being able to make choices was a way of coping for them. Most felt that they had little control over educational policy or administrative issues and that being able to choose various aspects related to classroom teaching helped to provide a general sense of balance. In particular, teachers mentioned choosing levels, work shift starting times and preferences for working in various departments as helpful in keeping their stress levels down.

Look at the Big Picture

Putting the job in perspective was also noted as a coping strategy throughout the interviews. One teacher's recollection was succinct, stating that 'at really stressful times, I remember why I got into teaching in the first place and just focus on my students' (Teacher 5, Lines 169-170). Another teacher recalled what it was like to work at an inner city public school in the United States:

> I mean it's very easy to hold these platitudes here because I've had real stress. I taught in a school where teachers got taken out in ambulances. We were actively told by the principal of the school 'don't call the police, we don't want you to bring the law in, even though you've been assaulted by a 14 or a 15-year old kid who's bigger than you' ahm, and who's violent and is bringing violence into the classroom... the first year I was at that school I did, I went out and I cried at least once a week. And cried until I could make myself walk back into that school, because it was the middle of the day and I'd have to go back into that school and then do my job, you know, to the best of my ability... so, yes I try to keep a world view of it all and keep things in perspective. (Teacher 8, Lines 513-523)

A third teacher compared it to jobs outside of the ELT industry:

> I mean, let's face it, you know, you're working from 8 till 2? That's a part-time job! You're doing a part-time job for a full-time salary, you know? At 2 o'clock most of my colleagues are thinking 'home time', most of the human race are thinking 'lunchtime', you know?... I used to work as a solicitor before I came into TEFL teaching and that was extremely stressful...I was working like 16 hours a day, six days a week. (Teacher 6, Lines 458-464)

All of the teachers in this cohort had more than ten years of teaching experience and had taught in a variety of situations in different countries; two of the teachers had also experienced previous careers in other fields prior to switching to English language teaching. Looking back at previous positions which they considered to be more difficult and then comparing those to their current teaching position was common among this group. Many teachers also tried to pick out positive aspects about their current job for which they were thankful.

Discussion

The present study sought to explore the sources of stress for university-level EFL teachers in the UAE and how they rated various occupational stressors. There are at least two important observations that can be made based on the findings. First, the topic of stress itself is seen as a serious concern among university-level English teachers, as the quantitative data from the present study resulted from an online self-report questionnaire that received a high response rate of 68%. Second, with the exception of teaching multiple repeaters, the types of stressors identified by the participants are consistent with those identified in the literature on teacher stress. This is important because the present findings may extend to previous findings from other contexts, suggesting that there may be some similarities.

An additional finding was that many teachers perceive multiple repeaters as contributing to stress levels in the classroom. Every day, educators serve a variety of students and designing classes to suit the needs of individuals requires careful balancing of a complex set of issues. Troudi (2007) conducted a study in the UAE within a university English program and found that multiple repeaters had their own specific points of view as to their linguistic wants and needs. From these needs and in some cases, demands, it is clear that catering to the specific needs of multiple repeaters could prove to be a challenging or, in some cases, a stressful event for some instructors. Further research is needed as to how multiple repeaters impact educational systems and teachers in the Middle East.

Participants also identified teacher assessment issues and 'too many course objectives' as important sources of stress and these are perhaps explained best in light of the educational reform currently sweeping the UAE and other Gulf countries, especially reform related to external crediting boards amongst the tertiary intuitions. As was previously mentioned in the literature review, increased globalization has lead to an emerging market of transborder education in the Emirates. While one effect of this movement has been to raise the standards of higher education, it has also resulted in greater scrutiny of both teachers and students alike. For teachers, this has translated into intensified annual performance reviews and working conditions that have been brought about by swift and ongoing movements in quality assurance; students have been re-positioned to meet the challenges associated with high stakes testing.

The latter is of paramount concern, as abrupt shifts of 'new and revised' curricula have become common place in the Emirates, and they are often put into place without providing proper training or support for teachers and management. Policy makers need to proceed with caution when realigning programs, especially those that emphasize international exit exams, as such changes can have a profound impact on the stress levels of all involved. Mathison and Freeman (2006) conducted a study that focused on testing within a high stakes accountability environment and found that emphasizing one measure of academic success could lead to multiple sources of stress in the workplace. They suggest that:

> ...accountability creates a domino effect that has resulted in the disintegration of the physical, social and emotional context meant to support the work of teachers. Excessive, unrealistic and ambiguous demands of the workplace...have resulted in an increase in the amount of ethical, psychological and physical conflicts experienced by teachers...accountability structures result in practices that restructure the nature of teachers' work as well as the nature of their workplace...indeed they are likely to have unhealthy effects and lead to stressed teachers who struggle along, get sick, or leave the profession. (pp. 61-62)

Findings by Jacobs and Chase (1992) also support the present study. They found that teachers rated assessment and assessment-related activities as the least enjoyable aspects of their job because of the stress it entailed.

The third research question of the study addressed the coping strategies used by teachers who exhibited low levels of stress. The results showed that teachers coped in specific ways that were psychological, physical and proactive. Wiley (2000) maintains that teachers who are able to identify and develop a repertoire of coping strategies can become more effective in helping their students. Other researchers assert that individuals who are able to identify their sources of stress are less prone to teacher burnout (Bourne, 1995; Gmelch & Chan, 1994). The findings of the present study have also been echoed and confirmed by other studies in the literature (Dunham, 1994; Griffith, Steptoe, & Cropley, 1999; Lazarus & Folkman, 1984). The results were those of a subgroup of the population and due to the numbers involved in the sample, care should be taken when considering their application to other contexts.

Conclusion

The study described in this chapter explored a number of occupational stressors as well as the coping strategies used by a small cohort of tertiary expat teachers in the UAE. The types of stressors that were considered were those that pertained to student issues, teacher assessment and classroom teaching. The study also revealed that there are many other potential sources of stress that need to be addressed in future research, especially those that relate to the changing institutional contexts of the Arab world.

References

Al-Mohannadi, A., & Capel, S. (2007). Stress in physical education teachers in Qatar. *Social Psychology of Education, 10*, 55-75.

Barlow, L. (2009). *The effect of nonnative speaker accent on EFL students' listening comprehension.* Unpublished doctoral dissertation. University of Exeter, UK.

Bourne, E.J. (1995). *The anxiety and phobia workbook.* Oakland, California: New Harbinger.

Brimblecombe, N. (1995). Teachers' perceptions of school inspections: A stress experience. *Cambridge Journal of Education, 25*, 53-63.

Brown, J.D. (2001). *Using surveys in language programs.* New York: Cambridge University Press.

Byrne, B. (1996). Burnout: Testing for the validity, replication, and invarience of causal structure across elementary, intermediate, and secondary teachers. *American Educational Research Journal, 31*, 645-673.

Chaplain, R. (1995). Stress and job satisfaction: A study of English primary school teachers. *Educational Psychology, 15*(4), 473-489.

Dornyei, Z. (2003). *Questionnaires in second language research: Construction, administration and processing.* London: Lawrence Erlbaum Associates, Publishers.

Dunham, J. (1994). A frame work of teachers' coping strategies for a whole stress management policy. *Educational Management and Administration, 22*(3), 168-174.

Dussalt, M., Deaudelin, C., Royer, N., & Loiselle, J. (1999). Professional isolation and occupational stress in teachers. *Psychological Reports, 84*, 943-946.

Elbow, P. (1986). *Embracing contraries: Explorations in teaching and learning.* Oxford: Oxford University Press.

Forlin, C. (2001). Identifying potential stressors for regular class teachers. *Educational Research, 43*, 235-245.

Gmelch, W.H. (1988). Educators' response to stress towards a coping taxonomy. *Journal of Educational Administration, 26*(2), 221.

Gmelch, W.H. (1993). *Coping with faculty stress.* New York: Sage Publications.

Gmelch, W.H., & Chan, W. (1994). *Thriving on stress for success.* Thousand Oaks, California: Corwin Press.

Griffith, J., Steptoe, A., & Cropley, M. (1999). An investigation of coping strategies associated with job stress in teachers. *British Journal of Educational Psychology, 69*, 517-531.

Hui, E., & Chan, D. (1996). Teacher stress and guidance work in Hong Kong secondary school teachers. *British Journal of Guidance and Counseling, 24*, 199-218.

Jacobs, L.C., & Chase, C.I. (1992). *Developing and using tests effectively: A guide for faculty.* San Francisco: Jossey-Bass.

Kyriacou, C. (2000). *Stress-busting for teachers.* Cheltenham: Stanley Thornes.

Kyriacou, C. (2001). Teacher stress: Directions for future research. In E.C. Wragg (Ed.), *The RoutledgeFalmer reader in teaching and learning.* London: RoutledgeFalmer.

Kyriacou, C., & Sutcliffe, J. (1987a). A model of teacher stress. *Educational Studies, 4*, 1-6.

Kyriacou, C., & Sutcliffe, J. (1987b). Teacher stress and satisfaction. *Educational Research, 21*(2), 89-96.

Lazarus, R.S., & Folkman, S. (1984). *Stress, appraisal, and coping.* New York: Springer.

Manthei, R., Gilmore, A., Tuck, B., & Adair, V. (1996). Teacher stress in intermediate schools. *Educational Research, 38*(1), 3-19.

Manthei, R., & Soloman, R. (1988). Teacher stress and negative outcomes in Cantebury state schools. *New Zealand Journal of Educational Studies, 23*, 145-163.

Mathison, S., & Freeman, M. (2006). Teacher stress and high stakes testing: How using one measure of academic success leads to multiple teacher stressors. In R. Lambert & C. McCarthy (Eds.), *Understanding teacher stress in an age of accountability.* Greenwhich, Connecticut: Information Age Publishing.

McShane, S., & Von Glinow, M.A. (2005). *Organizational behavior.* New York: McGraw-Hill/Irwin.

Millicent, A., & Sewell, J. (1999). Stress and burnout in rural and urban secondary school teachers. *Journal of Educational Research, 92*, 287-299.

Mohammed, M.A. (2000). *Teacher stress.* Unpublished dissertation. Physical Education College, Cairo.

Osmond, K.B. (2008). *Emirati nursing students' perception and experiences of studying nursing and science through English.* Unpublished doctoral dissertation. University of Exeter, UK.

Okebukola, P. (1992). The concept of village schools and the incidence of stress among science teachers. *Human Relations, 45*, 735-751.

Pithers, R.T., & Fogarty, G.J. (1995). Symposium on teacher stress: Occupational stress among vocational teachers *British Journal of Educational Psychology, 65*, 3-14.

Sari, H. (2004). An analysis of burnout and job satisfaction among Turkish special school headteachers, and the factors effecting their burnout and job satisfaction. *Educational Studies, 30*(3), 291-306.

Schonfield, I. (1990). Coping with job-related stress: The case of teachers. *Journal of Occupational Psychology, 63*, 141-149.

Troman, G. (2000). Teacher stress in the low-trust society. *British Journal of Sociology of Education, 21*, 331-351.

Troudi, S. (2007). Negotiating with multiple repeaters. In C. Coombe & L. Barlow (Eds.), *Language teacher reseach in the Middle East.* Alexandria, VA: TESOL Publications.

Tuetteman, E., & Punch, K.F. (1990). Stress levels among secondary school teachers. *Educational Review, 42*(1), 25-29.

Wiley, C. (2000). A synthesis of research on the causes, effects, and reduction of teacher stress. *Journal of Instructional Psychology, 27*(2), 80-87.

Wilson, V., & Hall, J. (2002). Running twice as fast? A review of the research literature on teachers' stress. *Scottish Educational Review, 34*(2), 175-187.

Part II: Educational Reforms in the Arabian Gulf

ROBIN DADA

Chapter 10
Teacher Leadership in the Arab Gulf: Expatriates and Arab Educators Mentor Each Other

Abstract

Teacher leadership is a part of participatory leadership (Tolbert & Rook, 2005) and the maximization of educator teams in schools. This chapter reports on the results of a qualitative study into the attributes and roles of teacher leaders and the interplay of bureaucratic and organic leadership systems in Arab schools. Eleven middle level (Grades 6-9) teacher leaders in the United Arab Emirates (UAE) were the key informants in the study, with data drawn from teachers and principals. The data collection included their weekly reports about their work, as well as the field notebook of conversations with principals and teachers kept by the Academic Program Coordinator for the Middle Schools (the researcher), all of whom were a part of a systemic school reform program in the UAE entitled Madares al Ghad (Schools of Tomorrow). The results describe the attributes of good teacher leaders as strong relationship builders and listeners, both by the teacher leaders and their principals and colleagues. The most important role identified by teacher leaders was the responsibility for professional development experiences. More difficult roles for the teacher leaders included the scheduling of these experiences. Obstacles to the role included the random scheduling patterns, absenteeism, and sporadic Internet connectivity in some schools. Commitment to and support of teacher development by the principals was an asset to the teacher leadership role. The interplay between the organic nature of teacher leadership and the hierarchical nature of educational organizations in the UAE was suspect in the implementation and requires continuous effort. The study has a number of implications for educational reform efforts and the maximization of human resources within schools.

Introduction

This study describes the introduction of foreign master teachers as teacher leaders into the government schools in the Madares al Ghad (MAG) program in the United Arab Emirates (UAE). This reform program was initiated as a systemic reform with a broad focus on whole school reform. The teacher leadership component of this larger program was built on the platform of helping local teachers understand participatory leadership and teamwork, as well as develop skills of collaboration to increase student achievement. The study described in this chapter focused on the preparation of local teachers to engage in participatory leadership, support collaborative planning activities, contribute and learn from shared professional development experiences, and develop communities of practice that critique current practice against desired outcomes, developing sustainable professional development in UAE schools and local development of teacher leadership skills.

The UAE, less than 40 years old, has been engaged in educational reform to support a resource rich country to find its place in the global marketplace. There is an expressed need for a highly skilled Emirati workforce committed to preserving the cultural identity of the UAE while helping the country to operate competitively in the 21st century and citizens who possess the capabilities and skills needed for a knowledge-based society (Al Jaber, 2010). A variety of reform discussions and plans have come and gone over time; their failure to thrive often explained by a perceived inability of schools to implement new methods or innovative practices (Bardsley, 2010). The current bureaucracy in the educational system in the UAE supports educators' deference to directives rather than proactive adjustment of teaching to student needs. In the current curriculum of the Ministry of Education there is emphasis on the development of knowledge and skills, but less of a focus on life and career skills, information literacy, or management, and their integration with current issues and themes important to the 21st century. Higher order thinking, critical analysis of knowledge and skills, and local/global themes are limited in the current curriculum. The introduction of participatory leadership at the teacher level was a purposeful move toward creating organic structures in the school organization that encouraged interaction and thought drawn from the needs of students and the contextualization of the curriculum in the 21st century UAE culture. In the next sections, a brief description of the MAG program within the UAE education system is given followed by a review of the literature on teacher leadership.

Background

Teachers and Schools in the UAE Context and the MAG Program

The creation of a unified country in the 1970's prompted efforts to standardize schooling across the Emirates and the development of prescribed curriculum and assessment frameworks. Until recently, schooling in the UAE remained focused on religion, Arabic language, English literacy, computation, the sciences, and civics to serve the needs of citizens of the past era. A holistic reform process is currently under way being driven by an indigenous theory of modernization that simultaneously values a diversified economy, a successful exploitation of ICT, an open Arabic and Islamic knowledge society, and thus, an educational system of international character and quality. The process is fundamental and will redefine for the UAE what it is to be Arabic and Islamic in a globalizing world (Macpherson, Kachelhoffer & El Nemr, 2007).

In 2009-2010, the Dubai Statistics Center (2010) reported that 76% of the teaching workforce in Kindergarten and Primary schools were Emirati teachers, but the expatriate workforce made up approximately 95% of the middle level and secondary boys' schools and nearly 29% of the workforce in the same levels of the girls' schools. Throughout the region, women who desire to work in schools as teachers of young children or elementary grades enter an educator preparation program. Teachers who complete this type of program develop knowledge and skills about child and adolescent development, pedagogy, and assessment. Men and women who plan to teach secondary students typically prepare as subject matter specialists and rarely prepare as teachers, but complete Baccalaureate degrees in a content field (physics, mathematics, English literature). Many do not have pedagogical knowledge in support of their content knowledge when they graduate (Ridge, 2010). Expatriate teachers are frequently not included in professional development programs that target Emirati teachers. Men become teachers by default when they fail to be admitted to courses of study leading to their desired profession, such as engineering and medicine. These teachers graduate and register with the Ministry of Education to arrive at the school under-enthused with their career circumstances, typically unskilled for teaching, and struggle to make a living from the limited salary and benefits they receive. They turn to tutoring after hours or second jobs to make ends meet and support their families, leaving little time for preparation and collaboration. While this practice is not condoned by the Ministry of Education, it is practised throughout the region (Lewis, 2010a; Lewis, 2010b).

In order to develop the UAE education system and replace the non-productive teaching and learning methods associated with low expectations, rote memorization, and silo teacher existence with productive strategies leading to active learning environments for students and collaborative and generative modes of work for teachers, the Madares al Ghad program was conceived. At its 2007 launch, it was comprised of 50 schools in all of the seven Emirates in the UAE. It was made up of 18 elementary schools, 13 preparatory schools, and 22 secondary schools with some schools operating at two levels. The program was a joint effort between the Ministry of Education (K-12) and the Ministry of Higher Education and Scientific Research as a systemic and comprehensive reform program for K-12.

Two types of foreign MAG personnel were employed in the schools, the School Level Team Leader (SLTL) and the Teacher Mentor (TM). The TM worked in the classrooms with local teachers as a team teacher and mentor, as well as a teacher for children. The teaching assignment provided for a 'best practice' demonstration classroom and gave the TM the chance to gain 'street credibility' among the local teachers and principal. Their work in the classrooms of their colleagues included support during experimentation with new teaching techniques and activities, including development of learning centers, differentiated learning activities, and development of a repertoire of learner-centered teaching methodologies. The SLTL worked with TMs to orchestrate professional development experiences for local teachers, to identify the best use of scheduled professional development time, and to organize collaborative team planning for instruction and assessment. The SLTL also served as a link to the principal and the two typically met weekly for an update and observed classrooms. The SLTL encouraged the principal to visit classrooms with him/her to learn about what was changing in his/her school and the two were responsible for teacher evaluation. The MAG program, currently in its fourth year, has encountered some changes in staffing patterns and roles.

The work of teacher leaders during the second year of the MAG program focused on the implementation of the action goals which consisted of four innovations. These included the creation of print and visually rich learning environments, the use of integrated language experiences, infusion of technology tools to support language learning and teaching, and collaborative planning for developmentally appropriate learner-centered experiences. All four of the action goals were identified to facilitate increased student achievement. Traditional classrooms were stark with individual desks for students. Students of Grades 1-12 remained in their classroom as their teachers passed through the door approximately every 45 minutes. There were many reasons given for why print rich environments were not possible in the UAE. Explanations ranged from, 'the students and other teachers remove things from the wall' (Male Teacher, School 7), 'the principal didn't allow things on the wall' (Male Teacher, School 9), 'there's not enough space for all subject teachers to put up a print rich environment' (Female Teacher, School 3), 'students will be distracted; it's better to put nothing on the wall' (Female Teacher, School 11), 'student work isn't perfect and things on the wall can be confusing' (Male Teacher, School 1), to 'there are no office boys in the school to provide this service' (Male Teacher, School 13).

Teachers grounded in language acquisition quickly accepted the concept of the print-rich environment with a variety of print-rich materials finding their way to the walls and doors of the classrooms that supported language learning. Teachers developed connections between word walls, illustrations, student work, illustrative posters of reading and writing strategies and grew an understanding of how to teach reading and writing more effectively and as a part of every interaction in the classroom. Teachers with less understanding of language development generally resisted longer and took 1-2 months longer to show signs of trying this innovation, but responded positively when they could see its impact.

The second innovation was collaborative planning, drawing upon the strengths of all grade-level teachers to identify the resources to be used and how. This innovation was welcomed by teachers who were always looking for good ideas. For teachers who only knew about following the pages of the required textbook or comfortable with their reliance on supervisors to direct the objectives and topics to be covered, this was an uncomfortable expectation. These teachers lacked confidence in their own ability to identify good teaching materials or did not want to be responsible for having chosen something that wasn't useful. Collaboration was met with resistance. Comments such as 'this is a lot of extra work and takes too much time; we're too busy to do this' (Female Teacher, School 4), 'the teachers are not used to working like this and will not accept all of this extra work' (Male Principal, School 1), and 'we are not free to change the materials; they are tested by the Ministry and our students will be disadvantaged without working through the curriculum' (Female Teacher, School 11), were heard more frequently in the early stages of collaborative planning, but still persist in some schools today.

The third innovation was the infusion of technology tools into teaching and learning. English teachers received laptops to facilitate their planning and instruction. Many teachers used the technology to create interesting lessons that drew upon a variety of Internet sources. Some teachers were so engaged with the technology that they sometimes failed to involve students in the whole enterprise, creating some missed learning opportunities for students. Others, particularly the uninspired, were found to only unpack their computer when someone would observe them. Progress was noticeable across the project, particularly in those schools with consistent Internet connectivity. Specialized training for these teachers using social networking tools in teaching English was provided in the fourth semester of the MAG program providing an impetus of student projects that engaged students in language production and sharing of products.

The fourth innovation of focus during the time period of this study was the implementation of developmentally appropriate practices in instruction, behavior management, procedures and routines, and learning experiences. Many of the schools had not been in the habit of providing explicit instruction to students regarding classroom procedures and routines, nor had teachers of a grade level developed consistent procedures and routines to maximize efficiency in the classroom. Classrooms became more orderly with the addition of this practice.

There was often discrepancy between the assumptions of male teachers as to how they thought students should conduct themselves and the students actual behavior. Male schools spoke about behavior problems more often than girls' schools and the male teachers found the issue more troubling, particularly where instruction was more traditional in approach. Girls' schools more often struggled with teacher absenteeism; however girls seemed to be more tolerant of change. Teachers were also beginning to work with differentiated instruction, but struggled in its implementation during this period. As the teacher leaders worked with colleagues on the aspects of this innovation, planning for materials management, expected behaviors, making arrangements to cover for colleagues, and smooth transitions helped in making learner-centered activities more productive.

Teaming and Leadership

The early literature on professional development in organizations focused on the need to 'fix' something. Conley and Muncey (1999) describe the trend toward the use of deficiency models for school reform based on the belief that teachers are unmotivated to improve their teaching. This mindset was followed by the *teacher professionalization* movement. Reformers realized that even the most highly motivated teachers fell short of their goals in poorly organized schools, where their professional judgment was not considered (Labaree, 2009; Lieberman, Saxl, & Miles, 1988). More recently, an emphasis in the literature on the *professionalization* of the school organization and management has emerged with two schools of reform: 1) creating change through enhanced teacher roles (Danielson, 2007; Berry & Ginsbert, 1990); and 2) enhancing teacher teaming to support change and diminish isolation (Main & Bryer, 2005; Kruse & Louis, 1997). The first approach changes the roles of individual teachers while the second changes the teachers' roles through new organizational configurations that draw upon 'teams' of teachers.

The Coalition of Essential Schools (2010) recommended engaging in reform that promotes both teacher leadership and teaming as strategies for change. Teachers are to be encouraged and supported to adopt and use skills, beliefs, and activities that increase collaboration and draw upon their professional responsibility to participate as leaders in the school (Benitez, Davidson, & Flaxmam, 2009). Portin (1999) presented a triadic model of leadership that described leadership as more complex than the authority of position. The triadic model described an interplay between transactional leadership (leader-centered, rational decision-making, and focused on the efficiency of the organization), transformational leadership (elevating the motives and goals of institutional members), and critical leadership (emancipation of organization members and power measured by the capacity of members involved in an interaction).

Teaming and leadership can seem at odds with each other unless viewed in the context of the early work of Burns and Stalker's (1961) distinction between 'mechanistic' and 'organic' organizational systems. Mechanistic systems emphasize a hierarchy of control and authority, as well as the vertical interactions of superiors and subordinates. Organic systems emphasize a network structure of control and authority, including a lateral direction of communication that consists of information and advice rather than instructions and demands. Both teacher leadership and teaming emphasizes task variety, professional learning, and lateral communication (Kruse & Louis, 1997; Pounder, 1995; Smylie 1994) as well as the changing roles of leader and follower.

The MAG Model drew upon this literature and expanded the influence of experienced and expert teachers, drawing mainly from foreign teachers in the first year and then adding more local teachers in the second, third, and fourth years. TMs and SLTLs were identified using the qualities of successful teacher leaders, drawn from the work of Danielson (2008), which include such characteristics as having:

- the ability to collaborate with others
- the confidence of other educators and persuasiveness.
- respect for their own instructional skills
- an understanding of evidence and information
- the ability to recognize the need to focus on those aspects of the school's program that will yield important gains in student learning

- an open mind and respect for others' views
- optimism and enthusiasm
- confidence and decisiveness
- perseverance
- flexibility and willingness to try different approaches
- expertise in their field

Challenges to teacher leadership are rooted in the school culture. The use of foreign teacher leaders increased the level of anxiety in the early stages of the program as the schools and teachers had received little preparation for the arrival of the TMs and SLTLs. Obstacles such as autonomy, egalitarianism, and deference to seniority made the work of the teacher leaders challenging, as it does in teacher leadership programs in general, requiring TMs and SLTLs to be particularly sensitive to developing good relationships with their colleagues in the schools. The teachers who were brought in as teacher leaders were excited about their specialized roles as teacher mentors and team leaders because of their experience and desire to be helpful. The MAG personnel, as in other research findings on teacher leadership (Munger Johnson, Fiarman, Papey, & Quzilbash, 2009; Donaldson, 2005), saw the assignment as an opportunity. Their experience and success let them feel competent and confident in their work, and they wanted to share their acquired expertise with others.

Although the TMs and SLTLs were initially enthusiastic, they encountered the challenges mentioned above. From these obstacles grew some ineffective coping mechanisms on the part of some of the

TMs and SLTLs, such as working only with the willing or choosing to work alongside teachers in support rather than in mentorship. These issues, coupled with the schools' limited preparation for their arrival and experiencing much of their day and surroundings in a language they did not understand, allowed the enthusiastic teacher leaders to feel left out of conversations, and sometimes wondering if they would be able to fit into their new environment. The orientation program in the second year included a large component of initial leadership training and an ongoing leadership program to enable the foreign teachers to make the transition from experienced classroom teachers to teacher leaders in the UAE with greater emphasis on relationship building at the school level.

A further issue with teacher leadership was the difficulty of principals to understand the role of the teacher leaders, worrying that there may be confusion about who teachers reported to. Teacher leadership, while experiencing a resurgence of support around the world, and it is particularly associated with educational reform movements, it is also experiencing the rub between hierarchical and networked structures of leadership and decision-making. Limited orientation for schools, particularly principals, contributed to this issue in the MAG program. The bureaucratic organization common in Arab schools was not serving the work of teachers who were responsible for individualistic learning outcomes in students (Burns & Stalker, 1961) and required a network of grade level educators and specialists to formulate curriculum plans, instructional activities, and engage in professional development. Principals became more comfortable with the role as they came to understand teacher leadership better as a support to their responsibilities.

The Study

The study reported in this chapter considers whether teacher leadership development is a promising strategy in support of UAE in-service teacher professional development. The following research questions were addressed:

- Which attributes of teacher leaders are most important in the UAE context?
- What are the important roles of teacher leaders in the UAE and are some more difficult than others?
- Do teacher leaders encounter obstacles? If so, what are the obstacles they encounter?
- Which strategies are the most productive in dealing with obstacles?
- What is the interplay between mechanistic and organic organizational characteristics with the introduction of teacher leadership in the MAG program?

The key informants for this study were eleven SLTL in eleven schools: five were males serving in boys' schools and six were females serving in girls' schools. TM comments were part of the SLTL weekly report and represented 17 TMs: 6 males and 11 females in the eleven MAG schools. Each school principal provided feedback throughout the year on the teacher leaders that were in their school. The 40 local teachers who provided perspectives and information were from the English language department in each school.

This study was carried out in the first two years of the MAG program. SLTLs submitted their weekly report of activities on a provided template that included day-to-day work accomplished, professional development experiences provided and/or participated in, identification of breakthroughs or difficulties in mentoring or leadership roles, requests for training/problem solving assistance.

TMs used a Daily Planner Template to identify activities, along with identifying concerns, successes, notes regarding calls/e-mails to make, and questions that support reflection on the day's events and their activities were submitted to the SLTL and informed the SLTL report. In addition, data about local teacher and principal perspectives were drawn from the field notebook of the researcher who functioned as the Academic Program Coordinator for the program. She worked consistently over two years with the eleven schools. All schools included Grades 6-9; Grades 6 was part of the MAG program in the first year, with Grade 7 joining in the second year. Grades 8 and 9 were preparing to become part of the MAG program in the third year. The MAG teacher leadership staff was mostly from English speaking countries (3 were bilingual).

The remarks and comments from the SLTL weekly reports were reviewed, coded according to themes and topics related to the research questions, and the frequency of responses was calculated. The field notebook of the researcher was also coded using the same system as the SLTL weekly reports. The results of the study are discussed in the next section according to the five research questions.

Results and Discussion

Which attributes of teacher leaders are the most important in the UAE context?

The foreign teacher leaders (TMs and SLTLs) repeatedly referred to the importance of patience, consistency, and the ability to listen as important attributes in their work. When they wrote about patience and consistency they explained this as the need to say things more than one time in different ways and having to hear the frequent reminder that others had tried to change things but the system was unchangeable. They also described these attributes in the context of enjoying people and developing relationships.

New teacher leaders were screened during the second intake for classroom experience and their ability to manage groups as this was part of the change that had to occur at the classroom and school level. Teacher leaders without classroom teaching experience were susceptible to failure due to their inability to manage classroom sized groups. There was also an importance to having teacher leaders who were well grounded in language acquisition and pedagogy of English as a Foreign Language (EFL) learners as school staff were lacking in these teaching skills. The TMs' classroom teaching assignment and their open class periods were valued. Local colleagues were invited to observe them at work, particularly when they were using a particular teaching strategy, or when they had collaboratively developed a lesson plan with the local teachers. TMs and SLTLs who understood how to manage a classroom and keep several activities going at once were admired; those who could not were dismissed as not credible by their local colleagues, rendering them ineffective. Local teachers and principals cited the need for a positive attitude, 'being active', and 'being willing to listen to others' ideas'.

Staying true to desired outcomes of the program, while possessing the ability to recognize alternative routes to the desired end, was important. In schools where there was a willingness to embrace the phrase, *in the best interest of the student*, as the measure against which all innovation or practice was considered, teacher leaders found a means to limit unproductive discussion, while encouraging teacher dialogue.

Generally speaking the important attributes of teacher leaders as found in this study were similar across the informants and consistent with the characteristics described by Danielson (2008), including ability to work with others, confidence and persuasiveness, respect for their skills, open mind and respect for others' views, optimism, enthusiasm, decisiveness, perseverance, flexibility, expertise, and focus.

What are the important roles of the teacher leader and are some roles more difficult than others?

All teacher leaders cited professional development (PD) as their most important role. They had a collective understanding that they needed to share what they knew and support local teachers' development. Many teacher leaders and principals initially perceived the formalized workshops that they scheduled as the PD work. The embedded PD provided in a shoulder-to-shoulder mode was harder to understand and value by principals who perceived that SLTLs did not have enough work to do or that they did not do enough PD. Once SLTLs began to share their weekly report with principals and outline the specific issues they were working on with each teacher, the embedded PD was more visible. One girls' school demonstrated a triadic model of leadership as the principal, who was clearly the recognized leader, encouraged MAG personnel at work in her school as leaders and supported the emergence of her local staff as they began to take on short-term leadership roles related to PD (Portin, 1999). Most schools saw PD from the perspective of a 'deficiency model' (Conley & Muncy, 1999) of professional development, i.e. the teachers do not have a skill that is desired.

The second most frequently cited role was that of encouraging experimentation with active strategies. For the local teachers, their experience with supervision was negative and equated to being given a list of things done wrong during an observation period. The teacher leaders identified things that were working well and then worked with teachers on the aspects that were not serving their students well, choosing to work with one or two issues at a time. Positive feedback was important and appreciated, as well as giving limited and specific recommendations. The TMs identified the importance of supporting teachers in trying new strategies; to be the extra hands and eyes available that allowed the teacher to experiment with more confidence. Teachers were afraid of someone noticing that activities did not go well or that students misbehaved. As one of the teachers commented: 'I can't let the students work together, I will lose control' (Teacher 3, in Boys' School 4). Teachers grew in their ability to manage classrooms with multiple activities.

The role that SLTLs cited frequently as being difficult was getting teachers to engage in collaborative planning. Some principals sabotaged the collaborative planning time by excusing teachers from school to run errands. Egalitarianism (Danielson, 2008) was problematic in three of the schools when local teachers expected TMs to make the plans for them and produce materials. Nine schools eventually developed a rhythm to planning and their efforts were noticeable in the students' achievement, the use of active strategies, and the collegial support they extended to each other in running learner-centered activities.

Do teacher leaders encounter obstacles and if so, what are they?

Schedule irregularities, changes, and failures contributed to the challenges encountered by teacher leaders. The traditional practice of scheduling each instructional period for each cohort of students individually provided randomness to the school day. The assignment of classrooms to cohorts of students, rather than teachers, made for stark and uninviting learning environments. On the surface, it seemed to be acceptable because students did not require passing time, they had a place to put their books, and supervision was not required between classes. However, it obstructed effective classroom use and management because teachers did not have teaching resources in the classroom. As the MAG program progressed, the rooms were reassigned to one or two teachers of the same subject and the students moved to the teacher. The teachers were responsible for creating a learning environment and having the resources at their disposal to use when needed. They were also responsible for the condition of the room as a learning environment. One school resisted the use of the dedicated classrooms, while others used the model well.

Another issue was teacher absenteeism and the lack of an effective substitution program. Substitute teachers were typically drawn from teachers who were not in class. This upset the collaborative planning or PD activities as teachers were sent to substitute for a class. Teachers with a chronic medical problem were not in school consistently enough to ensure student progress and each absence was covered by different teachers.

The degree of support by the principal made a difference in local teacher commitment. Principals were sometimes confused about the lines of authority and communication between all of the governing authorities that interfaced with the MAG program. The interplay between agencies was not clear in the two years of this study; greater communication and transparency was needed. Principal commitment to the program was important for success. When principals encouraged staff to work towards implementation, changes occurred. In two schools, principals were opposed to the changes and worked at cross purposes with the teacher leaders. A few principals struggled with their own assertiveness as they struggled between 'the best of students' and keeping the teachers happy. When teachers complained to the principals about PD or planning cutting into their errand time, these principals would ask the teacher leaders to limit the planning and PD, negatively impacting the program.

Some schools had sporadic Internet connectivity which became an obstacle for students and teachers. Two schools cited inability to manage utility bills, which varied significantly. Connectivity would cease prior to school holidays, breaks, or as the school year approached exam time to save money. Teachers were worried about technology being unavailable and they did not want to take the chance on being so dependent on it with a room full of students. This attitude eased in the schools with consistent connectivity.

The language and culture barrier was also an obstacle. One of the social norms of the region is to not disappoint. It is best not to say *no* too directly so as not to disappoint the asker. Foreign teacher leaders were confused by the use of *insha'allah* (if God wills) to mean *yes*, particularly at the start of the program when they were new to the region. The meaning that Islamists would ascribe to the phrase '*insha'allah*' is: *Yes, absolutely, unless there is some unforeseen intervention by God which keeps me from doing the task.* The phrase has been adjusted by some to mean something comparable to *let's see* or *maybe* and, in time, teacher leaders began to understand this phrase to mean *no, not likely* or *I don't want to.* Teacher leaders also confused a lack of response to one of their comments as a sign of agreement in the early days of the project and in time grew to realize the importance of talking with individual teachers. These issues were not insurmountable and were included in orientation programs to better support mutual understanding.

The use of metaphors and idioms were also a source of misunderstanding. Foreign teacher leaders had to think about the language that they wanted to use and consider how it would be understood once spoken. In time, both local and foreign educators developed the language they needed and an understanding of each other's words and phrases to express intended meanings. Colleagues developed trust of each other's intentions and an ease in asking about meanings intended. The development of trust and good collegial relationships between teachers was important.

Which strategies are the most productive in overcoming obstacles and in working with difficult roles?

Relationship building held the biggest pay off in problem solving and solution development. Spending time with the principal and with teachers to plan and work through challenges was pivotal to the success of the program. The teacher leaders who were adept in relationship building were able to work closely and more intensely with their team. Teacher leaders who were more reserved struggled with egalitarianism and seniority issues. Through the overt recognition of local teachers' improvements and progress, teachers grew confident and appreciative of feedback. SLTLs shared successes with principals, making it easier for principals to recognize their teachers' development. Recognition of small victories was valued by teacher leaders in measuring progress and was appreciated by the principal and teachers.

SLTLs found that when they could offer something of themselves to their school, it was valued. Some offered free English language lessons, tutoring for international English language exams (such as the International English Language Testing System (IELTS) exam), strategic planning support and specialized workshops requested by the teachers or principal. TMs and SLTLs reported feeling overwhelmed with the enormity of the task. In the second year teacher leaders and schools set goals to target the most important or achievable in the time span available and focused on these issues, always with an eye on increasing student success.

What is the interplay between hierarchical management structure and organic teacher leadership?

Although a formalized role in the MAG program, teacher leadership was discounted in schools with dissenting principals. Schools in the UAE have traditionally been hierarchical with the principal operating as the building manager and supervisors entering to evaluate teachers and manage curriculum. Collaborative planning, shared responsibility in professional development, and professional communities of learners were foreign concepts and mostly uncomfortable in the early days of the MAG program. Significant progress in this area was made over the first two years of the program; however, three boys' schools expressed consistent preference for less collaboration.

About half of the SLTLs and TMs struggled with their own comfort level in developing informal and organic structures in their roles. Teacher leaders often expressed frustration with not having 'authority' to compel teachers to do what they wanted them to do or would express signs of competitiveness with the people they were mentoring. Developing flexible relationships with local teachers enabled planning using a variety of ways to accomplish necessary tasks, commit to collaboration and share the development of weekly plans. While there was some stratification (the teacher leader was responsible for submission of the school's lesson plans for feedback from the academic program coordinator), the manner in which these plans were prepared for submission was different by school.

The hierarchical structure that is prevalent in the current Ministry organizational structure continues to make teacher leadership difficult. Talk of site-based management and other examples of teacher leadership is emerging. There remains a concern that no one will function in these roles without a salary stipend or increased status, however teachers can see the value of shared leadership. By the end of the second year of the MAG program, shared leadership roles between principals and teacher leaders were occurring more comfortably, particularly in girls' schools, but also in two of the boys' schools. It is also worth mentioning that teacher absenteeism appeared to be less problematic in schools where teachers felt more committed to each other and their students. This is an important area for further study.

Conclusion

The teacher leaders in the study were a part of the initial efforts to recast the eyes of UAE educators in a new direction, aligning professional practice, habits of mind, and skills that lead to student success. Most teachers were interested in learning new methods and working with students in different ways, but they were very cautious about losing control of their classrooms or being harshly evaluated if they did not complete their textbooks. Most teachers were able to embrace a new strategy when they observed impact on student.

The capacity to build relationships and develop team spirit, make a commitment to the mission, even during difficult times, and possess a knowledge base that allowed the teacher leader to stay focused on the desired outcomes emerged as important attributes of the teacher leaders in this study. The value of multicultural learning communities is an important finding of this study. There were many deeply rooted stereotypes from both sides in the beginning. The focus on relationship building was important at a variety of levels, but ultimately the relationships that developed did so in support of student achievement. What mattered to both the foreign and local teachers was getting along with others, respecting others, and collaborating together to do what was necessary for the benefit of students and the future of the UAE. For the expatriate teachers, there was much to learn about the rhythm of work in the UAE context. Local colleagues learned more about the cultures, similar dreams, and professional aspirations of the foreign teacher leaders, as well as their rhythm of work. Most of the teacher leaders in the MAG program struggled, to some degree, with issues of egalitarianism, seniority, and principal support. Patience and respectfulness of others was important to work through these issues. Principals requested more guidance about the lines of authority and communication between all of the governing authorities that interfaced with the MAG program. The interplay between agencies was not clear and greater communication and transparency is needed in the future. The principals who were not as supportive to the program often cited this as the rationale for their lack of support. The teacher leaders had clear lines of communication and reporting, but they were not always able to understand the complexities and political nature of the relationship between the Educational Zones, the Ministry, and the newly emerging Education Councils in the UAE. When attitudes about student background or family surfaced and were confronted by MAG staff and teachers together through a professional discussion, teachers recognized how these attitudes influenced the way they saw their students, their expectations for the students, and ultimately, the students' achievement.

The MAG program is in its fourth year and continues the teacher leadership component. To make the kind of difference it was intended to make, the program needs to work with both English and Arabic medium teachers and the languages of instruction noted as two compatible languages that do not compete, but that increase access for students. Teacher language development must become a significant part of the sustainability of the implementation of a bilingual or dual language environment. National identity remains a priority in this program and is evidenced by the attention to curriculum resource choices. Continuous professional development of educators, administrators, and educational executives is important. Ministry of Education policies related to use of the school day, teacher and principal standards, curriculum planning, assessment and reporting practices, and building use will be important facilitative measures to support educational development and sustain the development that has begun. The UAE has everything to gain by investing fully in its children and in professional educators by bringing educational practice into the 21st century. There are no great cities or great countries without great educational programs at all levels.

References

Al Jaber, S. (2010, June 6). Economic growth rests on research and education. *The National*.

Bardsley, D. (2010, February 9). A decade of pupils called the 'lost generation.' *The National*.

Benitez, M., Davidson, J., & Flaxman, L. (2009). *Small schools, big ideas: The essential guide to successful school transformation.* San Francisco: Jossey-Bass.

Berry, B., & Ginsberg, R. (1990). Creating lead teachers: From policy to implementation. *PhiDelta Kappan, 71*(8), 616-621.

Burns, T., & Stalker, G. (1994). *The Management of Innovation.* USA: Oxford University Press.

Clark, D. (1997, updated 2010). Concepts of Leadership. Retrieved Oct 2, 2010 from http://www.nwlink.com/~donclark/leader/leadcon.html

Conley, S., & Muncey, D. (1999). Teachers talk about teaming and leadership in their work. *Theory into Practice, 38*(1), 46.

Coalition of Essential Schools (n.d.) CES benchmarks reflection and self-assessment tool. Retrieved October 1, 2010 from: http://www.essentialschools.org/system/school_benchmarks/13/a ssessment_tools/original/Professional_Learning_Community_S A.pdf

Coalition of Essential Schools (2010). Benchmarks. Retrieved October 1, 2010 from: http://www.essentialschools.org/items/5

Danielson, C. (2008). *The handbook for enhancing professional practice.* Virginia: Association of Supervision and Curriculum Development.

Danielson, C. (2007). *Enhancing professional practice: A framework for teaching.* ASCD: Alexandria, VA.

Donaldson, M.L., Kirkpatrick, C.L., Marinell, W.H., Steele, J.L., Szczesiul, S.A., & Johnson, S.M. (2005). "Hot shots" and "Principal's pets": How colleagues influence second-stage teachers' experience of differentiated roles. *American Educational Research Association.* Montreal, Canada.

Dubai Statistics Center. (2010). *Employment in Governmental Education by Stage, Nationality, Sex—Emirate of Dubai (2007/2008 – 2009-2010).* Retrieved on September 8, 2010, from http://www.dsc.gov.ae/Reports/DSC_SYB_2009_04_06.pdf

Kruse, S.D., & Louis, K.S. (1997). Teachers' reflective work: School based support structures. *Educational Administration Quarterly, 33*(3), 89-216.

Labaree, D. (2006). Power, knowledge, and the rationalization of teaching: A genealogy of the movement to professionalize teaching. In Hartley, D., & Whitehead, M. (Eds.), *Teacher education: Major themes in education, Volume IV,*

Professionalization, social justice, and teacher education (pp 127-163). New York: Routledge.

Lewis, K., & Shaheen, K. (2010, January 9). Low-wage teachers take on second jobs. *The National.*

Lewis, K. (2010, August 24). Private tuition 'needs regulation.' *The National.*

Macpherson, R., Kachelhoffer, P., & El Nemr, M. (2007). The radical modernization of school and educational leadership in the United Arab Emirates: Towards indigenized and educative leadership. *International Studies in Educational Administration, 35*(1), 60-77

Main, K., & Bryer, F. (2005). *What does a good teaching team look like in a middle school classroom?* Griffith University Research Online: AU. Retrieved on October 1, 2010, from: http://www3.griffith.edu.au/03/ltn/issue_02/article_12.php

Munger, M., Johnson, S., Fiarman, S., Papey, L., & Quzilbash, R. (2009). *Shared responsibility for teacher quality: How do principals respond to peer assistance and review?* A paper presented at the annual meeting of the American education Research Association, San Diego, April 2009. http://www.gse.harvard.edu/~ngt/new_papers/MSM_AERA_20 09.pdf

Portin, B.S. (1999, January). What shapes my leadership? *Primary Practice, 18*, 4-6.

Ridge, N. (2010). Teacher quality, gender, and nationality in the UAE: A crisis for boys. Working Paper (10-6). Dubai School of Government: Dubai.

Rook, D., & Torbert, W. (2005). *Seven transformations of leadership*. Boston: Harvard Business Review.

NETTIE BOIVIN

Chapter 11
The Rush to Educate: A Discussion of the Elephant in the Room

Abstract

While literacy is commonly viewed as an autonomous set of measurable skills acquired in school, it is also understood as an ideological construct framed within a socio-cultural, in-school and out-of-school learning context. The latter viewpoint is shared by the New Literacy Studies (NLS) movement (Street, 1996). Similarly, Hornberger (2003) assesses the biliteracy continua as being housed within a larger socio-cultural power discourse. Since 1995, Qatar has been undergoing dramatic national educational reforms. These are part of a broader national reform process and as such provide an ideal context from which to compare competing views of literacy while examining the impacts of reforms on national literacy. In this chapter the theoretical frameworks of the NLS movement and Hornberger's (2003) biliteracy continua, are applied to an analysis of the recent rapid and revolutionary K-12 educational restructuring in Qatar. Upon careful assessment of the educational reform process (including the analysis, assessment, implementation and testing in the K-12 school system), it becomes apparent that while the vision to create a modern global educational system is underway in Qatar, the rush for the process to occur, along with the unintentional, hegemonic implementation from Western educational experts, could disadvantage rather than benefit the reform process, if not addressed.

Introduction

Qatar is a tiny resource rich country which prior to the discovery of gas, relied on pearl diving and fishing as a means of economic prosperity. The indigenous population, presently only 20% of the total population, were predominately nomadic Bedouins and fishermen. Qatar was under British protectorate from 1868 (Brewer, Augustine, Zellman, Ryan, Goldman, Stasz, & Constant, 2007). In 1939, a small oil reserve was discovered, and after World War II, the British helped the Qatari government with extraction. This new influx of capital enabled educational reforms to begin in the 1950's. After 1971, immediately after gaining full independence, that natural gas was discovered in Qatar. This vast increase in wealth, (Qatar has one of the largest natural gas reserves in the world), enabled further reforms to take root (Moini, Bikson, Neu, DeSisto, Al Hamadi, & Al Thani, 2009; Brewer, Goldman, Augustine, Zellman, Ryan, Stasz, & Constant, 2006; Brewer, et al., 2007) while prompting an increased sense of responsibility to the citizenry (Al-Misnad, 2010). Societal changes were implemented including those at the educational level. This chapter examines the educational reform process that Qatar has followed over the past 50 years with emphasis on the more radical reforms of the last decade.

Education in Qatar

Prior to the 20th century the educational system in Qatar was grounded on religious scholarship. The 'Kuttab' approach taught literacy skills, such as reading and writing, from the Quran (Al-Misnad, 2010; Brewer, et al., 2007). The first Ministry of Education (MoE) was created around the mid 1950's and the first wave of reforms ushered in a policy move towards a slightly more secular style of education based on the Egyptian school and curriculum model (Brewer, et al., 2007). The pedagogical style remained teacher-centered with the core approach of rote-memorization (Brewer, et al., 2006). The primary school education system was an all male domain, but shortly afterwards girls were allowed the opportunity to obtain an education. However, education was still segregated (Al-Misnad, 2010; Brewer, et al., 2007). Moreover, teachers were the same sex as the students until the 1970's when the system of model schools was developed to aid boys' transition from the home to school, and then into business. This new model allowed male primary school students exposure to female teachers while providing job opportunities for the female teachers (Brewer, et al., 2007). It should be noted that at this time, teachers were not only poorly paid, but attitudes from the community towards the profession were low (Brewer, et al., 2006; Brewer, et al., 2007).

Further reforms would wait until a new financial revival. After the Qatari independence from the British, and the beginning of the natural gas wealth in the 1980's, education again became a priority. However, implementation occurred haphazardly with little overall vision or framework (Al-Misnad, 2010). The top-heavy, bureaucratic MoE controlled all the final decisions and all funding for the schools (Erman, 2007). It was not until 1995, after the present Emir overthrew his father that greater comprehensive reforms occurred. In 1998, new legislation was introduced and the creation of an elected municipal government included the provision for women to run for election. The educational reforms were part of a larger shift towards democratization and globalization. However, it would not be until 2001 that consultants were approached to assess and overhaul the education system (Brewer, et al., 2007). The Emir approached the RAND Corporation, a non-profit U.S. research institution, to undertake one of the largest educational reform including: policy, bureaucratic structure, educational framework, curriculum development, community outreach, and testing and assessment. The RAND Corporation undertook assessment at both the K-12 level and university level, therefore affecting the entire educational process.

The RAND Corporation: Assessment, Re-Design and Implementation

In 2001, Qatar contracted the RAND Corporation to assess the K-12 educational system in Qatar. Classrooms in both private Arabic schools and MoE Model schools were observed and it was found that students in secondary education were not prepared to enter university and they lacked critical thinking skills. At that time, the pass rate for exiting high school students was only 50% for all subjects combined (Brewer, et al., 2007). Qatar's illiteracy rate of 13.6% underscored this fact (UNESCO, 2006). The RAND Corporation felt that the students were not able to access technical jobs in the oil and gas fields which were presently filled by expatriate workers (Al-Misnad, 2010; Brewer, et al., 2006). Moreover, they found that the overall K-12 curriculum lacked standardization, locally produced textbooks, and an overall coherent educational policy framework (Brewer, et al., 2007). The educational system was devoid of performance indicators and standardized testing, while the school facilities were poor and needed upgrading. Finally, the pay for teachers was low and there was little opportunity for professional development. However, the report did reveal that the teachers in the schools were highly motivated and willing to work hard (Brewer, et al., 2007). The RAND Corporation recommended a radical revamping of the overall system (Erman, 2007; Brewer, et al., 2007; Zellman, Ryan, Karam, Constant, Salem, Gonzalez, Orr, Goldman, & Al-Thani, 2009) including autonomy of schools, accountability of performance, variety of school content and choice for parents (Zellman, et al., 2009).

After analysis, the RAND Corporation submitted three types of educational systems to the Emir. The first choice was a similar version of the existing central model (Zellman, et al., 2009). The second was a voucher school model considered too risky as Qatar 'had no market for information on school performance' and therefore the country was ill-equipped for an educational marketplace to guide the consumer parents' (Brewer, et al., 2007, p. 56). The final accepted model was a charter school system or as it became known, the Independent School system (Zellman, et al., 2009). The Independent Schools would be accountable through audits, reporting mechanisms and student assessments. The designing of the school system was to allow businesses, such as Qatar Petroleum, to create a particular type of school based on their needs for skilled employees, e.g. a math- and science-based curriculum school. In addition, any interested party could theoretically open an Independent School, allowing the market to dictate educational need (Zellman, et al., 2009; Brewer, et al., 2007). This was quite a revolutionary approach compared to what had previously existed in Qatar.

Moreover, the RAND Corporation oversaw the development and design of the curriculum of the entire K-12 curriculum. They identified four main curricular subjects: English, Arabic, mathematics, and science. For reasons never explained, English, which was originally to start at Grade 3, now begins in Grade 1 (Brewer, et al., 2007). Moreover, the RAND Corporation decided that the Arabic curriculum would use the same pedagogical approaches used to teach English (Brewer, et al., 2007). From the initial assessment of the education system in 2001 to curriculum evaluation, design and implementation of the first twelve Independent Schools in 2004, the whole process took only two years (Zellman, et al., 2009).

The next stage in the educational reform was the testing process. Standardized testing was lacking in the Qatari educational context. The RAND Corporation chose to approach the problem from two angles. First, an annual assessment of the Independent School system established examining all levels of student performance, teacher methodology, classroom content, and attitudes of all stakeholders (teachers, students, and parents) (Brewer, et al., 2007). The second angle was the use of two different international assessment tests comparing the literacy skills of Qatari students to those of students from other countries. The first test was the Programme for International Student Assessment (PISA), which is an international testing organization that tests reading, mathematics, and science literacy for 15 year olds. The second test was the Progress for International Reading Literacy Study (PIRLS) which assesses reading literacy of Grade 4 students worldwide (*Education for a New Era Magazine*, 2008). Testing occurred after the independent schools were operational for only two years and the RAND Corporation decided to use the results as baseline data (Brewer, et al., 2006). Qatar performed poorly in comparison to most other countries (falling in the bottom percentile of the testing group); however, it was ahead of other Arab countries like Kuwait and Morocco (Supreme Education Council, 2008). The RAND Corporation also produced annual school evaluations that compared the Independent Schools to the private Arabic schools and the MoE Model schools but failed to show any statistical significance in the test results (Supreme Education Council, 2008).

Next in the educational reform process was a re-evaluation and assessment of the successes and failures of the reforms, again overseen by the RAND Corporation. Shortly after the implementation in 2004, a reassessment occurred from 2004-2006 with findings presented in 2009 (Zellman, 2009; Gonzalez, Le, Broer, Mariano, Froemel, Goldman, & DaVanzo, 2009). As stated in the preface of the report 'the timeline for developing a fully designed standards-based assessment system was too short' (Gonzalvez et al., 2009, p. XIV). Moreover, due to the rushed timeframe, proper community outreach was unable to occur, for both the parents and the business stakeholders (Gonzalvez et al., 2009). Workshops and meetings meant to communicate action plans were often scheduled when working parents could not attend (Gonzalez et al., 2009). However, according to Brewer et al. (2007), there is a link between community, policy, curriculum, students and teachers and 'policies designed to affect one part of a system will often affect other parts' (p. 90) sometimes unintentionally. During the educational reform overseen by the RAND Corporation little attention was paid to the local community and its first language (L1). However, literacy cannot be untangled from its context.

Models of Literacy

The ideological assumptions held by the RAND Corporation during their assessment and re-design of the Qatari education system are consistent with an autonomous model of literacy. The autonomous model views literacy taught as a set of skills or techniques, using scientific in-class methodology and as such it ignores or denigrates other narratives and genres that exist outside of the classroom (Hull & Schultz, 2001). The notion of western literacy posits the usage of literacy as a measurable tool for advancement in the modern global society (Street, 1996; Hull & Schultz, 2001). Furthermore, the autonomous model of literacy negates, as Street (2003) argues:

> the cultural and ideological assumptions that underpin it, so that it can then be presented as though they are neutral and universal and that literacy as such will have these benign effects...[This] is simply imposing western conceptions of literacy on to other cultures or within a country those of one class or cultural group onto others. (p. 77)

Research studies conducted by several educators on workplace literacy point towards the need to expand the view of out-of-school literacy, especially for those who do not attend tertiary education (Hull, 1999; Dias, Freeman, Medway, & Pare, 1999; Heller, 1997; Street, 2003). If literacy, is a form of discourse then as Vygotsky, (1962) argues it is culturally bound in the socio-cognitive interactive activities which vary from culture to culture and therefore context to context. This more all encompassing view of literacy learning is housed in a more ideological viewpoint.

The ideological model of literacy includes both in school and out-of-school contexts when assessing students' abilities. The New Literacy Studies (NLS) are at the forefront of this approach moving away from viewing literacy as just acquisition of skills towards regarding it as a social practice (Street, 1995). This varies from the autonomous model, which regards in-school literacy learning as the only important literacy practice. Conversely, Heath (1982) regards formalized education as only a small component of the overall literacy process. The long term study by Heath (1982) in the 1960's and 1970's of three diverse communities (white working class, mixed race middle class, and black working class) illustrated that children develop their language learning differently depending upon their culture. In addition, Hull and Schultz (2001) report there is a worrisome trend 'to build and reify a great divide between in-school and out-of-school contexts...(which) dismisses the engagement of children with non-school learning as merely frivolous or remedial or incidental' (p. 3). However, Scribner and Cole (1981) view literacy to be 'socially organized practices' not just in reference to reading and writing skills, but moreover comprehension of when, how and in what community cultural contexts these practices occur.

From the above discussion, it becomes apparent that literacy practices need contextualizing within other communicative modes not just reading and writing used for testing and assessment purposes. As Hornberger (2003) states, in her biliteracy continua model, successful attainment of literacy contains context, content, and media. Hornberger's (2003), research demonstrated in many different cultural contexts, that there is a complex interrelationship between bilingualism and literacy. She states 'We as educators, researchers, community members or policy makers need to take account of all the dimensions represented by the continua' (Hornberger, 2003, p. 98). Therefore, we cannot separate the contexts of the home community from that of the school community as literacy is an interconnected community event that exists within cultural confines, not just housed within the walls of a formal classroom (Street, 2003). Furthermore, in Qatar, how language is learned and cultural identity processed differs from the way in which Western literacy is processed (Clachar, 2004; Sayed, 2003). Therefore, the idea of implementing a curriculum not based on indigenous cultural ownership imposes a particular foreign ideology onto a population.

A Discussion of the Elephant in the Room

There are several issues raised in the investigation of the Qatar K-12 educational reforms such as the particular viewpoint of literacy adopted in the reforms, oversights in testing and assessment, hegemonic implications, and finally policy constraints. Addressing the first issue of the literacy model it is clear that the RAND Corporation's view of literacy is firmly entrenched in the autonomous model. For example, their examination of students' learning of Arabic and English was based on in-class observation using Western pedagogical practices, rather than on the integration of cultural context and usage of the literacy skills (Brewer, et al., 2007). Concerning the learning style of the Qatari students, the 'Maktab' or 'Kuttab' methodology was dismissively identified and labelled as rote memorization without any discussion or attempts to synthesize the inherent cultural learning style of the Qatari students with the new, western learning style advocated by the RAND Corporation (Brewer, et al., 2006, 2007). The RAND Corporation never investigated out-of-school learning as Street (1984, 1995) did in the 1970's during the oil boom in Africa. Through examination Street discovered that after school the students would gather to discuss passages from the Quran. This revealed a less rote learning method and a more socio-interactive one.

There are other genres of literacy that exist outside the rules of formal academic literacy and therefore must be included for a comprehensive evaluation of education and literacy. While critical thinking, engagement and learner-centred pedagogy are truly effective and essential they should not force all cultures to abandon their language culturally transmitted in favour of Western academic testable practices. Literacy stems from cultural discourse therefore it should not be imposed upon or denigrated by others based on differences in socio-cultural learning styles (Gee, 1996). The RAND Corporation went to schools to observe classroom interaction, however they admitted to comprehending methodology in only

English-medium classrooms. While they interviewed teachers, administrators and students (Brewer, et al., 2007) there was no mention of interaction with the wider community, nor any attempts to understand the socio-cultural needs of the community (Zellman, et al., 2009). Moreover, the RAND Corporation implemented English western style pedagogy also for the teaching of Arabic (Brewer, et al., 2007). This lack of socio-cultural recognition during the assessment and implementation of the educational reforms is evident upon examination of the testing process.

Within the Qatar framework, the RAND Corporation pushed for accountability as a principle of the educational reform. To compensate for the prior lack of performance indicators, the RAND Corporation devised a series of annual surveys investigating parental communication, teacher pedagogy, student motivation, and subject assessment. Furthermore, they implemented tests comparing student performance between the Independent Schools, the MoE Model schools and the private Arabic schools (Gonzalez, et al., 2009). These tests started in Grade 1. One would question the need and rationale to test the lower grades when researchers such as Cummins (2001) state that children learning two languages take between five to seven years before catching up in the second language (L2). Therefore, testing at this early stage seems premature and lacks sound judgement. Moreover, the international tests mentioned earlier (PIRLS and PISA) are in English. However, this is not the Qatari students' L1 (Supreme Education Council, 2008). One would question why there is less emphasis on testing in the students' L1. Moreover, why is the testing for science and mathematics occurring in an L2?

Such issues raise questions as to not only the validity of the test results but also the underlying motives of the testing. While global standardization in testing is an excellent goal, when it happens at the expense of the students' L1, it is subtractive in nature and relies on assimilative approaches rather than accommodative ones. Furthermore, research has proven subtractive bilingualism is less effective in L2 learning (Cummins, 2001; Baker, 2000). Futhermore, any evaluation tool can have a covert, often hegemonic, effect (Tam,

2001). It is true that the international tests were performed as baseline testing, however, the fact remains that no other types of culturally sensitive testing occurred. As Tam (2001) states, the effectiveness of testing depends on what testers believe is relevant to measure. In addition, Larson (2001) reconfirms there are difficulties in applying the 'scientific approach' as it is inadequate when measuring subtle cultural nuances that affect learners. Constraints raised by issues in testing reveal an unintentional, hegemonic push on the part of the RAND Corporation. Further exploration of this issue, investigation into the framework, ideology, and methodology behind the reforms, are needed.

Another major concern regarding the reforms is why allow the same company to analyse the educational situation, create the educational framework, oversee the curriculum development, re-examine the progress, and finally set the tests. This seems lacking in objectivity. Also a notable flaw is the framework of the Independent Schools. One of the principles of the Independent School system is to allow anyone the ability to open a school. In theory, this is a positive alternative, however, in practice, it can become a possible tool used by business as a controlling mechanism rather than to educate the citizenry.

Furthermore, the way that the RAND Corporation's ideological bias colour the reform process poses a larger concern. The RAND Corporation is a U.S. non-profit institute originally started by the U.S. Department of Defence (RAND Website, retrieved May 2010). Their mission statement declares that they plan to 'Further promote scientific, educational, and charitable purposes, all for the public welfare and security of the United States of America' (RAND Website, retrieved May, 2010). In assessing the educational reform put together by the RAND Corporation, one must also assess their biases. While the reforms were visionary and all encompassing, they were too rapid and lacked attention to the socio-cultural identity of the Qatari students thereby keeping power within a Western autonomous framework. This gives the appearance that the reforms had some outside imperialistic purpose. As Lemaitre (2002) argues, 'globalisation has become a new way of describing the imposition of cultural, political and economic priorities formerly associated with imperialism' (p. 6).

In addition, upon careful scrutiny of the methodology employed by the RAND Corporation, it appears to be less based on a scientific model and more on a rushed indistinct approach. For example, the RAND Corporation conducted classroom 'observations at approximately 15 schools: boys' and girls' schools at all three levels (primary, preparatory, and secondary), Ministry schools, and private institutions' (Brewer et al., 2007, p. 35). Only 15 schools, half of which are boys' and half are girls' schools. Then of the seven schools per gender one third were primary schools, one third middle schools, and the final third were secondary schools (that is about 2-3 schools per educational level). After this, they had to observe MoE Model schools and private Arabic schools. The total number of schools observed was approximately two per type therefore, with a population of 100,000 students this seems statistically insignificant (Brewer, et al., 2007).

The educational and business policies that were implemented further constrained the rushed framework devised by the RAND Corporation. People spoke of creating an excellent education system yet without enough time for community outreach or the much-needed teacher training to manage the classroom modifications this seemed impossible (Brewer, et al., 2007). At the same time as the school reforms were happening, Qatar University implemented a policy to switch the medium of instruction from Arabic to English. Thus, Qatar University put more pressure on the students to attain a higher level of academic English (Moini, et al., 2009). Even though, countries in the surrounding region are all Arabic speaking, Qatar seemed to be moving away from securing a higher level of Arabic in Qatari students. This resulted in a generation of students whose 'Arabic isn't a second language, but it isn't a strong first language either' as declared by Dr. Mathes, Associate Dean of Academic Affairs at Qatar University in an interview (Cupp, 2009). However, researchers have shown a strong L1 will increase the chances of a strong L2

(Cummins, 2001; Bailystok, 2002; Garner & Bochna, 2004; Sagasta Errasti, 2003). Moreover, research has also shown that later introduction of a L2, for example in Grade 5, is more effective (Garner & Bochna, 2004).

All of these educational policies put pressure on the students in the K-12 to progress at an unrealistic pace. However, the underlying policy driving the speed of the reforms is not an educational one but rather a political one referred to as 'Qatarization' (Brewer, et al., 2007). In 1990, Qatar initiated plans to replace 75% of expatriate workers with locals, by the year 2010, which would coincide with the expiration of 75-year lease by British Petroleum of the natural gas reserves (Brewer, et al., 2007). The Qatarization policy prescribes that vacated job positions be filled by Qatari citizens and it has been dictating the unnecessary speed of the educational reforms, despite the well-known fact that education as with cognitive development in general takes time (Cummins, 2001). The RAND Corporation's failure to synthesize the cultural context of the community's L1 into the new educational framework combined with the weakening of the primary students' L1 literacy creates a subtractive situation which research has shown is not positive for the community (Baker, 2000; Cummins, 2001). The imposition of western pedagogy, curriculum and testing at the expense of the students' L1 and cultural identity is a giant elephant in the room that needs addressing.

Some Implications

Educators must realize that culture can inform our pedagogical choices and implementation practices. Qatar's Supreme Education Council, when discussing results from the PISA and PIRLS, admitted that there was a need to improve the relationship between the home community and its involvement in the school (Supreme Education Council, 2008). They also suggested a push for positive attitudes towards reading among parents to increase students' performance scores. However, again there was no discussion of increasing reading in Arabic, the students' L1. Questions arise as to why most of the performance indicators embedded in the educational reforms are in the students' L2 (math, science and reading skills) rather than their L1 at the primary level (Moini, et al., 2009). At present parents are somewhat excluded from the educational process as many are not proficient enough in English to aid their children with their math and science studies. Moreover, many Qataris are worried about the weakening of their children's Arabic language skills (Pasaniuc, 2009; Cupp, 2009).

A recommendation for the Supreme Education Council would be to focus on the L1 of the students, at the lower primary level, that would allow for the inclusion of the parents in the educational reform process. An increase in literacy skills in Arabic as a L1 would positively affect proficiency in the L2 (Cummins, 2001). The desire to strengthen the local L1, does not denigrate the overall educational reform; which in breadth of curriculum, structure, principles and content is a wonderful display of vision on the part of the country. Rather, altering early parts of the framework would strengthen rather than weaken what has already begun. Otherwise a weak L1 would result in more socio-cultural problems that ultimately would create dissatisfaction among members of the local community with the new Qatar school system and English language acquisition overall. The community needs to feel ownership of the process for the reforms to be effective (Street, 2003; Hull & Schultz, 2001; Hornerberger, 2000). As Street (1996) discusses, people need 'to see themselves as agents who have the power to transform practices and not merely recipients' (p. 9).

A second recommendation would be to alter or include other types of testing to obtain a better assessment of student performance. It is easy to teach to the test but harder to educate. Education should not be contingent on programs that only adhere to scientific approaches and allow global politics to dictate educational policy as this is a dangerous hegemonic paradigm. Amending the literacy viewpoint to one that addresses embedded ideologies and cultural biases would allow for the implementation of constructive pedagogical goals such as critical thinking, learner centered teaching, and standardized curriculum without ignoring the socio-cultural context that is especially important at the primary education level (Cameron, 2004; Genesse, 2007).

As Cummins (1981, 1988) suggests, examining policies, which cause indistinct power relationships in schools, is important in providing equitable education for all. The rush to globalize appears to be an unintentional, hegemonic desire for western countries to impose English as a power in countries of the Middle East, such as Qatar. One cannot ignore the elephant of socio-cultural literacy and identity in a rush to create a modern global citizenry. Inclusion of past historical and cultural learning styles is imperative to a successful future society even at the cost of slowing down the reforms for a chance of reflection on the overall process. Moreover, literacy is not indistinguishable from culture rather it stems from the community. As Oakes (2009) argues, 'Understanding these cultural roles with the assistance of an insiders' perspective can make for better formulated literacy interventions which draw upon home-school connections in literacy practices and their linkages to culture, ability, and access issues' (p. 3). Instead of carelessly rushing to impose western standards of literacy, policy-makers, educators and parents need to reflect on the current state of education in Qatar and carefully plan the next step. Moreover, other Gulf States must also pay attention to lessons learnt from the Qatari educational reform or face similar problems in the future.

References

Al-Misnad, S.A. (2010). *Education Reform in Qatar the Big Picture.* Doha: Qatar University.

Al-Misnad, S.A. (2010). *Qatar Univeristy – Presidents' Office.* Retrieved March 2010, from http://www.qu.edu.qa/offices/president/president_educational_re form.php

Baker, C. (2000). *The care and education of young bilinguals- An introduction for professionals.* Clevedon: Multilingual Matters.

Brewer, D.J., Goldman, C.J., Augustine, C.H., Zellman, G.L., Ryan, G., Stasz, C., & Constant, L. (2006). *An introduction to Qatar's primary and secondary education reform.* Santa Monica: The RAND Corporation.

Brewer, D., Augustine, C.H., Zellman, G.L., Ryan, G., Goldman, C.A., Stasz, C., & Constant, L. (2007). *Education for a new era: Design and implementation of K–12 education reform in Qatar.* Santa Monica: The RAND Corporation.

Cameron, L. (2003). Challenges for ELT from the expansion in teaching children. *ELT Journal, 57,* 105-112.

Clachar, A. (2000). Opposition and accommodation: An examination of Turkish teachers' attitudes toward Western approaches to the teaching of writing. *Research in the Teaching of English, 35*(1), 66-100.

Cummins, J. (2001). *An introductory reader to the writings of Jim Cummins.* Clevedon: Multilingual Matters Ltd.

Cummins, J. (1988). *Language proficiency, bilingualism and academic achievement.* New York: Longman.

Cummins, J. (1981). *The role of primary language development in promoting educational success for language minority students.* Los Angeles: Evaluation, Dissemination, & Assessment Center.

Cupp, J. (2009). *In Qatar and Egypt, education reform means learning in English.* Retrieved April 23, 2010, from http://www.huffingtonpost.com/journalism-boot-camp/in-qatar-and-egypt-educat_b_242656.html

Dias, P., Freedman, A., Medway, P., & Pare, A. (1999). *Worlds apart: Acting and writing in academic and workplace contexts.* Mahwah, N.J.: Lawrence Erlbaum.

Erman, A. (2007). *Think independent: Qatar's education reforms (Middle East).* Retrieved May 11, 2010, from http://www.entrepreneur.com/tradejournals/article/161065936.html

Garner, J., & Bochna, C.R., (2004). Transfer of a listening comprehension strategy to independent reading in first-grade students. *Early Childhood Education Journal, 32*(2), 69-74.

Gee, J. (1996). *Social linguistics and literacies: Ideology in discourses.* London: Farmer Press.

Genesee, F. (2006). Introduction. In F. Genesee (Ed.), *Educating Second Language Children* (pp. 4-5). Cambridge: Cambride University Press.

Glasser, S. (2007). Qatar's educational reforms trigger unease among Muslim leaders. *Washington Post.*

Gonzalez, G., Le, V., Broer, M., Mariano, L.T., Froemel, J.E., Goldman, C.J., & DaVanzo, J. (2009). *Lessons from the field developing and implementing the Qatar student assessment system, 2002–2006.* Santa Monica: the RAND Corporation.

Heath, S. (1982). Protean shapes in literacy events: Ever-shifting oral and literate traditions. In D.Tannen (Ed.), *Spoken and written language: Exploring orality and literacy* (pp. 91-118). Norwood, N.J.: Ablex.

Heller, C.E. (1997). *Until we are strong together: Women writers in the Tenderloin.* New York: Teachers College Press.

Hornberger, N.H. (2003) *Continua of biliteracy: An educational framework for educational policy, research and practice in multilingual settings.* Clevedon: Multilingual Matters.

Hull, G. (1999). What's in a label? Complicating notions of the skills poor worker. *Written Communication, 16*(4), 379-411.

Hull, G., & Schultz, K. (2001). Literacy and learning out of school: A review of theory and research. *Review of Educational Research, 71*(4), 575-61.

Larson, J. (2001). *Literacy as snake oil: Beyond the quick fix.* New York: Peter Lang Publishing.

Lemaitre, M.J. (2002). Quality as politics. *Quality in Higher Education,* 8(1), 29–37.

Moini, J.S., Bikson, T.K., Neu, C.R., DeSisto, L., Al Hamadi, M., & Al Thani, S.J. (2009). *The Reform of Qatar University.* Santa Monica: the RAND Corporation.

Oakes, L. (2009). Literacy in an extended family household in Kabul. *Language & Literacy, 11*(3), 1-14.

Pasaniuc, J. (2009, January 28). *Global English: Issues of language, culture, and identity in the Arab World.* Retrieved May 28, 2010, from http://www.caleidoscop.org/Members/janina/news/global-english-issues-of-language-culture-and-identity-in-the-arab-world

RAND Corporation (2009). *History.* Retrieved May 1, 2010, from http://www.RAND Corporation.org/about/history

Sagasta Errasti, M. (2003). Acquiring writing skills in a third language: The positive effects of bilingualism. *International Journal of Bilingualism, 7*(1), 27-42.

Sayed, Z. (2003). The sociocultural context of English language teaching in the Gulf. *TESOL Quarterly , 37*(2), 337-341.

Scribner, S., & Cole, M. (1981). *The psychology of literacy.* Cambridge, MA: Harvard University Press.

Street, B. (1996). Preface. In M. Prinsloo, & M. Breier (Eds.), *The social uses of literacy:Theory and practice in contemporary South Africa* (pp. 1-9). Bertsham: Sached Books.

Street, B. (1995). *Social literacies: Critical approaches to literacy in development.* London: Longman.

Street, B. (1984). *Literacy in theory and practice.* Cambridge: Cambridge University Press.

Street, B. (2003). What's 'new' in New Literacy Studies? Critical approaches to literacy in theory and practice. *Current Issues in Comparative Education*, 5(2), 77-91.

Supreme Education Council. (2008). *International test results underscore urgency of reforms*. Retrieved March 13, 2010, from: http://www.english.education.gov.qa/content/resources/?parent= &type=Education+for+a+New+Era+Magazine.

Tam, M. (2001). Measuring quality and performance in higher education. *Quality in Higher Education*, 7(1), 47–54.

UNESCO (n.d.). *UNESCO Country Statistics*. Retrieved March 21, 2010, from http://stats.uis.unesco.org/unesco/TableViewer/document.aspx? ReportId=121&IF_Language=eng&BR_Country=6340&BR_Re gion=40525

Vygotsky, L. (1962). *Thought and language*. Cambridge: The M.I.T. Press.

Zellman, G.L., Ryan, G.W., Karam, R., Constant, L., Salem, H., Gonzalez, G., Orr, N., Goldman, C., & Al-Thani, H. (2009). *Implementation of the K--12 education reform in Qatar's schools*. Santa Monica: the RAND Corporation.

STEPHANIE L. KNIGHT, ATMANE IKHLEF, DAWN PARKER,
MALATESHA JOSHI, ZOHREH R. ESLAMI, HISSA M. SADIQ,
MUBARKA AL-AHRAF, AHMAD AL SAAI

Chapter 12
An Investigation of Math and Science Teaching and Learning in Qatari Independent Elementary Schools

Abstract

Following the establishment of a set of key elements for educational reform in Qatar, this chapter presents the findings from a research study in 67 randomly selected third and fourth grade math and science classrooms in Qatari Independent Schools on the status of the key educational reform elements. Observations were conducted to determine teacher and student classroom behaviors related to student-centered teaching and learning. Surveys were administered in these classes to investigate students' perceptions of inquiry and learning environment and teachers' perceptions of reform-based instruction and teacher efficacy. Achievement data were obtained from reports of the Qatar Comprehensive Educational Tests. Findings indicated a mismatch between observed behaviors, including achievement performance, and participant perceptions of student-centered teaching and learning. In general, participant perceptions indicated greater implementation of reform-based elements than were evident in observations and achievement data. Few differences in profiles of higher- and lower-performing schools were found, although lower-performing schools exhibited more student-centered classroom characteristics with more student off-task behavior. Implications of the findings are also discussed in the chapter.

Introduction

In 2002, after analysis of the Qatari educational system (Brewer, Augustine, Zellman, Ryan, Goldman, Stasz, & Constant, 2006), 'Education for a New Era' (Law Decree No. 37) reform was enacted. The decree established development of national curriculum standards in math, science, English, and Arabic; emphasis on critical thinking; establishment of charter schools (Independent Schools); development of standards-based assessment; instruction in English in math and science; and extensive teacher professional development. A new governing organization with less centralized control consisting of the Supreme Education Council, Education Institute, and Evaluation Institute was established to provide policy and to oversee implementation. The reform incorporated many aspects of current movements in other nations (Calderhead, 2001), and represents an important accomplishment for a small country that did not institute public schooling until 1951.

In the classroom, the reform provides '...emphasis on encouraging a spirit of inquiry and hands-on learning' (www.education.gov.qa). Two standards in particular of the *National Professional Standards for Teachers and School Leaders* (Education Institute, 2007) highlight skills and dispositions that teachers need in order to be able to implement the reform. Standard 4, establishing learning environments that 'engage all students in purposeful and intellectually challenging learning experiences, encourage constructive interactions among teachers and students, and enable students to manage their own learning and behaviour' (p. 25), and Standard 5, 'Construct learning experiences that connect with the world beyond school' (p. 30) reflect an emphasis on student-centered teaching.

While considerable study of organizational structures and outcomes of Qatar reform has been planned and implemented (Brewer et al., 2006), little attention has been placed on the actual site of teaching and learning - the classroom. The purpose of this chapter is to present research findings on the status of reform-based teaching and learning in Qatari elementary math and science classrooms. This research provides information on classroom processes related to student-centered teaching and learning goals. The objectives of the chapter are to:

- outline instructional strategies related to Qatari educational reform observed in third and fourth grade math and science classes;
- describe the extent to which students engage in productive classroom participation and self-regulated learning needed for critical thinking and problem solving; and
- investigate patterns of teacher and student perceptions and behaviors related to school attainment of math and science standards.

The chapter also addresses implications for teaching and learning in Qatari classrooms. The nature of the cross-cultural collaboration of the project researchers brings to bear the views of insiders and outsiders on interpretation of findings and implications for practice.

Background

Qatari curriculum standards emphasize student-centered classrooms where students actively engage in critical thinking, inquiry and problem solving (Education Institute, 2007). The focus employs constructivist-based models of learning (Bransford, Brown, &

Cocking, 1999, 2000), pedagogical approaches (Grossman, 2005), and professional development (Putnam & Borko, 2000). These constructivist-based models emphasize the necessity to engage initial understanding so conceptual change can occur, the importance of deep foundational knowledge that allows meaningful conceptual frameworks to develop, the need to define, implement, and monitor learning goals and strategies, effective use of technology, development of dispositions that encourage critical thinking and reflection, and the need for professional development based on sound principles of teacher learning (Putnam & Borko, 2000).

The complexity of interactions in Qatari classrooms has been heightened by increased accountability and changing expectations for teachers and students. The paradigm shift from rote memorization to meaningful learning places tremendous pressure on students, who must assume responsibility for motivational and cognitive processes of learning, and on teachers, who must provide instructional and assessment strategies that foster student engagement and autonomy during inquiry (see e.g., Blumenfeld, Kempler, & Krajcik, 2006; Donovan, Bransford, & Pellegrino, 2000). While classrooms characterized by these reform elements should emerge as more successful on Qatari standards-based assessments, little research has been conducted to examine the relationship between these characteristics and standards attainment or even to determine whether these elements exist in the classroom.

Student Behaviors and Outcomes in Student-Centered Classrooms

Student engagement has been studied extensively as a predictor of student achievement (Good & Brophy, 2000). Current views of student active engagement reframe the notion of time-on-task in ways that connect it more closely to the disciplines that form the context for engagement (Engle & Conant, 2002). A recent National Research Council report (Duschl, Schweingruber, & Shouse, 2007) refers to 'productive participation' (p. 194) that goes beyond mere participation to participation in ways that facilitate disciplinary learning, specifies intellectual progress as a result of this participation, and is demonstrated by change over time in student behaviors related to argumentation and inquiry. This kind of engagement depends on the discipline, task, and topic being studied and is influenced by student characteristics (e.g., motivation and attitudes) as well as teacher behaviors and classroom environment. Although this is an area of increasing interest, few studies of productive participation have been conducted (Duschl et al, 2007).

While productive participation is a feature of student-centered classrooms that foster meaningful disciplinary learning, students must also develop strategies and dispositions that function outside of specific classrooms, activities or lessons. One requirement for students' intellectual autonomy is their ability to control motivation, persistence, and use of learning and problem-solving strategies. Self-regulation refers to students' thoughts and behaviors related to achievement of learning goals that enable them to transfer what they have learned to new contexts (Schunk & Zimmerman, 2008). The process leads to student control of learning and is necessary for effective outcomes in student-centered classrooms. Considerable research has been done in North America and Europe on processes that self-regulated learners use to learn and about the kinds of environments that foster self-regulation (Boekaerts, 1999). However, little research on student-centered classrooms has been conducted with Qatari students. Since individual and contextual differences play a role in acquisition of self-regulation (Zimmerman & Schunk, 2001), research needs to be conducted in the Qatari context with the added goal of providing Qatari teachers and administrators with information to be integrated into their classrooms.

Teacher Role in Student-Centered Classrooms

Learning in schools is traditionally dominated by adults; students rarely make decisions about their own learning. Even though educational philosophies aim to produce citizens capable of participating thoughtfully in society, our educational practices tend to foster dependence, passivity and a 'tell me what to do and think' attitude (Goodlad, 1984), especially in the Gulf States. In student-centered classrooms, decision-making, organization, and content are largely determined by students' needs and perceptions. The teacher's role changes to facilitator rather than director. This shift is effective in helping students make progress in academic achievement, social skills, and acceptance of diversity. Student-centered teaching techniques help teachers set up effective instructional environments for every member of the classroom, regardless of diverse learning needs (Stuart, 1997). Although the idea of learner-centered teaching is not new, it is a challenging task requiring instructional practice that focuses on student intellectual autonomy, motivation, persistence, and use of inquiry learning and problem-solving strategies. In student-centered teaching environments, instructors provide support to students, demonstrate flexibility in curriculum without compromising learning goals, and utilize a variety of assessments (Motschnig-Pitrik & Holzinger, 2002). In contrast to the traditional classroom characterized by the initiation, response, evaluation (IRE) discourse format, student-centered classrooms feature discussion among students with teacher facilitation rather than domination (Sawyer, 2006).

Teacher Perceptions and Beliefs

Research indicates that teachers' perceptions and beliefs influence their instructional practices and ultimately student achievement (Good & Brophy, 2000). Teachers' beliefs about their effectiveness (teacher efficacy) underlie many instructional decisions that shape students' educational experiences (Soodak & Podell, 1997). Teachers with high self-efficacy tend to teach in ways characterized by use of inquiry, they believe they can help students overcome learning problems and succeed, and they are more knowledgeable of their students' developmental levels (Rubeck & Enochs, 1997). Highly efficacious teachers are more likely to use open-ended, inquiry and student-directed strategies, while teachers with low efficacy are more likely to use teacher-directed strategies such as lecture or textbook reading. When teachers have low self-efficacy, their teaching tends to be characterized by authoritative, teacher-centered roles.

Challenges of Second Language Teaching and Learning

In previous sections, research highlights the importance of student interactions with the teacher and other students. While interactions based on discussion in one's native language are challenging enough, the added challenge of teaching and learning in a second language and in a reform context drawn from western cultures may make the task of developing self-regulated learners in an Arab country even more difficult (see e.g., Krashen, 1985; McInerney, 2008). Effectiveness of student-centered approaches may depend on teachers' abilities to provide comprehensible input in the second language together with linguistically and academically appropriate tasks in settings where students feel comfortable interacting with others in their second language (Grassi & Barker, 2010).

While teacher efficacy has been studied in other contexts, few studies have explored the perceived teaching efficacy of nonnative English-speaking teachers teaching content in a second language (Eslami, 2005). Teachers' target language proficiency determines their classroom teaching practices and their use or non-use of the target language (Kamhi-Stein & Mahboob, 2005, 2006). In spite of the common-sense nature of this statement, research in this area is limited. There is a need to examine Qatari teachers' perceptions of their self-efficacy in terms of capabilities to teach science and math in English, their second language. These perceptions may mediate effects of professional development for student-centered classrooms.

The Study

The purpose of this study was to develop profiles of schools implementing Qatari reform to examine relationships among classroom processes, teacher and student perceptions, and student achievement in math/science classrooms in higher- and lower-achieving elementary schools. The findings represent the first phase of a multi-phase study still in progress. The first phase provides descriptions of teaching and learning in reform-focused schools, while subsequent phases (not yet completed) will use these findings to focus on development, implementation, and impact of professional development models for student-centered teaching. The phase described in this chapter addressed the following research questions:

- What instructional strategies do teachers implement in third and fourth grade math/science classes in Qatari Independent Schools?
- To what extent do their students engage in productive classroom participation during math/science?
- To what extent do students exhibit self-regulated learning (motivation and strategy use) during math/science?
- How effective do teachers perceive themselves to be when providing instruction in third and fourth grade math/science classrooms?
- How do the teaching and learning profiles of higher- and lower- performing elementary schools differ?

Participants

Participants included teachers and students from a sample of math/science classes in independent elementary schools. Elementary schools were targeted since the need to use strategies for self-regulation of motivation and problem-solving begins between 5-10 years of age and continues to develop throughout the elementary years (Donovan et al, 2000). The study was confined to math and science classes since productive participation is discipline-based. Data were collected in 17 schools randomly selected from 46 schools that comprised the first two cohorts of Independent Schools. Each school had implemented the Qatar standards for at least 3 years. The sample included 7 boys' and 8 girls' schools. Three to five third and fourth grade math/science classrooms were randomly selected from each school. The sample included 67 teachers and approximately 1150 students.

Procedures

The extent to which classroom interactions and activities were student-centered was determined through observations using two instruments: *The Stallings Observation System Snapshot* (Stallings, 1975) and the *Teacher Attributes Observation Protocol* (TAOP; Fouts, Brown, & Thieman, 2002). The *Snapshot* documents materials, activities, grouping, instructional strategies, and teacher-student interaction patterns, and establishes student engagement rate (Stallings & Giesen, 1977). The *Teacher Attributes Observation Protocol* is a combined qualitative/ quantitative measure (qualitative scripting followed by summative Likert-type items) designed to capture constructivist teaching approaches. The Likert-type items represent seven components (conceptual understanding, reflection, student active participation, real world applications, consideration of diversity, challenging curriculum, and assessment) consisting of 27 indicators. Interrater reliability for the *Snapshot* was .85 and .79 for the TAOP. Internal consistency for the TAOP was .93. Teachers also were asked to conduct a 'typical' class and were observed during a math/science lesson. While the observations do not provide an exhaustive profile of classroom interactions and we cannot guarantee that teachers provided typical lessons, the data provide a snapshot of what is occurring on a given day in Qatari elementary math/science classrooms.

Teachers completed the *Teacher Efficacy Scale* (TES; Gibson and Dembo ,1984). The TES contains 16 items in two scales: *Personal Teaching Efficacy* (PTE; teacher's perceptions of her ability to affect student learning), and *General Teaching Efficacy* (GTE; teachers' beliefs about the general relationship between teaching and learning). Teachers also completed the *Inventory for Teaching and Learning* (ITAL; Ellet & Monsaas, 2007) to determine perceptions of instructional practice and the extent to which they engaged in practices consistent with *Traditional, Standards-based,* and *Inquiry* teaching. Reliability for the TES was .98 and for the ITAL .95. To investigate teachers' perceived English language proficiency, a 13 item questionnaire investigating both productive and receptive language skills was administered to a subset of 29 teachers (Eslami & Fatahi, 2008).

On a day separate from classroom observations, students completed the *Individualized Classroom Environment Questionnaire* (ICEQ; Fraser & Fisher, 1991; Spinner & Fraser, 2002) and the *How Do You Solve Problems* inventory (HDYSP; Howard et al, 2000) to determine perceptions of self-regulated learning including classroom environment, strategies, and problem-solving. The ICEQ contained five scales: Personalization, Participation, Independence, Investigation, and Differentiation and exhibited internal consistency of .79. The HDYSP consisted of 25 items in five scales (Problem Representation, Objectivity, Evaluation, Knowledge, and Monitoring Subtasks) measuring problem solving and self-regulation perceptions. Internal consistency was .79.

Instruments were in English since English was the language of instruction for math/science. However, assistance was provided in Arabic. For student instruments, six Qatari elementary math/science teachers assisted in adapting the language and response format and in pilot-testing instruments with students not in the study. Native, Arabic-speaking research team members administered surveys to classes, translating as needed. Each survey required approximately 30 minutes to complete. Teachers completed surveys in English independently, but Arabic-speaking survey administrators were available for assistance. Arabic survey versions, translated by researchers fluent in Arabic and English, were also available.

Results from the *Qatar Comprehensive Educational Tests* (QCET), administered yearly in grades 4-6, were obtained for each school in math/science from reports of the Qatar Evaluation Institute (2009). Three classification lists provide a picture of overall school performance in three areas: extent to which schools meet standards, level of academic achievement, and academic progress from 2007-2008. Each list was divided into three performance levels. Schools in the top tiers of the three lists were used to define higher-performing schools in comparison with lower-performing schools in the remaining tiers. Third grades were not included since they were not eligible for testing until the following year. Nevertheless, the achievement results provide an indication of overall school performance within the timeframe of the study.

Schools were considered higher-performing if they appeared in the top tier of any of the three categories. Our results yielded 2 top tier schools for Meets Standards; 5 for Academic Achievement; and 4 for the Overall Change category. Some schools were represented in the top of more than one level. Eight schools were classified as higher-performing and 9 schools as lower-performing. Descriptive data for school profiles were analyzed qualitatively.

Results and Discussion

To address the four research questions, descriptive statistics were generated in four categories matched to the research questions: Instructional Strategies, Productive Classroom Participation, Self-Regulated Learning, and Teacher Efficacy (Tables 1-5). For the fifth research question, school profiles were developed to compare higher- and lower-performing schools (Tables 6-7).

Instructional Strategies

The *Snapshot* yielded information about classroom grouping, activities, and materials. An aggregate variable including activities and materials characteristic of student-centered instruction (amount of discussion, project-based instruction, student use of manipulatives, technology integration, and cooperative learning) was compiled from the data. Classrooms emerged as teacher-centered with over 70% of instruction occurring in teacher-directed large groups and about 25% involvement with small group/individual configurations. Student-centeredness, as defined by the aggregate variable, was observed less than 20%. However, there was a great deal of variation by school as determined by the large standard deviations (Table 1). Student-centeredness ranged from a low 0% to a high of almost 70% across schools, but Discussion and Projects, key elements of student-centered instruction, were observed infrequently in all schools.

Table 1: Stallings Observation System Snapshot - Means and Standard Deviations
    (n=56)

GROUPING	Mean %	SD
1 student	8.89	17.52
Small	17.38	18.53
Large	48.04	29.64
All	24.10	24.28
STUDENT INVOLVEMENT	**Mean %**	**SD**
*Discussion	4.82	10.99
Practice/drill	4.91	10.01
Kinesthetics	2.89	6.42
*Projects	.62	4.92
Classroom Management	3.40	7.64
Receiving Assignments	9.16	16.22
Computers/Calculators	.63	3.53
*Manipulatives	4.44	10.44
*Multimedia	6.15	14.09
Visual Aids	24.58	20.11
*Cooperative learning	3.04	8.22
No Materials	41.83	21.23
Total Student Off Task	29.66	19.34

TEACHER INVOLVEMENT	Mean %	SD
Monitoring Seatwork	10.56	17.60
Interactive Instruction	67.25	24.88
Organizing/Managing	20.29	22.47
Working Alone	1.59	5.45

*Indicates a student-centered activity

While the Snapshot documented activities and materials, the *Teacher Attributes Observation Protocol* investigated the nature of the content of classroom instruction, including depth of conceptual understanding elicited and the degree to which the curriculum challenged students (Table 2). Overall results were low, with the key elements of student-centered instruction (Real World Applications, Active Student Participation, and Differentiation in Strategies and Curriculum) observed rarely. Teaching for Conceptual Understanding and Challenging Curriculum were observed more often than other variables, but were still low. Again, there was considerable variation across schools.

Table 2. Teaching Attributes Observation Protocol - Means and Standard Deviations
    (n=56)

Attributes	Mean	SD
Conceptual Understanding	.86	.31
Reflection	.63	.30
Real World Applications	.23	.26
Active Student Participation	.37	.33
Differentiation	.51	.39
Challenging Curriculum	.84	.03
Assessment	.48	.01

Note: Scales range from 0 (Not Observed) to 4 (Observed Very Often)

The results depict an emerging set of instructional strategies consistent with the direction of educational reform in Qatar, but not yet fully implemented. While teacher-centered instruction prevailed, student-centered instruction occupied a fifth of the time observed. Superficial structures such as grouping and discussion were more prevalent than evidence of depth of content or active student participation which underlie productive classroom participation. During one observation, field notes indicated that a particular teacher would turn to the observer frequently and give the 'label' for the instruction she was providing (e.g., this is tying the content to student lives). However, the observer noted that the examples were either incorrect or at a low level and that students were not involved actively in instruction.

Productive Classroom Participation

Productive classroom participation refers to student engagement in discipline-based activities in ways that lead to self-regulation and motivation. This construct was measured by comparing the amount of off-task behavior and kinds of activities observed. (see Table 1). Results indicated that students overall were off-task and not productively engaged about a third of class time. This is disturbing since it reflects reduced opportunity for student learning of any type. This finding may be related to the type of school. Classroom management in boys' schools is perceived as more difficult than in girls' schools (Personal Communication with Qatar University professor) and higher off-task rates in boys' schools, which comprised 7 of 17 schools included in the analysis, could have affected off-task level. Comparison of off-task rates revealed about 10% more in boys' schools, and the range for off-task was much greater compared to girls'. The off-task level for both girls' and boys' schools may be related to difficulties in teacher management of higher-level learning activities noted in previous research (Brophy & Good, 2000; Doyle, 1986).

Examination of the aggregate variable representing elements of classrooms characterized by student-centered inquiry reveals some use of Discussion, Manipulatives, and Multimedia, but little evidence of Projects or Cooperative Learning that are key characteristics of inquiry-based classrooms (Duschl et al., 2009). The small groups noted in the previous section do not appear to be cooperative groups, but more superficial structures. While there was considerable variation as noted by the standard deviations (see Table 1), percentages were generally low across classrooms for discipline-based activities that underlie Productive Classroom Participation.

Contrary to the results of the observations, teachers perceived they emphasized more elements associated with student-centered inquiry than traditional teacher-centered instruction (see Table 5 below). The mismatch between teacher perceptions and observed behaviors needs to be considered by those implementing the reform as well as those providing professional development for teachers. Perhaps teacher use of structures such as small group learning, although not necessarily accompanied by inquiry activities or conceptually challenging content, gave them the illusion of student-centered inquiry. Conversely, this mismatch between actual strategy use and teacher perceptions of strategy use may represent an initial stage in moving from teacher-centered to student-centered instruction. In fact, although observations revealed low levels of conceptual understanding and challenging curriculum, these variables were higher than other elements of student-centered inquiry instruction and may be emerging in the classroom.

Self-Regulated Learning

Self-regulation refers to students' dispositions and strategies (motivation, persistence, and strategy use) that enable them to achieve learning goals related to inquiry and problem solving (Schunk & Zimmerman, 2008). Students reported high levels of problem-solving (problem representation) and self-regulation (objectivity, evaluation, and subtask monitoring) with the exception of one area (see Table 3). Students reported less knowledge available for problem solving. This finding may be related to observation data described previously that reported low levels of conceptual understanding and challenging curriculum – the knowledge base was not provided.

Students' perceptions of classroom environment that facilitates development of self-regulation were more mixed. Students reported high degrees of Personalization and Participation and to a lesser extent, Involvement. However, students' perceptions of Independence and teachers' Differentiation of student work/activities were considerably lower. While results of the *Inventory for Teaching and Learning* (see Table 4) indicated that teachers perceived they gave students opportunities for autonomy and individualized assignments/ activities according to Qatari standards, students did not perceive these elements to the same extent. Students felt that teachers gave them personal attention, cared for them, and gave them opportunities for participation and involvement in class activities. However, without autonomy and differentiation, student-centeredness could not be fully achieved.

Table 3. Students' Surveys: Means and Standard Deviations

I. Individualized Classroom Environment Questionnaire* *(n=1151)*		
	Mean	**SD**
Personalization	4.11	1.30
Participation	3.66	1.41
Independence	2.15	1.41
Involvement	3.42	1.44
Differentiation	2.82	1.60
II. How Do You Solve Problems* *(n=1151)*		
Problem Representation	4.06	1.22
Objectivity	4.03	1.25
Evaluation	4.15	1.18
Knowledge	3.76	1.42
Subtask Monitoring	4.01	1.19

*Scales range from 1 (Strongly Disagree) to 5 (Strongly Agree)

Teacher Efficacy

Teachers with high teaching efficacy typically impact students more positively than low-efficacy teachers. In this study teachers reported high levels of Personal Teaching Efficacy and somewhat lower levels of General Teaching Efficacy (see Table 4). In other words, they had less confidence that other teachers teach in ways consistent with development of problem solving and self-regulation, but they perceived they personally could impact student performance in these areas. This is consistent with findings of other research (Tschannon-Moran & Hoy, 2000). However, the high efficacy did not appear to generate positive findings for this study.

When investigating efficacy for teaching in English, the results showed that overall efficacy for the subset of teachers was high and similar to the larger set of teachers for General Teaching Efficacy and Personal Teaching Efficacy (see Table 4, Ia & Ib). Self-reported English proficiency was also high. Listening was lower than the skills of Speaking, Reading, and Writing, but all were high (Table 4, II). Since teachers were recruited to teach math and science in Independent Schools partially based on their English ability, this finding is not surprising. However, while confidence in English ability is desirable, confidence alone may not be enough to implement reform. Results of observations indicated that teachers were doing most of the talking in English. Students were doing very little talking in English. The lack of English proficiency among students may have contributed to the observation findings of a lack of student-centeredness. Students' confidence in their English proficiency and their opportunity to participate in linguistically appropriate tasks are key elements since students would benefit most from an active role in classroom discussion. The findings indicate that teachers' ability to facilitate this confidence and proficiency and scaffold classroom discussion needs to be further investigated.

Table 4. Teacher Surveys: Means and Standard Deviations

	Mean	SD
Ia. Teacher Efficacy* TOTAL SAMPLE *(n=67)*		
General Teaching Efficacy	4.11	1.68
Personal Teaching Efficacy	5.41	.89
Ib.Teacher Efficacy* SUBSET (n=29)		
General Teaching Efficacy	4.28	1.09

Personal Teaching Efficacy	5.47	.23
II. Teacher Perceptions of English Proficiency *(n=29)*		
Overall Proficency	4.01	.87
Listening	3.86	.92
Speaking	4.10	.87
Writing	4.04	.94
III. Inventory for Teaching and Learning*** *(n=67)*		
Standards	5.31	.55
Traditional	3.78	.57
Inquiry	5.11	.26

*Scales range from 1 (Strongly Disagree) to 6 (Strongly Agree)
**Scales range from 1 (No Proficiency) to 5 (Very Proficient)
***Scales range from 1 (No Emphasis) to 6 (Very Strong Emphasis)

Profiles of Higher- and Lower-Performing Schools

Tables 5-7 provide results of the comparison of higher- performing schools (HPS) and lower- performing schools (LPS). Findings indicated few differences by performance level, perhaps because both achievement and behaviors related to standards were quite low. The top tier of Meeting Standards only achieved 10-20% of standards (Qatar Evaluation Institute Report, 2009). The *Teacher Attributes Observation Protocol*, which focused on instruction from a constructivist perspective consistent with the standards, provided support for more use of student-centered instruction by Lower-performing schools than Higher-performing schools, but also showed very low use overall by both groups (see Table 5). For observed behaviors using the *Snapshot*, three composite variables related to student-centeredness were considered: Teacher interactions with individuals and small groups, Student-centered activities, and Student off-task behavior. Higher-performing schools were characterized by more teacher interactions with individual students and small groups and less student off-task behavior than Lower-performing schools, although both groups had high off-task behavior. LPS, surprisingly, exhibited almost twice as much student-centered activity, although both groups were extremely low in this area (see Table 5).

Table 5. Classroom Observations by Higher- and Lower-Performing Schools:
Means and Standard Deviations

I. Teaching Attributes Observation Protocol*	Mean		SD	
High-Performing *(n=6)*	.44		.23	
Low-Performing *(n=9)*	.60		.33	
II. Stallings Observation System Snapshot				
Variables	High Performing *(n=6)*		Low Performing *(n=9)*	
	Mean%	SD	Mean%	SD
1 Student or small group	14.19	13.19	13.46	13.9
Student-Centered activities	2.25	3.73	4.19	5.74
Student Off-Task Behaviors	30.59	20.92	40.8	13.35

*Scales range from 0 (Not Observed) to 4 (Observed Very Often)

Results from teacher (see Table 6) and student (see Table 7) surveys show some differences by school performance. Teachers in both HPS and LPS reported similar high levels of efficacy for teaching in reform-oriented schools. However, differences across groups consistent with the findings from the classroom observations emerged when teachers were asked about the type of instruction they provided in classrooms. Although both groups indicated they implement high levels of standards-based and inquiry practices and lower levels of traditional instruction, teachers in LPS reported higher levels of standards-based and inquiry instruction than teachers in HPS (see Table 6). Students' perceptions of classroom environment (ICEQ instrument) and problem-solving (HDYSP instrument) were high and similar across groups (see Table 7). In general, observations of inquiry practices were much lower compared to teacher and student reports of these practices.

Table 6: Teacher Surveys by Higher- and Lower-Performing Schools: Means and
Standard Deviations

I. Teacher Efficacy*	High-Performing *(n=7)*		Low-Performing *(n=8)*	
	Mean	SD	Mean	SD
GTE	4.20	1.69	4.25	1.55
PTE	5.42	.79	5.43	.67
Total	4.82	1.24	4.84	1.11

II. Inventory for Teaching and Learning** (n=69)				
Standards	5.25	.81	5.40	.89
Traditional	3.91	1.30	3.78	1.46
Inquiry	5.09	.81	5.22	.82

*Scales range from 1 (Strongly Disagree) to 6 (Strongly Agree)
**Scales range from 1 (No Emphasis) to 6 (Very Strong Emphasis)

Table 7. Student Surveys by Higher- and Lower-Performing Schools: Means and
Standard Deviations

	Mean	SD
I. Individualized Classroom Environment Questionnaire*		
High-Performing (n=8)	3.29	.91
Low-Performing (n=9)	3.27	.77
II. How Do You Solve Problems*		
High-Performing (n=8)	4.05	1.18
Low-Performing (n=9)	4.02	1.19

*Scales range from 1 (Strongly Disagree) to 5 (Strongly Agree)

In summary, some variations by achievement level were noted, with LPS *exhibiting* and teachers in LPS *reporting* greater student-centeredness. Several explanations might address this unexpected finding. Since schools were randomly drawn from eligible schools, the possibility of bias should be mitigated. Nevertheless, due to teacher absenteeism, many substitutions had to be made, raising the possibility that teachers who were absent were somehow different than their colleagues who were present. In addition, some schools were unable to be observed due to scheduling problems. Scheduling observations was a major challenge due to scheduling uncertainties and last-minute changes that appear to be common in Qatari schools. In addition, the length of the observation may not have captured classroom teaching and learning to the extent needed, even if there were no problems with the schedule. However, since both LPS and HPS had similar problems with absenteeism and were observed for the same amount of time, these are probably not factors in the differences that emerged. Overall, the fact that multiple data sources support similar findings suggests that the limitations presented above probably were not responsible for the unexpected findings.

Another possibility, and one common in the U.S., is that the assessments may not be consistent with the standards. Teaching to the test, particularly if the test is more oriented to basic skills, often works against student-centered approaches. Traditional direct instruction has been successful in raising standardized test scores (Good & Brophy, 2000). Teachers in HPS report more traditional instruction than teachers in LPS, an indication that this may be a possible factor in the results.

Another explanation is that student and teacher behaviors related to student-centeredness are emerging and have not yet been implemented to the extent that we can see a relationship between achievement and instruction. Previous evaluation of the processes, activities, and outcomes of Qatari reform highlighted challenges, including the ambitious scope of the reform, the short time period for implementation, and the limited capacity for implementation (Brewer et al., 2007, p. 24). The important factor of the language of instruction was not noted, but it may be a significant barrier. Overall, both observations and student outcomes indicate low levels of standards implementation. Additional investigation of barriers confronted in classrooms that might contribute to low levels of implementation, including possibility of linguistic and cultural difficulties, needs to be conducted.

The dispositions for student-centered instruction, or at least awareness of the goals, are prevalent as indicated by teacher and student survey responses. However, teachers and students may not yet have acquired the skills needed to implement student-centered instruction and impact achievement. Change in performance may lag behind changes in teacher and student perceptions and dispositions due to the pressures this approach places on participants (see e.g., Boekarts, 1999; Schunk & Zimmerman, 2008). The high student off-task rate signals problems in general with management of the new and often unfamiliar behaviors related to student-centeredness. That the classes in LPS have higher off-task rates and more evidence of student-centered activities, but with lower achievement, supports the hypothesis of increased pressures due to the approach.

Conclusion

Findings from this study indicate mismatches in two areas: 1) observations of student and teacher behaviors related to implementation of Qatari educational reforms and student and teacher perceptions of the extent to which they are implementing reform; and 2) perceptions of teachers versus students on selected variables related to student-centeredness. Survey results indicate that teachers and students perceive progress in key components related to implementation of student-centered learning environments. Teachers perceive they can impact student outcomes related to reform positively and students recognize skills in problem solving and self-regulation, although they also perceive they have less independence and individualization than reported by teachers. Observations reveal few student and teacher behaviors that constitute student-centered instruction; teachers and students report much higher levels. Student off-task behavior is high, indicating reduced opportunity to learn. Test results exhibiting low levels of standards achievement across schools support the findings from observations. Observation of classroom processes necessary for actualization of student-centered approaches and results from the achievement data provide little evidence that reform has been fully implemented. In addition, some evidence exists from quantitative and qualitative observations that the level of the content is not as challenging as needed to achieve goals set through the standards.

The differences in schools and the mismatch among participant perceptions, observed behaviors and achievement have implications for the implementation of educational reform in general and professional development in particular. First, evaluators of the reform need to go beyond self-report of impact and include observation and performance measures. Another step might include examination of the measures used to gauge progress to insure a match between standards and assessment of standards. Additionally, case studies of schools that are making progress could provide models to assist teachers and administrators in the implementation of the standards, with particular emphasis on behaviors related to student-centered instruction and opportunities for students to engage in tasks at appropriate linguistic and cognitive levels. The lag between recognizing and implementing standards-based instructional activities will require considerable professional development and extensive coaching in the implementation of reform elements as well as the facilitation of second language acquisition. In particular, targeted professional development that goes beyond general aware-ness of appropriate instructional strategies and includes intensive practice and coaching with feedback (Hawley & Valli, 1999) could help close the gap between participant perceptions and observed behaviors and achievement and may be the key to the successful implementation of educational reforms in Qatar and other Gulf States where similar reforms are being trialed.

Acknowledgement

This study was funded by a grant from the Qatar National Research Foundation, National Priorities Research Program, Grant # 13-6-7-1.

References

Bransford, J.D., Brown, A.L., & Cocking, R.R. (1999). *How people learn: Brain, mind, experience, and school.* Washington, DC: National Academy.

Bransford, J., Brown, A., & Cocking, R.R. (2000). *How people learn: Brain, mind, experience, and school* (expanded edition). Washington, DC: National Academy.

Brewer, D., Augustine, C., Zellman, G., Ryan, G., Goldman, C., Stasz, C., & Constant, L. (2007). *Education for a new era: Design and implementation of K-12 Education reform in Qatar.* Santa Monica, CA: Rand.

Boekaerts, M. (1999). Self-regulated learning: Where are we today. *International Journal of Education Research, 31*, 445-457.

Calderhead, J. (2001). International experiences of teaching reform. In V. Richardson (Ed.), *Handbook of Research on Teaching* (pp.777-800). Washington DC: AERA.

Chinn, C.A., & Malhotra, B.A. (2002). Epistemologically authentic inquiry in schools: A theoretical framework for evaluating inquiry tasks. *Science Education 86*(2), 175-218.

Duschl, R., Schweingruber, H., & Shouse, A. (2007), *Taking science to school: Learning and teaching science in grades K-8.* Washington, DC: National Research Council, National Academy.

Education Institute. (2007). *National Professional Standards for Teachers and School Leaders.* Doha, Qatar: State of Qatar Supreme Education Council.

Ellet, C., & Monsaas, J. (2007, April). *Cross-sample validation of a measure of teaching and learning environments in science and mathematics.* Paper presented at the Annual Meeting of the American Educational Research Association, Chicago, IL.

Engle, R., & Conant, F. (2002). Guiding principles for fostering productive disciplinary engagement: Explaining an emergent argument in a community of learners classroom. *Cognition and Instruction, 20*, 399-483.

Eslami, Z.R.,(2005). Raising the pragmatic awareness of language learners. *ELT Journal, 59*(2), 199-208.

Eslami, Z.R., & Fatahi, A. (2008). Teachers' sense of self-efficacy, English proficiency, and instructional strategies: A study of nonnative EFL teachers in Iran. *TESL EJ, 11*(4), 1-19.

Fouts, J., Brown, C., & Theiman, G. (2002). *Classroom instruction in Gates Schools: A baseline report.* Seattle, WA: Bill and Melinda Gates Foundation.

Fraser, B., & Fisher, D. (1983). Development and validation of short forms of some instruments measuring student perceptions of actual and preferred classroom learning environment. *Science Education, 67*, 115-131.

Gibson, S., & Dembo, M.H. (1984). Teacher efficacy: A construct validation. *Journal of Educational Psychology, 76*, 569-582.

Good, T., & Brophy, J. (2000). *Looking in classrooms.* New York: Longman.

Grassi, E., & Barker, H. (2010). *Culturally and linguistically diverse exceptional students.* Thousand Oaks, CA: Sage.

Hawley, W.D. & Valli, L. (1999). The essentials of effective professional development: A new consensus. In L. Darling-Hammond, & G. Sykes (Eds.), *Teaching as the learning profession.* San Francisco: Jossey Bass.

Howard, B., McGee, S., Shia, R., & Hong, N. (2000, April). Metacognitive self-regulation and problem-solving: Expanding the theory base through factor analysis. Paper presented at the Annual Meeting of the American Educational Research Association, New Orleans, LA.

Kamhi-Stein, L., & Mahboob, A. (2006). *TESOL virtual seminar: Teachers' language profeciency in English language teaching.* Alexandria, VA: TESOL.

Kamhi-Stein, L., & Mahboob, A. (2005). *Language proficiency and NNES professionals: Findings from TIRF-funded research initiatives.* Paper presented at the 39th Annual TESOL Convention, March 30-April 2, San Antonio, Texas.

Krashen, S. (1985). *The input hypothesis.* London: Longman.

McInerney, D. (2008). The motivational roles of cultural differences and cultural identity in self-regulated learning. In D. Schunk, & B. Zimmerman (Eds.), *Motivation and self-regulated learning: Theory, research, and applications* (pp. 369-400). Mahwah, NJ: Lawrence Erlbaum.

Motschnig-Pitrik, R., & Holzinger, A. (2002) Student-centered teaching meets new media: Concept and case Study. *Educational Technology & Society, 5*(4), 115-131.

Putnam, R., & Borko, H. (2000). What do new views of knowledge and thinking have to say about research on teacher learning? *Educational Researcher, 29*(1), 4-15.

Rubeck, M.L., & Enochs, L.G. (1991). *A path analytical model of variables that influence science and chemistry teaching self-efficacy and outcome expectancy in middle school science teachers.* Paper presented at the annual meeting of the National Association for Research in Science Teaching, Anaheim, CA.

Sawyer, K. (2006). *Cambridge handbook of the learning sciences.* New York: Cambridge.

Schunk, D., & Zimmerman, B. (2008). *Motivation and self-regulated learning: Theory, research, and applications.* Mahwah, NJ: Lawrence Erlbaum.

Soodak, L.C., & Podell, D.M. (1997). Efficacy and experience: Perceptions of efficacy among preservice and practicing teachers. *Journal of Research and Development in Education, 30*, 214-221.

Spinner, H., & Fraser, B. (2002, April). *Evaluation of an innovative math program in terms of classroom environment, student attitudes, and conceptual development.* Paper presented at the annual meeting of AERA, New Orleans, LA.

Stallings, J. (1975). Implementations and child effects of teaching practices in Follow Through Classrooms. *Monographs of the Society for Research in Child Development, 40.*

Stallings, J. & Giesen, P. (1977). The study of reliability in observational data. *Phi Delta Kappa*, Occasional Paper 19.

Stuart, A. (1997). Student centered learning. *Learning, 26*, 53-56.

Zimmerman, B., & Schunk, D. (2000). *Self-regulated learning and academic achievement.* Mahwah, NJ: Laurence Erlbaum.

IQTIDAR ALI SHAH & NEETA BAPORIKAR

Chapter 13
The Suitability of Imported Curricula for Learning in the Gulf States: An Oman Perspective

Abstract

Curricula play an important role in education as they focus not only on what should be taught but also on who the learners are and their social context. Little attention has been paid to curriculum design and development in the Gulf Cooperation Council's (GCC) countries and especially in Oman. Higher Education Institutions (HEIs) in the GCC countries mostly rely on imported/foreign curricula. This chapter explores the importance of curricula development in the educational process in Oman and the suitability of imported curricula for students' understanding, learning, and professional development. Data were collected from the faculty and students in a number of HEIs who have adopted imported curricula using a questionnaire. Findings indicate an overall dissatisfaction among faculty and Omani students with the imported curricula. The chapter concludes with some recommendations for primary stakeholders in the Omani higher education system.

Introduction

Throughout the world significant steps have been taken by governments to improve the quality of higher education to meet the challenges of globalization. With the number of higher education institutions increasing, the quality of education has become a critical issue worldwide. According to Yamani (2006):

> Education is a universal concern for both developing and developed countries. Developing countries continually aspire to modernize their education systems, and developed countries pursue the adoption of the best education reforms and structure for their systems. In the end, all countries hope to gain from their education systems more effective citizens who can be productive participants, domestically and abroad, in markets and communities. (p. 3)

The higher education sector in the GCC countries has made significant developments during the past decade. There is considerable improvement in the education infrastructure and education opportunities have been increased for male and female students equally. Equity in education has been insured through the regional spread of all types of HEIs with diversified programmes of study and accreditation councils have been established to assure quality across HEIs.

In the last ten years, a large number of foreign universities established their branches/campuses in GCC member states bringing the total of HEIs to 200. In the UAE, branches of foreign universities have been established in the 'Free Education Zones'. In Qatar's 'Education City' a number of American and Australian universities are providing tertiary qualifications in various fields. In addition, most of the local universities have affiliated with foreign universities and signed cooperation agreements with them. Oman and Saudi Arabia have formed partnerships with a number of foreign universities to carry out their joint programmes (UNESCO, 2009). In Oman, 'Knowledge Oasis' was established in Muscat where two HEIs in the field of engineering and management opened their doors as early as 2001. The Middle East College of Information Technology is the first dedicated Information Technology College approved by the Omani Ministry of Higher Education and Waljat College of Applied Sciences offers degree programs of the Birla Institute of Technology (BIT), one of India's premier universities and a full member of the Association of Commonwealth Universities with internationally recognized degrees. The result of these partnerships among foreign and local institutions is a mixed type of tertiary education with most of the HEIs adopting the readily available foreign curricula.

Despite continuous efforts to improve higher education in the GCC region, there is still widespread criticism about the quality of higher education in GCC countries. According to Sabry (2009) there is severe decline in universities and research centers in the region. In the higher education sector, none of the GCC institutions is prominent in producing significant research (Sabry, 2009). Only two Saudi universities, i.e. King Saud University and King Fahd University of Petroleum and Minerals entered into the list of the top 500 universities in the world in 2010 (ARWU, 2010).

There is much debate in the literature about the low quality of higher education in the region and various causes have been identified. Fergany (2000) and Al-Rashdan (2009) mention the rapid expansion of HEIs, the low research activities, the low level of knowledge attainment, the weak analytical and innovative abilities, the unclear goals and the lack of academic freedom as the main causes for the low quality of higher education in the Arab World. HEIs have been criticized for not contributing much to the cultural and intellectual activities in the GCC and their role is seen as limited to providing instruction and granting academic certificates (Al Eisa, 2010). According to the World Bank report, across all levels of education the main classroom activities are copying from the blackboard, writing, and listening to the teachers. Group work, creative thinking, and proactive learning are rare (World Bank, 2008). Similarly, some national reports have identified the weakness of educational curricula and their unsuitability in terms of course duration. Moreover, curricula had not been upgraded to match scientific and technical progress (UNESCO, 2009).

Given the widespread adoption of foreign curricula in HEIs, the question is whether the foreign curricula meet the local market needs, students' learning abilities and required skills for employment. This chapter provides a close look at one of the GCC states, i.e. the Sultanate of Oman, and discusses the issue of suitability of foreign curricula for the local students.

Background

Oman has a fast growing and diverse higher education sector consisting of sixty-two HEIs (twenty-four private and thirty-eight public) offering various programmes of study. Of the sixty-two HEIs, six are universities (one public and five private), two are university colleges and fifty-four are colleges (Al Shmeli, 2009). HEIs are owned and governed by a variety of entities, including the Ministry of Higher Education, the Ministry of Man Power, the Ministry of Defense, the Ministry of Health, the Ministry of Commerce and Industry, other governmental entities, and private owners (OAC, 2006).

The total number of students in these institutions was approximately 80,000 in 2009: 45,337 students were enrolled in 38 government HEIs and 33,521 students in 24 private HEIs. About 12,000 Omani students are currently studying abroad. For the academic year 2007-08, the percentage of enrollment in science majors (engineering, information technology, health, natural sciences, physics, agricultural, architecture, and construction) accounted for 45.5% of the overall enrollment; humanities 35.4%; and commerce and economics constituted 19.1% (Al Shmeli, 2009).

Major challenges to higher education in Oman are: imported language (English as the medium of instruction), foreign faculty, and curricula developed overseas. In recent years, some practical steps have been taken to address these problems, such as recruiting native speakers of English to help Omani students improve their English language skills, and reducing overreliance on imported faculty for content areas through Omanization. However, there has been no focused work on creating a policy for locally produced curricula which will meet the regional needs in terms of learning, culture and human resource development.

This chapter discusses the importance of curriculum development in the educational process and explores student and faculty satisfaction with imported curricula adopted in most of the HEIs in Oman. More specific objectives are:

- To find out the level of students' understanding and learning from foreign curricula.
- To determine the extent to which foreign curricula are suitable to develop professionals according to the local market requirements.
- To identify the challenges faced by faculty using imported curricula.

Curriculum Development Framework

Institutions can be places where students articulate a preferred social future and exercise informed judgment with others toward that goal. The fundamental purpose of curriculum development is to ensure that students receive integrated, coherent learning experiences that contribute towards their personal, academic, and professional learning and development (IBE, 2003). Murdoch and Hornsby (1997) emphasized an integrated curriculum approach which provides students a more holistic view of the content. This approach is also called the 'understanding-driven' approach because it strengthens students' understanding of concepts as they are explored through different topics (Murdoch & Hornsby, 1997). Good curricula are sensitive to the learner background and relevant to the needs of their society (World Bank, 2009). The development and review of curricula should take into account national education policies and the socio-economic environment within which graduates will work.

Curriculum development and implementation is a process in which two stakeholders, students and teachers interact to efficiently transfer knowledge and skills to the students. In the GCC, the curriculum is considered as a package of educational materials purchased from American, British or Australian universities for local use. By purchasing foreign curricula GCC countries believe that they adopt quality education of international standards ignoring to a large extent the characteristics and abilities of their students and the specific requirements of their local market. The higher education system aims to prepare individuals who are capable of learning and of effectively participating in human development rather than just receiving education. Cornbleth (1990) and Jeffs and Smith (1990, 1999) have argued that curriculum theory and practice only makes sense when it considered alongside notions like class, teacher, course and lesson. It is not a concept that stands on its own. According to the policy on curriculum, developed by Rhodes University, South Africa (1998), the term 'curriculum' is more than a list of subjects, topics and text included in a course of study. It incorporates skills, the manner of teaching and assessment, the philosophical outlook of the teacher and who the learners are. Curriculum is the planned process, the actual implementation of the teaching, and the students' 'experiences' of the learning process.

Though for the moment academic faculty have to operate within a policy environment that prizes the productive and technical, the discourse has become so totalizing that forms of education that do not have an imported curriculum basis are marginalised in the GCC region. The temptation then is always there to join the bandwagon rather than work out suitable alternative options which make sense in terms of the processes and commitments involved. The analysis presented in this chapter intends to provide an incentive for change.

However, there is no guarantee that higher education will move in a more edifying direction.

Globalization impacts every aspect of society. The higher education sector may be one of the most affected by global trends, and economics and business degree courses seem particularly influenced by them (Marcelo, 2007). In recent years, new types of curricula (i.e. internationalized curricula, joint venture curricula and imported curricula) have been developed and adopted by HEIs around the world. Internationalization of the curricula means to introduce an international, intercultural, or global dimension into course content and materials and into teaching and learning methods (AUCC, 2006, 2009). The main rationale for the internationalization of curricula is to prepare students with the international knowledge, perspective and skills needed to excel in an increasingly globalized economy and society. Joint venture curricula are curricula designed by two or more institutions jointly keeping in view their local and international requirements. Internationalized curricula and joint curricula received much attention in developed countries and in some developing countries as well. Finally, imported curricula, also called foreign curricula, are exported to countries where the level of education is comparatively low. Imported curricula are used in most of the Arab countries.

Initially the Gulf universities relied on imported teaching materials from Egypt, Syria, and Lebanon. These contained examples and information not entirely compatible with the needs of Gulf higher education (Davidson, 2009). These days, HEI in the Gulf countries have affiliations with well-known universities in the USA, Britain and Australia for adopting their curricula. According to Rice (2006) universities in the GCC region that are establishing new graduate programmes wish to attract students by showing that their curriculum leads to a degree that is comparable to that of a well-known Tier 1 university (Tier 1 refers to high-performing, nationally competitive research universities) such as Harvard, Stanford, Massachusetts Institute of Technology, George Washington University, or Oxford University. Thus, HEIs in the GCC region use imported curricula as a sign of high quality in tertiary education. The HEIs attract students under the assumption that they are using the curricula of advanced countries and their education standards are equal to that in advanced countries of the world. However, curriculum is the interaction of teachers and students and both have high stakes in its development and design as well as certain expectations in its implementation. The extent to which students' and teachers' needs and expectations are met, is an important indicator of high-quality curricula. According to Al-Rashdan (2009), the educational curricula in the Arab universities are mostly theoretical and philosophical which created a low harmony between the students' learned skills and the needs and problems of society.

In Oman, too, the adoption of foreign curricula is considered a mark of quality and it is used to attract students into tertiary degree programmes. However, the suitability of foreign curricula for student understanding and learning has always remained an issue of serious concern. To address this issue, most of the HEIs in Oman have adopted a one-year Foundation Programme which aims to adequately prepare students' language skills (English), basic mathematics/ science skills, and IT skills for studying the foreign curricula. However, to date there has been no study conducted to analyse the suitability of foreign curricula for the Omani students. The study described in this chapter is an attempt to fill this gap.

The Study

To assess the suitability of foreign curricula in Oman, this study looked at the faculty and students of the various HEIs who have adopted imported curricula for economics and management courses, and the course outlines and expected learning outcomes of these programmes. Figure 1 shows the framework adopted for the data collection in an effort to tease out the different facets of curricula satisfaction and measure faculty and students' perceptions.

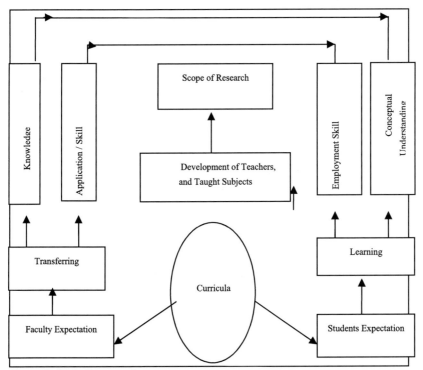

Figure 1: Study Framework

Using the above framework as a guide, data were collected using two questionnaires (one for faculty and one for students) employing a 5-point Likert scale. The questionnaires sought to obtain the teachers' and students' views on the suitability of the curricula in terms of students' understanding, learning, skill development, flexibility, market need, relevancy to culture, enhancement of teacher knowledge and scope for research. Using the Statistical Package for Social Sciences software (SPSS), descriptive statistics were generated.

Results

Faculty Perceptions

Data were collected from 15 faculty members teaching business and economics courses in Colleges of Applied Sciences, Ministry of Higher Education, Oman. Details of their teaching experience including teaching experience in GCC countries along with their qualifications are given in Table 1 below.

Table 1: Faculty Experience and Qualifications *(n=15)*

Experience in GCC (in years)	Frequency	Percentage
1-3	7	46.7%
4-7	7	46.7%
8-12	1	6.7%
Total	15	100%
Total Experiences (in years)	Frequency	Percentage
1-3	2	13.3%
4-7	3	20.0%
8-12	4	26.7%
13-16	3	20.0%
17-20	3	20.0%
Total	15	100%
Qualification	Frequency	Percentage
Master	9	60.0%
PhD	6	40.0%
Total	15	100%

The participating teachers were well-qualified with all of them having a Master's degree and even 40% of them holding a doctorate. The majority of them had extensive teaching experience (86.7% had taught for 4 years of more), and more than half of them had taught in the GCC region for 4 years or more. With regards to the teachers' perceptions of imported curricula adopted by their institution in Oman, the results are summarized in Table 2 below.

Table 2: Faculty Satisfaction from Imported Curricula *(n=15)*

Questionnaire item	Mean*	Standard Deviation
According to international standard	3.33	1.05
Suitable for teacher knowledge development	3.07	1.03
Scope for conducting research	2.73	1.10
According to country needs	2.53	0.99
According to Job Market	2.40	0.91
Easy for teaching	2.33	1.05
Relevant to working life	2.27	1.03
Suitable to develop students' skills	2.20	0.77
Relevant to socio-cultural context	1.93	0.96
Flexible (teacher can change)	1.87	0.83
According to local level	1.80	0.77
Easy for student understanding	1.53	0.64
Easy for student learning	1.50	0.66
Overall Satisfaction	2.26	0.90

*Scale: 1= Strongly Disagree, 2=Disagree, 3=Neither Agree nor Disagree, 4= Agree, 5=Strongly Agree

Faculty members of HEIs in Oman slightly agreed that the curriculum in their respective institution is of international standard (Mean 3.33, SD 1.05) and suitable to enhance teacher knowledge (Mean 3.07, SD 1.03). They moderately disagreed with six facets of curricula satisfaction: having scope for faculty research (Mean 2.73, SD 1.10), country needs (Mean 2.53, SD 0.99), job market (Mean 2.40, SD 0.91), easy for teaching (Mean 2.33, SD 1.05), relevant to working life (Mean 2.27, SD 1.03), and suitable to develop students' skills (Mean 2.20, SD 0.77). The participants showed disagreement with regards to the imported curricula being relevant to the socio-cultural context (Mean 1.93, SD 0.96), flexible (Mean 1.87, SD 0.83), or according to local level (Mean 1.80, SD 0.77). Faculty members also thought the imported curricula are not easy for students' understanding (Mean 1.53, SD 0.64) or for student learning (Mean 1.50, SD 0.66). The overall satisfaction level for faculty was 2.26, which shows moderate dissatisfaction.

Students' Perceptions

Data from 132 students of business and economics were collected from Colleges of Applied Sciences in Oman. 11.4% of the students were in Semester 2, 27.3% were in Semester 4, 26.5% were in Semester 6, 1.5% in Semester 7 and 33.3% in the last semester of their study programme. With regards to their GPA, 2.3% students had a CGPA of 2.00 or less, 55.3% students had a CGPA between 2.0-3.0, 34.1% students had a CGPA of 3.0-3.5 and 8.3% students had a CGPA of 3.5-4.0. Students' perceptions regarding imported curricula of their courses of business and economics are summarised in Table 3 below.

Table 3: Students' Satisfaction with Imported Curricula *(n=132)*

Questionnaire Item	Mean*	Standard Deviation
According to country needs	3.52	0.98
According to Job Market	3.44	0.98
According to local level	2.47	0.99
Relevant to socio-cultural context	2.45	1.06
Easy for students' understanding	2.39	0.91
Easy for student learning	2.27	0.92
Suitable for skills development	2.20	1.02
Relevant to working life	2.01	0.97
Overall Satisfaction	2.50	0.97

*Scale: 1= Strongly Disagree, 2=Disagree, 3=Neither Agree nor Disagree, 4= Agree, 5=Strongly Agree

The results show that students of various HEIs in Oman slightly agreed that the curricula in their respective HEIs are according to the needs of their country (mean 3.52, SD 0.98), and the job market (Mean 3.44, SD 0.98). Students moderately disagreed with five facets of curricula satisfaction: according to local student level (Mean 2.47, SD 0.99), relevant to socio-cultural context (Mean 2.45, SD 1.06), easy to understand (Mean 2.39, SD 0.91), easy to learn (Mean 2.27, SD 0.92), and suitable for skills development (Mean 2.20, SD 1.02). Furthermore, students disagreed that the curricula are relevant to their working life (Mean 2.01, SD 0.97). The overall student satisfaction was 2.50, which was slightly higher than the teachers' satisfaction level but still showed that even students were dissatisfied with the imported curricula.

Discussion

Curricula are in the heart of the teaching and learning process. Quality education means achieving learning objectives and requires more than recruiting qualified teachers and developing infrastructure. Without looking into the appropriateness of curricula to students' level, a high standard of education cannot be achieved. Curricula need to fulfill the expectations of both the faculty and the students. Good curricula also include scope for research and subject development. Looking at the results from this perspective, it is apparent that the imported curricula adopted in Oman are unable to successfully fulfill their objectives as both the faculty and students are dissatisfied the suitability of these curricula for the students' ability level, their relevance to students' future working life and their socio-cultural context, how easy they are to understand and learn, and their suitability for students' skill development. This is mainly due to the fact that these imported curricula have been developed to meet international standards rather than the needs of local students and their level of ability. Consequently, teaching these curricula is a challenge for faculty who find themselves unable to fully transfer skills and knowledge to learners who are weak.

Learners at all levels of education have their own interests and these can be used as an impetus for making the curricula more effective and relevant leading to enjoyable learning. The notion of relevance has a different meaning for each learner, depending upon perceived utility. Relevance is about deep connections between the student, his/her emerging interest in a given area and the complex learning challenges that define that area. This relevance involves a balance between student interests and the curriculum (Bloom, 1985).

In addition, skills such as literacy, numeracy, innovative problem solving and self-development, may not be possible through an imported curriculum as the ability to learn and retain knowledge is based on the schooling system which is country specific. Thus, such skills need to be deliberately grounded in the student's own areas of interests as the relationship between theory and practice is interdependent in real life.

According to Caplan students are not products of an institution. The only thing an institution can claim as a product is the learning environment (cited in Washor, 2008). In order to create a better learning environment, the GCC countries, including Oman, need to focus on the suitability of the curricula adopted in their higher institutions. Merely importing curricula from well-known foreign institutions is not the right approach as the imported curricula may at the most not be the right fit and at the worst be irrelevant. It is worth ensuring that the curriculum is relevant to the students' needs as this facilitates the creation of learning opportunities. It also ensures better and deeper student engagement, and it challenges learners intellectually and personally within their areas of interest and beyond.

In order for Oman to position itself competitively in the global economy, it needs to create new opportunities for better education based on curricula that allow individuals to move from being teacher dependent to being self-directed and hence better prepared for a globalised world.

Conclusion

In the 21st Century individual learning in all contexts is likely to assume more importance than teaching and learning in formal settings. Thus the concept of curriculum, its suitability and relevance is also likely to change dramatically. Elliott (1998) talks of a curriculum above and beyond school boundaries and Young (1998) presents the idea of a 'connective curriculum' to promote connections in all types of knowledge from formal and informal contexts.

In the context of modern global economic competition nations around the world are experimenting with different strategies to make their educational systems relevant to the economic needs of their countries. Oman and the rest of the GCC States have made leaps of progress in their education systems, however, a gap still exists in terms of curriculum development, and the GCC countries need to work harder and realize that having a suitable and relevant curriculum that serves the educational needs of their Arab students involves vast technical and contextual knowledge.

It is our recommendation that under the aegis of the Ministry of Higher Education, Oman must develop suitable, uniform, and comprehensive curricula to meet the local needs in terms of culture, learning, and understanding, skills development and manpower requirements. The higher education sector in Oman is now mature enough and has the requisite expertise, national and international, to design an effective curriculum.

References

ARWU. (2010). 2010 Academic Ranking of World Universities. The Center for World-Class Universities of Shanghai Jiao Tong

University, China. Retrieved August 15, 2010, from: http://www.arwu.org/

AUCC. (2006). Internationalization of Curriculum, Association of Universities and Colleges of Canada.

AUCC. (2009, March). *Internationalization of the Curriculum: A Practical Guide to Support Canadian Universities' efforts.* Association of Universities and Colleges of Canada. Retrieved August 15, 2010, form: www.aucc.ca/_pdf/english/publications/curriculum-primer_e.pdf

Al Shmeli, H. (2009). Higher education in the Sultanate of Oman: Planning in context of globalization. IIEP/SEM 293/10 Policy Forum, 2-3 July, 2009. Retrieved August 15, 2010, from: www.iiep.unesco.org/fileadmin/user/Pol/Alshmeli_Oman.pdf

Al-Eisa, A. (2010, February 17). The realities of higher education in the Gulf. Retrieved August 15, 2010, from the Middle East Online database.

Al-Rashdan, A.F.A. (2009). Higher education in the Arab World: Hopes and challenge. *Arab Insight, 2*(6), 77-90.

Bloom, B. (1985). *Developing talent in young people.* New York: Ballantine Books.

Cornbleth, C. (1990). *Curriculum in context.* Basingstoke: Falmer Press.

Davidson, C.M. (2009). Higher education in the Gulf States: Challenges and trends. Presidential Inauguration, Faculty Symposium, May 3, 2009, American University of Beirut.

Elliott, J. (1998). *The curriculum experiment: Meeting the challenges of social science.* Buckingham, Philadelphia: Open University Press.

Elliot W. (2008). Relevance and the quest for rigorous student learning. *Curriculum Leadership: An Electronic Journal for Leaders in Education, 6*(8).

Fergany, N. (2000). Arab higher education and development: An overview. Almishkat Centre for Research. Retrieved August 15, 2010, from: www.ties-project.eu/public/Arab%20HE%20and%20development.pdf

Jeffs, T., & Smith, M. (1990). *Using informal education: An alternative to casework, teaching and control?* Milton Keynes: Open University Press.

Jeffs, T.J., & Smith, M.K. (1999). *Informal education: Conversation, democracy and learning.* Ticknall: Education Now.

IBE (2003). Challenges of curriculum development in the XXI century, Perspectives from Belarus, Moldova, Russia and Ukraine. Final Report of Regional Workshop held in Minsk, Belarus, 22-23 June 2003. International Bureau of Education, National Institute of Education, Belarus. Ministry of Education.

Murdoch, K., & Hornsby, D. (1997). *Planning curriculum connections: Whole-school planning for integrated curriculum.* Armadale, Australia: Eleanor Curtain Publishing.

Marcelo, R. (2007). The effects of globalization on economics and business curriculum contents in Argentina. Paper Presented at the annual meeting of the International Studies Association 48th Annual Convention, Hilton Chicago, CHICAGO, IL, USA.

OAC. (2006). *Plan for an Omani higher education quality management system (The Quality Plan).* Oman: Oman Accreditation Council.

Rice, D.V. (2006). Curriculum joint ventures and their implication for graduate programmes in the GCC. Paper presented at the Symposium for Graduates Studies in the Universities of GCC Countries, November 26-27, King Faisal University, Saudi Arabia.

Rhodes University (1998). Policy on curriculum development and review. Rhodes University, South Africa. Retrieved August 15, 2010, from https://www.ru.ac.za/documents/Academic% 20Planning/curriculumdevelopment.pdf

Sabry, M. (2009). Funding policy and higher education in Arab countries, *Comparative & International Higher Education 1,* 11-12.

UNESCO. (2009, June 29). *A decade of higher education in the Arab States: Achievements and challenges (Regional Report).* Arab Regional Conference on Higher Education, Cairo May 31, June

1-2, 2009, UNESCO Regional Bureau for Education in the Arab States, Beirut. Retrieved August 15, 2010, from www.educationdev.net/educationdev/Docs/arab_ higher_education_report.pdf

World Bank. (2008). *The road not travelled: Education reform in the Middle East and North Africa.* Washington DC: The World Bank.

World Bank. (2009). *The towers of learning performance, peril and promise of higher education in Sri Lanka.* The World Bank, Human Development Unit, South Asia. Retrieved August 15, 2010, from: http://siteresources.worldbank.org/SOUTHASIAEXT/Resources /Publications/TOLreportfinal. pdf

Young, M.F.D. (1998). *The curriculum of the future.* London: Falmer Press.

Yamani, S. (2006). Toward a national education development paradigm in the Arab World: A comparative study of Saudi Arabia and Qatar. *The Fletcher School Online Journal for issues related to Southwest Asia and Islamic Civilization,* Spring 2006. Retrieved August 15, 2010, from fletcher.tufts.edu/al_nakhlah/archives/spring2006/yamani.pdf

MARY ELLIS, ANITHA DEVI PILLAI, & ALI AL RABA'I

Chapter 14
Bilingual Academic Discourse Skills: A Pre-service Teacher Training Program in Bahrain

Abstract

Building on the curricular development work done by the National Institute of Education (NIE) of the Nanyang Technological University in Singapore during a multi-year consultation with the Ministry of Education of Bahrain, the international faculty members of the Bahrain Teachers' College (BTC) are now adapting the program to reflect the needs of pre-service teachers in Bahrain. The *English for Educators* module (Ellis & Pillai, 2009a) was developed to equip pre-service teachers with academic reading, writing and oral skills. The learning needs of these pre-service teachers were best met when BTC introduced bilingual team-teaching, i.e. Arabic and English language teachers co-teaching the module. Pre-service teachers and instructors were able to instruct and participate in a bilingual context providing pre-service teachers with the necessary skills to bridge their content and pedagogical knowledge between the two languages. It was also observed that when both Arabic and English language teachers were in the same classroom, there was an increase in the level of participation from pre-service teachers. Both staff and pre-service teachers benefited from the mutual cross-cultural exchange of pedagogy and teaching practices. This chapter provides an overview of the module and its implementation. From a broader perspective, this chapter will also provide recommendations for curriculum planners developing English language course materials for pre-service teacher training in other Gulf States.

Introduction

The use of English in educational institutions has become increasingly important in the Kingdom of Bahrain, a member of the Gulf Cooperation Council (GCC), which is located in the Arabian Gulf. The GCC, which consists of six states (Bahrain, Kuwait, Oman, Qatar, Saudi Arabia and the United Arab Emirates) is one of the fastest-growing markets in the world and has become progressively more significant to the global economy. The Bahrain Economic Development Board (Al-Alawi, Al-Kaabi, Al-Kahleefa, & Rashdan, 2009) identified education in Bahrain as important for the country's economy and prompted the need for educational reform. This provided impetus for the government of Bahrain to improve educational opportunities and adopt new methodologies to ensure high quality education programs. In November 2007, the Quality Assurance Authority was established to carry out the initiatives of the Bahrain Economic Development Board in the academic sector, which included the University of Bahrain (UoB) Board (Al-Alawi, Al-Kaabi, Al-Kahleefa, & Rashdan, 2009).

Current Educational Reforms in Bahrain

As the first country in the Gulf region to provide publicly-funded education for both sexes, Bahrain is considered a leader in educational reform. Bahrainis have a literacy rate of 85% which is one of the highest in the region (Bahrain Economic Development

Board, 2008a). Bahrain's *Economic Vision 2030* has been influential in current educational reforms. Driving the success of the vision is an education system which is effective and relevant to the current global labor market (Baby, 2008). Providing a link between education and training to the workforce is the focal point of this initiative. Vocational learning in secondary education curriculum has been emphasized, thus enabling students to have greater career options in terms of employment or future study (Economic Development Board, 2008b). Innovative practices at the Bahrain Teacher's College, such as the teaching of science and business courses primarily in English, may soon be applied in government schools.

University of Bahrain

The UoB was formed in 1968 through a merger of the Gulf Polytechnic and the University College of Bahrain. It has colleges in the arts, business, education, engineering, information technology, law, science and applied studies. It is the only public university in Bahrain and its graduates are sought after in the Bahrain employment market (Al-Alawi, Al-Kaabi, Rashdan, & AL-Kahleefa, 2009).

Previously, students were admitted to UoB based solely on their high-school grade point average (GPA). A newly instituted policy by the UoB requires high school graduates to pass a university entry exam in mathematics, English and Arabic. These test scores combined with a high school GPA are used to obtain entry to the various programs offered at UoB. Thus, UoB recognizes the importance of both Arabic and English as mediums of instruction and places emphasis on both throughout its curriculum.

UoB's unique emphasis on bilingual (Arabic-English) lesson delivery was a crucial tenet in their newly established Teachers' College (Al-Alawi, Al-Kaabi, Rashdan, & AL-Kahleefa, 2009). The Bahrain Teachers' College (BTC) was set up in 2008 after a multi-year consultation with the National Institute of Education (NIE) of Nanyang Technological University in Singapore. NIE, the sole teacher training institute in Singapore, was chosen for its expertise in the area of teacher education and since 2007 the institute has been engaged with the Bahrain Ministry of Education in teacher recruitment, performance assessment, establishment of the teachers' training college and in the enhancement of a professional development framework (Lek, 2009). The BTC was established with the following focus:

> ...to develop our most important educational resources, our teachers, by improving their recruitment and training, enhancing the management of their performance, improving their image in society, and increasing the attractiveness of careers in teaching. (UoB-BTC, 2009)

BTC specifically aims to produce teachers who demonstrate core personal and professional knowledge, skills and values appropriate for appointment within the teaching cadre of the Ministry of Education in the Kingdom of Bahrain. Broad professional and personal competencies include skills necessary to operate effectively in both Arabic and English as well as leadership and teamwork skills. The Bachelor of Education and Postgraduate Diploma in Education programs comprise five strands: Education Studies, Curriculum Content Studies, Curriculum Studies, Educational Communication and Professional Practice.

The BTC embraces an approach to teacher education that is learner-centered at every level; primary, elementary, intermediate and post secondary. The BTC encourages pre-service teachers preparing to teach in the K-12 system to explore and engage theoretical knowledge, practical knowledge, formal and informal learning, and establish innovative pedagogy and best practice. Bilingualism in Arabic and English is emphasized, particularly since much leading research in teacher preparation is done in English and is not available in Arabic. Additionally, developing research programs and establishing global connections will frequently necessitate working in English (UoB-BTC, 2009).

This chapter provides an overview of the implementation of a bilingual module, *English for Educators*, at UoB-BTC and makes recommendations for curriculum planners in other pre-service programs across the GCC region.

Background

Throughout Asia and the Middle East, there is an emphasis on the development of knowledge-based economies. A combination of global literacy, strong foundations in mathematics and science, ability to create knowledge and an environment supportive of innovation are seen as essential for a knowledge-based economy (Teo, 1999). Two important components of global literacy include proficiency in English and information technology literacy. In this section, each of these two essential components is discussed in an effort to provide a rationale for the structure of the module, which is reviewed in the following section.

One of the challenges of the 21st century learning environment is providing teachers with the ability to process and use information effectively. Recent studies strongly advocate information literacy instruction in pre-service teacher education (Mokhtar & Majid, 2006; Choy, Wong, & Gao, 2008; Ozdemir, Akbas, & Cakir, 2009). Advances in the application of information technology have allowed access to a vast amount of resources which can result in confusion and uncertainty for users (Kuhlthau, 2004). Thus, 'the ability to critically seek, evaluate and use information and tools for information seeking is a competence that is given increasing importance in contemporary western society' (Limberg & Sundin, 2006, p. 2).

Studies on information literacy in the Arab world (for example, Al-Saleh, 2004; Al-Suqri, 2007) have emphasized the need for more research in the area. Findings from Al-Saleh's study of 502 graduate students at three Saudi universities indicated that one of the main obstacles to utilizing information was insufficient instruction for using the library's electronic sources. English language proficiency was also a barrier in the use of electronic databases (Al-Saleh, 2004). In Al-Suqri's (2007) study the information needs and information-seeking behavior of social science scholars at Sultan Qaboos University in Oman were investigated. Findings were similar to the results from Al-Saleh's (2004) study: lack of adequate training in the use of library resources and language/cultural barriers. As Shamo (2001) noted there may be cultural differences in the approach to information-seeking, 'for example, in the Arab world, the values and beliefs are different. Access for information and the use of the Internet are perceived differently than the countries in the Western world' (p. 124). Apart from cultural barriers, English language proficiency also appears to be a major obstacle to developing information literacy. In their discussion of the importance of English and technology, McCawley and Zurstrassen (2002) noted that 'large populations require a special type of English for the Internet where the content is 80% English at present' (p. 1). Shoham and Mizrachi (2001), in their study of library anxiety among Israeli undergraduate pre-service teachers, stress the importance of English in today's academic community:

> Most databases are in English, the language of the Internet is English, and most scientific information is in English. All of this has the potential to harm scholastic achievement of students whose native language is not English. (p. 311)

Given the central role of information literacy to education, Moore (2002) reports that there is pressure to adequately prepare students for the vast amount of information available as a result of technology:

> Such information retrieved typically reflects only the language, culture and lifestyle of creators and as a consequence, information literacy gains a high profile as central to education. However, it is recognized that even in the most technically advanced countries, efforts to prepare students for the information age have been only partially successful. (p. 2)

Information literacy is most optimally taught in close relationship with content or subject areas. It is not an end to itself, but a means to an end. Teaching methodologies and learning approaches which are more student-centered such as inquiry, problem and project-based learning are instrumental in the acquisition of information literacy competencies.

Apart from information literacy, the development of English proficiency was another important tenet in the conception and implementation of the *English for Educators* module. Academic writing modules in universities have traditionally been developed based on research in the field of English for Academic Purposes (EAP). Research in this field focuses on academic discourse, on the teaching of that discourse, and informs instructors on how pre-service teachers can be taught to gain control over linguistic and social constraints in their writing.

Higher institutions in the GCC region, including Bahrain, require their pre-service teachers to take an EAP module in the course of their study (Malcolm, 2003). EAP modules traditionally emphasize information literacy, academic writing and oral presentation skills required by university pre-service teachers.

Recently, there has been a shift within the EAP field away from studying formal features of genres to considering socio-contextual aspects of genres (Pillai, 2010). This means that the same text may serve one (or multiple) purpose(s) for the writer and yet another (or others) for the reader. This makes the notion of genre and the purpose of texts and the components of texts dynamic, i.e. the function of a genre changes and evolves according to the needs of writers and readers. Being dynamic also makes the genre less prototypical as it is dependent on the writer's own understanding of the genre itself and of the reader's expectations.

Based on this view that genres are dynamic, a pedagogical approach to teaching academic writing in the university was developed by North American New Rhetoricians. New Rhetoric studies are primarily associated with composition studies whose main audience consists of mother tongue pre-service teachers. Generally speaking, mother tongue pre-service teachers have a stronger sense of their own discourse community than do second language pre-service teachers. More specifically, New Rhetoricians (Miller, 1994; Berkenkotter & Huckin, 1995) have studied how to assist university pre-service teachers in understanding the social functions and the contexts of genres (Hyon, 1996). Pre-service teachers are socialized into each genre through a series of activities aiming to facilitate the acquisition of appropriate academic writing discourse features.

Such pedagogical principles and theory deriving from research studies in the development of information literacy and academic English skills in undergraduate pre-service teachers were the basis for the structure of the *English for Educators* module described in the following section.

English for Educators Module at Bahrain Teachers' College

The 15-week *English for Educators* (Ellis & Pillai, 2009a) module was designed to equip pre-service teachers with various strategies to read educational expository texts, and to help them develop their academic oral and written skills in order to communicate competently and confidently in English in educational settings. The module integrates information literacy skills throughout the various units, with particular emphasis on evaluation, organization and synthesis of information, culminating in the final group project. Emphasis is on analytical reading skills with practice in vocabulary development. Academic writing is taught as a process, and awareness of information literacy is developed with an emphasis on database searching and avoiding plagiarism. Oral presentation skills are practised, and teamwork is emphasized in a final group research project which synthesizes skills learned throughout the course. The module is learner-centered, encouraging active student participation.

The activities in the module were developed to encourage group work and peer-coaching as Bahraini pre-service teachers had responded favourably to teaching methods that encouraged problem-based learning (Kassab, Abu-Hijleh, A-Shboul, & Hamdy, 2005) and collaborative fieldwork (Al-Ahemd, 2000). Alumrun (2008) recommended that Bahraini pre-service teachers should be encouraged to take an active role in processing information. Previous research conducted in the region indicated that Arab pre-service teachers in Jordan reported that they needed library research, knowledge about how to conduct and write research projects involving secondary data and academic oral presentation skills in order to be effective teachers in the future (Al-Rabai, 2004). The module was then designed to facilitate the learning of academic writing skills and oral presentation conventions through a group-based research project that required pre-service teachers to carry out a small scale research study in Bahraini classrooms and to present the findings at the end of the course.

As Bahraini pre-service teachers had been observed to prefer and excel in problem-based learning and group-based learning situations, the primary task in the module was designed to engage students in a collaborative learning environment. Project-based learning empowers pre-service teachers by providing sufficient activities with pre-defined goals and procedures for both individual learners and small groups (Ellis & Pillai, 2009b). The group task included in the module requires pre-service teachers to design a project-based assignment for any level in the primary/secondary school classroom and evaluate its effectiveness. In doing so they are required to show an understanding of project-based learning principles, describe the proposed project, describe how they carried out the project, and evaluate the lesson/activities. Pre-service teachers first write a report of about 2500-3000 words which also provides them with an opportunity to show their understanding of the local schools. After submitting their reports, they also give an oral presentation as a team. Students are assessed on the clarity and fluency of their presentation, their confidence in delivery, their ability to engage the audience and to respond to questions about the project.

Both the written and oral components require a joint process of negotiation and input from all the pre-service teachers in the team. Lecturers facilitate the learning of research skills and academic conventions throughout the semester through tutorials that incorporate student-centred activities. Such activities encourage pre-service teachers to become self-directed learners.

The task assigned in the module *English for Educators* for Bahrain Teacher's College was developed from a socially oriented EAP perspective with an additional focus of equipping pre-service teachers with information literacy skills. The task was designed to facilitate future academic writing classes particularly since graduate pre-service teachers from the Middle East were reported facing problems in understanding and producing discourse organizational structures and formal academic language in the EAP classrooms (Aljamhoor, 1996). Other studies have also found research projects to be the most common writing tasks in the undergraduate (Hale, Taylor, Bridgeman, Carson, Kroll, & Kantor, 1996) and graduate curriculum (Cooper & Bikowski, 2007).

Bilingual Delivery of the English for Educators Module

After the first cohort graduated from BTC, the Ministry of Education requested that the pre-service teachers' Arabic needed more reinforcement. As previously stated, the languages of instruction, study and research at the BTC are Arabic and English. As a result, BTC pre-service teachers and faculty members need to be able to instruct and participate in a bilingual context (BTC, 2009). It was this need for bilingual proficiency which resulted in changing the *English for Educators* module (which was originally designed to be taught only in English) so that it can be taught bilingually.

In October 2009, a capacity-building team from NIE Singapore came to BTC to evaluate the programs that had been put in place and to consult with BTC staff on any needed changes. In discussion with the English and Arabic language instructors, it was decided that team teaching between the *English for Educators* and *Arabic for Educators* modules be implemented. The two groups would share their expertise and have a cross-cultural exchange benefiting both staff and pre-service teachers. Logistics would be implemented so that teaching load and assessment could be shared. It was hoped that this arrangement could help improve oral and written communication in both Arabic and English for all pre-service teachers. This plan was implemented in January 2010 and feedback on the effectiveness of the module was elicited from course coordinators and teachers at department meetings.

The following assessment of the new bilingual module was given by Dr. Al Raba'i, Head of the Languages Academic Group (English, Arabic and Islamic Studies):

> We had a situation where English education is a need. Our problem arose from the fact that teacher candidates' levels varied within the same group and most of them would need clarification and guidance in Arabic. Most of our teachers, however, were not bilingual (at least Arabic was not one of their languages). As a head of the department, I had to come up with a solution. My department also offers a course in *Arabic for Educators* which focuses exactly on the same issues offered in *English for Educators*. Besides, all my Arabic language teachers know some English. Hence, I came up with the idea that all the *English for Educators* modules are co-taught (one teacher Arabic and one English. (Al Raba'i, personal communication, January 9, 2010)

Dr. Al Raba'i further discussed the benefits of the merger: pre-service teachers learned to bridge their content and pedagogical knowledge between the two languages; the presence of both Arabic and English language teachers increased class participation; and staff benefited from a cross-cultural exchange of pedagogy and teaching practices. The teaching methods and strategies in the Arabic and English language classrooms are different. Yet, the instructors were able to identify similarities and address the differences effectively. An unexpected outcome of this bilingual module was that the English instructors gained an understanding of students' first language interference in their writing. While the bilingual delivery of the module was found to be for the most part beneficial, there were some administrative limitations that emerged. For example, it may not be viable or feasible for two teachers to be deployed to teach in the same classroom. Hence, efficacy of the bilingual module has to be demonstrated to stakeholders.

Conclusion

The bilingual approach applied at the Bahrain Teacher's College has shown to be effective in teaching Arab university pre-service teachers. The emphasis on academic English equips pre-service teachers with language skills that they require for tertiary study. Instructors reported that attending the *English for Educators* module was more effective for students than the remedial English language programs as the module focused on academic discourse and communicative competence rather than grammatical accuracy.

Secondly, the results of bilingual tutoring have suggested an increase in pre-service teachers' motivation and participation level. Some instructors involved in this program indicated a positive change in their language classroom environment. Pre-service teachers were more forthcoming in the Arabic classroom and there was greater class rapport and participation. Bilingual teaching created a non-threatening environment for the language instructors to share their experiences and to learn from each other.

There are some implications for pre-service teacher programs in other GCC countries based on the implementation of the *English for Educators* module at the Bahrain Teacher's College. Language courses for pre-service teachers should include an information literacy module for the purpose of teaching students how to retrieve and utilize both conventional and electronic sources of information. The module should also include a component focusing on how to socialize pre-service teachers into the educational discourse community. The guiding principle of developing such a module is to ensure that the materials, products and assessments are relevant to the context of teaching in schools. It is imperative that this is not categorised as an English language proficiency course, but a course on communicative skills for the Arab pre-service teachers. Based on the implementation of the *English for Educators* module at the BTC, it is our belief that such course is best delivered bilingually.

References

Al-Ahmed, F.H. (2000). Multi-media input to a foundation ESP course at university level. *British Journal of Educational Technology, 31*(4), 374-376.

Al-Alawi, Y., Al-Kaabi, D., Rashdan, S., & AL-Kahleefa, L.(2009). Quality assurance and continuous improvement: A case study of the University of Bahrain. *Quality in Higher Education, 15*(1), 61-69.

Al-Saleh, Y.N. (2004). *Graduate teacher candidates' information needs from electronic information sources in Saudi Arabia.* Retrieved August 21, 2009, from Pro Quest Dissertations and Theses database (University Microfilms, 31560530).

Al-Suqri, M.N. (2007). *The information needs and seeking behavior of social science scholars at Sultan Qaboos University in Oman: A mixed method approach.* Retrieved August 21, 2009, from Pro Quest Dissertations and Theses database, (University Microfilms, 3294687).

Al-Rabai, A. (2004, December). *English Proficiency at Jordanian Universities: A case Study – Al al-Bayt University.* Cairo Studies in English (CSE), Cairo University, Egypt.

Aljamhoor, A.A. (1996). *The English writing process of two Saudi graduate teacher candidates before and after ESL instruction.*

Retrieved February 10, 2010, from Pro Quest Dissertations and Theses database, (University Microfilms, AAT9706443).

Alumran, J.I.A. (2008). Learning styles in relation to gender, field of study, and academic achievement for Bahraini university teacher candidates. *Individual Differences Research, 6*(4), 303-316.

American Library Association. (1989). Presidential committee on information literacy: Final report. Retrieved August 7, 2007, from: http://www.ala.org/ala/acrl

Baby, S. (2008, November 4). Education reform projects on way. *Gulf Daily News.* Retrieved October 5, 2010, from: http://www.gulf-daily-news.com/NewsDetails.aspx?storyid=233610

Bahrain Economic Development Board. (2008a). Bahrain opens Gulf's only Polytechnic. Retrieved October 5, 2010, from: http://www.ameinfo.com/169369.html

Bahrain Economic Development Board. (2008b). Focus on the right skills. Retrieved October 5, 2010, from: http://www.bahrainedb.com/EDBInBahrain.aspx?id=1226

Berkenkotter, C., & Huckin, T. (1995). *Genre knowledge in interdisciplinary communication: Cognition, culture and power.* Hillsdale, N.J.: L. Erlbaum.

Challenges Arab universities face in teaching English. (2004, March 25). *Khaleej Times.*

Choy, D., Wong, A., & Gao, P. (2008). *Singapore's pre-service teachers' perspectives in integrating information and communication technology (ICT) during practicum.* Paper presented at Australian Association for Research in Education (AARE), International Educational Research Conference, 2008, Brisbane, Australia.

Cooper, A., & Bikowski, D. (2007). Writing at the graduate level: What tasks do professors actually require? *English for Academic Purposes, 6,* 206-221.

Ellis, M., & Pillai, A.D. (2009a). *Communication for Educators: English for Educators Handbook.* Bahrain: Bahrain Teachers College.

Ellis, M., & Pillai, A.D. (2009b). Addressing digital literacy in the English language class. *TESL Reporter, 42*(1), 66-71.

Hale, G., Taylor, C., Bridgeman, B., Carson, J., Kroll, B., & Kantor, R. (1996). *A Study of writing tasks assigned in academic degree programs (Research Report 54)*. Princeton: NJ: Educational Testing Service.

Hyland, K. (2008). English for specific purposes. In J. Cummins & C. Davison (Eds.), *International Handbook of English Language Teaching* (pp. 391- 402). NY: Springer.

Hyon, S. (1996). Genre in three traditions: Implications for ESL. TESOL QUARTERLY, 30/4: 693-722.

Kassab, S., Abu-Hijleh, M., Al-Shboul, Q., & Hamdy, H. (2005). Gender-related differences in learning in student-led tutorials. *Education for Health,18*(2), 272-282.

Kimmo, T., Reijo, S., & Sanna, T. (2005). Information literacy as a social practice. Library *Quarterly, 75*(3), 329-345.

Kuhlthau, C.C. (2004). *Seeking meaning: A process approach to library and information services (2nd Ed.)*. Westport, CT: Libraries Unlimited.

Lek, C. (2009). NIE/NTU, Singapore congratulates Bahrain Ministry of Education on opening of Bahrain Teacher's College. National Institute of Education, Singapore News. Retrieved March 30, 2010, from: http://www.nie.edu.sg/news/feb09/

Limberg, L., & Sundin, O. (2006). Teaching information seeking: Relating information literacy education to theories of information behaviour. *Information Research, 12*(1). Retrieved January 3, 2008, from http://InformationR.net/ir/12-1/pap12(1) paper 280er280.html

Malcolm, D. (2003). Investigating successful English learners in Arab medical schools. In *Supporting independent English language learning in the 21st century: Proceedings of the Independent Learning Association Conference* (pp. 103-112). Australia: Melbourne University.

McCawley, P., Henry, D., & Zurstrassen, M. (2002). *The virtual Colombo plan: Addressing the ICT revolution.* Paper presented at the 2002 Global Summit of Knowledge Networks, Adelaide, Australia. Retrieved May 13, 2008, from http://globalsummit.educationau.edu.au/globalsummit/papers.htm

Miller, C. (1994). Rhetorical community: The cultural basis of genre. In A. Freedman & P. Medway (Eds.), *Genre and the new rhetoric*. London: Taylor and Francis.

Mokhtar, I.A., & Majid, S. (2006). *Information literacy education in the context of project work: Application of multiple intelligences and mediated learning*. Paper presented at the Asia-Pacific Conference on Library and Information Education and Practice 2006. School of Communication and Information, Nanyang Technological University, Singapore.

Moore, P. (2002, July). *An analysis of information literacy education worldwide*. White Paper prepared for UNESCO, the U.S National Commission on Libraries and Information Science and the National Forum on Information Literacy, at Information Literacy Meeting of Experts, Prague. Retrieved May 13, 2008, from www.nclis.gov/libiner/inforlitconf&meet/moore-full paper.pdf

National Forum on Information Literacy. (2003, October 3). Meeting Summary. Retrieved May 22, 2008, from: http://www.infolit.org/meetings/Summary_NFIL_Oct03.pdf

Neely, T.Y. (2002). *Sociological and psychological aspects of information literacy in higher education*. Lanham, MD: Scarecrow Press.

Ozdemir, S.M., Akbas, O., & Cakir, R. (2009). A study on the relationship between pre-service teachers' information literacy skills and their attitudes towards distance education. *Procedia Social and Behavioral Sciences, 1*, 1648-1652.

Pillai, A.D. (2010) *Discourse analysis of research papers and the acculturation experiences of novice writers*. Unpublished doctoral dissertation, Nanyang Technological University, Singapore.

Shamo, E.E. (2001). *University teacher candidates and the Internet: Information seeking study*. Retrieved December 31, 2004, from

ProQuest Dissertations and Theses database, (UMI No. AAT 3042834).

Shoham, S., & Mizrachi, D. (2001). Library anxiety among undergraduates: A study of Israeli B.Ed. students. *Journal of Academic Librarianship, 27*(4), 305.

Sinno, Z.S. (2009). *The impact on language learning of Lebanese teacher candidates' attitude towards English in the context of globalization and Anti-Americanism.* Doctoral dissertation, University of Leicester, UK.

Teo, C.H. (1999, October 19). *Building competitiveness in the knowledge economy: How is Asia facing up to the task?* Paper presented at the 1999 East Asia Economic Summit Plenary Session. Retrieved September 11, 2001, from http://1.moe.edu.sg/speeches/1999/sp191099.htm

University of Bahrain- Bahrain Teachers College (UoB-BTC). (2009). Retrieved March 30, 2010, from: http//btc.uob.edu.bh/Programmes

HALA AL-YAMANI

Chapter 15
Drama as a Pedagogy in Arab Teacher Education Programs: Developing Constructivist Approaches to Teaching

Abstract

Educational methods and approaches in Palestine are mostly traditional with the teacher as the Maestro in this teaching and learning process, and educational policies inevitably aimed more at controlling students than enlightening them. In the wake of the 21st century there is an interest in Palestine in developing innovative teacher training programs in order to reform the Palestine education system. Teachers need to learn new pedagogical approaches, methods and techniques if they are to use them in their classrooms. This chapter aims to document this educational reform movement by reporting on two research projects conducted with pre-service and in-service teachers. The focus of the research was to show how the use of drama as a pedagogy worked with the participants in the teacher training programs. Qualitative research methods and the interpretative approach were used to elicit the views and opinions of the participants. The analysis of the data demonstrated that drama is an effective pedagogy as it developed the participants' professional motivation and enhanced their perception of their own role as teachers and their attitudes towards more constructivist approaches to teaching and learning.

Introduction

Educators all over the world think about education and the way the educational systems have failed to keep up with the needs of contemporary society. O'Toole (2003, p. 2) noted that: 'educational theory, practice and praxis all emphasized that traditional schooling systems through the twentieth century were not coping with the demands and precepts of modern, let alone post – modern, society, if indeed they ever had.' Educators around the world have worked to update curricula and to focus on the creative aspects of the human being as a whole person. They have started to embrace creativity and team work and emphasise the role of artists, musicians and performing arts in education.

In Palestine there has been some movement towards educational reform, but the educational system has been greatly affected and marked with certain traditional characteristics particularly in the teaching and learning process (Hashweh, 1998; Sfeir, 2006). Teaching methods and approaches used in the classroom are mostly traditional and teacher-centered and limited to 'fact learning'. The aim of the different educational institutions is to provide learners with knowledge that has to be uncritically absorbed. Students are memorizing rather than creating and generating new ideas (Sfeir, 2006). This educational approach concentrates on only one part of human development, i.e. the intellectual part, and even then it does not develop all aspects related to this part. It provides opportunities for few mental processes and skills to be developed. It constraints all other high order thinking skills which are important for being an independent creative learner (Jawad, 1993; Hashweh, 1998; Sfeir, 2006).

In the Palestinian traditional education system, the teacher behaves as s/he knows everything and makes no mistakes whereas the learner knows nothing. The relationship between the teacher and the learner is arranged in a hierarchical order. Knowledge is very important and it is extrinsic rather than intrinsic. For educational reform to occur the Palestinian educational system needs to be developed in line with modern approaches to education and new teaching methods and techniques need to be integrated in the classroom in order to activate the role of the learner. Teachers need to use methods that aim at developing an independent, creative, critical citizen. Teacher educators need to train teachers in new and different approaches in order for teachers to be able to work differently with the new generations and to integrate such innovative approaches in their work in the classroom. Teacher education programs search for more powerful instructional methods to prepare teachers for the increasingly complex schools of the 21st century. This chapter presents the outcomes of a research study which investigated the inclusion of drama as a new pedagogy in teacher education programs in Palestine. It presents how trainees experienced drama and how it helped them in developing new teaching and learning approaches.

Background

Constructivism

Constructivism is an educational approach (Vygotsky, 1978) that places the learner in the centre of the educational process, and it emphasizes learning not teaching. It relies upon knowledge construction more than knowledge transfer (Jawad, 1993) as learners build or re-structure their concepts and knowledge through active interaction with experiences (Pineau, 1994; Cook, 2001).

   A constructivist educational approach promotes the active participation of the learner through providing a rich educational environment which gives learners the opportunity to discover the knowledge which surrounds them and to use different strategies of thinking, to explore experiences, and to implement and critically evaluate all that is related to their world. Through such an approach, education becomes an act of knowledge, as the learner experiences new learning through all aspects as a person (Pineau, 1994).

Social constructivism sees knowledge as a product of social interaction mediated by activities and cultural tools, such as language (Vygotsky, 1978; Gredler, 2001). Learning is not confined to the classroom, but it includes learning in and outside the school premises. Kamii and Lewis (1990, p. 35) referred to the constructivist classroom as 'a culture which students are involved not only in discovery but in a social discourse involving explanation, negotiation, sharing, and evaluation'. This happens when the person experiences this world through all aspects of herself/himself as a person who can formulate their own concepts and perceive the world around them. Learning in this way has two parts as De Groot (2006, p. 2) said: 'it is an autonomous process sustained by one's natural desire to explore, to find answers but foremost to raise questions; secondly, we almost always learn of and with others because we all have our limitations so we need others to deal with our limitations.'

Drama in Teacher Education Programs

Teachers need to be highly qualified and trained in order to make a real difference in the classroom. Changing teachers' concepts, attitudes and practice is the best way to integrate progressive teaching strategies and methods in the classroom and bring about educational reform. Teachers need new techniques that empower them as people, and as professionals to be able to create a better educational system. For teachers to become effective professionals and be able to make a real change, they need to understand how to learn using new and innovative approaches. As Pinar (1985) mentioned 'before we learn how to teach in such a way, we must learn how to learn in such a way' (cited in Norris, 1995, p. 280) Teachers need to experience new and different ways of teaching and learning. They need to be taught in the same way that they, in turn, will teach others (Richardson, 1990; Haberman, 1991; Kerekes, 2010).

In drama, as a process and art, the person is acting 'as if'. It is a process where the person is engaged in 'practice living' as Way (1967) described it. The person is playing other roles whether imaginative or realistic. Educational drama allows participants to be engaged, motivated, empowered, and active agents of learning (Heathcote, 1984; Wagner, 1999). The use of drama in the educational process has been described as a research process by Henry (2000) and Somers (2005):

> it starts with a defined topic of study, generates hypotheses, tests those hypotheses through experimentation or improvisation, gathers the data that flows from this experimentation, selects and orders it into a report by a mini performance, communicates outcomes to classmates or wider group. (Somers, 2005, p. 9)

Drama as an art provides a unique opportunity to the student teachers to live different kinds of experiences by using creativity and imagination - sometimes with no previous preparation (Somers 2005; Kerekes, 2010). The person improvises according to how they understand the experience or how their imagination allows them to deal with it. By using drama, teacher education programs can create opportunities for trainers to train teachers who are able to play different or new roles in their professional work (Whatman, 2000; Griggs, 2001). In this way the student teachers can learn the difference between teaching and learning. In the Palestinian context, drama would play an effective role in developing new understanding and new attitudes towards teaching and learning.

There is little literature discussing drama and teacher education. What exists is confined mostly to the use of drama in training teachers or the experiences of those teachers whose students use drama. Norris (1995) wrote about his experience of teaching teachers by using drama. He discovered that this method and especially the different scenes prepared by students, touched them deeply and reminded them that teaching is a human activity. Drama helped them develop their attitudes towards teaching as a profession as well as towards drama as a teaching method. Somers and Sikorova (2002, p. 112) found in their research with in-service teachers in the Czech Republic that the use of drama affected teachers' 'values congruence, knowledge, skills, and new awareness.' In their view, the drama course they taught had an impact on the practice of those teachers. Furthermore, Laakso (2005) in studying the learning potential of process drama with student teachers discovered that:

> Process drama proved to be a rich working method offering diverse and very individual experiences. The learning potential of process drama became apparent in the areas of empathy, self knowledge, group dynamics and of artistic experiences. (p. 356)

Finally, Kerekes (2010) in working with four team teachers at the College of State Island in New York mentioned that:

> Drama affords many important opportunities for today's teachers and learners. Developing young learners who have passion for learning as relevant, interdisciplinary discovery that involves creativity and others is a significant leap forward in developing independent thinkers and astute leaders. (p. 56)

These studies illustrate the positive effect of drama on the development of both teachers and students and how this has a profound impact on the life of the person as well as on their relationships and the quality of their professional work. The question remains: would drama work with pre-service and in-service Palestinian teachers? Would it develop their understanding of learning as a process and of their role as teachers? This is the focus of the studies described in this chapter.

The Studies

This paper is based on two research studies that the researcher conducted with two groups of trainees. The first one was a group of students in the pre-service teacher education program at Bethlehem University in Palestine. The pre-service teachers attended two consecutive courses, the first one was drama for teachers of young children and the second one was introduction to early childhood education which focused on the principles of early childhood learning and teaching. In both courses, drama was the main teaching method in presenting the various concepts such as imagination, developing tableaux, mime, improvisation and role- play. The students attended these courses twice a week for around 100 minutes in each session. In total students spent 45 hours in each course. In the first course there were 20 students in the group. For the second course that number of students was reduced to 14 as six students withdrew from the course.

The second research study was conducted with in-service teachers of the lower primary stage. Teachers attended a training program which focused on drama aspects and the principles of Early Childhood Education. The group of teachers represented different schools and teachers were chosen according to their interest and commitment to professional development. There were 17 teachers who represented ten schools of the Bethlehem district. The training workshops were once a week for twenty weeks with each weekly session lasting for four hours.

Both studies sought to explore the possibilities of using drama for teaching and learning and investigate the interaction and behavior of pre-service and in-service teachers in drama-based training. Data were collected by using qualitative research methods:

- Interviews: There were three main interviews with the participants: one at the beginning of the study, the second one near the end of it and the last one after they had finished the training. These interviews focused on the experiences of the participants and their impact on themselves and on their practice in the classrooms. The questions were open-ended which allowed the participants to express their thoughts and feelings.

- The participant's journals: participants wrote their own reflections on the individual sessions of the training workshops.
- The researcher journal and reflections.

In analyzing the collected data the researcher used the interpretative approach which was concerned with interpreting the thoughts and opinions of the participants. Data were categorized in themes so that patterns in the responses of the trainees to the drama activities could be highlighted. Even though these two studies were conducted with two different groups of participants, there were common aspects related to their interaction with drama as a pedagogical technique. This chapter focuses on how the two groups experienced drama as a pedagogy and how it affected them.

Results and Discussion

Attitudes towards the Workshops

Many of the pre–service and in-service teachers in the programs faced challenges through experiencing the various activities in the workshops. Both groups tried to convince the researcher to cancel the reflection journals because they did not know how to write their reflections:

> When the teacher asked us to write our own journals, I felt very angry and I asked myself; why did I study education? I feel it is the most difficult subject at

the university. It needs lots of work. I felt unhappy because it needs a high level of boldness and I do not have it. I do not like hard work and I would prefer traditional methods to any other teaching methods. (GHAS, Pre-service, Journal)

Writing our reflections is annoying and it disturbs me... It is not easy to think of the session and find a good time for doing this.... The trainer questions related to our reflections are similar to Why? and How? They are difficult questions and sometimes it is not easy to answer them. She asks about why we were enjoying a specific activity, but we were enjoying it, it is an answer and it is enough... (L.N. In-service, 2nd Interview)

The participants' feelings and thoughts about the drama-based workshops reflected the effect of the traditional approach in educating them. They were not ready yet for the new way of learning and teaching. They were much used to rote learning. Thus, they raised their concerns about attending this sort of sessions where they were busy working on various experiences and there was no teaching or explanations. One of the participants made the following comments which largely reflected the views of other participants:

Sometimes I feel upset of the work since it needs deep thinking and to discover the proper way of doing these activities with small children. Other participants could not understand reasons of doing specific activities. It's true that we discussed some activities, but it's necessary to know the objectives of all activities and how it relates to the curriculum that we are teaching. (T.F., In-service, 2nd interview)

It was clear that the expectations of the participants were based on the traditional model of teaching and learning. They expected to play a very simple role, that of the passive participant. The challenge in participating in the drama-based workshop activities was that it was difficult for participants to deal with something so new and unexpected. They noticed that the new teaching approach needs various abilities and skills that they do not have, such as concentration, imagination and working with others and in front of others. One of the participants commented:

> I faced difficulties in imagination, improvisation and to deal easily with the
> dramatic situations. (F.T., In-service, 1st Interview)

Facing the challenges pushed them to develop themselves and gave
them a chance to live the role of an active learner and understand
what it means to learn through the experience. They became more
positive about writing in journals and they continued to do so even
when it ceased to be a requirement:

> These days I read what I am writing and I keep it with me to follow my
> development and how I am expressing myself. Sometimes I study it to see what
> I wrote and how I felt at that time. (MAHA, Pre-service, 3rd Interview)

For some of the trainees whether pre-service or in-service, the journal
became part of their 'daily routine' since it helped them to think of
themselves, their actions and thoughts as well as their surroundings.

Communication Skills

Through the drama activities, trainees further developed their
communication skills. They became able to use verbal and non-
verbal expressions. They developed the skill of listening to other
people and paying attention to them. For a teacher, such skills are
essential for the development of a productive relationship with the
pupils.

Pre-service teachers discussed how they developed their verbal
and non-verbal communication skills. Drama empowered them to
express their feelings and thoughts. They became more able to
completely discuss what they thought and how they felt. They
discussed their non-verbal expression and how this had developed.
The following reflect some of the participants' thoughts:

> I became more aware of my expressions and more able to control them. Now I
> use my expressions much more to communicate with other people because I
> want others to know how I feel. I am also more aware of how others feel by
> looking at their facial expressions. (KAOT, Pre-service, Journal)

> I developed my ability to act in different situations whether verbally or non verbally. This helped me to communicate with others. I learned how to express myself freely. (KH.L., In-service, 3rd Interview)

Participants became more able to express themselves and to communicate clearly with others:

> I developed my ability in sending and saying the information to the pupils but in a positive and easy way. My communication skills have developed particularly in interacting with the pupils. This helped me in knowing them more and feels closer to them. (M.SH, In-service, 2nd Interview)

Participants also wrote about their ability to listen to other people and they mentioned the qualities they developed through drama. They discussed drama and how it developed their communication skills with both children and adults:

> I learned how to listen to others, how to be patient and how to deal with all pupils since they need to be listened to in order to understand what they say. I have learned how to communicate more effectively .... I grew up believing that a loud and strong voice is unacceptable for a girl but now I realise the importance of voice volume especially in classroom. (MITO, Pre-service, 3rd Interview)

> My abilities in expressing myself have developed a lot. These days I enjoy talking, listening and working with children. (H. N., In-service, 2nd Interview)

These comments show the participants' development of communication skills in different areas and the practical application of those skills in school.

Imagination

The trainees discussed how drama freed their thoughts and imagination. Both groups discussed how drama provided them with the opportunity to use different imaginative situations through which they discovered the importance of imagination and developed their ability to use their own imagination. The following excerpts reflect the participants' thoughts:

> I used to feel unhappy with the limitations of my imagination but I feel it has improved. For example, I told a story to pupils at the school ………and I used my imagination to add interesting events to the story... (INSU, Pre-service, 2nd Interview)

> I used my imagination through telling the story. I saw the beauty of the flowers nature, bright colors and I smelled the various smells of the flowers….Through this imaginative journey I learned to value imagination in our life as people and how to use stories and events we are living in. How to think and to make reflective thinking . (H.Z., In-service, Journal)

Through different kinds of drama techniques, participants explored and practised their skills in thinking and imagination. They discovered the importance of these activities for developing these aspects with young learners.

Play Attitude

From the midpoint of the training courses and onwards participants showed development in acting and playing:

> Honestly I did not expect that one day I would jump quickly from one chair to another one chasing others. I never thought I would feel as joyful as I felt today since we are living in a sort of closed shell. It has clear borders and red lines that we should not pass. (SHHI, Pre-service, Journal)

Participants played and enjoyed playing:

> I felt very happy that I could not hide it. When I was pulling my arms up and shouting 'let's, let's' like a bird that wants to fly…In this game, I took away all restrictions imposed, by society. (NAAB, Pre- service, 2nd Interview)

> On one hand drama took me back to my childhood and I became much freer in life, teaching and working with my pupils. On the other hand, I felt upset

because I learned this just recently, but not at the beginning of my work otherwise I have done many different things but in a better way. (MSH, In-service, 2nd Interview)

Games and drama activities helped me to use my energy and to become active and full of energy...Today I feel that I am able to interact, move and play with my pupils in the classroom. (H.Z, In-service, 2nd Interview)

Trainees wrote about how they discovered that there was no fault in acting freely and playing with enjoyment. Drama and the particular atmosphere created in the sessions helped them to rediscover the child within and gave them permission to enjoy playing and later on to play with their young students in their schools and their classrooms.

Critical Skills

Participants criticized the traditions and customs of Palestinians in terms of their effects on people's lives, especially children. While the participants had full awareness of the position of children in the Palestinian society, they also became aware of how 'cultural traditions and customs allow unkind treatment of children by adults. The rules and customs of our traditions create a very bad psychological situation for the child' (SAQI, Pre-service, 2nd Interview). They recognized how their society and the educational system restrain the individual from developing and feeling free. Through the workshop activities, participants tried to understand how traditions support or restrain the individual:

...our society does not care about children nor the importance of childhood. The most important thing is preparing her/him for the future. They give great care to some aspects, but not to the child as a whole person. (AMSH, Pre-service, Journal)

The educational system is not suitable for children, on the contrary, it's a negative system. It works against the needs of the child and against her\his needs and abilities. It works on constraining the child's thoughts and all other aspects. Teachers prefer working with the best pupils and forgetting that the weak pupil is one of their victims... Is it possible to make the child who is filled with energy, life, and action to sit silently as long as the teacher explains the lesson? What do we expect to achieve by using the boring traditional system of education which works against the ability, creativity and imagination of the child? (F.R. In-service, Journal)

The participants became critical thinkers; they showed deeper understanding and they were empowered to take action as well as to participate in changing and developing the situation for the better.

Understanding the Role of the Teacher

Participants related their experiences in drama with their role as teachers working with children in primary schools. They discussed how they '... can encourage each child to talk and express herself\ himself in front of the group in order to help others know her\him well so as to help her\him develop self as a person' (SUSA, Pre-service, 2nd interview). They realized their roles as teachers in 'encouraging pupils to use imagination and help them grow up as creative people' (MITO, Pre-service, Journal).

Participants also discussed the role of the teachers in relation to what they had learned through partaking in the activities:

These activities help us to know how sensitive children are to everything around them and to take more care when working with children. In each activity I should put myself in the shoes of children in order to provide what suits them. (NAAB, Pre-service, Journal)

I thought discipline and low movement are most important aspects in teaching small children. I believed in the various methods of punishment.... Even at the university when we were students we learned that the most important role of the teacher is controlling the classroom and keeping discipline. (W.R. In-service, Journal)

These reflections indicate that drama helped both pre-service and in-service teachers in developing their thoughts and attitudes towards the learner and entering into the world of the child. Drama helped them to understand this world and to better understand their role towards young learners. It also developed their curiosity to use new methods with children in the classrooms.

Understanding Children's Needs and Actions

The drama experiences also helped most participants in both groups to understand the world of the child and how they learn and adapt to the environment. They mentioned how drama and its associated activities helped them understand children's needs, feelings and actions:

> After these sessions, I understood the needs and characteristics of children. This affected my way of dealing with children and cares for their needs... I feel involved with children and I prefer to be with them most of the time. Now I understand the needs of children and how to deal with them. (KAOT, Pre-service, Journal)

> The child in the school needs care and attention. I did not know this before, so I was focusing on teaching and explaining the various materials. Drama helped me to give the attention to each learner and to think of her\his needs. I became much understandable to children and to think of their needs. I became a good listener to the pupils and they feel much released and free in working in the lessons. (H.L., In-service, 2nd Interview)

> I was much interested in teaching children and how to read and write, thus I felt this anger if they could not do it. I was developed through this training course and I learned many things about children. I became more interested in them.... I think of their circumstances and I think of their behaviors and reasons behind these behaviors. (H.I, In-service, Journal)

Living through different situations either by going back to their childhood or by playing the role of the child increased the participants' recognition and understanding of children. This reflected a positive attitude towards children and their needs which, in turn, would create a positive relationship between teachers and pupils.

New Educational Beliefs and Attitudes

Participants talked about their experiences and how they developed their attitudes towards the active role of the learner because they considered themselves to be the main agents of the educational process.

> Drama helps me in developing the concept of the progressive teacher who has an important and effective role in creating the new generation. This generation should be different from ours and we are using new methods, different from those we were learned by. (INSU, Pre-service, Journal)

> Learning through living the experiences is part of the new educational approach. I learned the importance of the experience through this training. I learned new ideas about teaching and learning. (T.F., In-service, Journal)

Participants were concerned mostly with their attitudes towards using drama and the creative arts with the children. They were interested in combining it with other new educational techniques.

> I believe in the effect of drama on the personality of the pupils. I think they become creative by exercising drama. In addition, I don't like the traditional method of memorizing to achieve good grades. (AMSH, Pre-service, 2nd Interview)

Trainees wrote about using new techniques such as drama and music in their teaching, encouraging pupils to use imagination and playing. They learned how to work with 'small groups of pupils instead of teaching the whole class as they used to in schools' (MAHA, Pre-service, 2nd Interview). They also became more understandable to children, they used 'open' questions and showed interest in the children. Participants became more interested in developing the child as a whole person. They understood and respected the main principles of Early Childhood Education.

> I noticed a big difference between the other teachers and myself specifically in the concept of childhood and how to deal with children. I focused on developing their language skills, physical skills, concentration and on what it is to be human. Other teachers are focusing on imparting knowledge, mostly treating the child as an object. Their concern is solely on improving academic performance rather than the child as an individual. (DIJA, Pre-service, Journal)

> I feel that I am going to change my methods in dealing with children and to use new active methods. These simple drama activities helped me a lot in teaching and learning. (H.Z., In-service, Journal)

This positive attitude is of utmost importance for future and in-service teachers alike if they are going to start breaking the vicious cycle of the traditional way of teaching and learning.

Conclusion

The two studies described in this chapter showed that the trainees faced challenges with drama as a training method especially at the start of the program. These challenges stemmed from the features of the traditional educational system in Palestine that these participants were used to. It was not easy for some of the participants to act and interact in the various activities. They expected the traditional, teacher-centered way of teaching and learning. However, once they were exposed to the new method, they enjoyed drama as a pedagogy and even their attitudes to play were developed. They participated fully in the various activities and they thought of what they were doing and how it was related to teaching and learning. They used the full range of their own resources: body, voice, senses, feelings, emotions and mental process (Way, 1967) in each of the sessions where they had to act out different sorts of situations whether as individuals or in small groups. Drama provided an open and easy environment for learners to feel 'released and become freer' (Hornbook 1989, p. 21). Despite the initial apprehension by many of the participants, drama proved to be a successful training technique with both pre-service and in-service teachers.

There was good evidence for the effect of drama as a teaching pedagogy in developing the teachers' basic understanding of their role in relation to young learners. Teachers adopted new beliefs and attitudes either towards the learner or in how to deal with learners and how to arrange the educational environment and plan for interesting activities. These aspects of development match the findings of other researchers such as Laakos (2005), Norris (1995) and Kerekes (2010) who found that drama developed the attitudes of teachers towards the teaching profession as well as towards drama as a teaching method. Somers (2002) also discovered the importance of drama in helping students understand the theory that was given to them during pedagogy lectures and the development of their practice in the schools. This became evident in the study with the pre-service teachers who got a chance to model and practice what they learned in the lecture rooms.

Undergoing drama experiences in which trainees became active learners grounded their understanding of this sort of pedagogical approach and helped them develop positive attitudes towards constructivist educational approaches as well the notion of seeing children as active learners. Participants had a better understanding of the classroom environment and the needs of their pupils. Griggs (2001, p. 24) also mentioned that 'such techniques increase the participant's own-self knowledge, their awareness of their classroom environments and their sensitivity to their learner's lives and needs-or the roles they play in seeing them realized.'

In dealing with a dramatic situation involving many kinds of internal and external processes, participants were engaged in investigating, experimenting, negotiating, synthesising, thinking of different possibilities and alternatives and concluding (Watkins 1983;

Somers 2005). Through drama, learning took place while learners experimented in action (Henry, 2000). In this process, the autonomy of the individual increased, especially through the 'rational self-critical and reflective procedures' (Gauthier, 1992) that were used in the workshops.

The studies described in this chapter have shown the positive effects of drama on pre-service and in-service teachers who appeared to develop constructivist approaches to teaching as a result of their training. There is a strong possibility that having experienced themselves what it is like to be an active learner, they will apply the same techniques in their classroom to actively engage their students in learning. The drama-based workshops also revealed the participants' need for this sort of experiences to develop as autonomous and creative professionals who are able to lead and implement innovative teaching approaches in the classroom. It would be interesting to see if drama-based teacher training could accelerate the pace of educational reforms in Palestine and other Arab countries with similar traditional educational systems.

References

Cook, D., & Collins, J. (2001). *Understanding Learning: Influences and Outcomes*. London: Paul Chapman Publishing Ltd.

De Groot, D. (2006). *The new learning*. Paper presented in the educational conference of the Arab Educational Institution in Bethlehem, Palestine.

Gauthier, D. (1992). The liberal individual. In S. Avineri, & A. De-Shalit (Eds.), *Communitarianism and individualism* (pp.151-164). Oxford: Oxford University Press.

Gredler, M.E. (2001). *Learning and instruction: Theory into practice*. New Jersey: Prentice-Hall.

Griggs, T. (2001). Teaching as acting: Considering acting as epistemology and its use in teaching and teacher preparation. *Teacher Education Quarterly, 28*(3), 23-35.

Haberman, M. (1991). *The dimensions of excellence in programs of teacher education.* Wisconsion: Teaching and Teacher Education.

Hashweh, M. (1998). Education and training in Palestine. Paper presented at the International Conference on Employment in Ramallah, Palestine.

Heathcote, D., O'Neill, C., & Johnson, L. (1984). *Collected writings on education and drama.* London: Hutchinson Education.

Henry, M. (2000). Drama's ways of learning. *Research in Drama Education, 5*(1), 45-62.

Hornbrook, D. (1989). *Education and dramatic art.* England: Basil Blackwell Ltd.

Jawad, R.M. (1993). *Arab education and civilization: Difficult choice.* Beirut: United Arab Studies Centre.

Kamii, C., & Lewis, B.A. (1990). What is constructivism? *Arithmetic Teacher*, 38(1), 36-37.

Kerekes, J., & King, K.P. (2010). The king's carpet: Drama play in teacher education. *International Journal of Instruction, 3*(1), 39-60.

Laakso, E. (2005). Encountering drama experiences. The learning potential process drama in the light of student teachers' experience. *Research in Drama Education Journal, 10*(3), 355-356.

Norris, J. (1995). The use of drama in teacher education: A call for embodied learning. In B. Warren (Ed.), *Creating a theatre in your classroom* (pp. 278-302). Ontario: Captus University Publications.

O'Toole, J. (2002). Drama: The productive pedagogy. *Critical Studies in Education, 43*(2), 39-52.

Pineau, E.L. (1994). Teaching is performance: Reconceptualizing a problematic metaphor. *American Educational Research Journal, 31*(1), 3-25.

Richardson, R. (1990). *Daring to be a teacher*. England: Trentham Books Limited.

Sfeir, J. (2006). *Developing basic education in Palestine: A holistic integrated perspective*. Palestine: MaDad & Italian Cooperation.

Somers, J., & Sikorova, E.(2002). The effectiveness of one in-service education of teacher's course for influencing teacher's practice. *Journal of In-Service Education, 28*(1), 95-114.

Somers, J. (2005). Drama as alternative pedagogy. NUFFIELD review of 14-19 education and training: Aims, learning and curriculum series, Discussion Paper 10.

Vygotsky, L.S. (1978). *Mind in society: The development of higher psychological processes*. Cambridge, MA: Harvard University Press.

Wagner, B.J. (1999). *Dorothy Heathcote: Drama as a learning medium*. London: Hutchinson.

Way, B. (1967). *Development through drama*. England: Longman.

Watkins, B. (1983). Drama as games. In C. Day, & J.L. Norman (Eds.), *Issues in educational drama* (pp.42-51). London: The Falmer Press.

Whatman, J. (2000). Learning new roles: Drama in teacher education. In O'Toole. J, &. Donelan, K. (Eds.), *Drama, culture and empowerment: The IDEA dialogues*. Brisbane: IDEA Publications.

Part III: New Approaches to Teaching and
Learning in the Arab World

Rida Blaik Hourani, Ibrahima Diallo, & Aleya Said

Chapter 16
Teaching in the Arabian Gulf: Arguments for the Deconstruction of the Current Educational Model

Abstract

Since the 1970s, the Arab Gulf countries have attracted a large number of expatriates from around the world. The presence of expatriates in the field of education is visible and sensitive because it brings together players with opposing education philosophies and traditions. This chapter analyzes the teaching context in the Gulf countries and argues for the deconstruction of education as advocated and practiced by early Islamic scholars. It calls for the adoption of a constructivist pedagogy in the field of humanities.

Introduction

The Gulf Cooperation Council (GCC) is an economic regional integration that comprises the Arabian Gulf countries of Bahrain, Kuwait, Oman, Qatar, Saudi Arabia, and the United Arab Emirates (UAE). The GCC countries are among the world's wealthiest nations because they are the world's largest oil and gas exporters and have the largest oil and gas reserves (Reinert & Rajan, 2009). As a result, these Gulf countries continue to attract massive influx of expatriates from around the world in order to sustain and expand their economies. For example, in the UAE, more than 80% of the population are expatriates, while in Qatar expatriates comprise nearly 60% of the population (Reinert & Rajaan, 2009). Expatriates operate in a wide range of socio-professional sectors. Education is one of the sectors where their presence is visible and sensitive. Education brings together in one area players with opposing education philosophies, different scholastic traditions and different didactic models. On the one hand, there are the Arab students, influenced by the pedagogical approaches and the conceptions of knowledge inherited from their Arabo-Islamic culture and traditions of the GCC countries and, on the other, there are the expatriate teachers educated in western teaching theories, mostly influenced by western traditions and liberal values. As a consequence, teaching and transmission of knowledge between these two opposing traditions face serious pedagogical challenges in the GCC countries. First, this chapter reviews teaching and education from the perspective of the constructivist theories and analyzes them with reference to the education practices in the Islamic world. Second, based on the authors' experiences teaching different subjects (social studies, literature and language) in the region, the article discusses challenges facing western trained teachers who operate in the Arabo-Islamic context of the Gulf. Finally, this chapter argues for the need to deconstruct education in the Gulf countries by incorporating the Islamic education and pedagogic traditions as defended by early Islamic scholars.

Constructivist Education

Since the seminal contribution of Europe's 18th century rationalists in the field of knowledge, e.g. Descartes (1596-1650) and Kant (1724-1804), and empiricists, e.g. Locke (1632-1704) and Hume (1711-1776), western education has made significant leaps forward. Such strides have had significant impact on our understating of the cognitive abilities of learners and have helped reformulate learning theories, in particular the theories of learning advocated by such major constructivists as Piaget (1937, 1967) and Vygotsky (1978).

Constructivist theorists have revolutionized learning and teaching theories by emphasizing the cognitive abilities of learners, the development of inquiry skills and encouraging learners to formulate their own opinions using their own experiences. Learning is no longer seen as mere repetition of patterns or mimicry, but a cognitive, deliberate, and active process leading to knowledge-building.

According to Cannella and Reiff (1994) and Richardson (1997), one of the most crucial contributions of the constructivist theorists is their emphasis on developing systematic methodological skills, such as encouraging learners in the active learning process, developing inquiry processes and problem-solving skills, and working collaboratively with others. Therefore, learners are prepared to engage in a range of activities that offer multiple perspectives and present information and data in a variety of formats (Nuthall, 2000). Zevin (2000) and McKay (1995) believe that providing correct answers and imposing single interpretation can be regarded as a de-emphasized learning process because learning from the constructivist view is primarily based on imparting skills and oriented to problem-solving. The next section summarizes the main aims of the constructivist learning theories.

Aims of Constructivist Learning

One of the most important aims of the constructivist learning is to enhance skills and ensure that learners take full advantage of their abilities. To achieve this aim, it is expected that learners engage in a process of discovering and analyzing facts presented on multiple levels and which involves high level of thinking. As such, learners are prevented from dwelling strictly on factual information. For example, Marlow (2000) found out that in the field of social studies there is a need 'to use a variety of methods and procedures to assist each pupil to achieve as optimally as possible' because 'learners individually possess diverse learning styles and intelligences' (p. 35). Zevin (2000) focuses on the importance of teaching (e.g. in social studies) in a reflective manner, which means that the learning process should revolve around questioning, making assumptions, and engaging in creative problem-solving in learning activities. In such learning framework, students need to monitor their own comprehension, make use of their previous knowledge, assess their own point of view, and question and interpret continuously facts and evidence in the light of their own experiences.

In fact, constructivists advocate that the curriculum should recognize children as active constructors of knowledge who can engage in mediating their own meaning by using their own knowledge and who can participate in any forum or learning setting by contributing in social and cultural negotiation in order to share meanings. In the light of this contribution, Sunal, Szymanski, and Haas (2002) supported the ideas put forward by Zevin (2000) and argued that a meaningful and relevant education aims at developing reflective and inquiry skills.

In short, it can be concluded that the aim of the constructivist learning endeavors are not only restricted to in-depth construction of knowledge, but also address issues that include a range of topics such as pedagogy and strategies of teaching (Giroux, 1992). In the following section, Islam and education are discussed with a focus on their historical perspectives and key figures that shaped and influenced them, while Islamic education is compared at times with the western education perspective.

Islam and Education

Generally people, including Muslim intellectuals, still talk about Islam as if it were a simple and unified entity. However, throughout the progress of Islamic civilization and Islamic thought, different ideas and different thinking approaches emerged (Panjwani, 2004). Since the early medieval times, Muslims acquired knowledge and were involved in processing and constructing it through inquiry, discovery, and questioning. The works of such figures as Avicenna and Averroes are a testimony of this process (Badi & Tajdin, 2004). Indeed, there was a wealth of concepts featuring how Muslims perceived knowledge because Islamic faith has been shaped by Muslims who came from diverse socio-ethnic and cultural back-grounds. For example, Panjwani (2004) portrayed a dichotomy of education in an Islamic context. He indicated that Muslim educators view this dichotomy as: western style of education being bad, while an Islamic style of education being good.

Islamic style of education can be described from two angles. The first posits that 'Islam is a comprehensive way of life. It is vision and civilization and a great blessing which flowered from the revealed knowledge delivered by the Almighty Allah'(Ali, 1984, p. 49). This view of education, supported by Ould Bah (1998), described education as intimately related to Islam and Islamic teachings which God completed and perfected over fourteen centuries ago. As for the second angle, it is defended by Sardar (1989) and it is based on the idea that 'Islam, after all, makes it a duty for everyone to seek knowledge and discover facts, and increase the welfare of mankind' (p.25).

In the current socio-cultural transformation in the Arabian Gulf states, the dichotomy of *East-West* education is controversial as to how much Arabs should adopt from the *western* model of education (for example teaching thinking and inquiry). Arab countries tend to overlook the fact that leaders of the Muslim *Umah* during the Ummaid, Abbasid and Andalusian times borrowed from the Greeks,

Byzantians and Persians among others. They are said to have had contributed tremendously to the flourishing of sciences, philosophy, scientific thinking, and knowledge acquisition. Subsequently, those Islamic thoughts and sciences contributed and enormously influenced the expansion of modern knowledge (Butterworth, 1983). Averroes and Avicenna are typical examples of Muslims who borrowed from the *west* and simultaneously contributed to the *west*. These well-known Islamic scholars not only made significant contributions to modern thought, but they were also proactive in terms of using logical reasoning and scientific arguments to discuss theology and religious ideas (Dallal, 1993; Haque, 2004).

Islamic Contribution

When Islam started in the seventh century A.D. and as the Muslim society grew exponentially, the place of knowledge in that society also grew. This led to diversified secular scientific and literary learning and knowledge to emerge. Subsequently, manuscripts produced in the eighth and ninth centuries travelled in all major centres that were under the Islamic dynasties. At the same time Muslim scholars endeavoured to search for both literary and scientific knowledge.

Günther (2005) indicates that in the past centuries, and especially during the ninth century, Muslim intellectuals contributed to discussions on educational theory, pedagogy and didactics, including social sciences that flourished since the 10th century and well into the 11th century. Avicenna and the theologian-*sufi* philosopher Al-Ghazali were proactive in terms of using logical and scientific arguments to discuss theological and religious ideas where the tools of logic were manifested to interpret theological matters. According to Günther (2005) those diverse thinking styles existed since the 10th century, i.e. during the medieval Muslim dynasties. This is also applicable to the pedagogical framework of education which reflected the process of using thinking during the teachings in that period. As for Kadi and Billeh (2007), they indicated that a tremendous change occurred during the Safavid and Ottoman empires during which pedagogy and teaching catered for the secular demands of the Safavid and Ottoman empires. The next section gives a background to education in the Islamic model and discusses the main challenges faced by this model.

Background to the Islamic Model

According to Panjwani (2004) Islamic education in pre-modern times was the vehicle for transmitting knowledge rather than processing it. He added that this transmission of knowledge was different from what prevailed in the medieval times, where teaching and pedagogy were genuine and derived from the very nature of Islamic scientific thought. Even though this approach was highly textual and based on memorization, it involved critical thinking and inquiry. Furthermore, education in the Islamic medieval time was an auxiliary science underlying the practice of education (Panjwani, 2004). Panjwani added that education was considered to underpin all areas of scholarly inquiry. However, the focus on memorization, recitation and the lack of thinking and knowledge processing, which prevailed, stems from the following three major observations:

i- First, as indicated by Kadi and Billeh (2007), the assumption that since the *Qura'an* and the *Hadith* are taught and learnt through recitation and memorization, secular subjects are taught in the same pedagogical manner.

ii- Second, Islamic education faced increasing pressure in the nineteenth century or earlier because some Muslim scholars strongly advocated inquiry and thinking. (Kadi & Billeh, 2007).

iii- Third, is the fact that in the postcolonial era the GCC countries have resorted to a defense mechanism manifested through their educational system. This defense mechanism

was characterized by the preservation and the revival of
their ethnic identity dictated by a fear of innovation and
changes in educational patterns. As a result, they held tight
to their traditional and conservative ways of teaching
(Barakat, 1993).

Since the education model in the GCC countries was linked to Islam
even until the middle of the nineteenth and twentieth century, the
conventional ways of teaching continued to be adopted from the
kuttabs[1]. Therefore, integrating inquiry and thinking in the teachings
was not part of the educational practices.

The Main Challenge of the Islamic Model

According to Gesink (2009), the challenge to the Islamic form of
education, from the hermeneutic and pedagogical perspectives, began
in the first half of the nineteenth century. It was propelled by such
modernist advocates as Tahtawi, Afghani and Rida who put forward
the Islamic principle of Ijtihad (reasoning). On the contrary, such
conservative opponents as al-*Safti* and al- *Mahdi* defended the
Islamic principle of Taqlid (following precedents).

In most recent times, especially starting from the mid-twentieth
century, education experienced a significant twist marked by the rise
of Arabic and Islamic identities and a self- realization of Arabic and
Islam as the foundation of post-colonial Arab independent nation-
states. Throughout this context, the field of education swang between
two edges of pedagogies: the Islamic model, characterized by
memorization and recitation, and the western education model
characterized by secular teachings.

---

1   The Kuttabs were non-government co-educational Muslim schools. Kuttabs
     were conducted in private houses or in mosques and destined for children
     between 5 and 12. Although they focused on reading, writing and some basic
     precepts of Islam, teaching was clearly religious and moral in content. Some
     arithmetic was added to the curriculum.

Between the 1950s and the 1970s, education in the GCC countries witnessed attempts to reshape educational institutions, especially in the public education sector. However, in some Muslim Arab countries such as in Lebanon, Syria and Jordan, both French and British missionary schools existed and these helped to reshape education, while in the GCC countries there were none or very few missionary schools. As a result, there was little foreign influence and their schools continued to be associated with the Islamic pedagogy of recitation and memorization that prevailed in the Kuttabs. Since the GCC countries were protectorates and not subject to the mandate system, as was the case in some Arab countries, their education neither borrowed from the modern western educational model, nor did it retain the medieval Islamic trend of teaching thinking. Therefore, 'secular' and modern 'raison d'être', or the pedagogical association between modern and medieval Islamic 'teaching thinking' and 'reasoning' were not prevalent. As mentioned by Badi and Tajdin (2004), creative thinking advocated in the modern Muslim World and inherited from an Islamic perspective is lacking in the GCC countries.

Generally speaking, learning in the medieval Islamic context, which included *ijtihad* and *qiyas* (analogical reasoning in Islamic law), required secular inquisitive and rational thinking. Such features are the roots of constructivist learning, which existed in the medieval Islamic context of teaching and learning, but these are now lacking in the current pedagogical context in the GCC countries. The following section discusses Islamic education in the GCC countries.

The Islamic Education Framework in GCC Countries

Due to socio-political and historical factors, learners in the GCC countries are strongly influenced by methods of learning and epistemologies inherited from their Islamic and Arabic traditions.

Learning, namely in the areas of languages, literature and social studies, remains confined within the norms of their socio-cultural context. As such, the practical application of the constructivist theories seems to face a number of challenges due to the relative conservative nature of these societies and to the strict adherence to their social norms and their education traditions. In these societies, since learning and knowledge acquisition are primarily based on socialization and adherence to their own national culture, attitudes, opinions and values are societal rather than individually constructed (Barakat,1993)

According to Teague (2000), due to social constraints, multiple perspectives are sometimes challenging and difficult to attain in such ethnocentric and conservative societies. Relatively, prior knowledge and experiences that are in harmony with the learners' communal norms remain the shared values of the group, while 'other' views or personal and independent perspectives, which do not conform to communal views, may be rejected. To illustrate this view, Gergen (2009) argued that in such communities 'the meaning of words and actions is not derived by comparing them against the subjectivity of their authors, but against the governing conventions of the communities in which we [people] reside' (Teague, 2000, p. 22). Consequently, in such a learning context, promoting a reflective inquiry is restricted and implementing constructivist teaching-learning principles is hindered. At best, teaching thinking and developing individual learning become restricted because education is intimately related to the socio-cultural norms and practices which should be strictly adhered to. As stressed by Wagner and Lotfi (1980, p. 239), 'the main goal of traditional Qur'anic education was, and remains, the complete mastery or memorization of the Qur'an'. This results in the exclusion of 'the possibility of subjecting these beliefs to rational critical investigation, which might erode their certainty [...] it does not allow for knowledge to be open to revision when new evidence comes to light that challenges its reality' (Halstead, 2004, p. 527). In the Islamic education framework, learning is focused only on the principle of *tafakkur*, that is thinking in the perspective of the revelation of the Qur'an and the teachings of the *Hadiths* and accepting every single Islamic truth.

Islamic knowledge is based on two major principles: First, constructing and processing knowledge in the realm of the sacred Islamic-religious concept known as *A'kida* or religious creed. As such, some teachings derived from Islamic faith remain untouched and nonnegotiable and faith is given priority over reasoning. Second, according to Muslim sociologist Ibn Khuldun, learning in Islam has many types of knowledge, including: 'alum al-Sharia' (science of Sharia), 'alum al-Aqliya' (sciences of reason), 'ulum al-marzula' (harmful sciences), and 'ulum-mahmooda' (praise worthy sciences). In these types of knowledge, there is a 'hierarchy of knowledge' in the sense that some are preferred over others because of the moral hierarchy associated with them (Panjwani, 2004, p. 23).

The situation is no better when teaching literature, language and social studies in the current context of the GCC countries. Issues that may be considered controversial or divisive are overlooked or avoided because simply they may lead to classroom conflict or even parental objection. Most of the time, deliberate rebuttal of learners' knowledge processing and formation of experiences stems out from socio-cultural justification because these may lead to views that may be perceived as against Islamic teachings and values. As supported by Halstead (2004) '...anything outside the divine truth of the Qur'an is at best superfluous, and at worst dangerous' (p. 517). As a result teaching pedagogies and practices are restricted and revolve within the realms of *al-haqiqa al-mutlaqa*[2].

As discussed earlier, constructivists' pedagogies encourage relativism that accepts pluralism of views against absolute truth. In this sense, western education relies on rational thinking, fact-based reasoning and free interpretation. These are in coherence with the pedagogies that prevailed and were practised during the medieval Islamic dynasties. However, due to ideological and social changes in

---

2   This is an important characteristic of Islamic beliefs that highlights that there is
     one absolute truth.

the history and evolution of Islam, these pedagogic approaches were abandoned and are hardly practised in the 21st century pedagogies in the GCC context, primarily due to socio-cultural constraints. Although Halstead (2004) argued that 'independence of thought and personal autonomy do not enter into the Muslim thinking about education, which is more concerned with the progressive initiation of pupils into the received truths of the faith' (p. 519), it can be said that such a view is applicable mainly to matters relevant to faith and Islamic religious creed rather than educational pedagogies. It is essential to note, there is a fine line between the two types of knowledge: one based on adoption of knowledge and the other based on acquisition through inquiry and discovery. Seemingly, the educational framework of modern pedagogy in the GCC countries has not been able to integrate successfully these two sources of knowledge into their education model. The following sections highlight major issues in implementing constructivist education in the GCC countries, in particular they focus on the social, cultural, and religious constraints.

Socio-Cultural Constraints

According to Barakat (1993) the socio-cultural constraints imposed upon Arab learners are so entrenched that they hinder the promotion of constructivist teaching and learning theories. New values and opinions can be developed as long as they fit within the established and shared social, religious, and cultural norms, while personal autonomy or independent thoughts are given little space, or no space at all (Barakat, 1993). This indicates that some of the limitations facing constructivist pedagogy lie within the socio-cultural dimension.

Generally speaking, constructivist teaching and learning is not widely spread, especially in the areas of social and cultural studies, languages and literature. This is due to the fact that socio-cultural traditions and personalized religious values and morals are highly prioritized. These constitute constraints to the development of the learner (Barakat, 1993). Consequently, teaching practices and pedagogies in the GCC countries remain stuck between a rock and a hard place. On the one hand, the conservative GCC societies are strongly influenced by their socio-cultural norms and the misconceptions of the pedagogical practices of thinking in an Islamic context. On the other hand, there are constructivist pedagogies inspired by secular education models and liberal thoughts promoted through western education models.

In the past decade many attempts were made to modernize and westernize the educational systems and institutions in GCC countries. The impact and presence of North American, Australian, and European educators, academics, and institutions have been noticeable. Mills (2008) confirms that western academics in the UAE are 'deeply involved in the public higher-education system' and 'work closely with the government officials to fundamentally change the higher education system in the country's seven emirates' (p. 2). These pioneer educational reforms have led to a polarized divide, characterized by the cohabitation of two opposing traditions with regard to the concept of education and its purposes, leading to serious pedagogical challenges.

The following section analyses some critical challenges faced in deconstructing the strategies for teaching literature and languages. It addresses controversial issues students in the GCC education are exposed to, based on the authors' experience in the field. Critical thinking needs to be taken into consideration when dealing with a range of topics in the context described below. It requires preparation by training students to conduct objective and rational analysis, which will pave the way to knowledge processing and the construction of multiple perspectives. This ground preparation is desirable as it encourages students to defend their own point of view and, at the same time, be able to accept others' opinions in the educational context.

Literature Versus Religion

Most non-Muslim literature, especially western literature and artistic representations (such as paintings) may include visual or vocal representation of the gods or God as personae, i.e. religious figures and God may be given human attributes and interact with other human beings. However, in the Muslim culture such literary or artistic representations are strictly prohibited and are considered blasphemous. When teaching a dramatic or literary piece where the gods act and talk, as in a play like 'Everyman'[3], and where Gods fight and engage in sensual matters as is in a Greek or Roman drama, teachers in the Arabo-Islamic culture of the GCC countries may need to reconsider their choices to make sure that they are not likely to offend their readers' sensibilities. One way of overcoming the dilemma is to introduce the idea gradually to the students while stressing its specific context prior to reading the text. A brief background would be required on the multi-deism in ancient Greek and Roman cultures and the acceptance of the visual representation of Christ in western contexts. This is certainly very different from the Muslim's sacrosanct belief in *Tawheed* where any representations of *Allah*[4] or its Prophet Mohamed (PBUH) are considered profoundly offensive. Therefore, Muslim students would not readily accept the idea of visual representations of God or a prophet even though in western cultures and practices such representations have always been tolerated and even endorsed by their religious institutions as it is acceptable from the Judeo-Christian perspective that God, Christ or his followers be represented by simple human beings on stage and be reinvented, ridiculed and, even, mocked at[5].

---

3   *Everyman* is a morality play set in the medieval era. In the play God and the
      Angel of Death appear as main characters in the plot.

4   This is a fundamental belief in Muslim faith, i.e., the Oneness of God or there
      is only One God. *Allah* is the Arabic word for God.

5   Another interesting example is John Milton's epic *Paradise Lost* in which God
      is seen talking and participating in the action, where Satan is a challenger of
      God's omnipotence.

The teacher's religious affiliation may be crucial in such situations and may determine the level of ease in dealing with such topics. When the learners and the teachers are from the same religion, dealing with topics such as the one mentioned before may be less daunting as learners may feel that their teachers are 'closer to them' as far as faith is concerned. As long as there are no sensitivities associated with the 'other', students may be more willing to accept dealing with 'alien' or 'remote' realities and concepts. Therefore, the local culture and its level of conservatism should be taken into consideration as to where the borderline between religion and tradition lies. For example, in teaching 'Everyman' and 'Paradise Lost' in three different Muslim cultures (i.e. Egypt, Malaysia, and the UAE), concern over hurting students' feelings was more heightened in the UAE than in Egypt or Malaysia where the majority of the students would not find it offensive to read such works. While reading such literary pieces is in no way meant to challenge the students' socio-cultural practices or religious beliefs, exposure to these western topics in such a pedagogical framework enhances multi cultural perspectives for greater understanding of other cultures.

Traditions

While the domain of religion is one fine topic that has to be addressed with care on the part of the teacher, traditions are also another challenging domain as they are often intrinsically tied with religion. Teachings that involve discussions of topics that may question, challenge, or contradict existing social, cultural and traditional beliefs and practices may be also extremely sensitive issues. Traditions are so tied and intermingled with religion that any social practices may be considered, mistakenly, as Islamic legacies or values and, therefore, may not be subjected to questioning.

Indeed, topics on issues such as traditions and culture may raise schism when class opinions are sought and discussed. For example, the topic of gender segregation, especially in educational institutions, may be one such issue. Gender segregation is practised in most education systems in the GCC countries. It is accepted and deeply entrenched in social practices and justified on religious grounds. Therefore, discussing arguments in favor or against segregation may be perceived as a crusade against religious prescriptions and cultural traditions. To mention just one such example, in one language course in a male-only institution in the UAE, which required free and open discussion on whether the education institution should be desegregated, one student refused adamantly to participate in the class discussion on this particular topic. For him, it was absolutely a matter of faith and traditions and it was a pointless subject for class discussion since, from the student's internalized religious perception, women are not expected to mix with men. Therefore, any personal and independent thought on such a topic by simple human beings, who owe total submission and allegiance to the Creator, amounts to insubordination to the Holy Scriptures. In another example, students in one of the most prestigious UAE teaching institutions rejected gender desegregation at school. Such rejection was not based only on religious, social and cultural grounds, but also on scientific grounds supported by findings of a research study conducted in US educational institutions. This shows how facts and scientific findings can be accepted and adopted as long as they corroborate and validate students' religious beliefs and cultural practices.

Sensual Domains

Even though Islamic thought does not prohibit discussing male/female relationships and any matters related to it , based on the authors' experience, it is evident that topics of sensual nature are predominantly sensitive in the Arab world in general and the GCC teaching context in particular. Selecting readings and study material on topics of sensual nature are risky in the Arab learning contexts despite the fact that *'The Arabian Nights'*, which continues to be the pride of Persian/Arabic prose, included sequences of sensuality.

The gender of the teacher may play a significant role in the students' acceptance of topics of this nature. The level of acceptance decreases sharply when the genders of the learners and the teachers are different. Even in classes where learner and teacher gender are the same, such topics should be approached with a great degree of care. On one occasion, in a private tertiary institution in the UAE, a female teacher of Arab descent taught successfully 'The Lady with the Dog' by Anton Chekhov[6] after securing consent from the students prior to teaching the short story. The students did read the story and showed genuine interest, as it reflects possible life dilemmas. The course was taught without confrontation with students, but, as expected, with only few uncomfortable situations. However, a male colleague teaching the same female students Ovid's 'Metamorphosis'[7] in the same institution faced stern resistance and rejection from female students who found it confronting for a male to talk about such sensual topics with them. Following this experience, the text was removed from the curriculum. Similarly, students' reacted in the same way to a female teacher of western background teaching the same syllabus in the same institution. It appears that gender and, to a certain extent, the religious affiliation of the teacher seem to affect students' tolerance in studying literary works relevant to gender issues.

Conclusion

This article has discussed the constructivist education model which is the core around which modern education theories are founded. It has also reviewed the Islamic education model from a historical

---

6 *The Lady with the Dog* is a short story by Anton Chekhov set in Russian City of Yalta and focuses on the extra- marital affairs of the main characters.
7 A related discussion of Greek myths where a goddess is seen naked by one of the characters.

perspective starting from medieval Islamic education practices to the current education models in the GCC countries. The article shows that throughout its history, contrary to common beliefs, the early Islamic education model has always enhanced the teaching of thinking, analogy, and inquiry and it has always been proactive in adopting and integrating contributions from other cultures. As a result, the early Islamic education model became diverse and subsequently flourished for generations. However, due to social-historical reasons and political choices, the current education models in most Arab Muslim countries, especially those in the GCC, shifted away from the inquisitive education model. Consequently, the knowledge acquisition and processing that was prevalent in the medieval Islamic education model during the Muslim dynasties, deteriorated significantly over time. Education became synonymous with memorisation, recitation and lack of critical thinking and rational practices to such an extent that for most western-trained teachers in the Arabo-Islamic context of the GCC, there is ever a present dilemma. Western trained academics working in the Gulf region have to censor their academic thrust of knowledge in order for it to fit adequately to the sensitive social, cultural and religious contexts within which they are operating. It is important in the current context of globalization marked by large-scale movement of people and exchanges between cultures that GCC countries consider integrating constructivist pedagogies as the basis for redesigning the teaching of humanities subjects in order to articulate creative thinking both at the school level and at the higher education level. As this chapter argued, such an approach would be in line with the early Islamic education model and would help unleash the learning opportunities and potential needed to sustain the economic growth of the GCC countries.

References

Ali, S. (1984). Conflict between religion and secularism in the modern world and the role of education in preserving, transmitting and promoting Islamic culture. *Muslim Education Quarterly*, *2*(3), 40-54.

Badi, J., & Tajdin, M. (2004). Creative thinking: An Islamic perspective - Kuala Lumpur. *American Journal of Islamic Social Sciences*, *23*(1), 200-248.

Barakat, H. (1993). *The Arab World: Society, culture, and state.* Berkley: University of California Press.

Butterworth, C.E. (1983). Ethics in medieval Islamic philosophy. *Journal of Religious Ethics,* 11(2), 224-239.

Cannella, G.S., & Reiff, J.C. (1994). Individual constructivist teacher education: Teachers as empowered learners. *Teacher Education Quarterly*, *21*(3), 31-35.

Dallal, A. (1993). The origins and objectives of Islamic revivalist thought, 1750-1850. *Journal of American Oriental Society*, *113*(3), 341-359.

Gergen, K. (2009). *Relational being beyond self and community.* New York: Oxford University Press.

Gesink, I.F. (2009). *Islamic reform and conservatism.* London: Tauris Academic Studies.

Giroux, H. (1992). *Border crossings: Cultural workers and the politics of education.* New York: Routledge.

Günther, S. (2005). *Ideas, images and methods of portraying: Insights into classical Arabic literature and Islam.* Leidem: Brill.

Halstead, J.M. (2004). An Islamic concept of education. *Comparative Education*, *40*(4), 517-529.

Haque, A. (2004). Psychology from Islamic perspectives: Contributions of early Muslim scholars and challenges to contemporary Muslim psychologists. *Religion and Health*, 43(4), 357-377.

Kadi, W., & Billeh, V. (2007). *Education in Islam-Myths and truths.* U.S.A.: The University of Chicago Press.

Marlow, E. (2000). Psychology in teaching the social studies. *Journal of Instructional Psychology, 27*, 28-36.

McKay, R. (1995). Brain-based learning: Support for an inquiry curriculum. *Canadian Social Studies, 9*(4), 128-129.

Mills, A. (2008). Emirates look to the west for prestige. *Chronicle of Higher Education, 55*(5), 1-7.

Nuthall, G. (2000). The role of memory in acquisition and retention of knowledge in science and social studies units. *Cognition of Instruction, 99,* 1-39.

Ould Bah, M. (1998). *Islamic education between tradition and modernity.* Morocco: ISESCO.

Panjwani, F. (2004). *The Islamic in Islamic education; Assessing the discourse: Current issues in comparative education.* U.S.A: Teachers College, Colombia University.

Piaget, J. (1967). *Biology and knowledge.* U.S.A.: Chicago University Press.

Piaget, J. (1937). *La construction du réel chez l'enfant.* New York: Basic Books.

Reinert, K., & Rajan, R. (2009). *The Princeton encyclopedia of the world economies.* USA: Princeton University Press.

Richardson, V. (1997). *Constructivist teaching and teacher education: Theory and practice.* Washington, D.C: Falmer Press.

Sardar, Z. (1989). *Explorations in Islamic science.* London: Mansell.

Sunal, V., Szymanski, S., & Haas, R. (2002). *Social studies for elementary and middle grades: A constructivist approach.* Boston: Allyn & Bacon.

Teague, R. (2000). *Social constructivism and social studies.* Retrieved April 8, 2009, from: http://filebox.edu/users/rteague/PORT/socialco.

Vygotsky, L. (1978). *Interaction between learning and development.* Cambridge: Harvard University Press.

Wagner, D., & Lotfi, A. (1980). Traditional Islamic education in Morocco: Socio-historical and psychological perspectives. *Comparative Education Review, 24*(2/1), 238-251.

Zevin, J. (2000). *Social studies for the twentieth century: Methods and materials for teaching in the middle and secondary schools.* New York and London: Longman.

MICK KING

Chapter 17
Implementing Problem-Based Learning in the Gulf: A Case Study of Arab Students

Abstract

The increase in the number of foreign universities operating in the Arabian Gulf (Krieger, 2008; Lewin, 2008) has obliged Arab students to adopt more independent learning techniques and improve their English proficiency. This chapter describes a mixed-method action research study of how eight Arab students coped with a newly designed dissertation writing English course, which used pre-dominantly problem-based learning (PBL) techniques. The PBL style required students to work independently and see their tutor as a facilitator. Data were collected using a needs analysis, a teacher's reflective journal, a course evaluation and a student group interview. The most pertinent findings of the study suggest that Arab students can use PBL for English with relative success. However, the students' frustration with the difficulty of authentic texts suggests that semi-authentic texts and prior training in the tenets of PBL would facilitate learning even further. The study is significant as there is little, if any, evidence of research into PBL for English in the Arab world and it questions the widespread belief that Arab learners struggle to learn independently.

Introduction

As the number of foreign universities in Arab countries increases, Arab students need to adopt new learning styles that are more in line with western pedagogies. Usually, once students pass their English language pre-sessional courses, they see further language tuition alongside their content subject as unnecessary, despite their continuing problems with the linguistic demands of their courses. Using Problem-Based Learning (PBL) strategies for teaching content courses can be demanding on Arab students who usually struggle with the underlying learning patterns of the PBL approach. PBL depends on student-centred classroom activity, the tutor's facilitating role and the possibility of different perspectives as opposed to one definitive answer. All these are aspects that may clash with Arab students' perceptions of what constitutes good educational practice.

This chapter describes the development and implementation of a short English preparation course in dissertation writing at Stenden University in Qatar (SUQ, formerly CHNUQ) using PBL. The development of the course was necessitated by the Qatari students' inability to attain native-like English fluency after four years of University study. Given the students' reticence towards studying more English at the end of their University study program and their potential negativity towards traditional English study, it was imperative to develop a course that would encourage analytical learning, where the students would be challenged to investigate the requirements of dissertation writing independently.

This chapter starts by describing the background of the study, drawing on literature pertaining to PBL, Arab students' learning styles and their challenges with academic writing. Then, after the research methodology is described and justified, findings are evaluated and recommendations are made for the implementation of PBL English classes when teaching Arab students.

Background

PBL, as espoused by Moust, Bonhuijs and Schmidt (2001), is generally used in scientific fields but has been applied to other disciplines. Though used in the Arabian Gulf (see, for example, Das, Mpofu, Hasan & Stewart, 2002), there is little evidence of its application to English teaching. PBL requires students to wrestle with authentic situations from their field of study and decide what tools they would need in order to find possible solutions. The problems, or tasks, encourage students to learn independently and think critically. Thomas (2003) refers to PBL as a learning approach rather than a teaching theory. Teaching is replaced by facilitating and answers do not necessarily determine what is learned. In fact, as problems are ill-structured, there are no clear cut answers, and the process of seeking answers is where learning takes place (Abdullah, 1998).

There appear to be few examples of PBL in the field of English as a foreign language (EFL) writing in other regions of the world (see for example, Thomas, 2003; Matthews-Aydinli, 2007). Despite this, Reid (2001) states that writing course design increasingly employs problem-solving techniques. Mellor-Clark (2006) highlights how PBL offers task authenticity and raises awareness of form and genre, but continues that the lack of a right answer means it has not always found favour in EFL education. Dow and Ryan (2000) suggest that certain learning cultures reject PBL for English as students may not be risk-takers and find the indirect tutor role difficult to assimilate. In the Arabian Gulf learner autonomy is still quite new (Coombe & Al-Hamly, 2005) so it appears difficult to visualise how one could apply this method to an environment where more traditional teaching methods are preferred.

The field of EFL has successfully employed task-based learning (TBL) which bears a striking resemblance to PBL inasmuch as both require learners to work with (semi)-authentic tasks independently and make use of prior knowledge and skills to wrestle with real world problems (Willis & Willis, 2001; Skehan, 1996). PBL differs from TBL in often avoiding explicit task instruction and masking the objective of the task in some way (Moust et al., 2001), whereas TBL generally stipulates the working method on a task and a desired outcome (Skehan, 1996). PBL students have to work out independently via problem analysis techniques what the task requires and how to approach it, then present and share findings with each other before drawing global conclusions. In essence, there is no explicit task outcome but students, through testing their hypotheses, are better equipped to deal with similar situations in the future.

Can Arab Students Study Independently?

The belief that tertiary level Arab students struggle to learn independently has been widely researched in the Gulf. For example, Ricks and Szcerbik (2010) concluded that Arab students' overreliance on memorisation made them unprepared for independent learning. Ellili and Chaffin (2007, p. 300) highlighted Arab students' 'exposure to traditional teaching methodology, role beliefs and perceptions about the nature of learning which do not favour autonomy'; and Richardson (2006, p. 111) emphasised Arab students' 'passive, teacher-centred learning style [...] waiting for instructions and spoon-fed orientation'. While Scott (2006) recognised that 'Arab students are animated and enthusiastic conversationalists' (p. 91), he found they were 'hampered by avoidance of conflict' (ibid., p. 92), which could complicate any PBL type discussion. Ellili and Chaffin (2007) also noted that Arab students hold teachers responsible for classroom learning, while Das et al. (2002) found that medical students expected PBL tutors to provide input rather than searching for answers themselves. This reliance on teachers is underscored by Ward who refers to the teacher in the Gulf as the 'absolute patriarchal authority' (2009, p. 129). Finally, Richardson suggests that 'it is ethnocentric and unreasonable to expect that the same methodology and materials used in [non-

Arab] education should work [in the Gulf] with the same effect' (2006, p. 122).

Conversely, other Arab-based research has proposed that independent learning is feasible with Arab students. Lauder and Cozens (2008) implemented task-based instruction in the UAE with relative success, while in Saudi Arabia, Bin Daoud and Al Hamzi (2003) found positive outcomes from employing a reflective writing model. Two Egyptian studies (Khafagi, 2010; Sohdy, 2010) concluded that Arab students could learn to think critically. Finally, Eslami, Al-Buainain and Tzou's (2009) study conducted in Qatar showed that memorisation strategies were the least favoured among their Arab students. It appears, then, that the relative success or failure of independent learning models is context dependent and it would be unfair to paint all Arab students with the same brush. This is reinforced by findings showing Arab students in Saudi Arabia (Hor & Ismail, 2010) and Oman (Sancheti, 2008) able to learn in different ways.

Concerning Arab students' challenges with academic writing, Jordan (2005) cites written work as a major cause for concern for non-native speaker university students. In the Arab context, Bacha (2002) points to studies which show Arab students' difficulties with lexical variety, subordination and linking ideas, and Reid (1996) found that Arabs often avoid the passive and longer words - all of which are pertinent to academic writing. Scott's (2006) UAE research alluded to the discrepancy between Arab students' oral and writing capabilities, suggesting that 'although a student may appear very eloquent and articulate with the spoken word, translating [this] onto paper is quite another test' (p. 92). Finally, Ahmed's (2009) UAE study on students' attitudes towards advanced academic writing suggests that Arab students find the cognitive demands 'over-whelming' (p. 139) and, consequently dislike such courses. Despite difficulties with English and academic writing, Arab students often dismiss the need for more English tuition after they complete their pre-sessional courses. Studies by Coombe and Al-Hamly (2005) and

Ricks and Szcerbik (2010) suggest that this may be due to Arab students overestimating their competence in the language.

In summary, research indicates that there are conflicting views on the suitability of an inquiry-based approach to learning in the Arab context, with commentators divided on students' ability to cope with its independent nature. In the field of EFL, there is evidence of students' reluctance to study English beyond pre-sessional courses despite their apparent shortcomings in operating effectively in an academic environment with English as the medium of instruction. It is these factors which led me to test the suitability of PBL for academic English writing. My aim was to observe the extent to which it could be a valid model for counteracting student's negativity towards more English courses and promoting a more independent approach to acquiring advanced language skills.

The Study

The focus of the action research (AR) study described in this chapter was to analyse the extent to which a dissertation-writing course based on PBL principles can be successfully employed with Arab students. The AR model was based on a cycle of plan, act, observe and reflect (Cohen, Manion, & Morrison, 2008), whereby the course was planned and taught, entries were recorded in a reflective journal and course evaluation and interview data were analysed, before reflecting on the extent to which PBL was possible with Arab EFL students. The study participants were eight female Arab students who had passed the first three years of their Bachelor's degree and volunteered to take the course. All participants had previous training in PBL through their content courses.

The English PBL Course

The English PBL course was developed incorporating elements of TBL, which was appropriate for the participants inasmuch as they were familiar with the system and would need to work out the task focus, gain more self-confidence in academic writing and counteract fossilisation via consciousness-raising tasks, which use noticing as a key element. In addition, it was hoped that this would occur without the feeling of being 'punished' with more English study.

The first step in the course design was to conduct a needs analysis. Hutchison and Waters (2005) and Hamp-Lyons (2001) both emphasize the importance of conducting a needs analysis within the English for academic purposes (EAP) paradigm. Via an open-ended questionnaire student supervisors commented on genre-based and linguistic areas where their students had struggled. Dissertations of previous cohorts were also analysed to confirm the views expressed by the supervisors (see also Bacha, 2002). Student feedback was elicited using a Likert scale '*wants*' analysis in which students indicated which perceived needs of the dissertation supervisors resonated with them. Results showed that students favoured dissertation genre over grammar, which reflects Jordan's own findings (2005) that students consider grammar as less problematic than teachers do.

The next stage in the course development was to sequence the syllabus. Though Richards and Rogers (2001) recommend tasks be sequenced according to difficulty, and Nunan (2004) argues for the inclusion of scaffolding, recycling and reflection opportunities, the PBL tasks in the course were sequenced as per students' preferences by moving from genre-based to more specific language-related elements, thereby applying a 'holistic' to 'specific' model (Willis, 1996) for the course as a whole.

Although Nunan (2004) proposes that a combination of authentic, simulated and specially written texts optimises learning opportunities in the TBL classroom, the PBL course focused on authentic texts, such as old SUQ dissertation extracts and the SUQ

Dissertation Guidelines, in an effort to expose students to real world comprehensible input and to help them to first extract meaning from texts and later focus on form (Richards & Rogers, 2001). Exposure to a specific genre aimed to act as a model for learners (Derewianka & Hammond, 2001), providing them with real-world language based on their needs (Nunan, 2004). Where no suitable materials could be found, specially written texts were designed. It would seem logical that a writing course should provide plenty of writing opportunities. However, Dyer (1996) posits that tasks about writing are more beneficial than writing itself. In addition, the short course length (28 study hours) meant that writing was limited in favour of genre-based, language-related consciousness-raising.

According to Morley and Guariento (2001), authentic materials, focusing on target tasks (like writing a dissertation) should be supported by pedagogical tasks. Subsequently, the course included tasks that were PBL-oriented as students wrestled with the concept of 'dissertation', adding a TBL-style once explicit conventions and language items became prominent. The TBL-biased tasks made use of language activities such as noticing and consciousness-raising before assigning specific practice or task work like exercises or short writing tasks.

For PBL-style tasks, the desired outcomes were not always clearly stated, as students needed to determine themselves what they should do. These tasks had vague task titles, an emphasis on provoking discussion and the post task of researching to fill knowledge gaps and/or confirm hypotheses. In this sense, the teaching materials were often a catalyst for choosing a certain approach rather than an instruction on how to approach the task. For example, one task on the importance of organizing one's work according to guidelines had the title, '*Recipe for Disaster*' and contained a metaphorical vignette on how poorly planned cooking can go wrong. Students were then asked in the text: ***Discuss*** *this vignette.* ***Can you see*** *the link between this story and writing your dissertation?* On establishing the link through discussion, students were then directed to research the following for homework:

1. In each section, **what do you feel** you are actually supposed to do?
2. Can you find a thread between each section and the following one?
3. **In your opinion** what is the thread right through the report?

Though these questions appear to constitute the explicit task of answering questions, the phrases 'Discuss...', 'Can you see...', '...what do you feel...' and 'In your opinion...' allow for interpretation.

Materials were given to students on a class-by-class basis to enable assessment in real time of the extent to which expectations for each task were being met, to encourage reflection on how the students were dealing with the course demands, and to facilitate the revision of design elements accordingly. The three methods employed to assess the effectiveness of the course were a course evaluation questionnaire, a group interview with four of the eight students and my reflective journal. Consent procedures were followed where appropriate.

The students completed the Likert scale course evaluation questionnaire in the last class of the course to assess each task for clarity, relevance and its ability to challenge students. The following week, a 30-minute recorded group interview took place with four of the students who volunteered to participate. Students were invited to clarify and discuss the results of the course evaluation and comment on how they had coped with the PBL and the linguistic demands of the course. The course evaluation data were collated and analysed quantitatively using descriptive statistics and pertinent responses from the group interview were transcribed. Data from the interview and my reflective journal were then mapped against the research question and the questionnaire findings.

Results and Discussion

The main research focus of this assignment was to analyse the extent to which a dissertation-writing course designed to incorporate PBL principles could be successfully employed with Arab students. Due to the small number of participants, findings are given below in qualitative terms only. Whenever there are references to specific interview data, pseudonyms are used to protect the students' identity.

Clarity and Relevance of the Course Materials

Overall, there was strong agreement among students on the perceived clarity of the course materials. Students felt that the task instructions guided them sufficiently to the task outcomes. My own reflections were also that these students were able to follow the cryptic written pointers given in the tasks. Abeer opined, 'I found [the tasks] pretty obvious. It was very self-explanatory and to the point', although Hind did indicate that '[in two tasks] I didn't understand what I had to do'. In general, however, it appears that the content, materials and instructional design were clear.

With regards to the relevance of the course content, materials and design to the students' needs, although all students found the global content relevant, each respondent showed varying levels of satisfaction regarding the amount of time spent on dissertation genre and specific language elements. Ghetal commented, 'I think pretty much everything was covered. We went from what the whole layout would be; then we moved on to mistakes that are common'. Students also referred to particular tasks that they found most appealing. Hind felt that 'the recipe [structure] task was tough, but it was nice'. Ghetal mentioned two tasks which she found valuable: 'I really like the task where you asked to bring a proposal [and] the dissertation supervisor feedback [task] directed us'. Overall, findings suggest that the materials were relevant to the students' needs. Hind expressed the view of all when she said 'We are all more aware [of dissertation requirements] now'.

Coping with the PBL Style of the Course

Student responses indicated that they were able to make independent choices as a result of the course. This appears to contradict the findings of other UAE studies (see Ricks & Szcerbik, 2010; Ellili & Chaffin, 2007) which suggested that such a learner-centred approach is beyond Arab students. My own reflection was that students did require prompting at times and in the group interview students referred to this with Abeer stating, 'You didn't lecture us [...] you wouldn't give us the answer directly [and] you let us figure it out for ourselves'. Regarding independent choice, Samiyra's offering of 'I prefer to work things out for myself', reflected the views of the other respondents in using me as a last resort. Hind proffered that she did experience an awkward task, 'just once, but [the tutor] explained it'. This acceptance of my facilitating role again contradicts such studies as Ellili and Chaffin (2007) and Ward (2009) and reflects those of Khafagi (2010), Sohdy (2010), and Bin Daoud and Al Hamzi (2003), which showed Arab students' ability to think critically and independently.

The above findings indicate that although some tasks were quite vague, respondents felt that this had more to do with the challenge the task posed rather than unclear instruction. In other words, they understood what they had to do but they could not always find a way to do it. It was interesting to note their awareness of, and frustration with, how research can produce different answers (see also Mellor-Clark, 2006). Abeer commented that 'sometimes Internet research is not useful [because] when we look at other examples, it might confuse us'. Ghetal echoed this view: 'You go to different websites and they give you different ways [...] and there should be a universal way'. On the other hand, there was evidence that the PBL task process of analysing, setting learning goals, researching and discussing was beneficial in raising consciousness and dispelling misconceptions. This is clear in Ghetal's reflection on a task about writing a proposal: '[It] makes you really understand how much effort has to go in before you write your dissertation'.

I felt students struggled most on tasks involving defining an abstract and layout conventions. Students suggested that this was due to their existing misconceptions on the rules of writing abstracts and on layout, which led to them having to reconstruct their existing knowledge. From my perspective, they coped well with vague task titles with the exception of one of the last tasks on verb tense and passive mood where the title, *'The course is almost over so it's time to get tense and moody',* appeared to be beyond their cognitive and linguistic ability. However, I felt that any difficulty regarding wrestling with the task title was appropriate, as this was what the course was designed to do. Overall, there was evidence that the PBL approach did work and this would question Richardson's assertion that expecting non-Arab education methodology to work effectively in the Gulf is 'unreasonable' (2006, p. 122).

Coping with the Linguistic Demands of the Course

While coping with PBL refers to the learning approach used, coping with the linguistic demands refers to all aspects of the language content such as structure, layout, genre, vocabulary and grammar. Starting with structure, Abeer said 'When we had to list [the sections] from the beginning to the end of the dissertation; I think nobody had any idea how to do that'. The task on layout also appeared to cause some problems for the students as they expressed confusion about the norms given in the Dissertation Guidelines. Perhaps the biggest challenge was tasks on referencing and in-text citations. Even though the tasks seemed to interest them, they mentioned that they found them tough. I also sensed that they found noticing tasks quite problematic; especially those requiring them to notice conventions for reference lists and referring to sources. They argued that content teachers never seemed to give this much attention. While Abeer found the linguistic demands of the course acceptable, others did struggle with some language aspects. However, my overall impression was that the respondents did not overestimate their ability in English, which goes against the grain of other Gulf-based studies (see Coombe & Al-Hamly, 2005; Ricks & Szcerbik, 2010).

Regarding the predominant use of authentic texts, in one task, I used an extract from an old student's dissertation to highlight how *not* to write the problem statement and research questions but sensed that students really did not understand the text at all. As the extract was so poorly constructed, it appeared, in hindsight, to be too difficult to decipher. As I reflected, '[…]some of the authentic texts [I used] were just not appropriate as they were either too difficult or exhibiting worst, rather than best, practice' (Teacher's Reflective Journal). Despite most interviewees being non-committal on the use of authentic and semi-authentic texts, Abeer called for use of more student texts. She believed that '[we need to] look at more of our own work', and continued, 'we should have done more writing in class [as] it's better that we look at work of our [level]', reasoning that professional texts were difficult to process effectively and did not reflect the level of writing that they would produce. Despite these challenges, it appeared that the linguistic demands were not 'overwhelming' as found by Ahmed (2009, p. 139).

A final interview question was whether the subjects saw the course as a traditional English course or a PBL English course. Answers differed with Abeer and Hind sensing it was PBL and Samiyra reporting that she felt it was a traditional English course. Ghetal felt the course was a mixture, probably due to the PBL/TBL hybridity aimed for by the course. My own feeling is that the challenging vague PBL elements took it beyond a TBL course. While TBL can raise consciousness to a desired outcome, PBL may be a more realistic reflection of the world where learning outcomes may leave students not only more aware, but also more confused than when they started. As Ghetal reflected, 'I feel less confident [about the dissertation] now. I've seen all the mistakes that are possible and it's like...what am I gonna do?'

Conclusion

The study described in this chapter suggests that an academic writing course based on PBL principles can be successfully employed with Arab students. With few exceptions, respondents found the course materials and design clear and relevant. They also coped well with the PBL style of the course and did not seem necessarily perturbed by the need to think critically and research independently. In addition, they seemed comfortable with my role as a facilitator. Perhaps the only area where they showed some frustration and confusion was in discovering that different sources gave them different answers, but even that prepared them for real life learning. The linguistic demands of the course, though manageable, did make them aware of some misconceptions in genre and grammar and left some seeing the dissertation as a daunting task with many pitfalls. In the spirit of PBL, this negative consciousness raising may not be considered problematic; as students' awareness of their weak points would give them a specific focus, once they started writing their dissertation.

This research study, albeit small and limited, does propose that PBL has some role to play in advanced EFL learning of Arab students. However, this contextual study used subjects with previous PBL training. If the study were to be replicated with students who had no prior knowledge of PBL, it may not have such positive outcomes. To combat this, it is recommended that before implementing a PBL-based English course, there should be an initial training of the students on PBL principles, such as understanding the independent role of the tutor, having the self-confidence to make mistakes and learn from them and realising that real life scenarios rarely have one answer. Arab students get frustrated by multiple answers because they are often assessed on a one-right-answer basis in high-stakes assessments. PBL assessment needs to be either a formative or a summative reflection so students are allowed to conduct unrestricted research and learn to accept the fuzzy realities of the world in which they live. As for the genre and language elements of advanced academic writing, findings suggest that semi-authentic and specially constructed texts are preferable to authentic examples due to the difficulty that EFL students face in processing the more advanced language style. Similar research in the region should be encouraged to see if results resonate with those of this study. If PBL for EFL is implemented with Arab students, the road may be tough as they struggle with its demands. However, the long-term benefits for teaching and learning do make it a worthwhile endeavour.

References

Abdullah, M.H. (1998). Problem-based learning in language instruction: A constructivist method. *ERIC Clearinghouse on Reading, English and Communication Digest*, 132. Retrieved April 17, 2010, from:
http://www.indiana.edu/~reading/ieo/digests/d132.html

Ahmed, K. (2009). Connecting the 'blocks' of advanced academic writing: Making research writing less 'fragmented' and more 'whole'. In C. Gunn (Ed.), *Exploring TESOL practices in the Arabian Gulf* (pp. 138-141). Dubai: TESOL Arabia.

Bacha, N. (2002). Developing learners' academic writing skills in higher education: A study for educational reform. *Language and Education*, *16*(3), 161-177.

Bin Daoud, S., & Al-Hamzi, S. (2003). Teaching writing through thinking and reflection. In S. Safar, C. Coombe, & S. Troudi (Eds.), *TESOL Arabia 2002: Critical reflection in practice:*

Selected papers from the 2002 international conference Vol. VII (pp. 335-359). UAE: TESOL Arabia.

Cohen, L., Manion, L, & Morrison, K. (2008). *Research Methods in Education*. London: Routledge.

Coombe, C., & Al-Hamly, M. (2005). Self-assessment accuracy revisited: The Arab EFL context. In C. Coombe, P. Davidson, & W. Jones (Eds.), *Assessment in the Arab World* (pp. 291-306). Dubai: TESOL Arabia.

Das, M, Mpofu, D.J.S., Hasan, M.Y., & Stewart, T.S. (2002). Student perceptions of tutor skills in problem-based learning. *Medical Education, 36*, 272-278.

Derewianka B., & Hammond, J. (2001). Genre. In R. Carter & D. Nunan (Eds.), *The Cambridge guide to teaching English to speakers of other languages* (pp.186-193). Cambridge: Cambridge University Press.

Dow, A.R., & Ryan, J.T. (2000). Preparing the language student for professional interaction. In W.M. Rivers (Ed.), *Interactive language teaching* (pp. 194-210). Cambridge: Cambridge University Press.

Dyer, B. (1996). L1 and L2 composition theories: Hillocks' 'environmental mode' and task-based language teaching. *ELT Journal, 50*(4), 312-317.

Ellili, M., & Chaffin, E. (2007). Emirati students' readiness for autonomous language learning. In A. Jendli, S. Troudi, & C. Coombe (Eds.), *The power of language: Perspectives from Arabia* (pp. 306-326). Dubai: TESOL Arabia.

Eslami, Z., Al-Buainain, H., & Tzou, J. (2009). Language learning strategy use by Arabic speaking students learning English through content areas. In M. Al-Hamly, C. Coombe, P. Davidson, A. Shehadeh, & S. Troudi (Eds.), *Proceedings of the 14ᵗʰ TESOL Arabia conference: Finding your voice: Critical issues in ELT* (pp. 81-93). Dubai: TESOL Arabia Publications.

Hamp-Lyons, L. (2001). EAP. In R. Carter & D. Nunan (Eds.), *The Cambridge guide to teaching English to speakers of other languages* (pp.126-130). Cambridge: Cambridge University Press.

Hor, G., & Ismail, O. (2010). Learning styles: A case of female Saudi college students. In M. Al-Hamly, C. Coombe, P. Davidson, A. Shehadeh, & S. Troudi (Eds.), *Proceedings of the 15th TESOL Arabia conference: Learning in English: English in learning* (pp. 88-96). Dubai: TESOL Arabia Publications.

Hutchison, T, & Waters, A. (2005). *English for specific purposes.* Cambridge: Cambridge University Press.

Jordan, R.R. (2005). *English for academic purposes: A guide and resource book for teachers.* Cambridge: Cambridge University Press.

Khafagi, N. (2010). Integrating critical thinking skills in a discipline-based course. In M. Al-Hamly, C. Coombe, P. Davidson, A. Shehadeh, & S. Troudi (Eds.), *Proceedings of the 15th TESOL Arabia conference: Learning in English: English in learning* (pp. 81-87). Dubai: TESOL Arabia Publications.

Krieger, Z. (2008). An academic building boom transforms the Persian Gulf. *Chronicle of Higher Education, 54*(29). Retrieved September 3, 2010, from:
http://www.eric.ed.gov/ERICWebPortal/search/detailmini.jsp?_nfpb=true&_&ERICExtSearch_SearchValue_0=EJ790335&ERICExtSearch_SearchType_0=no&accno=EJ790335

Lauder, S., & Cozens, P. (2008). Experiments in English. In A. Jendli, C. Coombe, & S. Troudi (Eds.), *Best practice in English language teaching* (pp. 239-248). Dubai: TESOL Arabia Publications.

Lewin, T. (2008, February 10). U.S. universities rush to set up outposts abroad. *New York Times Online.* Retrieved September 3, 2010, from:
http://www.nytimes.com/2008/02/10/education/10global.html

Matthews-Aydinli, J. (2007). Problem-based learning and adult English language learners. *CAELA Brief.* Washington D.C.: CAELA, 1-7. Retrieved April 17, 2010, from:
http://www.cal.org/caela/esl_resources/briefs/Problem-based.pdf

Mellor-Clark, S. (2006). Probem-based learning in ESP: Lessons learned. In M.S. Lahlou & A. Richardson (Eds.), *English for specific purposes in the Arab World* (pp. 35-46). Dubai: TESOL Arabia.

Morley, J. & Guariento, W. (2001). Text and task authenticity in the EFL classroom. *ELT Journal*, 55(4), 347-353.

Moust, J., Bonhuijs, P., & Schmidt, H. (2001). *Problem-based learning: A student guide*. Groningen: Wolters-Noordhof.

Nunan, D. (1989). *Understanding language classrooms: A guide for teacher-initiated action*. Cambridge: Prentice Hall.

Nunan, D. (1992). *Research methods in language learning*. Cambridge: Cambridge University Press.

Nunan, D. (2004). *Task-based language teaching*. Cambridge: Cambridge University Press.

Reid, J. (1987). The learning style preferences of ESL students. *TESOL Quarterly*, *21*(1), 87-110.

Reid, J. (1996). Responding to different topic types: A quantitative analysis from a contrastive rhetoric perspective. In B. Kroll (Ed.), *Second language writing: Research insights for the classroom* (pp. 191-210). Cambridge: Cambridge University Press.

Reid, J. (2001). Writing. In R. Carter & D. Nunan (Eds.), *The Cambridge guide to teaching English to speakers of other languages* (pp. 28-33). Cambridge: Cambridge University Press.

Richards, J., & Rogers, T.S. (2001). *Approaches and methods in language teaching*. New York: Cambridge University Press.

Richardson, A. (2006). Learning how to question. In M.S. Lahlou & A. Richardson (Eds.), *English for specific purposes in the Arab World* (pp. 111-122). Dubai: TESOL Arabia.

Ricks, M., & Szcerbik, A. (2010). Independent learning & Gulf students: Culture clash? In M. Al-Hamly, C. Coombe, P. Davidson, A. Shehadeh, & S. Troudi (Eds.), *Proceedings of the 15th TESOL Arabia conference: Learning in English: English in learning* (pp. 159-167). Dubai: TESOL Arabia Publications.

Sancheti, P. (2008). Comparative study of teaching and learning practices. In A. Jendli, C. Coombe, & S. Troudi (Eds.), *Best practice in English language teaching* (pp. 65- 76). Dubai: TESOL Arabia Publications.

Scott, S.W. (2006). Adapting western teamwork model to higher academia in the Middle East. In M.S. Lahlou & A. Richardson (Eds.), *English for specific purposes in the Arab World* (pp. 85-94). Dubai: TESOL Arabia.

Skehan, P. (1996). Second language acquisition research and task-based instruction. In J. Willis & D. Willis (Eds.), *Challenge and change in language teaching* (pp. 17-30). Oxford: Heinemann.

Sohdy, R. (2010). Does negotiation role play affect critical thinking skills of EAP/ESP university students? In M. Al-Hamly, C. Coombe, P. Davidson, A. Shehadeh, & S. Troudi (Eds.), *Proceedings of the 15ᵗʰ TESOL Arabia conference: Learning in English: English in learning* (pp. 97-110). Dubai: TESOL Arabia Publications.

Thomas, M. (2003). Assessment and learner performance in PBL. *Journal of Language and Learning 1*(1). Retrieved April 17, 2010, from:
http://www.jllonline.co.uk/journal/jllearn/1_1/thomas_learn1_1.html

Tomlinson, B. (2001). Materials development. In R. Carter & D. Nunan (Eds.), *The Cambridge guide to teaching English to speakers of other languages* (pp. 66-71). Cambridge: Cambridge University Press.

Tudor, I. (2001). *The dynamics of the language classroom.* Cambridge: Cambridge University Press.

Ward, J.M. (2009). Teaching to learn: Advantages of student-centred learning. In C. Gunn (Ed.), *Exploring TESOL practices in the Arabian Gulf* (pp. 124-130). Dubai: TESOL Arabia.

Willis, D., & Willis, J. (2001). Task-based language learning. In J. Willis & D. Willis (Eds.), *Challenge and change in language teaching* (pp. 173-9). Oxford: Heinemann.

Willis, J. (1996). Consciousness-raising activities in the language classroom. In J. Willis & D. Willis (Eds.), *Challenge and change in language teaching* (pp. 63-76). Oxford: Heinemann.

Sabina Ostrowska

Chapter 18
The Effect of Course Content on Student Motivation: A UAE Study

Abstract

The idea that Arab students' motivation towards learning English can be increased by introducing local materials into the classroom has been an undercurrent of thought at many English as a Second Language (ESL) conferences and workshops in the United Arab Emirates (UAE) in the last few years. However, there is no actual research that explores the veracity of this claim. The small scale action research reported in this chapter was designed to test the assumption that integrating local topics into course content increases students' motivation to study English. Both quantitative and qualitative data were collected so as to compare the students' response to lessons based on their textbooks versus lessons developed using local articles. The quantitative survey revealed no significant difference between the students' interest in either textbook- or newspaper-based lessons. The factors that influenced the students' level of motivation and interest were individual and personal. These findings underscore a tacit assumption that has been adopted by many researchers working within the critical paradigm; that is the assumption of 'learner homogeneity'. This chapter argues that even though critical theory tries to jettison the old dichotomy of 'us' and 'them', it often results in reinforcing the unequal power structure under the guise of post-colonial fairness. The follow-up group interview with the students underscores the relevance of four themes: the students' poor linguistic abilities, the feeling that English taught in the classroom is disconnected from the students' lives, the teacher as a source of motivation, and a preference to read about topics directly related to individual students' lives. In conclusion, independent reading portfolios are suggested as a solution to recognize learner heterogeneity, and to increase learner autonomy, and consequently, motivation.

Introduction

The UAE is a vibrant and multicultural country, where English is spoken in shops, cafés, and on the streets. There are local newspapers written in English which report on local news. Many Arabic-speaking parents decide to send their children to private English-speaking schools, or schools with a British or American curriculum (Troudi, 2007, pp. 5-6). By and large, learning English is an important factor in many people's lives in the Emirates; a factor that should positively influence ESL learners' instrumental motivation, i.e. motivation 'pertaining to the potential pragmatic gains of L2 [second language] proficiency, such as getting a better job or a higher salary' (Dörnyei, 2001, p. 49). Despite the abundance of local texts and contexts in English, few of them reach the local classrooms. Most of the ESL coursebooks used at the primary, secondary, and tertiary levels are written for Western students and they are published by international companies, such as Harcourt, Cambridge University Press, Oxford University Press, and Longman. Some of them are adapted to conform to Muslim culture and religion, but the changes made to these adapted coursebooks are superficial, and are concerned mostly with cultural appropriateness. Even though English plays an important role in Emirati society, 'local students see no concrete links between English language ability and communicative require-ments' (Syed, 2003, p. 338).

According to Syed (2003, p. 337), ESL teachers in the Gulf regions have identified several distinct issues that they find challenging, i.e. student motivation, literacy, underachievement, reliance on rote learning and memorization, and a dependence on high-stakes testing. This observation is supported by Thabit (2009) who expresses her concern with high school students' poor level of motivation and reluctance to learn English via culturally distant course materials:

> The issue of motivation for the students I teach is an important one as many of my high school students show poor attitudes towards learning English. When asked about it informally they often associate this to *boring textbooks which are of no relevance or interest to them*. [Emphasis added] (p. 57)

Some ESL teachers in the UAE suggest that designing activities that 'reflect topics of local interest and [...] drawn from local sources such as newspapers and magazines' would solve the problems outlined by Syed (Poultney, 2009, p. 19). Barlow and Floyd (1999), cited in Bennani (2008, p. 86), 'advocate the production of in-house materials, materials designed locally to suit learners' local needs and culture'.

A number of researchers in the Gulf have been exploring the issues surrounding Arab students' motivation to learn English and the use of local and authentic materials in the ESL classroom (Midraj, Midraj, O'Neill, Sellami, & El-Temtamy, 2007; Harris, 2009; Thabit, 2009; Banville, 2009). Most of these studies take the correlation between using local materials for teaching English and increased student motivation for granted and there is no actual research that explores the reliability of this claim.

Background

The issue of course content is inevitably linked with student (and teacher) motivation. White (1988, p. 66) claims that 'interesting topics' can increase students' motivation to study English. Even though the literature on the topic of language learning motivation is vast, (e.g. Oxford & Shearin, 1994; Gardner & Tremblay, 1994; Tremblay & Gardner, 1995), only a handful of researchers point out a correlation between students' motivation and course content (Dörnyei, 1994; Julkunen, 2002). In his Language Learning Motivation Model, which draws on Gardner's socio-educational model of motivation, Dörnyei (1994, p. 280) distinguishes three aspects of learning that may influence the degree of motivation among language students and the level of persistence in studying a foreign language:

1. the linguistic, cultural and social aspects of the target language;
2. the learner as an individual; and
3. the learning context.

The linguistic level is related to the concepts of integrative and instrumental motivation which form the traditional focus of the majority of studies into motivation in second language learning. Gardner's concept of integrative motivation, defined as 'a positive disposition towards the L2 group and the desire to interact with and even become similar to valued members of that community' (Dörnyei, 1994, p. 274), has been questioned in the light of recent reconceptualizations of language learning motivation (Lamb, 2004; Dörnyei & Ushioda, 2010). The researchers argue that in the globalized world there is no longer a target reference group of English speakers with whom English language learners would like to identify. The ownership of English is now global. As Stribling (2003) emphasizes, the integrative model of L2 motivation developed by Gardner cannot be transposed onto new language learning contexts, such as in the Philippines, Bombay, or, for that matter, the Gulf. Thus, it is doubtful if integrative motivation has any significant influence on ESL learners in the context of the UAE, where most

ESL learners use English to communicate with other non-native speakers or among each other.

With respect to instrumental motivation, English in the Gulf is perceived as the language of education and professional advancement. Taking into account the ESL context in the UAE, we might assume that the 'instrumental role' of English in the students' lives would provide them sufficient motivation to study English. However, one of the pioneer studies into UAE students' motivation by Midraj, Midraj, O'Neill, Sellami, and El-Temtamy (2007, p. 56) showed that college students with a strong instrumental motivation had a lower level of English language attainment than the students with a strong intrinsic motivation, i.e. willingness to communicate in English. Furthermore, according to the researchers, any study of motivation among ESL students is unique and closely linked to the socio-cultural context in which the learners live. A possible explanation for the lack of motivation to study English can be found in demotivation research. According to Dörnyei (2001), a demotivated student is someone who used to be motivated but has lost his or her commitment to study. As Dörnyei (2001) explains:

> Demotivation does not mean that all the positive influences that originally made up the motivational basis of a behaviour have been annulled; rather, it is only the resultant force that has been dampened by a strong negative component, and some other positive motives may still remain operational. (p. 143)

This means that by removing the 'negative components' that demotivate students we can restore their motivation. The relationship between the components of the language learning situation and demotivation has been researched by Sakai and Kikuchi (2009) who delineated six demotivating factors, among which is course design in terms of its content and materials. Sakai and Kikuchi's (2009) results with respect to demotivating factors are similar to Chambers's (1993), Oxford's (1998), and Dörnyei's (1998) findings. Despite the fact that these studies were conducted in different contexts, they all mention teachers (i.e., teachers' attitudes, personalities, and level of professionalism), course materials, and teaching methods as common demotivating factors.

The notion that culturally alien course materials can demotivate students is evident in Midraj et al. (2007). Drawing on their research into Emirati students' motivation, the researchers conclude that:

> [m]aterials for UAE students should be authentic to develop and/or appeal to their integrative orientation and thus developing/adding to their desire to spend time on learning outside the classroom. In other words, materials should be relevant to the students' needs and interests, and they should be *naturally motivating* to students, both in content and in form. [Emphasis added] (p. 56)

There is a common sense assumption here that the type of text used in an ESL lesson can affect students' level of motivation. This assumption though has not been questioned. Most of the research into motivation of ESL students in the Gulf leaps to the same seemingly natural assumption. For example, Banville (2009, p. 234) arguing for the use of local newspapers in the ESL classrooms in the UAE, assumes that newspaper articles 'are directly relevant to the immediate lives of students'. According to this author, using local news redresses 'a 'relevance imbalance' in classroom materials away from Anglo-centric and perhaps culturally irrelevant texts' (Banville, 2009, p. 235). Like Midraj et al. (2007), Banville (2009) assumes that lessons based on local news are relevant to students' lives, but does not provide trustworthy evidence to support this claim. This common sense conviction is contrary to the research conducted by Harris (2009). Drawing on the intuition that local news attracts students' attention and increases their motivation to read in English, Harris (2009) prepared an activity called 'Unwrapping the News' which was available to the students at their college's Independent Learning Centre. The project gave the students opportunity to read about local issues in English. In contrast to the common sense expectations, the project was a complete failure; only 5 out of 522 students participated. As the researcher found out, 'topic alone was not enough to make students put in [the] time and effort to read' the newspaper articles (Harris, 2009, p. 118). The students would read the articles only if they were in a test format and helped them prepare for their high-stakes exams.

As can be seen from this brief overview, the debate on using local texts to teach English is dynamic, but most of the time the researchers focus on expressing their teaching philosophy rather than on providing solid research findings. One of the reasons why so many ESL writers in the Gulf feel so strongly about the problems of local versus global is because of the power relationships implicit in this discourse. Using local texts in local contexts is a political issue, and a valid one, but we should not forget who our most important stakeholders are: the students.

The Study

The main aim of this research was to see whether Arab ESL students feel more interested in language learning materials that concern local issues, and topics set in familiar contexts. The secondary aim was to explore students' opinions about their English language course content, specifically the reading materials and tasks in their textbook. The study sought to find out how relevant the reading passages from the coursebook were to students' realities, and whether they felt inspired or motivated by these passages. The study utilised an action research methodology. As a method, action research fits well with critical and interpretive paradigms, because it assumes that reality is transient and subjective, and that each social context is unique and worth investigating. In addition to this, action research 'enables us to explore and even 'discover' implicit theories and beliefs that we hold about our teaching' (Troudi & Riley, 1996, p. 2). With regard to this study, action research helped to test some common assumptions about UAE students' motivation to read locally produced texts.

The context of this action research is an English language foundation program at a tertiary level educational institution in Al

Ain, the United Arab Emirates. The aim of the English foundation program is to develop the students' language skills for further study at the college level. The curriculum of the foundation programme is organized around discreet language objectives. The syllabus is textbook-driven and based on the *Interchange* series (Richards, Hull, & Proctor, 2004). This coursebook series is supplemented by the reading and vocabulary textbooks entitled *Password 1, 2,* and *3* (Butler & Bonesteel, 2003).

The class that participated in this action research study comprised of 9 Arabic female students. The students were 18-21 years old. In a practice Test of English as a Foreign Language (TOEFL) administered in the classroom, the students' TOEFL scores ranged from 410 to 480 points.

The data were collected using a questionnaire with closed- and open-ended questions, and a recorded, semi-structured group interview. To avoid misinterpretations and superficial responses, the questionnaires were translated into Arabic, and the students were allowed to answer the open-ended questions in Arabic. The questionnaires that were answered in Arabic were translated into English and then coded.

During one academic semester, the students followed their regular syllabus and coursebook, which were supplemented with materials adapted from a local English newspaper, *The National*. For the purpose of the survey, three passages were selected from the coursebook and three passages from the newspaper. The three passages from the coursebook corresponded with the topics in the passages from the newspaper (see Table 1).

Table 1. Reading Passages Used in the Survey

Topics	Coursebook Passages	Newspaper Articles
Problems of adolescence	Sleepy Teens	National Anorexia Levels
Health and medical tests	Drug to Match Your Genes	Women Ill-Informed on Cancer
Service industry	Service with a Smile	Tourism Shake-up for Al Ain

The passages taken from *The National* newspaper referred to familiar names and locations, and touched on current issues in the UAE, whilst the passages from the coursebook were set in foreign contexts.

In order to explore the students' opinions of these six passages, a take-home questionnaire was distributed in the final week of the course. The students were informed of the general purpose of the survey, i.e. to improve their English courses. The participation in the survey was voluntary, and eight out of nine students returned the questionnaires. All of the participants of the survey signed a consent form which was written both in English and in Arabic on the front page of the questionnaire.

The questionnaire consisted of twenty four closed-questions with a 4-point Likert scale from 'strongly disagree' to 'strongly agree'. The students were asked four questions about each reading passage. The questions drew upon the Course-Specific Motivational Components outlined by Dörnyei (1994, p. 280) after Crookes and Schmidt (1991). The study focused on interest, relevance, and satisfaction. In the questionnaire, interest and relevance were measured with the following items:

1. The passage was very interesting.
2. I felt that the topic was relevant to my life.
3. I would like to read more passages on a similar topic.

Satisfaction with the outcome of the tasks was measured by asking the students about their perceived comprehension of the reading passages.

The data gathered in the survey provided only a general picture of the students' opinion of the reading passages. It was necessary to validate these results using a semi-structured group interview. The students were asked the following set of questions:

1. Are you motivated to study English? Why? Why not?
2. What do you think of the content of your English courses at the university? Please, describe the positives and negatives.

3. What topics would you like to discuss in your English class if you could choose them yourself?
4. Give an example of your most memorable English lesson?
5. Which reading passage from your coursebook do you remember the most?

The interview was transcribed and the data were thematically coded. To ensure the validity of the coding of the qualitative data, an independent rater was asked to also code the interview, and the results were compared. There were twelve themes of varied level of frequency identified in the data, which were then grouped into four distinct categories that are discussed in the following section.

Results

The results of the questionnaire were analysed using the Statistical Package for the Social Sciences (SPSS). The descriptive statistics are summarized in Table 2. The mean results indicate that 'Women Ill-Informed on Cancer', the passage about cervical cancer among Emirati women, was considered as the most interesting and relevant. Two other passages that scored high in these categories were 'Sleepy Teens', the passage about American teenagers' sleeping habits, and 'Service with a Smile', the passage about the Japanese service industry; both these passages were taken from the students' coursebook. Thus, there was no distinct preference towards the passages from the local newspaper.

Table 2. Questionnaire: Mean Results for Individual Passages *(n=9)*

	The passage was very interesting.	I felt that the topic was relevant to my life.	I did not understand the topic of the passage.	I would like to read more passages on a similar topic.
	Mean	Mean	Mean	Mean
Sleepy Teens	3.12	2.88	1.5	3
Drug to Match Your Genes	2.88	3	2.38	2.12
Service with a Smile	3.12	2.62	2	3
National Anorexia Levels	2.88	2.75	2	2.62
Women Ill-Informed on Cancer	3.38	3.12	1.62	3.25
Tourism Shake-up for Al Ain	3	3.12	2	2.5

Scale: 1-Strongly disagree, 2-Disagree, 3-Agree, 4-Strongly Agree

The cumulative results of the questionnaire items (Table 3) show that 88% of the students thought that the passage, 'Sleepy Teens', was interesting, and 75% found the topic of the passage relevant to their lives and would like to read more texts on a similar topic. When reporting on their opinion of 'Women Ill-Informed on Cancer', 88% thought that the passage was interesting, 63% found it relevant to their lives, and 75% would read more similar articles. With respect to 'Service with a Smile', only 37.5% thought it relevant to their lives, and only 62% would like to read more similar stories.

Table 3. Cumulative Results for Individual Passages *(n=9)*

	The passage was very interesting.		I felt that the topic was relevant to my life.		I did not understand the topic of the passage.		I would like to read more passages on a similar topic.	
	Agree/ Strongly Agree	Disagree/ Strongly Disagree	Agree/ Strongly Agree	Disagree/ Strongly Disagree	Agree/ Strongly Agree	Disagree / Strongly Disagree	Agree/ Strongly Agree	Disagree / Strongly Disagree
Sleepy Teens	62.5% 25%	12.5%	62.5% 12.5%	25%		50% 50%	50% 25%	25%
Drug to Match Your Genes	37.5% 25%	37.5%	25% 37.5%	37.5%	25/ 12.5	12.5% 50%	37.5%	25% 37.5%
Service with a Smile	50% 37.5%	12.5%	37.5%	12.5% 50%	37.5%	37.5% 25%	12.5% 50%	12.5% 25%
National Anorexia Levels	25% 37.5%	12.5% 25%	25% 25%	50%	12.5% 12.5%	37.5% 37.5%	12.5% 37.5%	25% 25%
Women Ill-Informed on Cancer	37.5% 50%	12.5%	12.5% 50%	37.5%		37.5% 62.5%	12.5% 62.5%	12.5% 12.5%
Tourism Shake-up for Al Ain	50% 25%	25%	12.5% 50%	37.5%	12.5% 12.5%	37.5% 37.5%	37.5% 12.5%	12.5% 37.5%

Scale: 1-Strongly disagree, 2-Disagree, 3-Agree, 4-Strongly Agree

This result is confirmed by the open-ended part of the questionnaire. When asked which passage was the most interesting and why, one student wrote about 'Sleepy Teens': 'Because it was very interesting and it has many information about us because now we are in this age. Also, it has many advice for teenagers' (Student 7, Questionnaire). In a similar manner, other students felt that the passage had an 'effect on [their] social and daily life' (Student 3, Questionnaire), it was 'related to [their] life' (Student 4, Questionnaire), and it 'was dealing with an important issue in the society' (Student 5, Questionnaire).

In order to see whether there is any significant difference in the students' perception of the passages from the coursebook and the passages from the newspaper, the answers to the questions about the passages from the coursebook were combined and compared with the responses to the questions about the newspaper passages using Wilcoxon Signed Ranks Test. The comparison of the mean results of each question showed that the students found the passages from the newspaper to be slightly more interesting, and relevant (see Table 4), however the difference was not found to be statistically significant ($Z = .738, p = .461$).

Table 4. Comparison of Students' Response to the Passages from the Coursebook versus Passages from the Newspaper

	Passages from the coursebook	Passages from the newspaper
	Mean	Mean
The passage was very interesting.	3.04	3.08
I felt that the topic was relevant to my life.	2.83	3
I did not understand the topic of the passage.	1.96	1.87
I would like to read more passages on a similar topic.	2.71	2.79

During the analysis of the transcribed interview, four themes emerged that are relevant to students' motivation to study English:

- Demotivation Due to Language Problems
- English Being Disconnected from Students' Lives
- Teacher as the Source of Motivation
- Preference to Read about Topics Directly Related to Individual Students' Lives

Each of these themes is discussed below.

Demotivation Due to Language Problems

When asked why many students are not motivated to study English, most of the students who were interviewed indicated problems related to their poor linguistic ability. Their immediate response was 'because this is very difficult' (Student 4, Interview, Line 3). Listening and speaking were perceived to be the most strenuous for the students. This observation is in agreement with Thabit's (2009) research into her students' perceived language problems. One of my students said that she finds it difficult to speak, and the others confirmed this; some students mentioned listening as the second-most difficult skill.

Another area that the students felt that affected their motivation to read was vocabulary. One student said: 'Grammar is easy but the vocabulary it's difficult' (Student 4, Interview, Line 12). Students gave several examples in which understanding vocabulary improved their self-esteem and gave them a feeling of achievement. Student 2 (Interview, Line 140) explained that the most memorable reading experience was when she 'translate[ed] all the words' and understood the text. Student 1 (Interview, Lines 184-190) recalled a graded reader she read a year before: 'It is very nice and the word easy. Vocab easy and the grammar easy.' The students' accounts of the most memorable reading materials did not refer to the topics but to their sense of achievement when they managed to understand the English in the reading passage.

English Disconnected from Students' Lives

One of the themes that recurred throughout the interview was the students' perception that the English they study in the classroom is disconnected from their lives and thus it is irrelevant to them. One of the students expressed her concern that what they study in the foundation programme is irrelevant to their future studies at the college: 'we take English course but we can't take another subject to benefit what we learn here [...] You learn in English course something else [than] we learn in other subjects; it's difficult' (Student 3, Interview, Lines 22-23). Another student commented on an activity in which the students had to bring their favourite food product to the class, talk about it in front of the class, and teach the students two new words from the label. She felt it was good to 'give the students exercise in their life' (Student 2, Interview, Lines 34-36). In general, the students considered projects that required work outside the classroom as the most motivating and relevant to their lives. One of the students commented that it is difficult to focus on reading in the classroom, and that it is easier to read when they have a clear task to achieve.

Teacher as the Source of Motivation

The relationship between teacher motivation and learners' motivation was found to be a significant factor in student achievement. As one of the students explained, 'the important things in teaching English is teachers. [...] If the teacher [is] hard working the student will work also' (Student 2, Interview, Lines 223-224). In addition, the teacher's approval in the form of praise, or a good mark, was mentioned as a motivating factor.

> I remember in grade 11 I like to read about amazing animals. It is very nice because I read different information from the internet and I wrote a topic about it and I get a very good mark [...] and the teacher was happy. (Student 4, Interview, Lines 110-113)

> In science, we have exercise about plants I collect different leave for plants and I put in the paper and when I get for the teacher I get good mark. (Student 5, Interview, Lines 145-148)

The observation that teachers motivate or demotivate students is in agreement with previous research on motivation (Chambers, 1993; Oxford, 1998; Dörnyei, 1998).

Preference to Read about Topics Directly Related to Individual Students' Lives

With respect to the topics in the reading materials, a few students mentioned science and technology as being boring and difficult. However, a few other students declared technology as interesting. All of the students agreed that topics related to teenagers are very interesting, even if they discuss teenagers from countries other than theirs. Furthermore, the students mentioned topics related to foreign cultures and health as attractive.

In response to the question about the reasons why particular passages from the coursebook stayed in their memory, the students provided personal rationales, e.g. 'Because that's very important for my health.' (Student 4, Interview, Lines 171); 'Because it's important for life. For me it's a nice subject.' (Student 2, Interview, Lines 181). The students were most interested in topics related to their personal life, i.e. being teenagers and being women. Two students expressed it very well, 'The topic is interesting for me because I am a girl. The subject increases our information about cancer' (Student 3, Survey) and 'now we have many information about some diseases in the women and teenagers. Also, they give us some advice and causes for these diseases.' (Student 6, Survey). With regard to the other topics, the students portrayed a variety of interests.

Discussion

The main question of this research study was to see whether Arab university students would find course materials based on their local issues and derived from local newspapers more interesting and relevant to their lives, and hence more motivating. The statistical analysis showed that there is no significant difference in the students' response to coursebook passages versus newspaper passages. The interview confirmed that the topics students found most interesting were those related to their individual lives and concerns; there was no common denominator across the group of students. The results of the study revealed a silent assumption on the side of the researcher, and many other advocates of using local materials in an ESL classroom (Holliday, 2003; Midraj et al., 2007; Poultney, 2009; Banville, 2009), namely the presumption of learners' homogeneity. The study assumed that the students were interested in local issues, or that they were all interested in similar topics. However, this assumption proved to be flawed because it did not acknowledge either the fact that it was the teacher who chose the materials that the students studied, or the heterogeneity of students in terms of their lives and personalities. This assumption is related to stereotypes in TESOL.

According to Kumaravadivelu (2003, p. 716), ESL teachers stereotype the learners to deal with 'the unknown and unmanageable' task of teaching a language. Generally speaking, a teacher's stereotyping of students is a result of the whole educational apparatus which fosters homogeneity and jettisons individuality. The operation of this system can be observed everywhere in the world. As Apple describes it (2004), this phenomenon is a side effect of unequal power relations between students and their teachers. Apple (ibid.) maintains that:

> Educators have developed categories and modes of perception which reify or thingify individuals so that they [the educators] can confront students as institutional abstractions rather than as concrete persons with whom they have real ties in the process of cultural and economic reproduction. (p. 126)

In recent years, there has been a conscious movement against such stereotyping of Arabic ESL students. In his TESOL (Teaching English to Speakers of Other Languages) Arabia conference presentation, 'The struggle against 'us'-'them' conceptualizations in TESOL as the ownership of English changes', Holliday (2003) outlined two positions taken by TESOL professionals. In the first position, depicted as 'us' versus 'them', English is brought to the students by foreign teachers and foreign coursebooks. In this position, the students are passive receivers of the language. In the second position, called 'we are all in it together', English is part of the local context, and thus part of the students' lives. While such conceptualizations sound democratic and egalitarian, they maintain the 'us' and 'them' divide. In other words, bringing the local context, i.e. Gulf based texts, to the classroom may not be what the so called 'local' students want.

Treating Gulf students as a homogenous abstraction leads to curricular decisions that are not informed by the students' real needs and interests, but rather by educators' assumptions about them. Forcing local texts on the students is just as undemocratic as using global coursebooks. The former position may seem to rid of the gap between 'us' and 'them', but it is just another guise for the traditional power structure. For example, Banville (2009, p. 236) claims that the situation in which 'teachers [...] tailor the news story to the interests and cultural composition of the class' fosters a democratic power relation in a classroom. This approach, however well-intended, is not democratic; it reinforces the traditional unequal power relation between students and teacher under the guise of cultural sensitivity. It renders students homogenous by assuming that because they come from the same region, they should share the same interests. Furthermore, it reinforces the teacher's central power position as the one who knows what they want to read.

Drawing on the findings of the current research study and keeping in mind students' individuality, I want to suggest the introduction of independent reading portfolios as a solution: (i) to motivate the students to read outside the classroom; (ii) to allow the students to read on topics relevant to their lives; and (iii) to foster autonomy. It is hard to foster good reading habits and pleasure of reading in the classroom. This does not mean that we should not teach reading; teaching reading skills and strategies is an essential part of teaching language. However, it should not end there. If we ensure that the students read outside the classroom, we will help them become autonomous readers. The implementation of independent reading portfolios requires a certain amount of initial preparation, and teacher-student conferencing during the term. A number of preliminary sessions, held in the library or in the computer lab, should be devoted to discussion on where to find reading materials, and how to select appropriate and interesting texts. It is essential that the students grasp the idea that reading is not a chore, and that they should choose materials that *they* find interesting and exciting.

Conclusion

The assumption that fostering learner autonomy increases students' motivation draws on research in humanistic psychology and educational psychology (Dörnyei, 2001). Dörnyei (ibid.) lists a number of strategies that can help increase students' autonomy: 'allowing students real choices, sharing responsibility with the students for organizing their learning process and giving them positions of genuine authority, and encouraging students' contributions, peer teaching and project work' (p. 131). One of the approaches associated with the development of autonomy is resources-based, i.e. it underscores students' independent interaction with learning materials. Introducing independent reading portfolios into the Arab educational context described in this chapter can prove to be beneficial in developing Arab students' autonomy, and their motivation to study, and specifically, to read in English.

References

Apple, M. W. (2004). *Ideology and curriculum*. New York and London: RoutledgeFalmer.

Banville, S. (2009). Bringing news into the classroom. In M. Al-Hamly, C. Coombe, P. Davidson, A. Shehadeh, & S. Troudi (Eds.), *Finding your voice: Critical issues in ELT* (pp. 233-243). Dubai: TESOL Arabia.

Bennani, A. (2008). L2 young readers and foreign cultural content. In A. Jendli, C. Coombe, & S. Troudi (Eds.), *Best practice in English language teaching* (pp. 79-94). Dubai: TESOL Arabia Publication.

Butler, L., & Bonesteel, L. (2003). *Password.* New York: Longman.

Chambers, G.N. (1993). Talking the 'de' out of demotivation. *Language Learning Journal, 7*, 13-16.

Crookes, G., & Schmidt, R.W. (1991). Motivation: Reopening the research agenda. *Language Learning, 41*, 469-512.

Dörnyei, Z. (1998). Demotivation in foreign language learning. Paper presented at the TESOL '98 Congress, Seattle.

Dörnyei, Z. (1994). Motivation and motivating in the foreign language classroom. *The Modern Language Journal, 78*(3), 273-284.

Dörnyei, Z. (2001). *Teaching and researching motivation.* Essex: Pearson Education.

Dörnyei, Z. (2010). L2 motivational self system. In Z. Dörnyei, & E. Ushioda (Eds.), *Motivation, language identity and the L2 self.* Bristol: Mutlilingual Matters.

Dörnyei, Z., & Ushioda, E. (2010). Motivation, language identities and the L2 self: A theoretical overview. In Z. Dörnyei, & E. Ushioda (Eds.), *Motivation, language, identity and the L2 self.* Bristol: Mutlilingual Matters.

Gardner, R.C., & Tremblay, P.F. (1994). On motivation, research agendas, and theoretical frameworks. *The Modern Language Journal, 78*(3), 359-368.

Harris, D. (2009). Establishing an L2 reading motivation framework for tertiary level. In D. Anderson, & M. McGuire (Eds.), *Cultivating real readers: Emerging theory and practice for adult Arab learners* (pp. 113-120). Abu Dhabi: HCT Press.

Holliday, A. (2003). The struggle against 'US'-'THEM' conceptualization in TESOL as the ownership of English changes. In Z. Syed, C. Coombe, & S. Troudi (Eds.), *Critical reflection and practice* (pp. 16-40). Dubai: TESOL Arabia.

Julkunen, K. (2002). Situation- and task-specific motivation in foreign language learning. In Z. Dörnyei, & R. Schmidt (Eds.), *Motivation and second language acquisition* (pp. 29-41). Manoa: University of Hawaii.

Kumaravadivelu, B. (2003). Problematizing cultural stereotypes in TESOL. *TESOL Quarterly, 4*, 709-719.

Lamb, M. (2004). Integrative motivation in a globalizing world. *System, 32*, 3-19.

Midraj, S., Midraj, J., O'Neill, G., Sellami, A., & El-Temtamy, O. (2007). UAE grade 12 students' motivation and language learning. In S. Midraj, A. Jendli, & A. Sellami (Eds.), *Research in ELT Context* (pp. 47-62). Dubai: TESOL Arabia.

Oxford, R. (1998). The unravelling tapestry: teacher and course characteristics associated with demotivation in the language classroom. demotivation in foreign language learning. Paper presented at the TESOL '98 Congress. Seattle.

Oxford, R., & Shearin, J. (1994). Language learning motivation: Expanding the theoretical framework. *The Modern Language Journal, 78*(1), 12-28.

Poultney, N. (2009). Reflections in the Gulf. *Perspectives: An English Language Teaching Periodical from TESOL Arabia, 16*(1), 18-19.

Richards, J.C., Hull, J., & Proctor, S. (2004). *Interchange*. New York: Cambridge University Press.

Sakai, H., & Kikuchi, K. (2009). An analysis of demotivators in the EFL classroom. *System, 37*, 57-69.

Stribling, P. (2003). *Motivation in the ESL/EFL Classroom: Rhetoric and reality. Proceedings of the 16th EA Educational Conference Melbourne 2003*. Retrieved May 10, 2009, from: http://www.englishaustralia.com.au/ea_conference03/proceeding s/pdf/034F_Stribling.pdf

Syed, Z. (2003). The sociocultural context of English language teaching in the Gulf. *TESOL Quarterly, 37*(2), 337-341.

Thabit, A. (2009). Exploring the use of authentic materials in a girls' government high school. In C. Gunn (Ed.), *Exploring TESOL Practices in the Arabian Gulf* (pp. 56-65). Dubai: TESOL Arabia.

Tremblay, P.F., & Gardner, R.C. (1995). Expanding the motivation construct in language learning. *The Modern Language Journal, 79*(4), 505-518.

Troudi, S. (2007). The effects of English as a medium of instruction. In A. Jendli, C. Coombe, & S. Troudi (Eds.), *The power of language: Perspectives from Arabia* (pp. 3-19). Dubai: TESOL Arabia Publications.

Troudi, S., & Riley, S. (1996). Action research: Using your classroom for professional development. 30th Annual Meeting of the Teachers of English to Speakers of Other Languages, Chicago.

White, R.V. (1988). *The ELT curriculum: Design, innovation and management.* Oxford: Basil Blackwell.

MELANIE GOBERT

Chapter 19
Cultivating Phonological and Orthographic Awareness in Arab Learners of English

Abstract

Despite the inclusion of English as a Foreign Language (EFL) and English as a Second Language (ESL) in the national primary and secondary school curriculum in most Gulf Arabic speaking countries since the early 70s, tertiary teachers have long remarked the poor reading standards of high school graduates (Al Kitbi, 2006; Cobb, 2007). Many Gulf Arab nationals cannot obtain terminal degrees because of their inability to demonstrate an effective reading ability in English on external standardized benchmark exams such as the International English Language Testing System (IELTS, 2006; 2007; 2008). Phonological awareness is not only necessary for success in reading achievement in English (Ehri, 2005; Lesaux & Siegel, 2003), but it is a precursor of reading ability. This chapter describes a quantitative pretest/posttest quasi-experimental study that was used to determine if direct phonics instruction would increase the phonological and orthographic awareness of 18 to 25-year-old students studying in a tertiary foundation program in English in the United Arab Emirates (UAE). The research suggests that phonics training of sixteen weeks duration does not significantly improve students' performance on a measure of phonological awareness.

Introduction

The Persian Gulf has been important as an oil-producing region since World War II. The UAE is a small country located on the Persian Gulf made up of a federation of seven emirates, with a population of about 4 million, of which only about a quarter are nationals. In modern times, English has replaced Arabic as the *lingua franca* for communication among the 200 various nationalities and linguistic groups working in the UAE (Randall & Samimi, 2010). English is also the medium of instruction for all government tertiary institutions in the country.

Poor English language standards among UAE citizens is a matter of concern for the government which is striving to nationalize jobs and maintain economic growth (Al Kitbi, 2006; Al Sayegh, 2004). Despite all the resources committed to the teaching of English, many UAE national students fail to achieve adequate standards in English literacy. This restricts them from earning a terminal degree and this, in turn, hinders them from entering the local job market. The average score for reading on the Academic Module of the IELTS exam for Arabic speaking students was 5.52 in 2006, 5.31 in 2007, and 5.09 in 2008. For the General Training Module the scores were 5.10, 5.04, and 4.73 respectively. For UAE test takers the average reading scores were even lower. The Academic Module was 5.10 in 2006, 4.96 in 2007, and 4.80 in 2008; on the General Training Module, the scores were 4.07 in 2006, 4.02 in 2007, and 3.91 in 2008 (IELTS, 2006; 2007; 2008).

This chapter reviews historical and contemporary perspectives on reading in English as a Second Language, and discusses the implications of the Arabic writing system, Arabic diglossia, and word-recognition research on Arabic learners.

Background

Alderson (1984) first posed the question of whether reading in a second language was a reading problem or a language problem and concluded that a threshold level of language acquisition is necessary before students' language (L1) reading ability can assist in reading a second language. The Threshold Hypothesis, also called the Linguistic Interdependence Hypothesis (Abu Rabia, 2001), or Central Processing Hypothesis (Geva & Siegel, 2000), proposes that learners transfer their language proficiency from one language to another. In other words, students who read well in one language will be good readers in an additional language without considering the possibility that language learners might not be proficient in reading their own language, or that they may be illiterate or semi-literate in their L1 (Burt, Peyton, & Adams, 2003).

In direct opposition to the Threshold Hypothesis is the Orthographic Depth Hypothesis (Geva & Siegel, 2000), also called the Script Dependent Hypothesis (Abu Rabia, 2001), or the Linguistic Coding Depth Hypothesis (Kahn-Horwitz, Shimron, & Sparks, 2006), which proposes that the more distance there is between two writing systems, the greater the difficulty in decoding the written language. The Orthographic Depth Hypothesis predicts that the irregularity of grapheme-phoneme conversion rules in English will create significant reading and writing problems for Arab students (Abu Rabia, 2002).

In Beland and Mimouni's (2001) case study of a 32-year-old bilingual male patient who suffered brain damage from a stroke which resulted in deep dyslexia in two languages, (Arabic and French), the researchers found a large number of letter reversal errors such as 'qird,' (monkey) for 'qidr,' (cooking pot). Because letter reversal errors were not observed in French, the researchers concluded that 'the Arabic consonantal trilateral root system constitutes a privileged unit of access to the Arabic mental lexicon' (p. 118).

Abu Rabia (2002) also proposed a model of reading unique to the Arabic reader when reading Arabic without the diacritics that mark the short vowels. These diacritics (for example, as in the word *résumé*) are removed from the native Arabic speaker's written script from about the age of nine (Maamouri, 1998). Early word recognition research on Arabic ESL learners mistakenly categorized Arabic as an orthographically shallow language when compared to English (e.g. Brown & Haynes, 1985; Randall & Meara, 1988). Orthographically shallow languages are phonetic, which means that they have a high level of one-to-one sound-letter correspondence. Orthographically deep languages are languages with a low-level of one-to-one sound letter correspondence. Today most researchers agree that Arabic is an orthographically deep language when the diacritics that mark the short vowels are removed (e.g. Abu Rabia, 2002; Abu Rabia & Awwad, 2004; Kahn-Horwitz, Shimron & Sparks, 2006; Mumtaz & Humphreys, 2001). Furthermore, in the Arabic trilateral, or triconsonantal, root system, words contain a three, or sometimes four, consonant root such as 'ktb' (Abu Rabia, 2002; Abu Rabia & Taha, 2006). The root 'ktb' means 'write.' Written without the diacritics that indicate short vowels for adult readers, the reader pronounces 'ktb,' 'kitab.' The vowel sounds 'i' and 'a' are part of the consonant sounds 'k' and 't.' In Arabic, the root 'ktb' combines with different affixes and suffixes to produce different words or units of meaning, such as 'ketaab,' *book*, 'yiktib,' *he writes*, 'katab,' *he wrote*, and 'kaatib,' *writer*, but the reader must put in the vowel sounds as appropriate according to the sentence context to determine the correct word for the specific context (Abu Rabia & Awwad, 2004). Subsequently, the phenomenon of homographs (words that are spelled alike but have a different meaning, such as 'bank' and river 'bank' in English) occurs in Arabic to a much greater extent than in English, with a proficient Arabic reader sometimes needing to finish an entire page of text in order to decode its meaning (Abu Rabia, 2002). Abu Rabia's model of reading in Arabic, proposes that the reader's eye identifies the trilateral or quadrilateral root of the word and conveys general lexical access and sentence comprehension. The

Arabic reader does not use phonological information for exact lexical retrieval purposes. Fluent English readers, on the other hand, access words lexically by both sight and sound as in Coltheart's (2006) Dual Access Route Theory.

The phenomenon of Arabic diglossia is another significant factor in the teaching of ESL to Arabic learners (Maamouri, 1998). Diglossia (a termed coined by Ferguson in 1959 cited in Saiegh-Haddad, 2004) is characterized by the following features: (a) a difference between written and spoken forms; (b) a rigid sociofunctional complementarity of two separate functions performed by two linguistic codes; (c) a dominant and rich written literacy tradition; and (d) linguistic relatedness between the two codes, written and spoken. Arabic diglossia accounts for the fact that Arabic, in its classical or literary form, is different from its colloquial or everyday spoken form (Abu Rabia & Awwad, 2004). To further complicate matters, Arabic speakers from Algeria, Tunisia, and Morocco, or Syria, Egypt, and Lebanon, do not speak the same everyday language as speakers from Kuwait, Saudi Arabia, and the UAE. In fact, even countries that are geographically close, such as the UAE and Saudi Arabia, do not speak the same dialect, although their languages are more similar to each other than to Lebanese Arabic or Moroccan Arabic (Saiegh-Haddad; Taouk & Coltheart, 2004).

In Arabic, there are actually two written codes (Saiegh-Haddad, 2004). One is Classical Arabic (CA), the language of the Islamic Holy Book, the Quran. The second written code, in which scholars attempted to modernize Classical Arabic at the turn of the 20th century, is Modern Standard Arabic (MSA) (Maamouri, 1998). These two written forms of the Arabic language are in stark contrast to the colloquial dialects spoken by the different groups that make up the Arabic world, known as Spoken Arabic Vernaculars (SAVs) (Saiegh-Haddad, 2004). SVAs are unwritten. Written Arabic language is either Classical Arabic, the language of the Quran, or Modern Standard Arabic, the written language of books, newspapers, magazines, and official papers and documents. Therefore, the day-today language spoken by an Arabic speaker is not the language that is written when the native Arabic speaker learns to read and write in Arabic (Taouk & Coltheart, 2004). The two languages, MSA and SAVs, are so far removed from each other that Arabic speakers themselves consider them as two separate languages (Saiegh-Haddad, 2004). The difference between MSA and SAV is so great that becoming truly literate in reading and writing MSA extends all the way through college (Maamouri, 1998). Therefore, high school graduates are not literate in reading and writing Arabic to the same degree that high school leavers in English speaking countries are literate in English (Saiegh-Haddad, 2004). Maamouri recounts how, in a diglossic situation such as Arabic, teachers show children who are learning to read a picture of a fish, known as 'huut' ('whale' in MSA) in their spoken dialect, and teach them that the picture/word is now a 'samak,' 'fish' in MSA (Maamouri, 1998). Learning how to read and write in MSA is similar to learning a second language. Furthermore, the student does not hear the language being spoken because SVA, MSA and CA are far removed from each other lexically, phonetically, and grammatically (Abu Rabia & Taha, 2006).

In addition to the dichotomy between the Orthographic Depth Hypothesis and the Threshold Hypothesis, much of the methodology on teaching reading in ESL emphasizes top-down processing models to the exclusion of bottom-up processing models (Birch, 2002; Koda, 2005). The Psycholinguistic Model of Reading, by Goodman (1967) and Smith (1994), is based on reading research into eye movements that indicated which words the eye lingered on when reading a page of text. The Psycholinguistic Model of Reading has heavily influenced the methodology of teaching reading in ESL which relies on a whole language reading methodology rather than on teaching learners how to decode words. In ESL methodology, teachers activate the students' schema, or background knowledge, for the topic in a pre-reading task and encourage students to understand the gist of the reading text without understanding every word. Goodman's model proposed that readers comprehend a text through a psycholinguistic guessing game in which efficient readers hypothesize, predict, and verify as they read based on their background knowledge of the topic. While the Psycholinguistic Model of Reading may adequately explain what happens in skilled adult native speaking readers' minds as they read in a language in which they are proficient, it does not address how beginning readers achieve automaticity in their first language or their second (Segalowitz & Hulstijn, 2005).

As a consequence of the popularity of the top-down model in explaining L1 reading efficiency, most research on reading ESL has been on top-down skills such as syntactical processing and rhetorical structure (Ridgway, 2004), conceptual and cultural schemata (e.g. Abu Rabia, 1995), as well as attitudes and motivation (e.g. Wang, Martin, & Martin, 2002). Top-down models of reading have led ESL teachers, course designers, and material writers to believe that the best strategy for helping second-language readers develop target language literacy is to provide them with the background knowledge to decode a text (Grabe, 1991). Adult ESL learners who are literate in their own language or whose languages have a similar orthography to English might have sufficient linguistic resources to do just that. However, top-down models of reading may be insufficient to enable adult ESL students, who may be semi-literate in their own language or whose languages are written with different alphabets, to read in English.

Birch (2002) and Koda (2005) questioned the Psycholinguistic Model of Reading and emphasized the importance of visual input, bottom-up processing, and automatic word processing in ESL reading. Lower-level processes include word recognition, letter recognition, phoneme-grapheme correspondences, and the utilization of orthographic redundancies such as rime identification (Birch, 2002). Rimes are multiple letter strings such as *ditch*, *witch*, and *pitch*, that readers process by analogy (Goswami, 2000).

Several studies have indicated that the ESL reading comprehension difficulties experienced by native speakers of Arabic may result from deficient letter and word recognition, a bottom-up process

(Hayes-Harb, 2006; Ryan & Meara, 1991). Fender (2000, p. 291) writes that 'Arab ESL students seem to experience considerable difficulties with word recognition processes in a prelexical access stage in word recognition.' Automatic word recognition is necessary for fluent reading and fluent reading is necessary for comprehension (Walczyk & Griffith-Ross, 2007).

While good readers may seem to recognize words instantly without decoding them letter by letter, in actuality, orthographic knowledge is what accounts for the seamless retrieval of lexical information from print (Koda, 2005). Firmly installed at the crossroads of top-down and bottom-up reading processes is the relationship between sound (phoneme) and spelling (orthography) (Liben & Liben, 2004). Knowing that in English fluent readers have a dual access route to meaning, both phonological and lexical as in Coltheart's (2006) Dual Access Route Theory, the acquisition of automaticity, the instant retrieval of a word's meaning at the word-decoding level, cannot be ignored (Segalowitz & Hulstijn, 2005).

Ryan (1997), when researching ESL Arabic learners' word recognition, emphasized the role that bottom-up decoding processes play in the acquisition of learning to read another language. Arabic learners often have written mistakes in which vowels are missing or in the wrong place with the consonantal word structure relatively intact, that is, writing 'sprt' for 'separate' or 'pulls' for 'plus' (Ryan, 1997). These types of phonological and orthographic errors provide support for a reconsideration of ESL methodology when teaching L1 Arabic students to read. Current mass-marketed ESL textbooks rely on whole language reading methodology and contain little emphasis on English phonemes, word decoding, or spelling.

Studies by Brown and Haynes (1985), Randall and Meara (1988), Ryan and Meara (1991), Fender (2003) and Hayes-Harb (2006) indicate that L1 Arabic learners face specific written word-processing difficulties when reading in English. Arabic learners may be transferring strategies from their first language to English that interfere with their acquisition of English. Knowing that Arabic speakers suffer significant language-specific problems when decoding English can help educators develop strategies for teaching Arabic learners to read and write in English. L1 Arabic speakers might need strategies specific to their L1 language deficits. One of these strategies might be incorporating a direct phonics approach into traditional ESL reading instruction methodology. This chapter reviews an attempt to apply such an approach to the teaching of English reading to a group of Arab learners.

The Study

The current research study sought to explore whether direct phonics instruction could significantly increase phonological and orthographic awareness among adult Arabic speaking students in a government tertiary foundation level ESL program. A pretest/posttest quasi-experimental research design was used. Direct phonics instruction was the independent variable. Phonological and orthographic awareness as measured by the pre- and post-tests were the dependent variables. The phonological awareness test was the Word Attack subtest of the Woodcock Reading Mastery Test—Revised/ Normative Update (WRMT-R/NU) (Woodcock, 1987-1998). The subtest is a selection of 45 pseudowords in English that can be read aloud according to English grapheme/phoneme correspondence rules, for example, 'raff' and 'cigbet.' The orthographic awareness measure was a combined task developed by Siegel, Share, and Geva (1995) and Massaro, Taylor, Venzky, Jastrzembski, and Lucas (1980) and used in cross-linguistic studies by Nassaji (2003), Abu Rabia and Siegel (2002), and Sunseth (2003). The items on the test had both alternative final two position consonant endings, such as 'filv' and 'filk,' or alternative beginning consonant positions, such as 'fant' and 'tnaf,' and alternative vowel and consonant positions, such as 'nmtaou' and 'mauton.' In the task, participants were asked to select which of two items looked like a word in English or looked like it could be a word in English.

The 16-week duration of the study was determined by the 18-week academic semester calendar specified by the Ministry of Higher Education and Research. A total of 74 UAE females aged 18-25 participated in the study. The treatment group (n=38) received direct phonics instruction in addition to regular ESL reading instruction. The comparison group (n=36) did not receive direct phonics instruction in addition to traditional ESL reading instruction. The *Get Reading* phonics website was developed by an instructor in the foundation program. The phonics program was delivered to the treatment group in two phases. During the first 8 weeks, the instructors concentrated on letters and words and used techniques such as alphabetizing, teacher-student dictations of short words, and alphabet-to-sound activities. These activities were repeated systematically with different sounds and rimes to develop letter knowledge, basic phonological awareness and orthographic awareness. The activities occurred twice a week for 20 minutes each time. Two units a week from a spelling patterns workbook with a follow-up spelling test were also included in the program. Students also read aloud from lists of words located on the phonics website for approximately 30 minutes a week. The *Get Reading* website was utilized in class twice a week for 15 minutes each time. Discrete item activities, such as soft and hard 'g' and soft and hard 'c,' were practised for about 10 minutes a week over the semester. The treatment group received a total of approximately 110 minutes per week of direct phonics instruction. Students received approximately 30 hours of direct phonics instruction during the 16-week study in addition to traditional ESL reading instruction. A post-test was given at the end of the study.

Results

After the 16-week instruction, the treatment group and the comparison group were re-tested on phonological awareness and orthographic awareness using different versions of the phonological and orthographic awareness tests to determine if there was a statistically significant difference between the treatment group and the comparison group. Table 1 shows the means and standards deviations of the two groups of students on the pre and post Phonological Awareness Test (PAT) and Orthographic Awareness Tests (OAT).

Table 1. *Means and Standard Deviations of PAT and OAT by Group*

		PAT1	PAT2	OAT1	OAT2
Treatment *(n=38)*	M	8.95	12.2	17.6	15.7
	SD	4.68	6.62	1.42	1.87
Comparison *(n=36)*	M	10.2	11.5	17.3	15.2
	SD	5.94	5.29	2.07	1.81
Total	M	9.57	11.9	17.5	15.5
	SD	5.34	5.98	1.76	1.85

The means show that the treatment group improved more than the comparison group in the phonological awareness test. The standard deviations of the treatment group (*M*=8.95, *SD*=4.68; *M*=12.2, *SD*=6.62) were greater than the standard deviations of the comparison group (*M*=10.2, *SD*=5.94; *M*=11.5, *SD*=5.29) on PAT 1 and PAT 2 which indicates a greater individual variation within the treatment group. With regards to the orthographic awareness test, both groups showed a decrease of similar level in their orthographic awareness. Independent samples *t-tests* were used to compare the mean differences between the two groups (see Table 2).

Table 2. *Differences in PAT and OAT between Treatment and Comparison Groups*

	Treatment Group *(n=38)*		Comparison Group *(n=36)*		Significance
	M	SD	M	SD	
PAT1	8.95	4.68	10.2	5.94	t(72)=1.0, p=.31
PAT2	12.2	6.62	11.5	5.29	t(72)=.49, p=.63
OAT1	17.6	1.42	17.3	2.06	t(72)=.86, p=.39
OAT2	15.7	1.87	15.2	1.81	t(72)=1.3, p=.19

The *t-tests* revealed no statistically significant differences between the two groups of students. Single sample *t* tests were used for the within group comparisons (see Table 3).

Table 3. *Differences in PAT and OAT within Treatment and Comparison groups*

	Increase in PAT2		Decrease in OAT2	
Treatment Group *(n=38)*	$t(37) = .31$	p=.76 (ns)	$t(37) = .91$	p=.37 (ns)
Comparison Group *(n=36)*	$t(35) = .40$	p=.69 (ns)	$t(35) = .97$	p=.33 (ns)

No statistically significant differences were found in the orthographic and phonological performance of students within each group. Figure 1 shows a graphic display of the changes in PAT and OAT pretest and posttest scores of the treatment group and the comparison group.

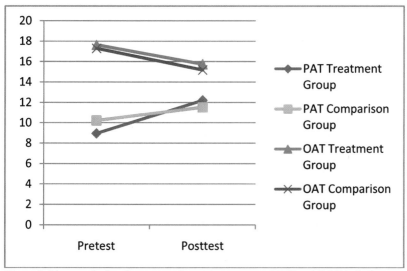

Figure 1. Line graph showing pre- and post-test scores on PAT and OAT in both groups

The lack of statistical significance could be the result of the short treatment period which was determined by the academic calendar in use at the institution where the study took place. Most studies on phonological awareness and orthographic awareness involve large groups of students and take place over a period of at least one year (e.g. Stuart, 2004; Lesaux & Siegel, 2003; Araujo, 2002; Lucey, 2002). The results of the study may have been different if the second measures of phonological and orthographic awareness had been obtained at the end of an academic year rather than at the end of a 16-week instruction period.

Discussion

Ehri's (2005) phase model of reading provides a possible explanation for the study findings. Ehri's model is a developmental model of reading based on research on native English speaking children, but since second language acquisition has been found to closely mimic first language acquisition, phases of phonological and orthographic awareness in adult second language learners might also mimic the acquisition of first language phonological and orthographic awareness, especially for those learners who come from a different alphabetic background to English, such as L1 Arabic learners. In Ehri's model, the four phases leading to the development of complete automatic sight word reading (automaticity) are characterized by the type of alphabetic knowledge used to form connections between graphemes and phonemes to bond spellings of the words to their pronunciations and meanings in memory. The four phases are (a) pre-alphabetic, (b) partial alphabetic, (c) full alphabetic, and (d) consolidated alphabetic. In the pre-alphabetic phase, the word is read by the reader looking at selected visual features. For example, the word 'look' is read by the reader recognizing the two tall letters at the beginning and the end of the word and the two circles in the middle. These readers are essentially non-readers. Their reading repertoire is limited to a few words. In the partial alphabetic phase, readers form connections between only certain sounds and letters usually the beginning and ending of words. For example the 's' and 'n' in 'spoon' allow them to read the word 'spoon' which might be the phase at which Arabic learners stagnate because of first language interference. Arabic readers may access the correct meaning of the many homographs that they encounter in Arabic via the sentence context of the word (Abu Rabia, 2002; Kahn-Horwitz, Shimron & Sparks, 2006; Saiegh-Haddad, 2004). There is a distinct possibility that they transfer this strategy to English (Kahn-Horwitz, Shimron, & Sparks, 2006). In the partial alphabetic phase, many words that share boundaries such as 'spoon' and 'skin' or 'bird' and 'boat' are confused by learners. Classroom evidence abounds of native Arabic speakers confusing words that share boundaries such as 'chapter' and 'character,' 'lunch' and 'launch', 'claps' and 'clasp,' 'aboard' and 'abroad' and 'commitment' and 'communicate.' According to Ehri (2005), readers at the partial alphabetic phase 'are limited to forming partial connections because they are unable to segment the word's pronunciation into all of its phonemes' (p. 173). They also 'invent partial spellings of words by writing only the more salient sounds and leaving out medial letters' (Ehri, 2005, p. 173). For example, as when Arabic speakers write 'sprt' for 'separate' and 'pulls' for 'plus' as reported by Ryan (1997). Stagnation in the partial alphabetic phase is also characteristic of native English speakers who have been diagnosed with a reading disability such as dyslexia (Ehri, 2005). Finally, full alphabetic phase reading occurs when readers learn sight words by forming complete connections between letters in spellings and phonemes in pronunciations (Ehri, 2005).

The participants in the current study may have moved from a pre-alphabetic phase to a full alphabetic phase in phonological awareness and orthographic awareness. Because of the interference of L1 reading strategies that rely on pre-alphabetic phase strategies, that is recognizing words by their visual appearance, participants began to recognize and segment words into grapheme-phoneme relationships in the second orthographic awareness test rather than rely on the same whole word, visual recognition strategies that they used in the orthographic awareness pretest. Because participants began to segment the words according to grapheme-phoneme correspondences rather than depend on whole word reading strategies in items such as 'jofy' and 'fojy', they may have scored lower in average. Additional evidence of using whole word reading strategies was found amongst dyslexic native English speakers who scored higher in the same orthographic awareness test than non-dyslexics native speakers who scored higher in the phonological awareness test (Siegel, Share, & Geva, 1995). Siegel, Share, and Geva concluded that the difficulties with phonological processing and the increased orthographic awareness of the dyslexics indicated a reading strategy that relied more on the visual (pre-alphabetic phase) than the phonological features (partial alphabetic to full alphabetic phases) of words. Because of first language Arabic whole sight-word reading strategies, the participants in the study may have begun to apply segmentation grapheme-phoneme strategies as in the English full alphabetic phase which caused them to score lower on the orthographic awareness test as non-dyslexic native speakers had in the Siegel, Share, and Geva (1995) study.

Conclusion

Native speakers of English are able to decipher the syllabic pronunciation of unknown words because of their early elementary educational phonics instruction in generalizing the pronunciation patterns of English sounds and spelling (Goswami, 2000; Treiman, Mullennix, Bijeljac-Babic, & Richmond-Welty, 1995). No research on the effect of direct phonics instruction on adult native Arabic speakers had been done prior to this study although there have been studies on systematic phonics training on ESL children from differing L1 backgrounds (e.g. Araujo, 2002; Lesaux & Siegel, 2003; Lucey, 2002; Stuart, 2004). These studies indicated that direct phonics instruction had a positive effect on phonological and ortho-graphic awareness and that the effect was maintained through future years of schooling. Tertiary ESL foundation programs in the UAE currently rely on whole reading ESL teaching methodologies. The connection that exists between bottom-up word decoding problems in English for Arabic speakers and successful reading instruction methodology for native English speaking children includes training in the English phonological system (Anderson, 2006), reading aloud in the classroom and listening to English being read aloud (Amer, 1997; Gibson, 2008), as well as extensive reading (Al Ansari & Bulaila, 2004; Hafiz & Tudor, 1989; Yamashita, 2008). To adequately address the reading needs of adult Arabic learners of English in tertiary institution foundation programs, English instructors need to adopt more of the methodologies used to teach reading in English to English-speaking children.

References

Abu Rabia, S. (1995). Attitudes and cultural background and their relationship to English in a multicultural social context: The case of male and female Arab immigrants in Canada. *Educational Psychology, 15*(3).

Abu Rabia, S. (2001). Testing the interdependence hypothesis among native adult bilingual Russian-English students. *Journal of Psycholinguistic Research, 30*(4), 437-455.

Abu Rabia, S. (2002). Reading in a root-based-morphology language: The case of Arabic. *Journal of Research in Reading, 25*(3), 299-309.

Abu Rabia, S., & Awwad, J. (2004). Morphological structures in visual word recognition: The case of Arabic. *Journal of Research in Reading, 27*(3), 321-336.

Abu Rabia, S., & Siegel, L. (2002). Reading, syntactic, orthographic, and working memory skill of bilingual Arabic-English speaking Canadian children. *Journal of Psycholinguistic Research, 31*(6), 661-678.

Abu Rabia, S., & Taha, H. (2006). Phonological errors predominate in Arabic spelling across grades 1-9. *Journal of Psycholinguistic Research, 35*(2), 167-188.

Al Ansari, S., & Bulaila, A. (2004). An attitudinal study of the status of extensive literary reading programmes in Bahrain schools: A study of two learning systems. *Journal of Educational and Psychological Sciences, 5*(2), 8-25.

Alderson, J.C. (1984). Reading in a foreign language: A reading problem or a language problem? In J.C. Alderson & A.H. Urquhart (Eds.), *Reading in a Foreign Language* (pp. 1-27). New York: Longman.

Al Kitbi, E. (2006). Gulf state's educational reform's real goals. *Arab Reform Bulletin, 4*(4), 23-24.

Al Sayegh, F. (2004). Post-9/11 changes in the Gulf: The case of the UAE. *Middle East Policy, 11*(2), 107-135.

Amer, A. (1997). The effect of the teacher's reading aloud on the reading comprehension of EFL students. *ELT Journal, 51*(1), 43-47.

Anderson, D. (2006). Why can't our learners read? 16th Annual TESOL Arabia Conference. Dubai, UAE.

Araujo, L. (2002). The literacy development of kindergarten English language learners. *Journal of Research in Childhood Education, 16*(2), 232-247.

Beland, R., & Mimouni, Z. (2001). Deep dyslexia in the two languages of an Arabic/French bilingual patient. *Cognition, 82*, 77-126.

Birch, B. (2002). *English L2 reading: Getting to the bottom.* Mahwah, NJ: Lawrence Erlbaum Associates.

Brown, T., & Haynes, M. (1985). Literacy background and reading development in a second language. In T.H. Carr (Ed.), *The development of reading skills* (pp. 19-34). San Francisco: Jossey-Bass.

Burt, M., Peyton, J., & Adams, R. (2003) *Reading and adult English language learners: A review of the research. Series on preparing adult English language learners for success.* Washington, DC: Center for Applied Linguistics. (ERIC Document Reproduction Service No. ED482785).

Cobb, T. (2007). The old vocabulary, the new vocabulary, and the Arabic learner. In P. Davidson, C. Coombe, D. Lloyd, & D. Palfreyman (Eds.), *Teaching and learning vocabulary in another language* (pp. 102-121). Dubai, UAE: TESOL Arabia.

Coltheart, M. (2006). Dual route and connectionist models of reading: An overview. *London Review of Education, 4*(1), 5-17.

Ehri, L. (2005). Learning to read words: Theory, findings, and issues. *Scientific Studies of Reading, 9*(2), 167-188.

Fender, M. (2003). English word recognition and word integration skills of native Arabic and Japanese speaking learners of English as a second language. *Applied Psycholinguistics, 24*, 289-315.

Geva, E., & Siegel, L. (2000). Orthographic and cognitive factors in the concurrent development of basic reading skills in two languages. *Reading and Writing: An Interdisciplinary Journal, 12*, 1-30.

Gibson, S. (2008). Reading aloud: A useful learning tool? *ELT Journal, 62*(1), 29-36.

Goodman, K. (1967). Reading: A psycholinguistic guessing game. *Journal of the Reading Specialist, 6*, 126-35.

Goswami, U. (2000). Phonological representations, reading development and dyslexia: Towards a cross-linguistic theoretical framework. *Dyslexia, 6,* 133-151.

Grabe, W. (1991). Current developments in second language reading research. *TESOL Quarterly, 25*(3), 375-405.

Hafiz, F., & Tudor, I. (1989). Extensive reading and the development of language skills. *ELT Journal, 43*(1), 4-13.

Hayes-Harb, R. (2006.) Native speakers of Arabic and ESL texts: Evidence for the transfer of written word identification processes. *TESOL Quarterly, 40*(2), 321-339.

IELTS Annual Review. (2006). Retrieved from http://ieltsexams.net/wp-content/uploads/2007/12/ielts-annual-review-2006.pdf

IELTS Analysis of Test Data. (2007). Retrieved from http://www.ielts.org/researchers/analysis_of_test_data/percentile_ranks_2007.aspx

IELTS Analysis of Test Data. (2008). Retrieved from http://www.ielts.org/researchers/analysis_of_test_data/test_taker_performance_2008.aspx

Kahn-Horwitz, J., Shimron, J., & Sparks, R. (2006). Weak and strong novice readers of English as a foreign language: Effects of first language and socioeconomic status. *Annals of Dyslexia, 56*(1), 161-186.

Koda, K. (2005). *Insights into second language reading: A cross-linguistic approach.* Cambridge: Cambridge University Press.

Lesaux, N., & Siegel, L. (2003). The development of reading in children who speak English as a second language. *Developmental Psychology, 39*, 1005-1019.

Liben, D., & Liben, M. (2004). Our journey to reading success. *Educational Leadership, 61*(6), 58-61.

Lucey, T. (2002). Environmental relationships to students' reading comprehension and development. *English Quarterly, 34*(3-4).

Maamouri, M. (1998). *Arabic diglossia and its impact on the quality of education in the Arab region. Paper presented at the World Bank Mediterranean Development Forum, Marrakech, Morocco.* (ERIC Document Reproduction Service No. ED456669).

Massaro, D., Taylor, G., Venezsky, R., Jastrzembski, J., & Lucas, P. (1980). *Letter and word perception: Orthographic structure and visual processing in reading.* Amsterdam: North Holland.

Mumtaz, S., & Humphreys, G. (2001). The effects of bilingualism on learning to read in English: Evidence from the contrast between Urdu-English bilingual and monolingual children. *Journal of Research in Reading, 24*(2), 113-134.

Nassaji, H. (2003). Higher-level and lower-level text processing skills in advanced ESL reading comprehension. *The Modern Language Journal, 87*(2), 261-276.

Randall, M., & Meara, P. (1988). How Arabs read Roman letters. *Reading in a Foreign Language, 4*(2), 133-145.

Randall, M., & Samimi, M. (2010). The status of English in Dubai. *English Today, 26*(1), 43-50.

Ridgway, T. (2004). Literacy and foreign language reading. *Reading in a Foreign Language, 15*(2), Retrieved from http://nflrc.hawaii.edu/rfl/ October2003/ridgway/ridgway.pdf

Ryan, A. (1997). Learning the orthographic form of L2 vocabulary: A receptive and productive process. In N.Schmitt & M.McCarthy (Eds.), *Vocabulary: Description, acquisition, and pedagogy* (pp. 181-198). Cambridge, GB: Cambridge University Press.

Ryan, A., & Meara, P. (1991). The case of the invisible vowels: Arabic speakers reading English words. *Reading in a Foreign Language, 7*(2), 531-540.

Saiegh-Haddad, E. (2004). The impact of phonemic and lexical distance on the phonological analysis of words and pseudowords in a diglossic context. *Applied Psycholinguistics, 24*, 495-512.

Segalowitz, N., & Hulstijn, J. (2005). Automaticity in bilingualism and second language learning. In J.F. Kroll & A.M.B. De Groot (Eds.), *Handbook of bilingualism: Psycholinguistic approaches* (pp. 371-388). Oxford: Oxford University Press.

Siegel, L., Share, D., & Geva, E. (1995). Evidence for superior orthographic skills in dyslexics. *Psychological Science, 6*(4), 250-254.

Smith, F. (1994). *Understanding reading (5th edition)*. Hillsdale, NJ: Lawrence Erlbaum Associates.

Sunseth, K. (2000). *The role of naming speed and phonemic awareness in reading, spelling, and orthographic knowledge.* Unpublished doctoral dissertation, University of Waterloo, Ontario, Canada (UMI No. 0-612-53519-3).

Stuart, M. (2004). Getting ready for reading: A follow-up study of inner-city second language learners at the end of key stage 1. *British Journal of Educational Psychology, 74*, 15-36.

Taouk, M., & Coltheart, M. (2004). The cognitive processes involved in learning to read in Arabic. *Reading and Writing: An Interdisciplinary Journal, 17*, 27-57.

Treiman, R., Mullenix, J., Bijeljac-Babic, R., & Richmond-Welty, E. (1995). The special role of rimes in the description, use, and acquisition of English orthography. *Journal of Experimental Psychology, 124*(2), n.a.

Walczyk, J., & Griffith-Ross, D. (2007). How important is reading skill fluency for comprehension? *The Reading Teacher, 60*(6), 560-569.

Wang, Y., Martin, M., & Martin, S. (2002). Understanding Asian graduate students' English literacy problems. *College Teaching, 50*(3), 97-101.

Woodcock, R. (1987-1998). *Woodcock reading mastery tests—Revised/Normative update (WRMT-R/NU)*. Bloomington, MN: Pearson Assessments.

Yamashita, J. (2008). Extensive reading and development of different aspects of L2 proficiency. *System, 36*, 661–672.

KATHERINE L. HALL

Chapter 20
Teaching Composition and Rhetoric to Arab EFL Learners

Abstract

Arab students studying in tertiary institutions through the medium of English, as is the case in the United Arab Emirates and other Gulf countries, face unique challenges not only with language acquisition but also in engaging in the written discourse of academia. Often teachers of composition and rhetoric in the Arab world do not have a mastery of Arabic and its culture, which may lead to misunderstandings about how native Arabic speakers interpret writing and reading tasks. This chapter examines the best practices for teaching composition and rhetoric to native Arabic speakers. The chapter discusses the definitions and origins of composition and rhetoric as an American modality and the issues that non-Arab teachers of writing face when teaching native Arabic speakers. The next section of the chapter focuses on specific EFL problems for Arabic speakers, their difficulties in transferring Arabic to English in writing, students' lack of critical analysis skills, and the traditional focus on rote memorization. Finally the chapter discusses practical pedagogical methods for teaching composition and rhetoric to Arabic-speaking students.

Introduction

Teaching composition and rhetoric to non-native English speakers often poses difficulties and requires a rethinking of traditional pedagogies, especially for university academics working in Arab countries who are not trained in teaching English as a foreign language (EFL). Often when students learn English as a foreign language, their education in the Arab speaking world has focused on memorization and rote learning. Arnold (2008), in his *US Today* article, revealed even at the university level, 'in much of the Middle East, the national universities are overwhelmed with hundreds or even thousands of students in mass lectures stressing rote memorization' (p. 11). The critical thinking skills that are required for students to participate in a composition and rhetoric course are often new and confusing to Arab students. Therefore, teachers of academic writing are often frustrated and find themselves refining traditional rhetoric and composition pedagogies to suit the needs of their students. These challenges are further compounded as the teacher must focus on teaching composition and rhetoric alongside teaching English as a language. As Zughoul (2003) asserted, 'the teaching of English in the era of globalization has put more demands on the teacher of English' (p. 29).

   In the Arab world, and in particular when examining Arabic native speakers in the composition and rhetoric classroom, there are a plethora of challenges faced by English teachers. Composition and rhetoric as a discipline is often the focus of American universities' core liberal arts curriculum. Arabic culture in general is historically an oral tradition-based culture. Often Arabic-speaking students struggle with reading assignments, particularly in comprehending content in literary pieces. Researchers found that the lack of reading skills in Arabic-speakers is mostly connected to the difficulties they face in learning the formal written Arabic that is used in the Qur'an (Gallagher, 1989). Even when religious leaders deliver their doctrine, it is rarely written in a text; instead the lessons are recorded and distributed by CD's or cassettes (Eickelman, 1992). Further, Eickelman discussed Arabs and how 'until recently most Muslims— and certainly those in the Middle East—were not sufficiently literate to read or directly comprehend the Qur'an or other religious texts' (p. 644).

This chapter examines native Arabic speakers and their challenges in a traditional composition and rhetoric classroom in an American university in the UAE and provides suggestions for helping these students overcome their challenges.

Composition and Rhetoric in American-Style Education

Rhetoric and composition has become a permanent part of the curriculum in American universities abroad in order to emulate their counterparts in the United States of America (USA). The courses are called different names at different universities: Freshman Composition; Developmental Writing; Expository Writing; Rhetoric and Composition; Introduction to Academic Writing. These are core courses required for a liberal arts education. In order to receive an undergraduate degree at an accredited USA university, a student must successfully pass a sequence of rhetoric and composition courses. Additionally, since these courses are offered to university students at any given American university, departments of rhetoric and composition have continued to evolve, separate from traditional English and ESL departments. This evolution is indicative to the importance that American universities now place on students' successful completion of composition and rhetoric courses. Although teachers of rhetoric may have varying definitions of what academic writing is, 'there is probably consensus that in whatever form, academic writing should have clarity of language, predictability of structure, and honesty in substantiating any claims' (Morley-Warner, 2009, p. 106). In addition, Steinberg (2005) described composition and rhetoric courses and their instructors by saying 'the feature that most distinguishes composition from its disciplinary siblings is its primary focus on pedagogy, and, more specifically, its conception of pedagogy as a mode of knowledge production, not merely a vehicle for knowledge transmission' (p. 130).

Universities handle the placement of students into writing courses differently, but many of them provide a written placement exam or require a writing sample to determine where a student should begin his/her writing sequence. Students who are non-native English speakers are frequently placed into a developmental writing course. Horner and Trimbur (2002) discussed how 'basic writers have commonly been described as immigrants and foreigners to the academy...' (p. 609), while Amey and Long (1998) pointed out that 'the knowledge gained in developmental courses in English, reading, and mathematics seems fundamental to the successful completion of other college courses' (p. 8). Developmental courses are non-credit courses preparing students to enter composition and rhetoric courses. American universities abroad almost always have a developmental writing course to prepare their students for the rigor of academic writing at the university level and 'the development of the writing abilities of individual students' (Sweigart, 1996, p. 13). Doyle and Fueger (1995) assessed students' progress in developmental writing courses and found that students' writing abilities increased by taking the course. They found that after completing a developmental writing course, the students wrote longer, more complex sentences and at the same time reduced the number of errors in those sentences. Not only are the results favorable, but also the percentage of change between pre- and post course papers is relatively consistent (p. 24). It is important to note that in this study participation in a developmental writing class provided positive gains in writing whether the student was a foreign language speaker or not.

After passing developmental writing, students must then move through the required writing courses. Rhetoric and composition, by their very nature, train students in the art of argumentation, which will prepare them for other courses in the academy. Pally (1999) detailed about argumentation that :

> It is involved in the range of academic/professional tasks, from lecture comprehension to research, and to all genres of written and oral presentation. Understanding it and being able to make it are among the fundamental needs of all students and professionals in an English-language setting. (p. 3)

As Pally acknowledged rhetoric and the ability to compose arguments are an integral part of 'English' courses that focus on academic writing in the American system of education, regardless of whether the universities are in the USA or abroad. It is within these courses of argumentation that students hone their critical thinking skills and develop analytical thinking. Such skills are now the focus of the entire educational system in the UAE and other Gulf countries in their effort to transform themselves into knowledge-based societies.

Teaching Arab Students Composition and Rhetoric

There are a variety of challenges that teachers of native Arab speaking students face in the composition and rhetoric classroom. Murphy (2005) detailed that 'Arabic-speaking students often have particular difficulties with written English, for a variety of reasons related to their linguistic and educational background'(cited in Rivard, 2006, p. 31). Additionally, for Arabic native speakers, 'English rhetoric is often construed as cold and highly impersonal rather than embellished as is the elite style of literary Arabic' (Santos & Suleiman, 1990, p. 5). Similarly, 'the rhetoric of a tightly organized, logical presentation of ideas is as foreign to Arabic-speaking students as the language of English itself' (Yorkey, 1974, p. 17). Lastly, we must know as teachers that 'learners may use their first language (L1) rhetoric when they communicate using the second language'(Aljamhoor, 2001, p. 26). It is crucial for teachers of composition and rhetoric to understand the nature of the native Arabic speakers they are teaching before they can attempt to amend their pedagogy to accommodate these students. This section will look at: specific ESL problems that are relevant to Arab students; difficulties that students have in transferring Arabic to English in writing tasks; critical analysis skills deficiencies; and finally the tendency toward rote memorization in the Arab world's educational system.

Specific ESL Problems

Arabic speaking students face problems in learning English, especially reading and writing, that stem from a variety of factors including poor home literacy practices, Arabic diglossia, and issues with reading in both English and Arabic (see Gobert, 2010; and also in Chapter 19 of this book). Additionally, students make writing tasks insurmountable for themselves by trying to translate their Arabic thoughts into English writing. Admittedly this issue is faced by many ESL students as they try to write their essays in English, but native Arabic speakers will often make patterns of errors that are sometimes so substantial that their essays become difficult to understand. Santos and Sulemin (1990) in their discussion of cultural and linguistic considerations mention that 'word order (*e.g. Dead Sea vs. *Sea Dead*), language typology (*e.g. Ali goes to school vs. *goes Ali to school*), [and] structural patterns (*e.g. that's the teacher whom I met vs. *That the teacher whom I met him*)...are different in both languages' (p. 177). Yorkey (1974) also referenced the study of Scott and Tucker who isolated four grammatical errors that most Arabic speaking students seem to make habitually: verbs, prepositions, articles and relative clauses (p. 14) (see also Chapter 21 in this book where Josephine O'Brien provides a more detailed account of the differences between English and Arabic that are particularly problematic for Arab ESL students). Johns (1997) reminded instructors that 'because some of our students do not share academic genre knowledge with their instructors, or with other readers and writers, they face considerable obstacles' (cited in Pally, 1999, p. 4). These obstacles that Arab students face are often compounded when their academic instructors are not trained to teach ESL students, as is the case with many foreign staff in foreign universities in the Gulf region.

Difficulties in Transferring Arabic to English in Writing

In addition to ESL problems, Arabic native speakers face further challenges in transferring ideas and words from their own language into English. Arabic, like many languages, has many dialects and these dialects let a trained ear know the difference between a student speaking Arabic from Iraq versus that of Palestine, for instance. Speaking Arabic is also tremendously different than writing it. The written Arabic that students learn during their pre-university education is completely different to the Arabic they speak. Written Arabic is based on the traditional Arabic language (like that of the Qur'an) and is not used in speaking. Fewer and fewer Arabic speakers master written Arabic into the modern generations, except for the religious verses and often only in oral recitation. Said (2002) discussed the role of classical Arabic in the literature and writing and made the following comments:

> ...classical Arabic, like Latin for the European colloquial languages until a century ago, has maintained a living presence as the common language of literary expression, and has done so despite the lively and readily available resources of a whole host of spoken dialects...Moreover, these spoken dialects don't at all have the large literature in the classical lingua franca, despite the fact that in every Arab country there seems to be a substantial body of colloquial poetry, for instance, which is liked and often recited if only to other speakers of that colloquial. Thus even writers who are considered regional tend to use the modern classical language most of the time and only occasionally resort to colloquial Arabic to render not much more than snippets of dialogue.

> So in effect, an educated person has two quite distinct linguistic personae in the
> mother tongue. (p. 222)

According to Yorkey (1974) 'even after years of study, few Arabs ever achieve a confident command of classical Arabic' (p. 3) while most young Arabic speakers admit they never completely learned classical Arabic and often struggled with courses focusing on Arabic writing.

Consequently, if students have not achieved mastery in their native language (L1) writing then it will be difficult for them to achieve competency in second language (L2) writing. As Rivard (2006) wrote Arabic-speaking students are 'trying to acquire L2 literacy on the foundation of a shaky L1 literacy' (p. 58). Even though, 'teaching literacy in the native language tends to enhance literacy and fluency in English' (Nordby, 2009, p. 42), as Pally (1999) discovered 'argumentation and rhetorical conventions vary among languages, (sub)cultures, and discourse communities' (p. 3). The variation of 'rhetorical conventions' between written Arabic and English are vast. Although Dweik and Hommos (2007) showed that students who were proficient writers in Arabic were also good writers in English, a great number of Arabic native speakers have had minimal practice in writing by the time they enter university. Although this chapter is not about the close relationship between reading and writing, a connection exists between students lacking sharpened reading and writing skills in their native language and their weaknesses in these skills in the foreign language.

Critical Analysis Skills Deficiencies

Further issues arise with native Arabic speaking students from critical analysis skills deficiencies. Critical analysis in a liberal arts education program is fundamental. According to Lunsford (1997) 'most of our basic writing students are operating well below the formal-operations or true-concept formation stage of cognitive development, and hence they have great difficulty in 'de-centering' and performing tasks which require analysis and synthesis' (p. 280). Arab students who write at the developmental level have difficulties with critical analysis of texts and writing academically. Pally (1999) found that 'the most persistently difficult challenges facing ESL/EFL students [is] exemplification and questioning material written by authoritative experts' (p. 12). For Arab students Rivard (2006) pointed out that 'since school [prior to university] is teacher-centered and based on a rote learning system, students who receive good marks are not necessarily the brightest or most able to succeed in a western-style college or university' (p. 26). Based on her personal experience in the Gulf, Rivard commented that 'the students I encountered in the Arabian Gulf States were struggling with decoding the English language at a level well below that required to read about abstract ideas in a critical manner' (p. 54). Academic instructors of native Arabic speakers must remember that when they ask students to do higher level writing tasks, they are asking them to utilize skills that they may have failed to develop before entering university.

The Arab Education System

Another challenge that academic instructors of Arab students face is the outdated form of education that most students receive before arriving at the university. Formalized education, particularly in the Gulf region, is a relatively new concept, especially when compared to the West. Many of the programs used for teaching Arabic-speakers, whether in Western modeled schools or government Arabic schools, follow educational curricula that have been adapted from models outside of the Middle East region. This adaptation is flawed in many instances as it does not always consider the students of the region. In a recent article in *The National*, a UAE based newspaper, Dr. Natasha Ridge of the Dubai School of Government said of the current UAE school curriculum: 'In terms of creating students who are knowledge-based rather than content memorizers, it's really hindering students a lot...It's creating students who are very good at memorizing, but not very good at applying knowledge' (Lewis, 2010). It should be noted that the UAE has the highest percentage of higher education institutions in the Gulf region and it is often the cited instance of teaching and learning in the Arab speaking world.

Pedagogically, Arab students are not used to being in charge of their own learning and text creation and they struggle to cope with the demands of critical thinking and independent learning. Arab students are well-equipped from their primary and secondary education to memorize large amounts of information while drill and repetition are the main pedagogies when students learn English. Maamouri (1998) reported in his study on educational concerns in the Arab world that:

> the profile of Arab education varies across and within countries. All Arab educational systems, however, seem to share the following negative charac-teristics: (a) a questionable relevance, (b) an unacceptably low quality, and (c) high repetition and drop-out rates, especially in the poor rural and urban communities. (p. 12)

Futhermore, a focus on exams across all levels in the Arab education system has discouraged teachers from applying more student-centered approaches to teaching and learning which are more in-line with Western pedagogies.

When Arab students enter university, they are taught through the medium of English. Even though Universities are well-resourced and employ foreign academics who have been trained in a western educational system, often 'it is not possible to create in one or two years that which has not evolved over the past twelve'(Rivard, 2006, p. 30). One student in a recent UAE newspaper article said, in reference to his high school education, 'there were two major issues for me, the first is language,' said Osama al Aashek... 'Number two is research. We did not do any. They did not tell us to research online or do papers. I had to learn it all from scratch at university' (Shaheen, 2010). These comments echo the opinions of my own students particularly in reference to their written assignments. After surveying my Arabic-speaking students about their previous educational experiences, one male student replied,

> I learnt to write essays in a proper format when I took the English 102 class with you. I owe you a lot because without you, there is no way I would have been able to write essays the way I do now. When I lived in London, the English they taught there was of a high standard, but the English in the schools here [UAE] is appalling compared to over there. I always had the creativity and the ideas, but you really did teach me how to put them all together, keep them organized, in proper order, and really help me to write the essays that I did.

Additionally, a female student replied,

> Although we were taught the basic elements of writing like 5 body paragraphs, introduction, and conclusion, there are still things like the thesis and the more spicif [sic] outline that we did not focus on. In addition, the concept of academic writing and its rules was almost not presented.

Unfortunately, Arab students, like students around the globe, resort to easy ways to complete assignments that they feel ill-prepared to do effectively. The under-preparedness of students often leads them to desperate measures in order to complete their writing assignments. No teacher of writing is exempt from receiving plagiarized assignments, but the widespread availability of the Internet has resulted in an increase in the incidents of plagiarism. Shaugnessy (1977) commented on the mentality of the developmental writer and said,

> The BW [basic writer] student both resents and resists his vulnerability as a writer. He is aware that he leaves a trail of errors behind him when he writes. He can usually think of little else while he is writing. But he doesn't know what to do about it. (p. 7)

This vulnerability and lack of preparation from previous education often leads university students to plagiarize.

Best Practices for the Composition and Rhetoric Classroom

As an instructor of composition and rhetoric to Arabic speaking students, I have reinvented many of my pedagogies to reflect my students' needs. As most instructors do, I have devised, revised and refined methodologies to help my native Arabic speaking students, find success in their writing courses.

Conferencing one on one with students and their drafts is one of the most effective ways to both help students feel 'ownership' of their writing as well as to work with their individual weaknesses and concerns with their writing. Because of intimidation in the social setting of the classroom, or because of the cultural stigma attached to asking questions and appearing ignorant to their instructor and their peers, Arab speaking students rarely, if ever, ask questions. Scheduling mandatory writing conferences and meeting with students one-on-one to discuss their writing, gives students the chance to openly discuss their writing concerns and difficulties. Sommers (1982) discussed at length the issues that both students and their instructors face with comments on essays. When conferencing with students, the commentary is more directly connected with students' writing experiences. Sommers also reminded us that 'as writers we need and want thoughtful commentary to show us when we have communicated our ideas and when not, raising questions from a reader's point of view that may not have occurred to us as writers' (p. 148). For native Arabic-speaking students the writing conferences provide the much needed 'thoughtful commentary' that Sommers talks about. Conferences for Arabic speakers provide the 'validation' that they need to feel successful in their writing endeavors. According to Rendon (2000), 'Validation occurs when faculty and staff let students know they are capable learners, are valued by the institution, and play an important role in their own learning' (p. 8). Finally, in Lambert's (1999) report on peer editing and conferencing, she attested that these two strategies together can strengthen students' writing ability.

Modeling in class using the students' essays has also been a successful pedagogy with Arabic- speaking students. I call these sessions in my classes 'group editing'. Seeing their work in class often encourages students to own their writing. This mini-publishing in the classroom helps students to feel less isolated in their writing and to confront the difficulties they may face. Learning in the composition and rhetoric classroom is not a solitary endeavor, but instead it is a community of writers learning to write better. For Laman and Van Sluys (2008), who studied writing experiences for non native English speakers, 'learning from a sociocultural perspective positions learning as a social work intimately tied to participants' identities; within this environment, learners actively negotiate their past practices with new options as they move across and within new contexts and cultures' (p. 2). Modeling a writing community for my students and 'teaching' them how to be active participants within this community has also been successful for my native Arabic-speaking students. One student in my class wrote about modeling: 'it was very useful because I got to know what were the right things I should do and what things I should avoid doing.'

Having students in closely guided peer editing pairs is another effective technique for helping Arabic speaking students understand and feel ownership of their writing. Instructors need to pair students of mixed writing abilities together and remember that 'without comments from their teachers or from their peers, student writers will revise in a consistently narrow and predictable way'(Sommers, 1982, p. 149). Bay (1999) discussed in her study with Japanese ESL students how peer editing provided more time for the students to interact with one another and also released the burden of additional marking for the teacher. Lambert (1999) in her studies with college students and peer editing reported that students become better writers as they learn from one another the 'processes involved in developing effective writing' (p. 20). Furthermore, Zen (2005) discussed in her paper how the 'process movement' in composition and rhetoric has affected how writing should be taught in stages (process) even in EFL courses, in which writing used to focus on grammar practice more than content writing; effectively students' writing processes must involve a variety of techniques for revising and editing. When these student writing pairs remain together for the course of a semester, they come to develop together as writers and begin to further move away from the idea that writing is a solitary process.

Developing writers also need multiple opportunities for minor writing assignments. Such 'low-stakes' writing assignments are not graded stringently nor weighted substantially for students' grade. Writing instructors need to keep in mind that 'writing is a learned ability' and that 'the best way, and maybe the only way, to learn how to write is by writing' (Witkowski, 1998, p. 54). Low –stakes writing assignments can be designed around mini-writing prompts that can be addressed in a short paragraph. For instance, students may watch a poignant film clip while given only a minimal amount of context for the film as a whole text, and then write a paragraph about it. Students demonstrate higher critical thinking skills when they can analyze a visual text and their replies for such a short writing assignment are often poignant and well-organized. Witkowski further demonstrated that 'as [students learn] to write, [they are] also finding out about the characteristics of good writing' (p. 55). This learning to write well through low-stakes assignments enables the development of confidence and skill in high-stakes assignments. As McKoski (1995) said, 'the principal pedagogical motive for expressive and process models of writing…are necessary tools for engaging the inexperienced and marginalized students in the act of writing' (p. 9).

Furthermore, students need to be involved in reading and many pre-research discussion activities revolve around that reading. This generation of students, and in particular Arab students, are not readers. Gobert (2010), in her presentation of her research about Emirati students and their lack of reading, found that students in the region do not read because reading is not encouraged at home, among other reasons. In order to assure that students come to class having read and prepared to discuss the reading, they are given a reading quiz. Even though students' grades are not majorly affected by the reading quizzes, they still slowly, but surely, begin to read to achieve good grades on the quizzes. What is important is that this technique allows students to have Socratic discussions in class based on the same reading because the majority of them have actually read the assigned article. Students are involved in breaking down arguments in the actual text of the article, discussing and debating main ideas, and describing what kinds of research the author chose to include in his/her article. Students do not only discuss content, but also look at the writing of the piece. To further analyze and understand a writer's choice of research, students unpack the research, determine its context (after discussing why it is important to know the context for the research), and analyze if the research is effective in helping the author to make his/her point. Similarly, students often compare and contrast two or more articles on the same topic to see how both sides may be presented and researched. Through this process, students begin to realize not only what research looks like but also what role effective research has in a piece of writing. Students are also taught to question sources and to understand how well-researched pieces of writing document and utilize sources. Students begin to enter the community of writers and to see themselves as part of that community, which is a tremendous accomplishment for Arab speaking students.

Another technique in preparing Arab students for writing their essays with a research component is having them participate in hands-on library instruction. Students attend a workshop with a librarian and they go through the library catalog, databases and other available library resources focused specifically on the topics of their upcoming writing assignment. The librarian walks them through step by step how to research their specific topic using the available sources. Research through databases and the actual library holdings is almost always a new endeavor for Arab students and the actual hands-on approach is particularly useful for them.

Last but not least, encouraging students to write their first drafts without including their research is another successful methodology that helps students to understand how to avoid plagiarism and to make their own writing more effective before including outside sources. Even if students have found their possible research sources for inclusion into their essays, they are made to put them aside until after they have written the 'meat' of their essay. By encouraging students to approach research as supplementary and support material instead of the main idea in their essays, the instances of plagiarism can be reduced significantly.

Conclusion

Finding ways to meet the special challenges that native Arabic speakers face in composition and rhetoric classes is an ongoing journey. Specific ESL problems, difficulties in transferring Arabic to English in writing, deficiencies in critical analysis skills, and a history of rote memorization in the Arab world all contribute to the challenges in teaching Arab students how to write academically. As a veteran instructor who continually reinvents the pedagogies of her classroom, I have tried many ways for helping my students achieve the most success in my composition and rhetoric classroom. Each methodology contributes a vital component to the overall learning process of my Arabic speaking students.

Conferencing individually, modeling students' own work in the classroom, peer editing partners, completion of 'minor' writing assignments, activities involving reading texts, library instruction and pre-writing drafts before integrating research, all are strategies that have worked successfully with Arabic speaking students in my writing classes. All of these methods of teaching in the writing class-room contributed to students' understanding, success and long term confidence as writers.

Though the pedagogical recommendations outlined in this chapter are by no means exhaustive, they are based on sound pedagogical theory and practical experience and they have proven successful with Arab students. All students are capable of learning to be good writers and native Arabic speaking students are no different. Arab students may be facing many challenges in their English-medium tertiary education but it is the instructors that must be prepared to guide them through and help them overcome these challenges. Native Arabic-speaking students are like all other students in that they, too, wish to find success in their classrooms and attempt their studies with the same intensity and dedication as do other students.

References

Aljamhoor, A. (2001). A cross-cultural analysis of written discourse of Arabic-speaking learners of English. *Journal of King Saud University: Language and Translation, 13*, 25-44.

Amey, M.J., & Long, P.N. (1998). Developmental coursework and early placement: Success strategies for underprepared community college students. *Community College Journal of Research and Practice, 22*(3), 3-10.

Bardsley, D. (2010, February 11). Initiatives fail to silence criticism. *The National*.

Bay, D. (1999). Internet discussion forums: A new modality facilitating peer writing in Japanese University-level EFL classes. ERIC (ED465299).

Beaubien, R. (1998). *The logical roots of argumentative writing: An adjunct to academic ESL/EFL writing students?* Lexington, KY: Paper presented at the Annual Meeting of Teachers of English to Speakers of Other Languages.

Doyle, M., & Fueger, K. (1995). Error analysis: Assessing developmental writing. *Journal of Developmental Education, 18*(3), 22-25.

Dweik, B.S., & Hommos, M.D.A. (2007). The effect of Arabic proficiency on the English writing of bilingual-Jordanian students. ERIC (ED458795)

Eickelman, D.F. (1992). Mass higher education and the religious imagination in contemporary Arab Societies. *American Ethnologist, 19*(4), 643-655.

Elliot, N., Paris, J., & Bodner, J. (1990). The teacher of writing in the ESL curriculum. *Viewpoints, 120*, 12.

Gallagher, E. (1989). Institutional response to student difficulties with the "Language of Instruction" in an Arab medical college. *Journal of Higher Education. 60*(5), 565-582.

Gobert, M. (2010). *Overcoming the reading challenges faced by L1 Arabic Emirati students: Presentation at the UNESCO Open Lecture Series*. Retrieved July 1, 2010, from: http://shct.hct.ac.ae/events/openlectureseries/

Horner, B., & Trimbur, J. (2002). English only and U.S. college composition. *College Composition and Communication, 53*(4), 594-630.

Laman, T.T., & Van Sluys, K. (2008). Being and becoming: Multilingual writers' practices. *College Composition and Communication, 85*(4), 265.

Lambert, G. (1999). *Helping 12th grade honors English students improve writing skills through conferencing.* Unpublished M.Sc. Dissertation, Nova Southeastern University.

Lewis, K. (2010, February 11). Outdated curriculum 'is holding pupils back.' *The National.*

Lunsford, A.A. (1997). Cognitive development and the basic writer. In Villanueva, V. (Ed.), *Cross-talk in comp theory: A reader* (pp. 3-14). Urbana, IL: National Council of Teachers of English.

Maamouri, M. (1998, September). *Language education and human development: Arabic diglossia and its impact on the quality of education in the Arab region. Marrakech, Morocco.* Paper presented at the Mediterranean Development Forum of the World Bank.

McKoski, M. (1995). A legacy of developmental writing. *Journal of Developmental Education, 19*(2), 8-12.

Morley-Warner, T. (2009). *Academic writing is...A guide to writing in a university context*. Sydney, Australia: Association for Academic Language and Learning.

Nordby, A. (2009). English language learners in the classroom. *English Language Learners in the Classroom, 36*(3), 42.

Pally, M. (1999). *Sustained content-based teaching for academic skills development in ESL/EFL*. New York, NY: Paper presented at the Annual Meeting of the Teachers of English to Speakers of Other Languages.

Rendon, L. (2000). *Fulfilling the promise of access and opportunity: Collaborative community colleges for the 21st century. New expeditions: Charting the second century of community colleges.* (Issues Paper No. 3). Washington, DC: American Association of Community Colleges.

Rivard, J.N. (2006). *An investigation into diglossia, literacy, and tertiary-level EFL classes in the Arabian Gulf states.* Unpublished Master's thesis, McGill University, Montreal, Canada.

Rosu, A. (1988, March). *Pragmatics and the teaching of writing.* Paper presented at the annual meeting of the conference on College Composition and Communication, St. Louis, MO.

Said, E.W.R. (2002). Living in Arabic. *Living in Arabic, 21*(4), 220.

Santos, S.L., & Suleiman, M.F. (1990). *Teaching English to Arabic-speaking students: Cultural and linguistic considerations.* Proceedings of the National Association for Bilingual Education Conferences.

Shaheen, K. (2010, February 11). The graduates: it was tough, but we learnt. *The National.*

Shaughnessy, M.P. (1977). *Errors and expectations: A guide for the teacher of basic writing.* New York: Oxford University Press.

Soliday, M. (1999). Class dismissed. *College English, 61*(6), 731-741.

Sommers, N. (1982). Responding to student writing. *College Composition and Communication, 33*(2), 148-156.

440 *Katherine L. Hall*

Stenberg, S. (2005). *Professing and pedagogy: Learning the teaching of English.* Illinois: National Council of Teachers of English.

Sweigart, W. (1996). Assessing achievement in a developmental writing sequence. *Research and Teaching in Developmental Education, 12*(2), 5-15.

Witkowski, S. (1998). Philosophy of writing from a developmental education perspective. *TLAR, 3*(1), 53-57.

Yorkey, R. (1974, July). *Practical EFL techniques for teaching Arabic-speaking students.* Paper presented at the Defense Language Institute, Lackland Air Force Base.

Zen, D. (2005, August). *Teaching ESL/EFL writing beyond language skills.* Paper presented at the 3rd International Annual LATEFL China Conference, Tonghua, China.

Zughoul, M.R. (2003). Globalization and EFL/ESL pedagogy in the Arab world. *Journal of Language and Learning, 1*(2).

JOSEPHINE O'BRIEN

Chapter 21
Teaching English to Arab Learners:
A case for a pedagogical grammar

Abstract

The chapter presents arguments for the development of a pedagogical grammar for Arab learners of English that involves consideration of elements of the target language (TL) that challenge all learners of English as a foreign language (EFL) and specific issues that arise because of transfer from Arabic. Arabic speaking learners of English illustrate developmental patterns common to all EFL learners but also have been observed to use transfer and translation from Arabic as strategies when expressing English tense, aspect, definiteness, indefiniteness, comparison, modality and conditionality. It is contended that though learners have studied the general rules for such concepts they frequently revert to translation from Arabic in written texts. It is argued, therefore, that a pedagogical grammar that considers developmental and contrastive factors between the structure of Arabic and English in identified problematic areas would provide materials to help learners understand correct forms and in addition provide them with a useful tool for editing and proof-reading their texts.

Introduction

In recent decades, English language teaching has been influenced by communicative approaches to language teaching with emphasis on English only classrooms (Krashen, 1988). While this approach has positive effects on students' communicative abilities, neglect of the local context particularly in education and language learning has given rise to a range of tensions (Barber, 1996) and has encouraged social theorists to focus on how to resolve tensions between cultural homogenization and heterogenization (Robertson, 1992). In the field of language teaching, references to the importance of considering local contexts when developing pedagogy for English language programs can now be found. Kumaravadivelu (2006) advocates developing strategies to 'advance a context-sensitive, location specific pedagogy that is based on a true understanding of local linguistic, socio-cultural and political particularities' (p. 224) with teaching techniques, methods and materials that depend on where, when and to whom, one is teaching. The current paper argues for the development of a pedagogical grammar to help Arabic speaking learners who take their third level education through the medium of English.

Theoretical Context

The theoretical perspective guiding education for decades has been that of constructivism (Gergen, 1995) built on beliefs that children mentally construct knowledge for themselves if presented with right input. Learners are encouraged to make connections, infer meanings, and build up patterns, in other words, take control of their own learning. Piaget (cited in Kitchener, 1986) pointed to the two principles of assimilation and accommodation that guide how we learn and teach. Learning is an active process in which learners discover and assimilate principles, concepts and facts for themselves and restructure prior knowledge to accommodate the new. Vygotsky (1978) believed that learning occurs through dialogue that takes place between learners and teachers (intermental) and within learners through internal dialogue (intramental). Learners take an active part in structuring their own internal knowledge map and how well they do so depends on purpose and motivation. Learners need help in accommodating new knowledge, a process described as 'scaffolding' by Vygotsky who believed that learners should be guided in their tasks by a mentor who could provide the necessary support.

The term 'scaffolding' was first introduced by Bruner (1960) to illustrate how children acquired language under parents' guidance with suitable input. The scaffold metaphor has become part of educational theory in second language learning. The necessary support is given to complete tasks that learners cannot do on their own. Bruner believes that understanding the fundamentals of a subject provides learners with general principles that can be transferred and adapted to new situations through 'transfer of training' (Bruner, 1960, p. 17). According to Bruner 'this type of transfer is at the heart of the educational process – the continual broadening and deepening of knowledge in terms of basic and general ideas' (p. 17). For Bruner, disconnected or unrelated sets of facts are not education and will not be remembered by the learners.

The constructivist model encourages learner independence through guided tasks and expects learners to construct their own mental model of knowledge from comprehensible input they receive. In the context of teenagers and young adults learning a foreign language (L2), a mental model of a language and language learning already exists. An approach that focuses exclusively on the target language may fail to consider the knowledge that learners bring to the L2 learning experience (Frankenberg-Garcia, 2000). Therefore, L2 programs in EFL environments must consider the effect of prior knowledge on subsequent language learning, and the kind of scaffolding necessary to facilitate learning an L2. Learners are not blank slates. As Jarvis (1987) points out 'learning is not just a psychological process that happens in splendid isolation from the world in which the learner lives, but it is intimately related to that world and affected by it' (pp. 11-12). Learners have had years of language and language learning when they begin their university English language courses and we need to understand how they try to accommodate the new linguistic knowledge to what they already know.

Practical Context

The current paper argues for the development of a pedagogical grammar to provide support for Arabic speaking learners of English who need English for university education. These learners need to communicate in English so the focus is on meaning but accuracy is essential in an academic context. Therefore, learners need to acquire both English function and form.

Descriptive grammars are often used in Arab schools and universities and while they provide a generic analysis and description of language points, they do not always address the challenges faced by Arab learners. The relevance of a pedagogical grammar with explanations and exercises designed to deal with the particular errors committed by Arab learners learning English is considered here. The contents of the grammar evolve from the practical needs of Arab learners, with language descriptions that are straightforward and accessible, and a range of focused exercises. The grammar seeks to present not a definitive description of the L2 but rather items relevant to learners with explanations designed to help them overcome the perceived difficulties they have with aspects of the L2 and forms part of a scaffolding process.

An initial investigation was undertaken to examine tense and aspect in the interlanguage of Gulf Arab learners (O'Brien, 2010).

The study explored two hypotheses to help explain non-conventional verb forms found in the written texts of Arab learners of English. The study considered developmental and contrastive factors as influences on the errors committed by Arab learners of English; both factors were found to be relevant in the analysis of learner texts. Differences between English and Arabic tense and aspect systems were concluded to account for some of the irregularities noticed in learners' texts. These included problems with understanding the function of present simple and progressive forms in English as a single verb form is used to perform a range of functions in standard Arabic, difficulties with the correct functional interpretation of the past progressive in English and the present perfect form.

Data collection from Emirati learners using English as a medium of instruction at university has been ongoing and over the last three years, approximately 2,000 essays of 800-1000 words have been collected and analyzed as sources of learner errors. Examples of non-conventional forms over a range of areas have been recorded in an Excel spreadsheet. An approach developed by Corder (1974) and adapted by Brown (1994), and Ellis (1995) of data collection, description, classification and explanation has been adopted with the objective of uncovering forms and emerging patterns that would explain how Arab learners perceive form to function relationships in English. The final step in this process is the development of focused materials to help Arab learners overcome the observed errors.

Linguistic Factors

Three developments, contrastive analysis (CA), error analysis (EA) and interlanguage (IL), in foreign language learning analysis influence perceptions of learners' progress in acquiring foreign languages. The original CA hypothesis (Lado, 1957) argued that L2 mistakes resulted from negative mother tongue (L1) interference that needed to be eradicated. Further studies indicated that the EFL narrative was more complex (Krashen, 1988) and error analysis led to the concept of IL defined by Selinker (1972) as a system 'distinct from both the native language and the target language' (p. 209). Learners are viewed within a constructivist framework as active participants developing an abstract set of principles on how the L2 works based on linguistic input, developmental features and prior language knowledge. Learners revise IL hypotheses based on meaningful corrective form and function input.

Developmental features manifested in overgeneralization of irregularities in past tense and plurals are common in the IL of all L2 learners including the Arab learners. Inherent elements of the English linguistic system contribute to some errors. Among these is the letter '*S*' which apart from its alphabetic role performs a number of grammatical functions: plural number, subject verb agreement in third person singular, possession in '*S''* and contraction in non-academic utterances with 'he's', 'it's', etc. Irregularities in the use of '*S*' are common in Arab learners' texts. Rutherford (1987) refers to the grammatical means available in elements such as '*S*' (plurals, possessives) and apostrophe (contractions, possessives) as 'grammaticization' and believes that 'for speakers of most other languages acquisition of these factors is no simple task' (p. 59). Other problematic multi-functional features of English for Arab learners include the morpheme '*–ing*', functioning as a verbal noun, an adjective and part of the progressive verb phrase. Experience suggests that the multi-functionality of '*–ing*' is challenging for Arab learners who tend to associate the morpheme with the notion of continuity. It is argued that explanations of the range of '*–ing*' functions should be clearly presented with detailed focused practice. Another multi-functional element noted to be confusing is the word '*that*' in its many roles of demonstrative adjective, pronoun, relative pronoun, particle to introduce noun clauses and as part of the '*so that*' phrase in clauses of reason and purpose. Additionally, common verbs '*to do*', '*to be*' and '*to have*' operate as main and auxiliary verbs in a range of complex syntactic structures. It is argued that a pedagogical grammar should illustrate the range of functions of each, and provide focused practice on each function relevant to the observed errors.

Arab Learners' Difficulties with English

It is now acknowledged that students' L1 may be a useful tool for learning a second language. Storch and Wigglesworth (2003) comment on the value of L1 as a 'psychological tool' and 'cognitive support' (p. 761). In terms of Arabic learners of EFL, it has long been hypothesized that transfer from the L1 accounts for much of learner non-target output. Kharma and Hajjaj (1989) suggest that Arabic speaking learners of English are confused by the form-function associations in the L2 as well as the differences between the L1 and L2. Noor (1996) suggests that the most common source of the irregular output he observed among Arab learners could be traced to the influence of Arabic. The following discussion focuses on some of the errors that are perceived to result from transfer from Arabic.

The influence of Arabic on English verb morphological form is observed in expressions of time with grammatical tense and aspect. Time and its linguistic expression are features of every social and linguistic culture. Time is a universal concept but the expression of time is culturally and linguistically specific. Klein (1994) explains that 'All natural languages have a rich repertoire of means to express temporality' (p. 15). The linguistic encoding of time is acquired when we learn our first language(s). At this stage, no prior linguistic associations exist between temporal notions and morphological and syntactic structures. It is generally accepted, therefore, that our early linguistic encoding of time is shaped by the semantic and grammatical focus of the first language (White, 1991). The acquisition and learning of all subsequent linguistic systems for the encoding of time occur against the background of existing associations formed during the L1 learning experience.

English and Arabic have grammatical systems for the encoding of temporal concepts through verb morphology. Deixis is central to tense (Comrie, 1976) or as Freed (1979) puts it 'the ordering of events' (p. 10). Tense involves events considered in terms of speaker location and ordering in relation to another event. Svalberg (1995) suggests that the fact that 'there is more than one reference point in the grammar' is 'what is peculiar about tense in English' (p. 69). She refers to these points as 'speaker time' and 'story time'. In each case, the 'axis of orientation' (Bull, 1971) differs; in speaker time, orientation is towards time of speaking (present, past simple, future, present perfect) and is referred to as primary tense while with story time vantage points may be from the perspective of another event (past perfect, conditional with 'would') and is viewed as secondary tense (p. 12).

In addition, there is grammatical aspect defined by Freed (1979) as linguistically encoding situations 'in terms of such things as inception, repetition, completion, duration and punctuality' (p. 10). The English morphological system encodes three aspects: simple for situations in their entirety as with the present simple and past simple, progressive (present and past) for phases of events located in different time frames and perfect for events seen as having occurred at least once before speaker reference time but retaining some current relevance (present perfect – resultative and continuative). Aspect as a grammatical idea has been less investigated than tense and is often subsumed under the category of tense in learner grammars, thus generating confusion for learners as they try to differentiate between the 12 tenses generally presented in descriptive grammars.

Aspect involves speaker perspective on events and languages manifest this perspective in a number of ways. It is arguably a much more complex concept semantically and syntactically than tense. Arabic is often classed as an aspect language, the primary focus of whose verb forms is to express aspectual features. The two Arabic morphological verb forms are often translated as present and past tenses whereas in fact, the focus is on the aspectual nature of events. Shlonsky (1997) says that Arabic verb forms have deictic (tense) potential because in the absence of all other functions 'sentences with a bare .... verb have a tense component' (p. 96). Cuvalay-Haak (1997) argues that Arabic verb forms are polysemous, a view that she says 'runs counter to traditionalist approaches' concluding that 'a simple verb form can thus be associated with two or more operators' (p. 127).

So what does all of this have to do with a pedagogical grammar? For simple tense situations, it could be argued that an exact correspondence exists between English simple tenses present, past and future, and Arabic imperfective (aal mu aari9), perfective (aal maa i) and future (aal mstaqbil) (see Table 1).

Table 1. Simple tense correspondence between English and Arabic

He eats bread.	yaakul khubz	يأكل خبز.
He ate bread.	aakul khubz.	أكل خبز.
He will eat bread.	sayaakul khubz	سف‖ سيأكل خبز.

However, several temporal notions (habituality, progressivity, duration, repetition, inception, completion, punctuality) are not encapsulated in this basic sentence. The following table illustrates the differences in tense and aspect between English and Arabic (Table 2).

Table 2. Differences in expression of aspect between English and Arabic

He <u>eats</u> bread <u>every day</u>.	<u>yaakul</u> khubz <u>kul yauum</u>.	يأكل خبز كل يَوم.
He <u>is eating</u> bread <u>now</u>.	<u>yaakul</u> khubz aalaan.	يأكل خبز الآن.
He <u>ate</u> bread <u>yesterday</u>.	aakul khubz <u>aamis</u>.	أكل خبز أمس.
He <u>ate</u> bread for three hours yesterday.	aakul khubz limuda thalaat saa9aat aamis. kaan yaakul khubz limuda thalaat saa9aat aamis.	أكل خبز لمدة ثلاث ساعات أمس. كان يأكل خبز لمدة ثلاث ساعات أمس.
He <u>ate</u> bread <u>every day</u> <u>last year</u>.	kaan yaakul khubz kul yauum aal sana aal maa iia.	كان يأكل خبز كل يوم السنة الماضية.

| He <u>ate</u> bread <u>all day</u> <u>yesterday</u>. | kaan yaakul khubz kul aal yauum aamis. | كان يأكل خبز كل اليوم أمس. |
| He <u>was eating</u> bread when his brother came. | kaan yaakul khubz 9ndmaa jaa' aakhhu | <u>كان يأكل</u> خبز عندما جاء آخه. |

Helping verbs, adverbs, adverbial phrases and prepositional phrases along with verbs contribute to the expression of temporal notions as observed in the examples above. Correspondence between English and Arabic forms is quite straightforward in simple tense situations; however, with additional temporal notions of habitual, progressive and repetitive, translation does not work and irregularities occur. English verb forms differentiate between simple and progressive aspects in the present whereas a single Arabic verb form covers both and disambiguation is achieved with adverb or adverbial/ prepositional phrase equivalent to 'now' or 'at the moment'. English past simple verb forms can express single punctual events, habitual series, duration, while Arabic encodes these temporal notions differently and employs the equivalent to the verb 'to be' with the imperfective form of the main verb to show habituality and progressivity. Adverbial phrases or subordinate clauses of time disambiguate the utterances.

The Arabic verb form is viewed as primarily aspectual, a semantic feature that may be transferred to English by learners who seek syntactic and morphological encoding of aspect rather than tense. The conflict between tense and aspect encoding may account for Arab learners' overuse of the –ing form to express habituality, duration and continuity. The application of the term 'continuous' to label progressive forms adds to learner confusion. Learners are wrestling with a range of form function relationships and Kharma and Hajjaj (1989) suggest that the fact that the English verb forms express many different meanings that do not always correspond or overlap with Arabic forms accounts for many of the difficulties Arab learners of English have.

In the following short texts, one Emirati learner's confusion with communicating a range of temporal notions is obvious.

In the past mothers <u>have</u> a big responsibility. She <u>working</u> and <u>getting</u> goats from the farm. She <u>was care</u> about her children. Mothers also <u>gets</u> water for her house. (Essay 5, Lines 10-11)

The first stative verb 'have' is present simple, a common developmental feature because of the stative nature of the verb; the verbs 'working' and 'getting' may suggest habituality to the learner while the attempt to reflect the past in 'was care' illustrates the incorrect combination of simple past and progressive (a tense aspect conflict). Simple present in 'gets' suggests an attempt to show the ongoing repeated event. A second learner shows a much clearer grasp of how to combine tense and aspect.

The writer and my grandmother again go side by side in <u>making us realize</u> that woman of the <u>past</u> <u>regularly did</u> painstaking tasks like <u>harvesting</u> dates from trees, <u>milking</u> the animals, <u>carrying</u> water home, <u>sowing</u> the seeds in the farm, <u>tending</u> the plants and then harvesting the fruits. They <u>stitched</u> their own clothes. Fire wood <u>was</u> at times scarce so ladies of a community <u>cooked</u> together on one fire. (Essay 8, Lines 15–19)

When learners try to find an exact correspondence between verb forms in English and Arabic, errors often result. A function to form approach in teaching is essential where learners learn the correct forms required to encode temporal functions.

Another verb form that is challenging is that of the present perfect. The difficulty here is that a number of functions are expressed through one form; Arabic uses a different form for each function as illustrated in Table 3.

Table 3. Form to function in English present perfect

1. Hind has lived in the UAE since 2004. (continuative)	t9iish hind fii al aamaaraat aal 9rbiia aal ltHda mundh 2004.	تعيش هند في الأمارات العربية المتحدة منذ 2004
2. Would you like some coffee? No thanks, I have just drunk coffee. (resultative)	hal triid finjaan qhwa? Laa shakraa, sharbtu ltuuh.	هل تريد فنجان قهوة؟ لا شكرا, شربت لتوه.
3. I have visited Cairo many times. (existential)	zurtu al qaahira maraat kathiira.	زرتُ القاهرة مرات كثيرة.

In (1) Hind still lives in the UAE and the Arabic imperfective (equivalent to present simple) is used. In examples (2) and (3), events are over; the Arabic perfective form shows completion. In English, speaker choice can encode these as present perfect in (2) to show current relevance of events (resultative), and in (3) to indicate that the speaker retains the possibility of visiting Cairo again. It is important to clarify the different functions encoded in a single verb form and to illustrate the use of each in text. Many grammar books tend to take a form approach, teaching learners how present perfect form combines with a variety of adverbs, adverbial and prepositional phrases.

Conditionality is a feature of natural languages; English simple present and past verb forms convey modality showing possibility or improbability in the conditional clause. Present simple forms generally indicate the likely nature of events occurring while past suggests improbability. The modality of Arabic conditions is expressed through a conditional particle while the verb in the conditional clause is an example of secondary tense in which a possible condition must be met before an event can occur. Consequently, a possible condition generally contains a verb equivalent to the English past as in:

- If I *had the money I will spend it on my friends and family.
- If I *had the weekend free, I gather my friends around for a camping trip.

Arabic perfective forms in conditional and time clauses illustrate the logical temporal relationship existing between two events. Realization of one event depends on the prior completion of another. Whether the main event refers to the past, present or future is irrelevant as Ingham (1995) points out, 'the preference is for the Time or Condition clause to precede the main clause and to contain a verb in the perfective' (p. 137).

Definiteness and indefiniteness are semantic concepts and the linguistic devices for encoding in/definiteness vary from one language to another. The acquisition of English in/definiteness system is problematic for Emirati learners and the parameters set by Arabic often interfere with the accurate use of definite and indefinite articles. In some languages, definite article equivalents indicate number, gender, phonetic sensitivity and case in addition to definiteness. Uses of English 'the' and Arabic 'al' are not affected by number or case, but are by usage. The differences between English and Arabic uses of 'the' and 'al'' lie in the limitations inherent in the English definite article. The generic use of the definite article could be considered one of the major problematic areas for Arab learners. In English, a singular noun preceded by the definite article may refer to a whole class of objects as in:

- The computer is a useful machine.

Reference here is to computers in general and not a single computer. The same generic reference can be made through the use of a plural noun without the definite article:

- Computers are useful machines.

The employment of the English definite article for generic reference is restricted to nouns that are countable rather than mass or abstract nouns.

- Sugar is expensive.
- Beauty is in the eye of the beholder.

Arabic 'aal' can be used in all the following examples unlike the English system:

- To refer to a general class of objects.
  The prices are high here.
  *The watermelon is good for you.
- To refer to abstractions.
  *The truth is stranger than fiction.

In addition, in definite utterances where an adjective precedes a noun 'al' is placed in front of both the noun and adjective as in *al walid al Tawil* = *the boy the tall*. Over-use of the definite article by Arab learners is the most common error found and hypothesized to result from the transfer of Arabic parameters to English. Focused exercises are needed to raise learner awareness; nevertheless, this is considered a very difficult error to eradicate and incidences of over-use of 'the' occur in the most sophisticated texts.

Indefinite articles 'a' and 'an' are employed to refer to persons, places, objects or ideas when no specific item or person is being referred to. The parameters on the expression of English indefiniteness include number, countability and noun type. With countable singular nouns, indefiniteness is expressed through 'a', 'an', 'each', and 'every'. Uncountable and plural nouns generally indicate indefiniteness either through a stand-alone noun or a noun preceded by 'some'. Arabic expression of indefiniteness is not number or noun type sensitive and shows case i.e. subject, object or indirect object through a system referred to as '*tanwiin*' or *nunation*. The sign of indefiniteness is not a separate lexical item, being attached to the noun as a superscript or subscript depending on the case of the noun (see Table 4).

Table 4. Indefiniteness

subject	A student //students came to the lecture.	جاء طالبٌ \\ طلابٌ إلى المحاضرة
object	I saw a student//students at the lecture.	رأيت طالباً \\ طلاباً في المحاضرة.
indirect object	Give the book to a student// students.	أعطى الكتاب لطالبٍ لطلاب .

In Arabic, mark of indefiniteness is part of the word; it is not number specific and is generally omitted in all but formal Arabic texts. In most writing, indefiniteness is understood from the context and the absence of the definite article 'al'. The following errors are those most frequently noted among Arabic speaking learners of English:

- My father teaches everybody to take *a responsibility for himself.
- Studying another language needs *a hard work.
- She teaches *a children what is important.
- You can study *another languages from TV by watching *a programmes.

The function of relative pronouns/ clauses in English and Arabic is similar. Both add more information to nouns and help clarify and define a person or thing. Rules of usage differ and some features of Arabic relative clauses may be transferred to English. An Arabic sentence contains a relative pronoun when the antecedent is definite as in 'the student'/'the students' but relative pronouns are not necessary when referents are indefinite. Btoosh (2010) explains that 'in English, the relative pronoun follows either definite or indefinite antecedent. However, the relative pronoun only occurs with a definite antecedent in standard Arabic' (p. 25). Errors illustrate transfer:

- It is a place *people, cultures, education, environment and public spaces are available.
- A number of people *face drug addiction in the UAE need help and support.
- I saw a boy *had left his father.

Another common error in English results from the transfer of the addition of a pronoun referent (a feature of the Arabic system) giving rise to the following structure in English: 'The film that I saw it'. Rutherford (1987) explains that English, unlike many languages, relativizes all positions and leaves no pronominal trace in relative clauses. Relative pronouns that indicate case as in 'who', 'whom', 'whose' make use of a referring pronoun unnecessary. However, when an Arabic relative pronoun refers to any part of the relative sentence which follows except the subject, it must be repeated in an attached pronoun. This retention of pronoun traces can be found in languages other than Arabic and may account for the following types of error in learners' texts: 'The man who I saw him' and 'The man who his son I met'.

In Arabic, particles are frequently used to perform functions that are grammaticized in English. A question particle in Arabic placed at the beginning of a declarative sentence forms a question. Speakers of English have to perform subject verb inversion in addition to the correct use of a helping verb in simple tenses. The tendency is for Arabic speakers to over-use 'do' mis-interpreting its function as a question particle rather than a helping verb as in 'Do you are going to the cinema?' Arabic negative utterances are constructed through the use of a particle whereas English negative sentences require an auxiliary verb that carries number and tense. Learner errors indicate failure to make the necessary transformations and may result in the overuse of 'not' as a negative particle irrespective of the structure of the whole sentence as in 'She not found her bag today'.

Implications for Teaching and Learning

The preceding discussion has highlighted some of the challenges (intrinsic – aspects of English grammar, and extrinsic – cross over from Arabic) faced by Arabic L1 learners of English. The paper has argued for the development of a pedagogical grammar that incorporates a large section on elements of transfer from Arabic. It must be pointed out that such a grammar would not solve all learner difficulties but would provide a powerful tool for learners, teachers and other stake holders such as government language planners involved in the language learning and teaching processes.

For learners, the grammar would provide a ready resource for error correction in written texts. The approach adopted in error analyses has been one of focus on form rather than forms involving an analysis of learner errors as observed in communicative tasks thereby ensuring that focus is on language in use. It has been observed that learners often revert to their own logic of linguistic practice to complete a task and that this logic is informed by their L1 Arabic. A grammar that raises consciousness about the nature of this transfer would facilitate editing and proof-reading because it takes a bottom-up approach and operates from learners' perception of form-function relationships rather than taking a top-down descriptive approach of the TL. By the time learners reach tertiary level, they should have moved through all the hypothesized language development phases after 12 years exposure to the TL but errors persist as Arab learners in an EFL environment still use the L1 as a crutch in writing texts. Therefore, focused attention should be given to the cause of the error and time dedicated to challenging instinctive intuitions based on the L1 that have often resulted in fossilization of an incorrect form and that do not work in the L2. Such an approach would provide a measure of intelligent scaffolding to help Arab learners overcome their difficulties. Tomasello and Heron (1989) and Carroll and Swain (1993) all point to the importance of metalinguistic awareness through which learners reflect on the nature of the error and learn to self-correct. Their research suggests that implicit instruction (communicative tasks) and explicit metalingusitic feedback on errors that are clearly L1 transfer such as in verb tenses, definiteness, indefiniteness, and conditionality help develop accuracy. The affective domain is another important area in language learning and learners' attitudes to the TL can affect the learning process. Incorporation of L1 knowledge would provide not just a pedagogical tool but also a powerful motivating factor as learners respond positively to the fact that recognition is given to the language knowledge they bring with them and the fact that Arabic is their mother tongue. Academic success based on achievement through the medium of a foreign language can result in negative affective factors if TL success interferes with progress in an unrelated language area. With the positive-affective factor of correction based on an explanation of the negative-cognitive input from L1, a more inclusive language learning environment would result.

From a teacher perspective, a pedagogical grammar has implications for both the native Arabic speaker teacher and the native English speaking teacher. For both it provides a ready-made analyses of learners' errors and a developed corpus of material to help with metalinguistic corrective feedback and consciousness raising for the former (Arabic speaking teacher) of areas of transfer that could be part of their own internal grammar and for the latter (English speaking teachers) a heightened awareness of a linguistic system that is often totally different to that of English and an understanding that learners bring a developed linguistic system with them to the language learning process. Both teaching environments would be enhanced with the use of a pedagogical grammar as it would allow focused attention to problematic areas.

In terms of other stakeholders in the language learning process such as decision makers and education systems, a pedagogical grammar could have profound cost-cutting implications in the financial planning process. In 1995, Al-Jassim identified the poor standard of English among undergraduate and post-graduate students as reasons for major governmental financial outlay in language learning to bring learners to the required standard for tertiary education. Unfortunately, this is still the situation both for those who remain in the UAE and go to study abroad (personal experience). If learners had the relevant corrective input, they would not require ongoing language instruction at postgraduate level as they do now to achieve the required IELTS Band 6 or 6.5 to undertake a M.A. or M.Sc. (personal experience working with Arab M.Sc. students 2009–2010). A pedagogical grammar would provide a useful tool for independent editing and proof-reading, develop a sense of independence and ownership of learners' own language evolution and eliminate the need for about 36 hours of language instruction per group per semester at upper tertiary levels. It would also allow professors of content subjects to concentrate on content areas rather than being distracted by learner errors.

References

Al Jassim, S. (1995). *Education, demographic structure, development and future challenges.* Dubai: Dubai Association for Culture, Arts and Theatre.

Barber, B. (1996) *Jihad Vs McWorld: How globalism and tribalism are reshaping the world.* Ballantine: New York.

Brown, D.B. (1994). *Principles of language learning and teaching.* New Jersey: Prentice Hall Regents.

Bruner, J. (1960). *The process of education.* Cambridge: Harvard University Press.

Btooshi, M. (2010). WH-movement in standard Arabic: An optimality-theoretic account. *Poznan Studies in Contemporary Linguistics, 46*(1), 1-26.

Bull, W.E. (1971). *Time, tense and the verb.* California: California University Press.

Carroll, S., & Swain, M. (1993). Explicit and implicit negative feedback. An empirical study of the learning of linguistic generalizations. *Studies in Second language Acquisition, 15,* 357-386.

Comrie, B. (1976). *Aspect.* Cambridge: CUP.

Corder, S.P. (1974). Error analysis. In J.P.B. Allen & S.P. Corder (Eds.), *Techniques in applied linguistics* (pp. 122-154). London: Oxford University Press.

Cuvalay-Haak, M. (1997). *The verb in literary colloquial Arabic.* Berlin: Mouton de Gruyter.

Ellis, R. (1995). *Understanding second language acquisition.* Oxford: Oxford University Press.

Frankenberg-Garcia, A. (2000). Using Portuguese in the teaching of English. In A. Pina, J.F. Duarte, & M.H. Serôdio (Eds.), *Do Esplendor na Relva: Elites e cultura comum de expressão inglesa.* (pp. 425-432). Lisboa: Cosmos.

Freed, A.S. (1979). *The semantics of English aspectual complementation.* Dordecht: Reidel Publishing.

Gergen, K.J. (1995). Social construction and the educational process. In L.P. Steffe & J.Gale (Eds.), *Constructivism in education* (pp. 17-39). Hillsdale, New Jersey: Lawrence Erlbaum.

Ingham, B. (1995). *Arabian diversions. Studies on the dialects of Arabia*. Berkshire: Ithaca Press.

Jarvis, P. (1987). *Adult learning in the social context*. London: Croom Helm.

Kitchener, R. (1986). *Piaget's theory of knowledge*. New Haven: Yale University Press.

Klein, W. (1994). *Second language acquisition*. London: Routledge.

Kharma, N., & Hajjaj, A. (1989). A contrastive analysis of the use of verb forms in English and Arabic. *Studies in Descriptive Linguistics, 10*, 103 – 137.

Krashen, S. (1988). *Theories of second language acquisition*. New Jersey: Prentice-Hall.

Kumaravadivelu, B. (2006). *Understanding language teaching: From method to postmethod*. New York: Routledge.

Lado, R. (1957). *Linguistics across cultures*. Ann Arbor: University of Michigan Press.

Noor, H. (1996). *English syntactic errors by Arabic speaking learners*. Microfiche ED 423, 600: King Abdulaziz University, Saudi Arabia.

O'Brien, J. (2010). *English tense and aspect in the interlanguage of Gulf Arab learners*. Verlag: Saarbrucken.

Robertson, R. (2002). Glocalization: Time-space and homogeneity-heterogeneity. In M. Featherstone, S. Lash, & R. Robertson (Eds). *Global modernities* (pp. 25 -44). London: Sage.

Rutherford, W. (1987). *Second language grammar: Learning and teaching*. London: Longman.

Selinker, L. (1972). Interlanguage. *IRAL, 10*, 209-231.

Shlonsky, U. (1997). *Clause structure and word order in Hebrew and Arabic: An essay in comparative semantic syntax*. Oxford: Oxford University Press.

Storch, N., & Wigglesworth, G. (2003). Is there a role for L1 in an L2 setting? *TESOL Quarterly, 37*(4), 761 – 770.

Svalberg, A. (1995). Meanings into pictures: Icons for teaching grammar. *Language Awareness, 4*(2), 65-68.

Tomasello, M., & Herron, C. (1988). Down the garden path: Inducing and correcting overgeneralization errors in the foreign language classroom. *Applied Psycholinguistics, 9*, 237-246.

von Glasersfeld, E. (1995). *Radical constructivism: A way of knowing and learning*. London: Falmer Press.

Vygotsky, L.S. (1978). *Mind and society: The development of higher psychological processes*. Cambridge: CUP.

White, L. (1991). Adverb placement in SLA: Some effects of positive and negative evidence in the classroom. *Second Language Research, 8*(2), 133–161.

List of Abbreviations

ADUPC	Abu Dhabi Urban Planning Council
AHDR	Arab Human Development Report
AR	Action Research
BANA	Britain, Australia & North America
BTC	Bahrain Teachers' College
CA	Classical Arabic
CA	Contrastive Analysis
CEPA	Common Education Proficiency Assessment
EA	Error Analysis
EAP	English for Academic Purposes
EFA	Education for All
EFL	English as a Foreign Language
ESL	English as a Second Language
GCC	Gulf Cooperation Council
GPA	Grade Point Average
GTE	General Teaching Efficacy
HCT	Higher Colleges of Technology
HDYSP	How Do You Solve Problems
HEI	Higher Education Institution
HPS	High-Performing Schools
ICEQ	Individualised Classroom Environment Questionnaire
IELTS	International English Language Testing System
IL	Interlanguage
IRE	Initiation Response Evaluation
ITAL	Inventory for Teaching and Learning
KHDA	Knowledge and Human Development Authority
L1	First Language, Mother Tongue
L2	Second Language
LPS	Low-Performing Schools

MENA	Middle East and North Africa
MGT	Matched Guise Technique
MIC	Ministry of Information and Culture
MoE	Ministry of Education
MSA	Modern Standard Arabic
NAPO	National Admissions and Placement Office
NIE	National Institute of Education
NLS	New Literacy Studies
OAT	Orthographic Awareness Test
PAT	Phonological Awareness Test
PBL	Problem-Based Learning
PD	Professional Development
PIRLS	Progress for International Reading Literacy Study
PISA	Program for International Student Assessment
PTE	Personal Teaching Efficacy
QCET	Qatar Comprehensive Educational Tests
SAV	Spoken Arabic Vernacular
SLTL	School Level Team Leader
SPSS	Statistical Package for the Social Sciences
SUQ	Stenden University in Qatar
TAOP	Teacher Attitudes Observation Protocol
TBL	Task-Based Learning
TES	Teacher Efficacy Scale
TESEP	Teachers who work in Secondary and Primary Schools
TESOL	Teaching English to Speakers of Other Languages
TL	Target Language
TM	Teacher Mentor
TOEFL	Test of English as a Foreign Language
UAE	United Arab Emirates
UAQ	Umm Al Quain
UNDP	United Nations Development Program
UNESCO	United Nations Educational, Scientific and Cultural Organisation
UoB	University of Bahrain

List of Reviewers

All papers included in this book underwent a rigorous review process. Initially 61 proposals were received of which 30 were selected for a double blind review process that involved a large number of notable academics from a range of universities based in the region. Through this process 21 papers were selected. These papers underwent further review and editing before being published in this book. Below is the list of academics (in alphabetical order) who were involved in the double blind review process.

Dr. Khawlah Ahmed, American University in Sharjah, UAE
Dr. Rozz Albon, Sharjah Higher Colleges of Technology, UAE
Dr. Iman Alghazo, UAE University, UAE
Dr. Ahmad Al Issa, American University in Sharjah, UAE
Dr. Othman Alsawaie, UAE University, UAE
Dr. Hala Al-Yamani, Bethlehem University, Palestine
Dr. Stephen Anderson, Zayed University, UAE
Dr. Costantine Antoniou, Higher Colleges of Technology, UAE
Dr. Naz Awan, British University in Dubai, UAE
Dr. Toni Briegel, UAE University, UAE
Dr. Mehmet Buldu, UAE University, UAE
Dr. Ken Carr, Zayed University, UAE
Dr. Christine Coombe, Dubai Men's College, UAE
Dr. Robin Dada, Zayed University, UAE
Dr. Georgia Daleure, Sharjah Higher Colleges of Technology, UAE
Dr. Peter Davidson, Zayed University, UAE
Dr. Christina Gitsaki, Sharjah Higher Colleges of Technology, UAE
Dr. Melanie Gobert, Higher Colleges of Technology, UAE
Dr. Mary Ellis, Nanyang Technological University, Singapore
Dr. Al-Sadig Ezza, Al-Majma'ah University, Saudi Arabia
Dr. Katherine Hall, American University in Dubai, UAE

Dr. Lorraine McLeod, UAE University, UAE
Dr. Katlin Omair, Sharjah Higher Colleges of Technology, UAE
Dr. Natasha Ridge, Dubai School of Government, UAE
Dr. Iqtidar Ali Shah, Ministry of Higher Education, Oman
Dr. Lauren Stephenson, Zayed University, UAE
Dr. Janet Thomas, Zayed University, UAE
Dr. Salah Troudi, Exeter University, UAE
Ms. Jane Truscott, Madares Al Ghad, Ministry of Education, UAE

Index